Exporting and Importing Fashion

A Global Perspective

Exporting and Importing Fashion

A Global Perspective

Elaine Stone
Fashion Institute of Technology

I(T)P

Delmar Publishers
Inc.

NOTICE TO THE READER

Cover photo by: Micheal Simpson/FPG

Delmar staff

Senior Acquisitions Editor: Mary McGarry
Project Editor: Theresa M. Bobear
Production Coordinator: James Zayicek
Design Coordinator: Karen Kemp
Art Coordinator: Megan Keane DeSantis

For information, address Delmar Publishers Inc.
3 Columbia Circle, Box 15-015
Albany, New York 12212-5015

Printed in the United States of America
Published simultaneously in Canada
by Nelson Canada,
a division of The Thomson Corporation

2 3 4 5 6 7 8 9 10 XXX 99 98

ISBN: 0-8273-5068-6

CONTENTS

P R E F A C E

Fashion, since the days of early civilization, has been global. Crude drawings depicting the mode of dress and societal customs were passed from century to century, and from culture to culture, with each period and country imprinting their mark of fashion.

Today, success in the international marketplace demands experience and the skill of a professional. Added to the difficult task of operating a successful domestic business, the intricacies of the global marketplace must be studied. *Exporting and Importing Fashion: A Global Perspective* provides students with an overview and introduction to exporting and importing theory, and offers a global perspective essential to anyone preparing to work in today's global fashion market. In addition to focusing on export/import procedures and government rules and regulations relevant to the fashion industry, the text also includes information on the demographics, psychographics, and socioeconomics of international fashion exporting and importing, as well as numerous forms vital to the import and export of fashion merchandise.

CONTENTS

As both an importer and an exporter, I found that there were few texts that covered the intricate factors of both exporting and importing that impact upon the fashion industries. Students interested in learning both exporting and importing procedures for fashion products had to go to a great many sources, most government books and manuals. So that the student can have a clear and concise view of the global fashion business, *Exporting and Importing Fashion: A Global Perspective* is presented in the following sequence:

UNIT 1: THE DYNAMICS OF THE INTERNATIONAL FASHION MARKETPLACE

To learn about the export and import fashion industry, students must first understand the dynamics of the international fashion marketplace. The first three chapters of this text focus on this topic. In Chapter 1, students are introduced to the nature and scope of global fashion marketing, learning about the one-world concept, the United States' role in the global marketplace, and the new role played by the U.S.

fashion industry. In Chapter 2, the diversity of regional environments is discussed, focusing on such topics as the importance of understanding other cultures, economic advancement among nations, and ethnocentrism as the biggest barrier to international trade. In Chapter 3, students are presented with an analysis of the international fashion market, with special emphasis on the impact of consumer demand on international fashion, developing an international perspective, and implications for the industry professional.

UNIT 2: GLOBAL SOURCING FOR AN INTERNATIONAL FASHION MIX

The focus centers on global sources in the global marketplace in Unit 2. In Chapter 4, students have an opportunity to learn who exports and why, examining the advantages and disadvantages of exporting as well as exporting by manufacturers and retailers and U.S. support programs for exporting. In Chapter 5, students study who imports and why, examining both the advantages and disadvantages of importing, the spread of importing, importing by manufacturers and retailers, tensions between retailers and manufacturers, and U.S. regulation of the textile and apparel industry. In Chapter 6, the focus is on product development for international trade, with an examination of the origins of product development, market research and analysis, and the factors affecting international market strategy.

UNIT 3: THE EXPORT MARKETING STUDY

The focus turns to the exporting of fashion products in Unit 3. In Chapter 7, students learn about getting into the export business, including the steps to developing and export strategy, product research and analysis, competitor research and analysis, foreign market research and analysis, and sources of export information. In Chapter 8, students study export distribution, promotion, and pricing strategy, with special emphasis on agents for distribution and promotion and developing a pricing strategy. In Chapter 9, the students are introduced to export procedures and learn about gathering documentation for exporting, getting paid for exports, terms of credit, tariff and nontariff barriers to exporting, and freight forwarders. In Chapter 10, the emphasis is on surviving in the global fashion marketplace, with special emphasis on preparation for international business and communication in international business.

UNIT 4: THE IMPORT MARKETING STRATEGY

The focus in Unit 4 is on import marketing. In Chapter 11, students examine import product strategy, learning about the analysis of the import product, locating sources of imported products, choosing the right import supplier, elements of import product decisions, specifications decision regarding imports, and factors affecting import prices. In Chapter 12, students examine import distribution and promotion strategy, with particular attention paid to factors in import distribution, the physical distribution of imports, import product promotion strategies, the role of price in sales strategies, and new trends in sales strategies. In Chapter 13, the subject of processing the import product is studied, including the process of imported goods, financing the import purchase, financing the payment, transporting the import purchase, and duties and quotas. In Chapter 14, the focus is on import procedures, with an examination of why import procedures exist, the role of the U.S. Customs Service, the entry process, the examination process, duties and quotas, and other constraints of trade.

UNIT 5: YOUR CAREER AND THE FUTURE OF GLOBAL FASHION MARKETING

The text concludes with Chapter 15, which focuses on careers and the future of global fashion marketing. This chapter examines the expansion of the international workforce, discusses building a career in international fashion, offers suggestions about how students can get the training they need, and provides valuable information about special opportunities for minorities and women, the job market, and getting an entry-level job.

APPENDICES

The following Appendices are included in this text:

- ⊕ *Export/Import Forms* is provided as a handy reference to the forms required for the exporting and importing of fashion products.
- ⊕ A *Glossary* of terms defined within the text narrative is included for student use as a reference.

- ⊕ An *Index* is also provided at the end of the text.

SPECIAL FEATURES

Many special features are incorporated into *Exporting and Importing Fashion: A Global Perspective* that highlight specific aspects of the global fashion marketplace. I believe these features will bring the text topics to life for the students and will help them envision a career in the international fashion business. All these features are appropriate for class discussion and library research projects.

GLOBAL GLIMPSES

This feature presents short, up-to-date stories about trends and topics in the global fashion industry, from the European Free Trade Association (EFTA), to fashion quotas, to the Export-Import Bank's attempts to untie tied aid, to the introduction of American advertising agencies into Eastern European countries.

GLOBAL GO-GETTERS

This feature includes suggestions for negotiating the intricacies of interpersonal relationships in a global marketplace. Topics covered include getting sick in a foreign country, intercultural communications, global toasts, global greetings, and social customs in other cultures.

GLOBAL GOODIES

This feature offers hints for the business person working in other countries, covering such topics as business cards, gift-giving as part of the business relationship in Japan, international banking, and traveling in Rome and Hong Kong.

TECH TALK

This feature focuses on technology in the global marketplace, and offers commentary on such subjects as laptop computers, exports software, global networking, and overseas conferencing.

UNIT READINGS

In addition to the five chapter features detailed, five unit readings excerpted from noted business publications and from the Fashion Institute of Technology (FIT) and focusing on specific aspects of exporting and importing fashion have been included in this text. Subjects include negotiating with business people in other cultures, making sense out of the new Europe, changes in the textile and apparel industries, and careers in international trade and marketing.

SKILL DEVELOPMENT

Exporting and Importing Fashion: A Global Perspective takes a "hands-on" approach to the technical material included in this text. In addition to providing a readable and accessible narrative, this text helps students to grasp the vocabulary of the fashion industry by boldfacing and defining new terminology at first use. These terms are presented again in a *Global Vocabulary* list at the end of each chapter to serve as a review of the new terminology introduced.

Also provided at the end of each chapter is a section entitled *Global Review.* This section presents a series of exercises which test students' grasp and recall of chapter content. This may be used as a review and study aid by students, and can assist students in focusing on the most important concepts discussed in each chapter studied.

Finally, each chapter concludes with a feature entitled *Global Digest.* This feature consists of a series of activities which allows students to discuss at greater length the significance of statements taken from the chapter, providing examples of how each applies to the exporting and importing of fashion products.

INSTRUCTOR'S MANUAL

An instructor's manual which provides many teaching and learning aids, as well as a test bank for each chapter, is available with the text.

Elaine Stone

ACKNOWLEDGMENTS

Without the experience of working in the global fashion world and having professionals work with me and teach me, this text could not have been written. To all those people here and abroad who helped me and shared in my success in exporting and importing fashion I say thank you. I also wish to thank the following reviewers, who donated time from their busy schedules to read the manuscript and whose insightful and helpful suggestions were instrumental to its development and completion:

June Baker, University of South Carolina

Annette Fraser, University of Wisconsin—Stout

Veronica Miller Mordaunt, The Fashion Institute of Design and Merchandising

Denise McGuire, Art Institute of Houston

Sarah Scavone, LeSelle College

Meg Tigard, Highline Community College

The Dynamics of the International Fashion Marketplace

CHAPTER 1

The Nature and Scope of Global Fashion Marketing

Until a few decades ago, most of the world's people still wore native dress. Japanese women wore kimonos; Indian women wore saris; even a small country like the Philippines had its own unique national dress. Today, ethnic dress is vanishing, especially in cities and sophisticated world capitals. Most of the world is adopting Western dress.

Although many people bemoan the loss of colorful national costumes around the world, others are delighted by what is to be gained from a world where nearly everyone dresses more or less the same. Fashion is becoming a huge global business.

To understand how enormous this change is, one must realize that even fifty years ago, almost everything that people used and needed in their daily lives—their food, furniture, appliances, transportation, and certainly their clothing—was grown or made in the country where they lived. A hundred years ago, people got almost everything they needed from their own towns or villages. Even a small town would have kept a weaver or two and several seamstresses and tailors busy sewing for its population; or often, clothes were made at home. Conversely, nothing that these small-town textile "industries" made was likely to travel farther than ten miles from its point of origin.

In the past fifty years, however, people's buying patterns have changed dramatically. Around the world, people have begun to buy goods from one another. Americans who once drove only American cars now drive cars from Japan and Europe. Eastern Europeans drive American-made tractors and pickup trucks. In the world of fashion, the array of choices is amazing. A woman looking for so simple a purchase as a pair of shoes can choose from shoes made in France, Italy, the United States, and Brazil, to name but a few of the world's major suppliers.

Fashion is one of the strongest sectors of this exciting, new world of international trade. Profits in consumer goods, which include textiles and apparel, increased by 19 percent in 1990.[1] Textile and apparel production is the largest source of worldwide employment, accounting for 25 million jobs around the world.[2]

Every nation has some kind of clothing industry. Clothes are made in glittering world capitals like Paris and Milan and in mud huts in the Andes Mountains of Latin America. In some parts of the world, fabrics are woven on small, handmade looms that turn out less than a yard of fabric a day. In other parts of the world, huge industrial looms churn out yards of fabric each hour. Around the world, fabric dyes

In today's global business environment, fashions reflect the glamor and influence of many countries and cultures. *Courtesy of I.B. Diffusion*

are made from natural sources, such as twigs and flowers, and in shiny, high-tech laboratories. The textile and apparel industry is a significant contributor to the economy of most nations.

THE ONE-WORLD CONCEPT

As nations are no longer able or willing to produce all the goods and services they need and want, they rely on one another to supply them with what they cannot or choose not to produce themselves. In the process, the world's nations are becoming economically interdependent in ways they have never been before. The world is, in effect, becoming one huge global market. Economically speaking, we are less and less a universe made up of individual nations and more and more one world in ways that were unimaginable even twenty years ago. Political scientists call this process—whereby the nations of the world are becoming more interlinked with one another—**globalization.**

Global marketing is the most important by-product of globalization. These days, to compete in the growing global market, a country must both sell to and buy goods from other countries. When a country sends its goods or products abroad, usually for purposes of selling them to other countries, it **exports** them. When a country brings in goods or products from another country, again, usually for purposes of selling them, it **imports** them.

THE UNITED STATES IN A GLOBAL ENVIRONMENT

The United States in general and the fashion industry specifically have been slower than the rest of the world to develop an international perspective. This lag in development can be attributed to several factors.

Because of its geography, the United States has not had to think globally in the same way that, for example, Europe has. All European nations are small, at least by U.S. standards, so small that fashion producers (indeed, all producers) could not rely on local populations to keep their factories at full production. European manufacturers have always had to sell in an international environment, even if this meant only the countries on their own borders.

In contrast, the United States is so large that in boom times, its factories have worked at full production to meet its own population's demand. U.S. industries have been a presence in the international marketplace, but until recently, they never needed foreign business to survive.

Although most of the world's nations are bordered by several other nations, the United States is bordered by only two. To its north is Canada, another large nation whose culture and values match those of the United States. To its south is Mexico, another physically huge nation that until recently has been too poor to participate in any kind of international fashion market.

This means that even the concept of a national border is different for Americans than for the rest of the world. Europeans, for example, routinely cross national borders—for vacations, for business, for shopping excursions. Many U.S. citizens spend their entire lives without crossing an international border.

Finally, language has been another barrier to the United States's ability to develop an international perspective. English has been the predominant language in the United States as well as in Canada. Few Americans speak any other language. In contrast, the typical European country is often home to several

Textile production contributes significantly to the economy of most nations. *Courtesy of the National Cotton Council.*

GLOBAL GLIMPSES

KEIRETSU AND AMERICAN BUSINESS

Because of trade frictions between Japan and the United States, the Japanese corporate groupings, or keiretsu, have been thrust into the limelight.

These groupings take several forms: bank-centered keiretsu, which horizontally link companies in different industries, and supply or distribution keiretsu, which vertically link the upstream or downstream operations of major manufacturers.

More than half of Japan's 100 largest companies belong to one of only six bank-centered keiretsu, the Mitsubishi Mitsui, Sumitomo, Dai-Ichi Kango, Fuyo, or Sanwa Group. Japan's most successful industries, automobiles and electronics, feature close and sometimes exclusive relationships between suppliers, manufacturers, and distributors.

Although some trade analysts attack keiretsu as exclusionary, others argue that they are penetrable by American companies and might actually help ensure their success in dealing with the Japanese firms. Another more controversial question is whether or not it would be desirable, or even possible, for Western corporations to form their own keiretsu.

There are ongoing dialogs and meetings to discuss the effects of keiretsu on economic efficiency and market access and the implications those effects have for American policy and business practices.

Based on information obtained at a one-day conference presented by Japan Society, 10/31/91, titled *Keiretsu and American Business: A Problem or a Solution?* and "Case Study: Anatomy of the Keiretsu" by David E. Huntley, *Export Today*, October, 1991, p. 42.

languages as well as being bounded by nations that speak other languages.

THE U.S. FASHION INDUSTRY IN THE GLOBAL MARKET

The biggest reason, though, that U.S. fashion producers have not become involved in the global market is that they have not needed to do so. For a long time, the climate for the U.S. fashion industry was so good that there was no need to look elsewhere for other markets.

But when the U.S. fashion industry experienced a serious and continuing downturn in the 1970s, in part fueled by large numbers of imports, U.S. manufacturers began to realize they had no choice but to turn to foreign markets to balance out the import boom. The U.S. fashion industry had flirted with the international markets on several occasions but, primarily, for the purpose of obtaining cheap imports or unloading its overproduced exports on the rest of the world.

Ironically, the import boom in fashion was fueled in part by the United States. After World War II, the United States helped to rebuild the economies of many nations around the world, often by introducing new textile and apparel training and techniques for emerging companies, or bolstering those in existence. Textiles and apparel manufacturing was a logical industry to introduce into foundering postwar econ-

omies because it required low skills and minimal investment.

Although the U.S. fashion industry did little to learn about exporting, other nations—those it had helped—learned their lessons well and began importing into the United States. Today, the primary task before U.S. fashion manufacturers is to learn how to export, or sell, their goods back to these same markets.

SELLING THE AMERICAN FASHION IMAGE

The United States has long exported its agricultural, telecommunications, chemical, and pharmaceutical products to the entire world. One third of all U.S. corporate profits, in fact, come from international sales. Only recently, though, has the United States seriously begun to sell its fashion to the rest of the world.

This is surprising to many people, because the American style of dressing—casual, sporty—has been known, admired, and copied throughout the world for decades. Names like Calvin Klein, Ralph Lauren, Donna Karan, and Levi's jeans spring to mind and bring instant recognition around the world. The world is ready to buy American fashion. And American fashion producers are interested in selling to the world. Yet, to date, the world has not bought a lot of U.S. fashion.

MCI. Making the world's business connections.

Success in today's business world knows no boundaries. With MCI's global network, services like world-wide direct dial long-distance, International 800, telex, electronic mail, fax, virtual private networks, MCI CALL USA,℠ and global private lines, makes communicating with the world as easy as communicating with the office next door.

In some parts of the world, MCI® is known through its subsidiaries, RCA Global Communications and Western Union International, which bring you the benefit of more than 70 years of international experience.

To make it easier for your business to make connections connect with us. For more information, in the U.S. call **1-800-999-2096.** Or send us a fax at **1-800-866-9329,** or a telex at **6731886.** Please direct your inquiries to operator 9.

© MCI Communications Corporation, 1991.

MCI®

In a global business environment, communications networks set up by companies like MCI and AT&T provide such valuable services as world-wide direct dial long-distance, telex, electronic mail, fax, virtual private networks, and global private lines. *Courtesy of MCI and AT&T. AT&T photography courtesy of Robert Ammirati and illustration courtesy of Oliver Williams.*

With an AT&T International 800 number your business has no boundaries.

AT&T International 800 Service   Don't let the border keep potential Canadian or Mexican clients away. Get an AT&T International 800 number. For them the call is free. And it's less expensive for you than accepting collect calls.

A toll-free number can also help cement the relationship once you've got their business. You can use it to take orders, provide customer service or keep in touch with your international salespeople so they can provide better service.

AT&T International 800 Service is available from over 60 countries. And there are more options than ever to make it just right for your business. So contact your AT&T representative, or call us toll-free at 1 800 222-0900, Ext. 2963 for more information. Because your growth doesn't have to stop at the border.

A World of Help℠ from AT&T.

AT&T

GLOBAL *GO-GETTERS*

JON C. MADONNA: OVERSEAS OPPORTUNITIES

"Today's opportunities are overseas, but American companies still hate to travel." So says Jon C. Madonna, Chairman of Peat Marwick, one of the country's leading accounting and management firms.

For years, American companies looked abroad when the cost of land, labor, and other essentials helped them produce a product more cheaply—one that could be brought home and sold at a profit. The United States used to be the world's largest single market, but it is now Europe that offers a market with a gross domestic product of $5 billion and 700 million potential consumers, if the Commonwealth of Independent States (CIS), formerly the Soviet Union and other Eastern bloc nations, is included.

We now pay closer attention to how our products are made. Production is more efficient. Prices are going down. We are becoming more competitive—but our competitors are doing the same thing! Therefore, the idea that our new production techniques and quality control will put us on top again—a view held by many American executives—is off-target, so says Mr. Madonna.

Europe has transformed itself from what many considered a sloppy, provincial competitor into a real powerhouse, prowling the world for markets. KPMG Peat Marwick recently surveyed more than 700 top executives at American companies to see what strategies they were pursuing in Europe. Among them are expanding production and service capabilities, entering into a joint venture or an alliance, and using good strategies and good business sense.

"The winners in this global competition will be world players and the United States should get into the game—now."

"If It's Markets You Need, Look Abroad," *New York Times*, FORUM, January 5, 1992, p. 50.

THE ROLE OF TRADE RELATIONS IN THE GLOBAL MARKETPLACE

To understand why the United States is becoming so interested in boosting its exports, it is necessary to know something about international trade relations.

Each of the world's nations has always been concerned with its own balance of trade. The **balance of trade** refers to the difference between what a nation sells to other countries and what it buys. If a nation sells more than it buys, it is believed to have a **trade surplus** in its trade balance. If a nation buys more than it sells, it is considered to have a **trade deficit**.

Throughout history, most of the world's nations have struggled at one time or another with their balance of trade. Generally, nations believe that they must operate at a trade surplus, but in recent years, some economists have suggested that operating at a deficit may not be as bad as it was once considered. These economists suggest that if a country does not worry about its balance of trade, but simply produces whatever it is best at producing and sells that product to the world, it will thrive. And, according to the theory, so will other nations.

Critics of this theory say that it does not take into account those nations that have few natural resources, no cheap labor supply, and in short, little or nothing to offer to the rest of the world.

Although economists discuss and debate this along with even more complicated theories about what a healthy balance of trade is, most nations continue to do what they have always done, which is to try to buy about the same amount that they sell in the international marketplace. For the U.S. fashion industry, besieged in recent years by the flood of imports, that means selling more American-made merchandise in the international marketplace.

THE U.S. FASHION INDUSTRY'S NEW ROLE IN THE GLOBAL ARENA

The time is riper now for the United States to enter the global arena than at any other time in U.S. history. In 1992, the European Community became a huge, unified, new market to the world. In 1991, the Iron Curtain melted, and the Soviet Union and Eastern bloc nations became another ripe new market for U.S. exports. Prior to that, the Soviet Union and its satellites bought some U.S. products, but U.S. fashion—with its worldly Western values—was not

TECH TALK

DON'T UNDERSTAND—JUST SWITCH ON—A COMPUTER

Once available to only those with huge mainframes, a working command of foreign languages is now accessible to anyone with a personal computer.

New software can save a business time and money by translating letters, proposals, invoices, and brochures in a matter of minutes. For example, professional translators often take an hour to translate a single page and charge $50, whereas software programs can do the work in minutes and are always available.

However, buyers must be cautious in using these programs. No translation program is 100 percent accurate, and many fail when it comes to idiomatic expressions, word order, verb tense, and highly technical or legal subject matter. One recent experience showed that a sentence saying the person's grandfather was a locomotive, really meant to say that he was a "locomotive engineer."

The ease, speed, and availability of translating power, however, should not blind language software converts to the basic rules of communications. After all, a computer can hardly be expected to spit out a grammatically correct letter in French if the user can't make verbs agree in English. Remember GIGO: garbage in, garbage out.

"Language Liberators," Rosalind Resnick, *International Business*, December 1991, pp. 61–62.

welcome. Now the latest U.S. fashions are a symbol of what these nations could become.

U.S. FASHION EXPORT ACTIVITIES

The U.S. fashion industry is in the midst of launching an all-out exporting effort to Europe and Japan. Designers and manufacturers have already begun to devise strategies for conquering the unified European market. For example, Silks, a silk-garment manufacturer, decided to enter the European Community market when its marketing experts discovered that European women did not have access to the new washed silks that had swept the U.S. market in the late 1980s. Leslie Fay, a maker of conservative women's dresses, targeted its market carefully to Great Britain, where women tend to dress conservatively.[3]

In still another example, Hue, a hosiery manufacturer, introduced young European women to an array of color in their hosiery wardrobes that they had never seen before. Hue's strategy is to sell an old product idea to a new market.[4]

Perhaps the most telling sign of the new demand for U.S. fashion occurred in 1992 when Au Printemps, the Parisian department store, staged an all-American promotion. This promotion looked much like the kind of storewide, international-theme extravaganzas that Bloomingdale's had used so successfully the previous ten years to capitalize on the import boom. Only now, the interest was no longer focused on Italy or China, but rather on fashion products made in the United States.

AMERICAN STRENGTHS AND WEAKNESSES

The U.S. fashion industry has many strengths that will make it successful in the international market; and it has some weaknesses to overcome.

American technology is still the best in the world. U.S. factories are the world's most efficient. Even during the 1980s production slump, American fashion producers were streamlining and upgrading production methods, improving services, and learning new ways to cut costs.

In recent years, the United States has also become a far less homogenous population in ways that will serve it well in the international marketplace. Spanish is now spoken by nearly a quarter of all Americans. An influx of immigrants from all over the world stands ready to revitalize the U.S. textile and apparel industry.

The industry's major weakness has been its failure to learn how to export. Fashion producers have been slow to enter the international market. They have resisted making the kinds of production changes that are necessary to accommodate a foreign market that grows more sophisticated every day.

The industry has been held back by its lack of know-how about export. Exporting takes specialized knowledge, and until recently, there have been few places for a prospective exporter to turn for information and advice.

Many fashion producers, who are small and mid-sized businesses, do not believe they are big

U.S. fashion exporters such as Hue have made significant in-roads in recent years in introducing European consumers to American products. *Courtesy of Hue Hosiery.*

enough to crack European markets. A recent survey shows that 70 to 80 percent of U.S. fashion producers have not even tried to export.[5]

But the idea that small companies cannot export successfully is a myth. Small Business Administration statistics show that of 90,000 firms that exported in 1988, 25 percent had fewer than 100 employees. Put another way, most were about the size of the average U.S. fashion producer.[6]

ENTERING THE GLOBAL ARENA

Although exporting and importing are two different processes, they are also like two sides of the same coin. As such, exporting and importing share some similarities. In fact, the basic process of moving goods from one country to another involves the fol-

lowing elements, regardless of whether one is exporting or importing:

1. Strategy.
2. Distribution and Promotion.
3. Processing and Procedures.

STRATEGY

No savvy fashion producer would begin a new venture without first thinking through and planning for the success of the venture. For most people, this means writing a business plan. A well-written business plan asks and answers the questions that ensure success in any venture. In addition, in the international market, a business plan shows the producer what he or she still needs to learn to enter an international venture.

The first question producers must ask is, What products will they—or should they—export or im-

GLOBETROTTING Gaffes

GETTING SICK

Nothing is more embarrassing (remember President Bush and his stomach flu in Japan) or more troublesome than becoming ill on your globetrotting trips. You will greatly reduce your risk of getting sick by avoiding some particularly "troublesome" foods. Keep away from produce of street vendors. (I know it looks good and smells wonderful, a real *no-no*.) Water, whether it is in the form of ice or is drawn from a tap—avoid it. Drink only bottled and packaged beverages. Raw or undercooked foods: these are havens for sickness-causing organisms. Avoid most dairy food; milks, cheeses, and, especially, unpasteurized dairy products are risky to consume. They are often regional delicacies but the safest thing is "thank you, but NO thank you." Even well-cooked foods can pose a risk if the dishes, utensils, or food preparers are not clean. Sometimes stale food is heavily spiced so that you will not notice its age; it can still make you sick!

Every year, millions of Americans are stricken with some form of ailment as a result of traveling and eating abroad. Third World countries, such as those in Latin America, Africa, Asia, and the Middle East, still pose a risk to travelers. To be a savvy globetrotter, contact the U.S. Public Health Service well in advance of your trip. For more detailed information on vaccine, disease, motion illness, water- and food-borne bacteria, you can write for U.S. government information. Send a $5 check, payable to Superintendent of Documents, addressed to same, U.S. Government Printing Office, Washington, D.C., 20402—or call (202) 783-3238.

port? Equally important, Where will they market them?

A producer who is marketing a high-style garment must find an area of the world eager for high style. One who is marketing a basic garment will want to find a region that needs this kind of product. Choosing where to sell exports and imports is as important as deciding what to import or export.

Where will producers get the raw materials for these products, that is, who will be their sources? With the world at their doorstep, as it increasingly is in today's business climate, fashion producers have a variety of sources from which to choose. The hard part is choosing the right ones, the ones that ensure success and acceptance in a global market.

What specifications, if any, of the proposed imports or exports need to be changed to suit the market? And finally, the producer must ask, How will these changes affect the final price? Can it be kept low enough to attract a customer, cover costs, and still earn a profit?

Another important strategic step is to contact sources of export/import information. No one should ever enter a foreign market without help from someone who knows it well. Help is available from federal and state agencies, all of whom are interested in promoting international business.

DISTRIBUTION AND PROMOTION

A careful plan for the distribution and promotion of exports and imports is also necessary. What must be done physically to move the product from one coun-

try to another? What sales-promotion tools are available to help sell the garment in another market? Should the producer emphasize the fact that it was manufactured abroad or play this down?

A fashion producer must learn about foreign agents who are invaluable in making sure that the products reach their intended market. Distribution strategies vary from culture to culture. A line that is sold in large department stores in the United States might do better in small boutiques in another country. In one country, a clothing line may be sold in malls and superstores. Another country may not even have malls and superstores.

Similarly, promotion must take into account regional markets and language differences. Is the same language or dialect spoken throughout a targeted sales region? Even slight changes in dialect can lead to problems in promotion. An advertisement that is witty in the United States may be indecipherable or even insulting in another country—even in a neighboring country.

Differences in values may affect how a garment is promoted. For example, in Japan where modesty is valued, it may be rude to promote a product by announcing that it is the "world's best."

PROCESSING AND PROCEDURES

Processing and procedures refer to the financing and documentation required to move goods from one country to another.

Producers must consider how they will finance their international venture. The first decision will be

Cultural differences must be taken into account when promoting products in another country. The above advertisement would be considered too racy, and therefore unacceptable, for use in an Arab country, where women traditionally bare little skin. *Courtesy of Guess Jeans.*

where to finance the product—at home or in the country to which one hopes to sell. Some foreign countries insist that import endeavors be financed by their own banks, and then the entrepreneur must learn to deal with what may be an entirely different banking system.

Financing methods also differ from country to country. In the United States, certain segments of the fashion market rely on **factors** for financing. (Factors are financial institutions that act as a credit and collection department for a manufacturer. For their services, the factor receives a fee known as a factoring commission.) However, they are not used in all international markets. One customer may want a letter of credit; another may view a request for one as a sign of distrust.

International entrepreneurs must figure out how they will receive payment and in what currency. Some currencies are impossible to translate into other currencies.

Numerous documents are required to import and/or export. One's own country must give permission to export. Fashion producers must learn to deal with customs, and the country to which one sells must give permission to import. Those operating in the global arena must familiarize themselves with import limits and bans as well as special taxes that are frequently levied on imported goods.

Fortunately, there are many sources of information and aid available to the fashion producer interested in working in the international arena. In the chapters that follow, you will learn about these and other important elements of exporting and importing in far greater detail. What often seems initially overwhelming becomes, with expert help, quite manageable.

GLOBAL Goodies
ROME . . . THE ETERNAL CITY

Despite the economic transformation Italy has gone through to become the fifth-largest industrial power, despite the fact that prices are up and shopping, once a reason in itself for visiting Rome, is best confined to "window-shopping," nothing has diminished the glory that is Rome! The Eternal City remains a beauty with magnificent domes, grand piazzas, and golden palaces. And drama is not confined to the stage in Rome. The price of a cappuccino gets you a front-row seat on a Roman square for hours of people watching. The trendy young Romans on the street in eye-catching fashions make this people watching a must.

Rome is also considered one of the greatest eating cities in Europe, with more than 5000 restaurants. The best and liveliest spots are the small family places and trattorias that cater to local neighborhood clientele.

If you are a fan of Italian fashion, remember that most of the time it can be less expensive in the United States, with the exception of a few weeks in January and July when fantastic sales take place in Rome. However, a large-volume fashion exporter has opened two shops worth looking into for bargains. Il Discount dell 'Alta Moda and Discount System carry clothes and accessories from all the top names in Italian fashion and some French designers at 50 percent off the marked prices. Pieces are from past collections, but you might find the proverbial something "smashing" to buy!

Based on "What's Up in Rome?" Martin Rapp, *TRAVEL & LEISURE*, April, 1992, pp. 88–140.

ENDNOTES

1. Phyllis Furman, "Fashion Houses Invading Europe," *Crain's*, June 6, 1991, p. 1.
2. U.S. International Trade Commission, *Emerging Textile-Importing Countries*, Washington, DC, 1982, p. 25.
3. Furman, pp. 1, 35.
4. Furman, pp. 1, 35.
5. Irving Vigdor, *Exporting: Get Into It*, Redwood Associates, 1989, p. 8.
6. William Delphos, editor. *The World Is Your Market*. Washington, DC: Braddock Communications, 1990.

VOCABULARY

balance of trade _____

_____

_____

exports _____

_____

_____

factor _____

_____

_____

globalization _____

_____

_____

imports

_____

_____

_____

trade deficit

_____

_____

trade surplus

_____

_____

_____

GLOBAL REVIEW   1. Why is the textile and apparel industry a significant contributor to the economy of most nations?

_____

_____

_____

_____

2. The lag in international perspective development by the U.S. fashion industry can be attributed to several factors. Name two and explain them.

_____

_____

_____

_____

3. There have been several theories about balance of trade deficit versus trade surplus. What are these theories and how do economists view them?

_____

_____

_____

_____

4. What are three basic elements that are common to both exporting and importing?

_____

_____

_____

_____

5. Why is a business plan essential for success in entering the arena?

    _____

    _____

    _____

    _____

6. Distribution strategies vary from country to country. What are some of the
    variances you would encounter?

    _____

    _____

    _____

    _____

7. Give some examples of a well-known U.S. slogan or ad copy for a fashion
    product that could be either indecipherable or insulting to a foreign
    consumer.

    _____

    _____

    _____

    _____

8. Explain the "one-world concept" and give fashion product examples of how
    it is affecting the U.S. fashion industry.

    _____

    _____

    _____

    _____

9. Why do you think the American fashion image has not yet successfully en-
    tered the global marketplace?

    _____

    _____

    _____

    _____

10. The textile and apparel import boom has been increasing since WWII. Why?
    Give examples that support your answers.

    _____

    _____

    _____

    _____

GLOBAL DIGEST   The following statements are from the text. Discuss the significance of each, giving examples of how each applies to the exporting and importing of fashion products.

1. "In the past fifty years, people's buying patterns have changed drastically."

_____

_____

_____

_____

_____

_____

_____

_____

2. "Because of its geography, the United States has not had to think globally in the same way that, for example, Europe has."

_____

_____

_____

_____

_____

_____

_____

_____

3. "The time is riper now for the United States to enter the global arena than at any other time in U.S. history."

_____

_____

_____

_____

_____

_____

_____

_____

CHAPTER 2

The Diversity of Regional Environments

To sell a dress in the United States, an American designer must put himself or herself into the mind of a familiar customer—the American woman. But to sell a dress in another part of the world, a designer must enter the mind of someone from another, often entirely different, culture. And that is not an easy thing to do, as many failed, would-be international entrepreneurs can testify.

Importing and exporting are not simply about making a garment and selling it in another area of the world; nor is global marketing simply about finding a garment in another country and bringing it home to sell. A successful importer or exporter is selling another culture's sense of style. In doing so, he or she must cater to its values, its esthetics, its economics, and sometimes even its politics.

THE IMPORTANCE OF UNDERSTANDING OTHER CULTURES

Successful exporters and importers must examine the world from many angles. You do not necessarily have to speak another language to do business inter-nationally (although it helps), but you do have to exhibit an understanding of other cultures.

Cultural, social, political, and economic characteristics are important because they affect the way we trade—and what we trade—with one another. For example, some countries are richer than others. With wealth comes a more advanced level of industrialization. The people living in more affluent countries will have more needs and wants than those living in a poor nation.

Affluent people often attach status to buying products that are imported from other countries. In the 1980s, when the United States enjoyed almost unprecedented wealth, people bought imported cars, computers, televisions, and clothes. A well-dressed man or woman was far more likely to be wearing a foreign label than an American one. The leading international fashion-exporting nations—France, Italy, and Japan—increased their presence in and their sales to the United States during this period.

In contrast, a poor or underdeveloped country is unlikely to be highly industrialized. Its primary work may be agricultural, and its people's main concern may be obtaining enough food to survive. When survival is at stake, people do not care about fashion. Their needs are minimal. They are not interested in the latest styles from Paris, Milan, or New York. The only kind of clothes that will be imported into a country like this are basic work clothes, if, indeed, any clothes are imported.

Ultimately, the more we understand others' cultures, the more we respect them. The more we respect others, the easier it is to do business with them. For many years, the nations of the world have mistrusted one another, and this mistrust has been a barrier to trade. As these barriers begin to break down, we can at last enjoy the benefits of the global marketplace.

CULTURAL TRAITS OF NATIONS

Even though we are all individuals, generally some traits are considered to be shared among the people of a nation. These are called **cultural traits.** The Japanese, for example, are known to be reserved as a culture, that is, many Japanese answer to this description, although, of course, some do not. Americans, on the other hand, are known for their gregarious, outgoing natures. Naturally, some Americans are not gregarious and outgoing, but many are.

The cultural traits of a nation affect how work is viewed. Do people work hard and long hours, or do they value time off and routinely take it? Do they take long lunches or short lunches? Can business be discussed over lunch? Do they gather on time for business meetings, or by unspoken agreement, do they typically start ten or even thirty minutes late?

What is beautiful—and what is not—also varies from culture to culture. What is acceptable with regard to the color, design, and shape of a product may have everything to do with cultural values. In much of Europe, chrysanthemums are considered a funeral flower and they would not be used, for example, to promote a new product. Nor would they be sent to someone with whom you hoped to do business. In Japan, the way in which a package is wrapped has special meaning, so much so that people from other countries would do well to take any business gifts to a Japanese firm that specializes in gift wrapping.

Sexual mores are another trait that varies from culture to culture. In Italy and France, nude women are routinely used in advertisements for lingerie and other products, something that would not be tolerated in the United States.

Fashion trends are also tempered by one's cultural outlook. Eastern Europeans love American jeans. They have long viewed them as a sign of Western liberation. Yet, they may not want exactly the same jeans that Americans are wearing. If Americans are switching to looser fitting jeans, eastern Europeans may still favor the tight jeans worn during the 1960s when jeans first became popular with youth. If the jeans that Americans export into these countries do not fit the way eastern Europeans want them to, they will not buy them.

SOCIAL TRAITS OF NATIONS

A country's social values also affect how business will be conducted. Do bosses and workers mix? Often class differences around the world are more rigid than in the United States. In countries like Great Britain and India, class differences may be very marked. Even in countries that do not have such fixed differences, there may be unwritten rules that must be observed if one is to do business successfully.

Social values affect the role men, women, and children play in the workplace. In some countries such as Japan, women are still not welcome in the executive ranks. In an Arab country, it is bad taste to ask a man about his wife. In Latin American countries, it would be bad taste not to inquire after a colleague's family before settling down to business.

Most countries ban child labor, but a few permit it. In some countries, sewing is exclusively women's work; in others, it is men's work.

How educated workers are, whether they read or write, and whether they speak other languages are all social traits that will affect how the business of the country is conducted.

POLITICAL TRAITS OF NATIONS

A nation's current political environment affects its ability to trade. A politically unstable nation may be difficult to do business with. Exporting or importing goods into a nation at war, for example, can be risky, if not impossible.

How a country is governed also affects how business will be conducted on an ongoing basis. Political structure is also closely tied to economic structure. Most governments tend toward one of two basic categories, authoritarian or democratic.

Does one ideology prevail, as in China, or are there many competing ideologies, as in the United States? If everyone is controlled by the same ideology, the government is **authoritarian.** Only people in power make decisions, and they make them for everyone. There are no competing constituencies, or they are not very powerful because they risk arousing the disapproval of those in power.

If everyone is involved in political decisions, and there are many constituencies or groups attempting to influence the political process, then the government is **democratic.** Many interest groups exist, each of whom tries to influence the elected leaders.

Not many airlines consider cargo
an ancient tradition.

As a culture, we were in the cargo business long before it was a business.

Though no one knows exactly how long, we do know that for centuries Japanese meals have been shipped in Bento boxes like the one above. A Bento box kept meals fresh for long periods of time by storing each course separately in its own sturdy compartment.

This long history of reliable perishables transport continues to this day at JAL Cargo, where our claim rate is an astonishing 1/100th the industry average.

After all, we didn't just get into the cargo business. You might say we were born into it.

JAL CARGO
No one takes cargo more seriously.

A nation's cultural traits, such as Japan's respect for tradition, are often reflected in its advertising. *Courtesy of Japan Airlines. Hing-Norton (c) 1991 NYC.*

In the United States, for example, the International Ladies Garment Workers Union (ILGWU) lobbies Congress for certain advantages for its members. For instance, it tries to restrict the number of imported garments that come into the country because they compete with American-made garments and have adversely affected the U.S. jobs.

In authoritarian governments, the ruling elite decides what is best for its garment industry and its buying public as well. Individuals and interest groups have little or no say in how their businesses will be run. If the government wants to expand exports, it will order businesses to take steps to do so. If it wants to cut down on exports, it will take steps to accomplish that, too, often with little regard for the rights of the individual entrepreneur.

In a democracy, the garment industry makes its own decisions regarding growth and profit, always taking into account customer demand.

ECONOMIC TRAITS OF NATIONS

Countries either have market-oriented economies or centrally planned economies. A **market-oriented economy** is geared both to profit and to consumers. The United States is a market-oriented economy.

GLOBAL *Goodies*
GIFT GIVING—JAPAN

The presentation of business gifts can be the final touch in a successful encounter or can turn a positive experience into a failure. Research into the gift-giving preferences and customs of the countries with which you plan to do business is well worth the extra effort, especially for Japan, which can be a tricky place when it comes to buying and presenting your host with a gift.

A gift should be given if visiting a company for the first time. This gift should be presented either after a meeting or at the business trip's conclusion. The Japanese are sensitive to corporate ranking where gift giving is concerned. Therefore, you should always give your best gifts to the most senior person in the group.

Some good gifts might include something special from your home state, maple syrup from Vermont, a nice bottle of wine from New York or California, or peanuts from Georgia or Alabama. Company logo-embossed items and commemorative plaques are also popular presents (as long as the company name is not tastelessly large!). Other welcome gifts include imported Scotch or cognac and frozen steaks. Just be careful to avoid gifts in multiples of four. The number four has morbid connotations in Japan.

Based on "Giving Gifts on Trips Abroad," by Jane Lansky. *Gannett Suburban Newspapers*, November 25, 1991, C Section p. 4.

Centrally planned economies generally go hand in hand with authoritarian governments. They are not geared to profit and are not run by consumer demand. At the moment, China is the only major country that has a centrally planned economy. Until the late 1980s, the Soviet Union and its Eastern bloc satellite nations were authoritarian, centrally planned economies, but this form of government crumbled, and one by one, those countries are now struggling to become more market oriented.

Most governments are a mixture of the two economic forms. In the United States, for example, labor laws designed to protect workers are limits set on the market. Usury laws, which limit the amount that money lenders can charge, are another example of a control on the free market. Although in theory, free-market economies work best with little regulation, in practice, most governments impose some restraints on free-market economies.

Centrally planned and free-market economies can run into trouble when they try to do business with one another. When China asked to join an international trade organization that many of the world's nations belong to, other nations opposed its admission to the group because they knew China wanted to export textiles. The textile-producing countries worried that because China was not profit oriented, it would be able to undersell the market-oriented economies of the world. Their textile industries would suffer unfairly, they thought, through no fault of their own.

ECONOMIC ADVANCEMENT AMONG NATIONS

Nations are also affected in their ability to engage in international trade by their level of economic advancement. Generally, the world's nations are classified as developed countries (DCs), less developed countries (LDCs), and newly industrialized countries (NICs).

DEVELOPED COUNTRIES (DCs)

Developed countries include all members of the Organization for Economic Cooperation and Development (OECD), which is the United States, Canada, Japan, Western Europe, Australia, and New Zealand.[1] The former USSR and several Eastern bloc nations were until recently included in this group, but with the disintegration of their economic systems, many are in a state of flux. With the two Germanies merged, Germany will be a powerful developed country, but Poland, Czechoslovakia, and Lithuania may no longer fit this category.

NEWLY INDUSTRIALIZED COUNTRIES (NICs)

Newly industrialized countries lag behind developed countries in industrialization, although they have some resources moving them toward greater

TEST YOUR BUSINESS SENSE

How well would you do conducting business in Japan? In each of the following situations, decide whether you would follow the approach indicated.

1. On meeting your Japanese counterpart, you return the man's bow with one of equal depth.

2. After greetings have been exchanged, you wait for your colleagues to seat themselves and then immediately begin negotiations.

3. Your Japanese business partner presents you with a gift. In return, you present your partner with a gift of a pair of cufflinks.

4. After you exchange your business card with your Japanese host, you tuck the host's card into your briefcase for safe keeping.

5. During a dinner conversation, you mention that your father is a World War II veteran.

6. After a meeting, a female executive declines an invitation to join her male colleagues at a geisha house.

7. While posing for a photograph, you throw your arm around your Japanese colleague.

8. During after-business drinks, you move your glass to make it easier for your Japanese host to pour. Not wanting to bother your host again for a second round, you help yourself.

ANSWERS

1. Although handshakes are gaining acceptance in Japan, the traditional bow is still considered the norm. Because you and your Japanese counterpart are equals, matching the depth of your bow to your colleague's is correct. However, if your Japanese host is your superior in business, you bow a bit lower.

2. The Japanese take their time. Before you get down to business, you should wait for your host to offer tea and try to get to know you and your company.

3. Gift-giving is customary for business associates. However, you should wait until your host offers you one first. Gifts normally are not opened in the giver's presence in Japan. Appropriate gifts include brandy, frozen steaks, and objects that come in pairs (considered good luck).

4. Business cards hold more importance in Japan than in the United States. Therefore, the card

should be extended with both hands and the type should face the receiver. (Ideally, the card should be printed in Japanese on one side.) Your host will examine the card and keep it on the table, which you should do as well.

5. Avoid talk about World War II with your Japanese host.

6. The Japanese have not yet felt the full force of feminism. If you are a woman, you may be invited out of politeness, but you are expected to decline. Women are not yet welcome in geisha houses, at sumo wrestling matches, or on certain mountains considered too sacred for women.

7. Wrong! The very reserved Japanese do not like public displays of affection.

8. When drinking alcoholic beverages, allow your drink to be poured, and then pour the other person's drink in return.

GLOBAL *GO-GETTERS*

MANFRED KRONEN: "A CONTINENTAL MANNER"

Courtesy of Igedo Düsseldorf.

Manfred Kronen, the owner of IGEDO in Dusseldorf, Europe's largest fashion fair, is in expansion throughout the Continent. In March 1991, he inaugurated *Moda Berlin*, the first modern fashion salon in the former Eastern Germany. In March 1992, he launched the Dusseldorf Gallery, a special section at IGEDO to showcase quality French, British, and U.S. fashion. The International Fashion Center, a joint venture with a leading German ready-to-wear (RTW) manufacturer, to be opened in Moscow, is nearing completion.

Mr. Kronen has some ideas on what U.S. companies must do if they are to conquer a slice of the giant European unified market. "American manufacturing is good, and its RTW is very good. But it's delivered too late for Europe."

In eastern Europe, the main problem as Kronen sees it is educational. "People still need to be taught how to operate the capitalistic system of buying and selling and a distribution system of retail stores. We need to help these economies so they can become good clients. But the first steps are being made. So the next 10 years will certainly be years of great opportunity."

As for Moscow, Kronen said he is convinced there is enormous potential there. Soviet companies that export are allowed to keep about 20 to 30 percent of their foreign currency and use this to buy consumer goods for their workers. "Fashion," according to Kronen, "is one of their first requests."

Information from "Manfred Kronen's Continental Manner," Godfrey Dieney, *Women's Wear Daily*, November 27, 1991, p. 18.

economic advancement. They often have large populations but a small share of the world's wealth.

The Eastern bloc nations, which, as of this writing, include Romania, Poland, Estonia, Hungary, Czechoslovakia, and Lithuania, are now considered newly industrialized nations. Once they successfully convert to a market-oriented economy, several, if not all, of these countries will undoubtedly be considered DCs.

Other NICs, whose recent growth can be largely attributed to their booming textile and apparel industries, include the city-state Hong Kong, which is due to become part of mainland China again in 1997; South Korea, whose standard of living is rapidly improving; and Taiwan. South Africa is sometimes classified as a developing country, sometimes as a newly industrialized country.[2]

LESS DEVELOPED COUNTRIES (LDCs)

Less developed countries suffer from a lack of exploitable resources and competitive industries. Existence may be at the subsistence level. These facts combine to keep LDCs from participating in any real sense in world trade. Because of a lack of industry, the less developed countries may depend on imports, but they rarely export their goods, a fact that also contributes to their remaining poor.

Thirty-six of the world's nations have been designated LDCs, including most of the African nations and some—Bangladesh, Afghanistan, Laos, Nepal—in Asia. In the Western Hemisphere, only Haiti is considered an LDC.[3]

NORTH-SOUTH DIALOGUE

Naturally, the world's LDCs, which are also sometimes referred to as Third World countries, are eager to join in the prosperity of the First and Second World nations. Because First and Second World nations do profit from trade with Third World nations, Third World nations have begun to insist that they receive economic aid from the richer nations.

To this end, in 1964, the United Nations convened the Conference on Trade and Development (UNCTAD) to coordinate and facilitate relations among First and Third World nations.

This led to what is usually called the **North-South dialogue**, which began in 1974. It was so named because the richest nations of the world occupied the Northern Hemisphere, whereas the poorest nations occupied the Southern Hemisphere. The North-South dialogues are a series of ongoing talks about how to help the LDCs, mostly through reduced trade barriers, investment, and improved exports.

Although the South wants to use trade with the North to advance its own ends, this has not always worked out, especially as the nations of the world become more economically interlinked with one another. Aid can be forthcoming only when the Northern Hemisphere countries are rich. Throughout the 1970s, these nations were riddled with inflation and unemployment, and were unable to extend as much help as they formerly had to Third World nations. All

Because of its booming textile and apparel industries, Hong Kong has now evolved from being designated as one of the world's less developed countries to one of its newly developed countries. *Courtesy of the Hong Kong Trade Development Council.*

the world's nations began to realize that the economy was now truly global and that help would have to go in both directions. Problems had to be viewed in less divisive terms.

Although the problems have not been erased, the international mood is one of growing cooperation rather than strife. Since the talks began, Third World nations have gradually begun to improve their trading status and are now exporting their products to new foreign markets.

CHOOSING AN IMPORT/EXPORT REGION

One important decision that international traders must make, regardless of whether they come from a DC or an LDC, is what to sell in the global marketplace. Another equally important decision is where to sell it. The world may be in the process of becoming a gigantic global marketplace, but this does not mean that all our regional differences have vanished. Nor does it mean that any one importer or exporter will do business with the entire world. Smart entrepreneurs learn that they must focus on a region of the world that will be receptive to their product.

To find a region ripe for importing or exporting entails considerable research, but before beginning this kind of specialized task, an entrepreneur needs to develop an overview of the business practices, customs, culture, and language of the world's trading nations. In the following pages, you will find general information about the major textile and apparel trading regions of the world.

CREATING FREE TRADE REGIONS

The worldwide dialogue on exporting and importing has produced at least one important change. Many nations have begun to form **free trade regions.** These are geographic areas in which there are few or no barriers to trade. These free trade zones are secure areas, usually located in or near customs ports of entry, which are regarded as legally outside a nation's customs territory.

BREAKING DOWN TRADE BARRIERS

Trade barriers are a product of the Industrial Revolution. Before the Industrial Revolution, most products were handmade by individuals, a time-consuming, laborious task that meant most products did not travel far from their producers. Producers worked hard enough to create products to meet local needs; the idea of international trade of most products seemed moot. Even if the interest in trading with others existed, the means did not.

With the advent of industrialization, though, products were mass-produced for the first time in history. With products being turned out in such huge numbers, producers could consider larger markets. The prospect of lucrative international trade loomed on the horizon as well.

Nations rushed to see who could earn the most profit from their mass-produced products. They began to sell their products in foreign markets and soon became aware that other nations were trying to sell their products right back. That is when the world's nations rushed to put special protections in place, protections that were designed to ensure that their own mass-produced products would be given preference over other country's goods.

Countries have several ways of preventing what they consider to be unfair competition from foreign producers. The most common are duties and quotas. **Duties** are special taxes on imports. **Quotas** are limits on the amount of a product that may be brought into a country. During the Industrial Revolution and continuing until recently, the nations of the world built many barriers to trade. Today, many countries, with Japan leading the way, are using standards as a restraint measure. By insisting on exceptionally difficult standards for the finished product, imports are likely to become noncompetitive because of added costs to meet these standards.

ADVANTAGES OF FREE TRADE

As the countries of the world have expanded their markets into all areas of the globe over the past few decades, they have become more interdependent on one another. The world's nations have begun to see the advantages of tearing down the old trade barriers. Without trade barriers, there can be true reciprocity. Each country welcomes the other's imports and knows that its imports will be welcomed in turn.

Imports and exports may even complement each other. The United States does not produce silk, for example, so it buys silk from China. China, in turn, might buy wool, which it does not produce, from the United States.

Other benefits to free trade include mutual growth and investment. China might invest money in the American wool industry while the United States might invest money in China's silk production industry. Each country's textile industry grows as a result.

MAJOR FREE TRADE REGIONS

The 1970s and 1980s saw the establishment of several major free trade regions in the world, and if all goes well, the 1990s will be a period to reap the benefits from them. To encourage and facilitate international trade, more than 300 free ports, free trade zones, and similar customs-priveleged facilities are now in operation in some 75 foreign countries, usually in or near seaports or airports. Many U.S. manufacturers and their distributors use free ports or free trade zones for receiving shipments of goods that are reshipped in smaller lots to customers throughout the surrounding areas.

ASSOCIATION OF SOUTH EAST ASIAN NATIONS (ASEAN)

Organized in 1977, the Association of South East Asian Nations (ASEAN) removed trade barriers among its members, Malaysia, Singapore, Philippines, Thailand, Indonesia, and Brunei. These nations are strong fashion-production centers, although they have yet to make a mark with their own designs.

In recent years, money has poured into ASEAN's garment industries from the other major Asian textile and apparel centers, Hong Kong, Taiwan, and South Korea, known as the Big Three. The Big Three were so successful selling garments to the rest of the world throughout the 1970s and 1980s that the United States and Europe imposed tighter quotas on them to protect their own fashion industries. In response, the Big Three shifted much of their production to ASEAN nations, where quotas were not so strict, and these nations' garment industries thrived as a result.

THE EUROPEAN COMMUNITY (EC)

Established in 1952, the European Community (EC), also referred to as the Common Market or the European Economic Community, organized with twelve member nations—Belgium, Denmark, France, Great Britain, the Netherlands, Spain, Greece, Ireland, Italy, Luxembourg, Portugal, and Germany—to become one trading entity.[4]

The EC's purpose is to eliminate all trade barriers. Member nations still govern themselves and retain national identities, but there are no duties or quotas among them. Exporting and importing among not only member nations but also other countries will be further facilitated by easy exchanges at national borders, centralized shipping, and unified billing and accounting systems.

TECH TALK

COFFEE, TEA, OR EXPANDED MEMORY?

As recently as a few years ago, international executives had only two options when it came to laptop computers: weak or cumbersome. Today, with over 350 companies designing laptops, and the technology advancing in leaps and bounds, the options have improved.

From "palmtops" weighing less than a pound to stylish notebook computers that fit in a briefcase and portable supercharged workstations, laptop computers now come in a variety of styles, sizes, and models, a variety wide enough to meet the demands of the most exacting international businessperson. Both physical size and weight, for instance, take on an additional significance when you travel frequently or travel over long distances.

If you are a "power" user or you want to use the same high-end software program on the road that you use at home, you will want a laptop with a fairly powerful processor. But remember: The more powerful the processor, the greater its battery consumption. Also true for laptop users, but particularly for international users, the keyboard is the most important element of your laptop to consider. And look closely at the screen. Along with the keyboard, a laptop's display will most affect your health and well-being. "Backlit" (as opposed to "edgelit") screens deliver the greatest clarity.

Battery life is another critical consideration for the international businessperson. If battery life is essential, you can usually purchase a second battery pack, essentially doubling computing time between charges. Of course, you will plug in your laptop whenever you can, and in Europe, as well as many other foreign countries, that means you will have to accommodate 220-volt power sources. Most major laptop manufacturers offer 220-volt or dual voltage power supplies, an absolute must for international businesspeople.

And what happens when your laptop breaks down abroad? Many of the larger laptop vendors have authorized dealers in other countries. If you spend much time in one or two foreign countries, check to see if the manufacturer has a dealer there. At least you will have someone to complain to.

Finally, if you are using a modem, make sure your laptop has a communications port or can support an internal modem. You may also need additional adapters for foreign phone jacks. Taking the time to choose the right laptop will save you hassles wherever business may happen to take you.

Based on Eric J. Adams, "The Latest Laptops For Global Executives," *World Trade*, October, 1991, pp. 104–108.

The EC will provide a wealth of opportunities for other countries interested in international trade. In 1990, 87 percent of U.S. exports went to western Europe.[5] American consumer goods, including textiles and apparel, are much desired by European nations, and trade will only become easier when western Europe is one trading area. The next few years will present an excellent window of opportunity for Americans to solidify their export position in western Europe. However, it is also probable that tariffs and quotas may be increased to nonmember nations, such as the United States. Therefore, it is essential that the United States have a strong export strategy that will build on the business already existing.

EUROPEAN FREE TRADE ASSOCIATION (EFTA)

In 1960, another free trade group was formed by Austria, Iceland, Norway, Sweden, Switzerland, and Finland. Member nations levy no tariffs on manufactured goods made by other members. Each member

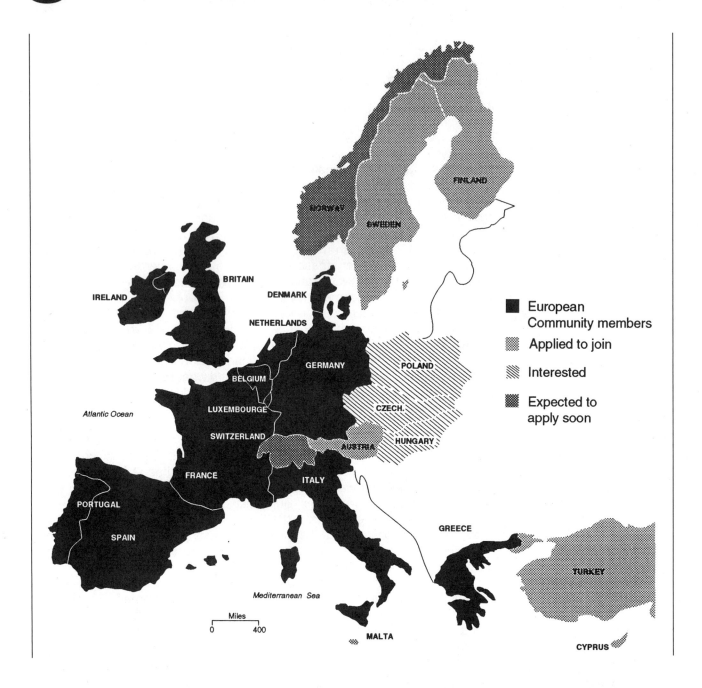

NORWAY

SWEDEN

FINLAND

BRITAIN

IRELAND

DENMARK

NETHERLANDS

POLAND

GERMANY

BELGIUM

Atlantic Ocean

LUXEMBOURGE

CZECH.

SWITZERLAND

AUSTRIA

HUNGARY

FRANCE

ITALY

PORTUGAL

SPAIN

GREECE

TURKEY

Mediterranean Sea

Miles
0   400

MALTA

CYPRUS

◼ European
Community members

▨ Applied to join

▧ Interested

▨ Expected to
apply soon

maintains its own external tariff structure for trade with other countries.[6]

The United States has not gone out of its way to trade with EFTA member nations, but with trade ties increasing around the world and EC emerging in 1992, the coming decade may offer an excellent opportunity to improve trade relations with this region as well.

At the end of 1991, after two years of negotiations, EC and EFTA agreed to form the world's largest trade bloc by 1993. The new European Economic Area will extend from the Arctic to the Mediterranean, embrace 380 million customers, and account

for 43 percent of world trade. In general, it requires EFTA to adopt most EC commercial practices, paving the way for nearly a doubling in the Community's size by the year 2000.[7]

THE CARIBBEAN BASIN INITIATIVE (CBI)

The Caribbean Basin Initiative (CBI) was enacted in 1983 between the United States and twenty-seven Caribbean nations and Mexico. Although most products became duty free, garments were subject to a tariff until 1986 when the Caribbean Basic Textile Ac-

GLOBAL GLIMPSES

EFTA: SEVEN BRIDES FOR SEVEN BROTHERS?

The European Free Trade Association (EFTA) is a seven-country trading bloc organized in 1960 as a counterweight to the European Community. EFTA consists of Austria, Sweden, Norway, Finland, Switzerland, Iceland, and since summer 1991, Liechtenstein. Although EFTA customs union allows goods to flow duty free among member states, EFTA has never sought the total economic integration that is the current goal of the EC.

Nonetheless, EFTA economies have much in common: Each boasts a high standard of living, an extensive network of social programs, and a skilled and educated workforce. EFTA members have among the highest GNP per capita in Europe. In fact, this prosperity has caused many people in those countries to oppose discussion of EC membership.

The question of how EFTA would fare when EC emerged in 1992 did not surface. A principal concern was whether EFTA economies could continue to prosper after "The Twelve" became a unified market. EFTA feared that its members would be isolated from EC and that its population of 33 million would be overwhelmed by EC's 343 million consumers.

In response, EFTA members have drawn closer to EC, moving both unilaterally and as an organization. Austria and Sweden have already formally applied for EC membership. Norway, Iceland, Finland, and even traditionally isolated Switzerland are seriously reassessing their roles in merging Europe.

Based on "EFTA: Europe's Other Prosperous Trade Bloc," Amy L. Wolfcale, *Export Today*, October, 1991, pp. 16–19; and "The 12 Become 19," *Newsweek*, November 14, 1991, p. 53.

cess Program was instituted. Under this program, Caribbean-made apparel can now enter the United States under a special tariff schedule #807 and #807A. Apparel that has the garment pieces cut in the United States of U.S.-made fabric, bundled, and shipped to the Caribbean, can reenter with duty charges only on the value added by the assembly.[8]

Since the Initiative, the Caribbean has become a strong production area for U.S. fashion. Labor is relatively cheap, and because the Caribbean nations are closer than the Asian fashion-producing nations, shipping costs are reduced as well.

UNITED STATES-CANADIAN FREE TRADE AGREEMENT (USCFTA)

In 1989, the United States and Canada began to organize as a free trade area. All barriers to textile and apparel trade will be phased out by 1999.

The American textile and apparel industry opposed the agreement. They feared that Canada would become a pipeline for cheap imported products.

The advantage of free trade with Canada probably outweighs any potential disadvantage. Canada's proximity and cultural similarities make it an ideal and natural export market for the United States. It is already the United States's major trading partner. Two thirds of Canada's trade is with the United States.[9]

NORTH AMERICAN FREE TRADE AGREEMENT (NAFTA)

The success in removing trade barriers between the United States and Canada spurred the two nations toward a similar agreement with Mexico, their neighbor to the south.

The North American Free Trade Agreement (NAFTA) is also expected to boost U.S. exports. Between 1987 and 1991, trade between the United States and Mexico doubled. Mexico is the United States's third-largest trading partner, after Canada and Japan.[10]

Past attempts to establish a convenient trade route between the United States and Mexico have failed in recent years, but the timing seems right this time. Mexico has made economic reforms that have bolstered its economic climate and raised business confidence.[11]

NAFTA is the most complex trade agreement the United States has ever undertaken and the first time it has signed an agreement with a developing nation.

The textile industry stands to benefit from the agreement because tariffs will be phased out for textiles and garment manufacturing, but American labor unions and human rights groups have raised concerns that the U.S. fashion producers will abuse the cheap labor in Mexico. Unions are also concerned that competition from cheap labor will force U.S. wages down.

A Few Examples Of What's Being Made In Mexico Today.

BANCA SERFIN

Investing in Mexico is truly a money-making proposition. Just ask a few of your competitors who have. Fortune 1000 companies in the appliance, electronic and automotive industries, to cite a few examples.

Companies in these and other industries are profiting from investments in one of the world's top-performing stock markets. And from direct investments in privatizations, low-cost production sharing plants and joint ventures.

So much so, in fact, that almost a full 65 percent of foreign capital invested in Mexico has come from corporations in the United States.

A significant portion of it from the clients of Banca Serfin. For as Mexico's most experienced international bank, no one has arranged more sales of state-owned industry. And no one can provide a better link to our country's fast-paced growth.

Because we offer every service from investment banking and export finance to M&A and maquiladora assistance. In short, all the capabilities you could need.

So talk with Banca Serfin about an investment in Mexico. And see what we can make of it.

Mexico City	New York	Tokyo	London	Toronto	Los Angeles	Nassau	Belize	Seoul
(525) 709-7644	(212) 574-9504	(8133) 273-5911	(4471) 408-2151	(416) 360-8900	(213) 955-0749	(212) 574-9500	(5012) 7-81-79	(822) 756-5186

For more information on investing in Mexico, call toll-free 1-800-336-7330 (U.S.); 1-800-336-6899 (Canada).

American investment in Mexican business has resulted in Mexican banks expanding their services in investment banking and export finance. *Courtesy of Albert Frank-Gunther Law. Art by Dom Algieri. Copy by Jon Sanders and Linda Edwards.*

GLOBETROTTING Gaffes

U.S. ETHNOCENTRICS

Three of our most popular national take-alongs on our global travels include the following. Try not to pack them on your trip.

1. *Why don't they speak English?* For the same reason we don't speak Catalan or Urdu.
2. *Take me to your fast-food emporium!* Scrambled eggs, showers, T.V., and all the other take-for-granted things here in the United States can be missing from your life on your travels. So what! Experiment! Try the local specialties.
3. *American know-how to the rescue!* Although we know how to cope with many things, bigger, smarter, and faster do not always add up to better. Remember, many of the cultures you will be working with were rich in art and technology when North America was still a glacier.

Despite these potential drawbacks, the free trade agreement will promote economic growth throughout Latin America, and everyone will benefit from stronger Latin American neighbors.

OTHER IMPORTANT TRADING AREAS

Apart from the free trade regions of the world, several other countries stand out as fashion centers eager to establish import/export relations with the rest of the world.

ASIA

Major fashion centers that are emerging in Asia include the so-called Big Three—Taiwan, South Korea, and Hong Kong—as well as China. Japan has been a major trading partner for the United States and other Western nations for a longer time.

BIG THREE   The economies of Taiwan, South Korea, and Hong Kong have improved significantly in recent years, in large part because of their successes in textile and apparel production. These countries would like to have a design impact on the rest of the world, and they are equally interested in buying Western design. Thus far, few U.S. exports have made their way to this part of the world, in large part because of the Big Three's resistance to imports. The United States has put intense pressure on the Big Three to permit more U.S. imports.

CHINA   The Big Three is sometimes amended to the Big Four when China is included as a major fashion producer. Textiles, especially silk and cotton, are important Chinese exports. China is Hong Kong's largest supplier of medium-priced piece goods, and if its technology were updated, it could become a major supplier to the rest of the world as well.[12]

China has pressured the United States to reduce trade barriers, although it remains to be seen whether it would be interested in buying American fashion. As the largest centrally planned economy and authoritarian government in the world, it has less interest in high fashion of the kind produced in the United States and western Europe than do most other nations in Asia.

JAPAN   Japan is the only Asian country whose designers have had a fashion impact on the Western world. In the 1970s, Japanese designers such as Kan-sai Yamamoto, Rei Kawakubo of Comme les Garçons, Yohji Yamamoto, and Matsuhiro Mastudo revolutionized the shape and texture of Western fashion. Their influence has continued.

In turn, as Japan's individual wealth has skyrocketed, the Japanese have become increasingly interested in Western fashion. Despite pressure from the United States, which sees Japan as a rich import market, Japan has not been especially cooperative about letting U.S. imports into the country.

TRADITIONAL EUROPEAN DESIGN CENTERS

For the United States, major western European sources of fashion imports are France, Italy, Germany, and Great Britain. These and other western European countries are also becoming increasingly important as export markets for American textiles and apparel.

FRANCE   France has been a fashion center—*the* fashion center—of the Western world since the reign of Louis XIV (1643–1715), when French designers began to dictate what would be worn in royal courts around the world.

New fashion is still created in the studios of France's haute couture designers. In recent years, France has also made inroads in prêt-à-porter, or ready-to-wear, which it exports throughout the world. It is impossible to step into a major American department store and not see French ready-to-wear imports.

ITALY   France's only fashion rival in recent years has been Italy, whose original designs in apparel and accessories, especially those in knitwear and leather, have swept the world. Italy is especially known for its innovative fabrics and yarns. It, too, has carved out a strong U.S. market for its exports.

GERMANY   Germany has not been a hot spot for American fashion buyers until recent years, when a number of young designers have caught the interest of American importers. Germany has also become a sophisticated, lucrative export market for the United States.

GREAT BRITAIN   For many years, London was for menswear what Paris has been for women's apparel—the fountainhead of fashion inspiration. In recent years, its dominance has diminished, and Italy has become the main source of European-styled menswear. But London still remains the major fashion center for impeccably tailored men's custom apparel.

Britain's most important fashion strength, however, lies in tweeds, woolens, and knitwear for both men and women.

WESTERN EUROPE'S INTEREST IN U.S. IMPORTS The United States has had less success in exporting to western Europe than western Europe has had in exporting into the United States, largely because of its own ambivalence about doing business abroad. American designers are well-known and respected, though, and this is a ripe potential market for U.S. goods.

EASTERN BLOC NATIONS

Democracy, along with economic reform, swept through eastern Europe and the Soviet Union in the late 1980s. Most of the Eastern bloc countries' economies are struggling, but the long-term outlook is good for them provided they make a successful shift from centrally planned to market-oriented economies.

The area is ripe for exports. U.S. exports to Romania doubled in 1990. Poland's freer economic policies make it a lucrative market for U.S. goods. The Commonwealth of Independent States, formerly the Soviet Union, has made it clear that it would like to do business with the Western nations, particularly the United States. And as their economies pick up strength, these nations will also begin to export their own fashions into the United States and other Western nations.

ETHNOCENTRISM: THE BIGGEST BARRIER TO INTERNATIONAL TRADE

Ironically, the single largest barrier to international trade is not the difference in political ideologies or the way economies are structured. Rather, it is each nation's ethnocentrism. **Ethnocentrism** is the belief, held by virtually every nation in the world, that its way of life is best or even superior to the way others live. Basically, this means that people apply their own culture to other peoples' cultures when developing products or conducting business negotiations. Ethnocentrism promotes prejudice. It hurts world trade. It gives offense. And it slows down the cultural understanding the world needs to become truly one global marketplace that will benefit everyone.

ENDNOTES

1. Care A. Nelson, *Your Own Import-Export Business: Winning the Trade Game.* Chula Vista, CA: Global Business and Trade Communications, 1988, p. 12. Kitty G. Dickerson, *Textiles and Apparel in the International Economy.* New York: Macmillan, 1991, p. 44.
2. Dickerson, p. 45.
3. Nelson, p. 12.
4. "Europe," *Business America*, vol. 112, no. 8, April 22, 1991, pp. 21–25.
5. Ibid., pp. 21–25.
6. Ibid., p. 22.
7. "The 12 Become 19," *Newsweek*, November 4, 1991, p. 53.
8. "Europe," *Business America*, vol. 112, no. 7, April 8, 1991, pp. 13–20.
9. Ibid., pp. 14–16.
10. World Institute White Paper, *US-Mexico Trade Agreement: What Can It Mean for New York and New Jersey Trade Policy?*, World Trade Institute, The Port Authority of New York and New Jersey, July 5, 1991, pp. 1–2.
11. Ibid., pp. 1–2.
12. Paul Charles Ehrlick, "The China Connection," *Women's Wear Daily*, September 28, 1987, p. 19.

VOCABULARY   authoritarian

centrally planned
economy

_____
_____
_____

cultural traits

_____
_____
_____

democratic

_____
_____
_____

developed country
(DC)

_____
_____
_____

duties

_____
_____
_____

ethnocentrism

_____
_____
_____

free trade regions or
zones

_____
_____
_____

less developed country
(LCD)

_____
_____
_____

market-oriented
economy

_____
_____
_____

newly industrialized
country (NIC)

_____
_____
_____

North-South dialogue

_____
_____
_____

quotas _____

_____

_____

GLOBAL REVIEW 1. Explain how the difference between the cultural traits of nations affects their international outlook.

_____

_____

_____

_____

2. The differences between social traits of various nations affect how business will be conducted. Give examples citing social differences for four different countries and how they affect international trade.

_____

_____

_____

_____

3. Explain how the political traits of a nation can affect its ability to be an international trader.

_____

_____

_____

_____

4. What are the major differences between a market-oriented economy and a centrally planned economy? Give a practical example of how these differences affect international trade.

_____

_____

_____

_____

_____

5. Explain and give an example of a "developed country" *DC*, a "newly industrialized country" *NIC*, and a "less developed country" *LDC*.

_____

_____

_____

_____

6. What is a Free Trade Zone and why were they conceived?

7. What are the advantages of "Free Trade"?

8. Give examples of U.S. laws that foster protectionism in the textile and apparel industries.

9. What are the major Free Trade Regions?

GLOBAL DIGEST

1. Give the "pros" and "cons" of "free trade" and "protectionism" as it affects U.S. apparel manufacturers.

2. Explain the purpose of EC and (a) give reasons why it will be beneficial to the U.S. international traders and (b) why it will be harmful for U.S. traders.

_____

_____

_____

_____

_____

_____

3. Discuss ethnocentrism as it relates to (a) making for more free trade, (b) moving more protectionism into trade, and (c) promoting exchange of customs.

_____

_____

_____

_____

_____

_____

_____

_____

CHAPTER 3

International Fashion Market Analysis

Even within a country as large as the United States, fashion producers enjoy a certain homogeneity in the marketplace. Sizes are standardized nationwide, and styles often sweep the country. If brightly colored silk trench coats are popular on the East Coast, producers of these coats can be reasonably certain that their success, in some recognizable form, will eventually travel across the country until it reaches the other coast.

Regional differences, of course, have always existed, and probably always will. New York women, for example, favor dark colors and tend to wear them year-round. On the sultriest summer day, Madison Avenue is dotted with sophisticated women dressed in black. In contrast, Californians fancy pastel colors and wear them year-round. It's true that few fashion products do equally well in all areas of the country at the same time or without some adaptations, but the potential for saturating the huge U.S. market always exists.

The homogenous nature of the U.S. market has made it difficult for fashion producers to imagine the differences that exist at every stage of production and promotion in foreign markets. U.S. fashion producers who would not dream of expanding into a new market at home without considerable advance planning think nothing of entering an international market with little or no preliminary market analysis and no solid strategy to justify their presence in the market.

A recent survey indicated that most business owners—two thirds, in fact—exhibited an awareness that their products could not be marketed in the same way around the world, but only one third reported developing a global marketing strategy before they entered the international arena. In this chapter, you will explore the kind of strategic thinking that is required to successfully analyze and conquer foreign markets.[1]

THE SPECIAL NATURE OF THE FASHION INDUSTRY

Analyzing a foreign market is not easy in an industry as individualistic as the fashion business. The same general principles that apply to all businesses apply to the textile and apparel industry, but they are magnified when the product is fashion. Market analysis for a fashion product is a far more complex task than, say, for a television or a computer.

THE EMOTIONAL NATURE OF FASHION

More than any other industry, fashion is based on a customer's needs, and those needs are largely emotional. They are not, for the most part, concrete needs. If you need to buy a house, for example, you may want a certain kind of house, but you can satisfy your need for a house without necessarily satisfying your want.

Fashion is different; here the whole point is to satisfy your wants. Few people need the clothes they buy. A human being could get by owning only three or four garments, but the fashion industry has helped to shape men's and women's wants in such a way that at any one time, most of us have a closet full of clothing. And most of those garments are based on emotional wants rather than basic needs. In fashion, unlike almost all other industries, the whole point is to satisfy the wants. This sets fashion apart from other industries, and makes the marketing of fashion a far more difficult task than the marketing of other products.

THE UNIQUE NATURE OF FASHION

The fashion business is unlike most other businesses in that its products are unique, that is, they are one of a kind. A producer may make 15,000 copies of a jacket, but that jacket design is unique. No one else is making an identical jacket. Every article of clothing starts with the imagination of a designer, who attempts to translate his or her essentially private idea into a garment that will appeal to a large public.

It is difficult enough to sell one person's ideas to a nation of consumers who share a language and a culture. The task becomes even more complex when the unique garment will be sold to individuals in different cultures who speak different languages and who also may wear different sizes, favor different colors, and have different ideas about how garments should be priced or even displayed in a store, to name just a few of the elements that come into play when one is analyzing a foreign market.

THE DYNAMIC NATURE OF FASHION

Another element that sets the fashion industry apart from other industries is its appetite for change, its dynamism. All businesses must change to survive, but the rate of change in the fashion industry is paced much faster than in other businesses. The world of fashion changes, quite literally, on a daily basis. Change is the lifeblood of the fashion industry. This

The appeal of fashions is most often based on emotional, rather than basic, needs. This wedding dress evokes the traditional aspects of African culture with its use of Kente cloth trim. *Courtesy of* Brides Today *Magazine; Leslie Coombs, designer & David H. Jenkins, photographer.*

poses special problems when a garment's life is about to be extended halfway around the globe.

THE CYCLICAL NATURE OF FASHION

Unlike most other industries, the fashion business is intensely cyclical. This **fashion cycle** is not haphazard, but rather, it follows an orderly pattern: introduction, rise, culmination, decline, obsolescence.

A new fashion may involve, among other things, a new shape, fabric, or color. After years of fashion leaders wearing natural fibers, for example, the introduction (or rather, reintroduction, because very little is truly new, even in the world of fashion) of rayon and other man-made fibers is a new event to a generation of high-fashion consumers. Fashions evolve through five distinct stages: introduction, rise, culmination, decline, and obsolescence.

INTRODUCTION STAGE   In the **introduction stage,** new fashions are usually met with some resis-

GLOBAL *GO-GETTERS*

JEROME CHAZEN: A GIRL'S BEST FRIEND

Liz Claiborne's corporate offices are in New York. The company owns no production facilities; instead, it contracts production in over 45 countries worldwide. It leases offices and showrooms in New York and has offices, warehouses, and distribution facilities in Pennsylvania, Rhode Island, Canada, Holland, the United Kingdom, and throughout the Far East and Western Hemispheres.

Liz Claiborne has been the focus of the U.S. apparel industry and a Wall Street favorite since the company was founded in 1976 by Liz Claiborne Ortenberg, her husband Arthur Ortenburg, Leonard Boxer, and Jerome Chazen. In 1989, the Ortenburgs retired to devote their time and energy to environmental causes; Leonard Boxer, the production and sourcing expert, also retired; and Jerome Chazen was appointed Chairman of the Board, where he truly proved that he was "a girl's best friend."

Chairman Chazen is credited with the fabulous marketing strategies that fuel the Liz Claiborne business. He also believes in a lean and streamlined corporate structure as well as being as debt free as possible and keeping the bottom line healthy.

A boost for Liz's bottom line has been the increase in sales internationally. In 1991, the sportswear lines were introduced to the United Kingdom in London's Harrod's and Selfridge's, both upscale department stores, and four House of Fraser stores. The firm expanded its U.K. account base to 26 stores in 1991 and expects to be in 81 stores by 1993. In 1993, there are plans for further expansion on the continent. Liz Claiborne is presently sold through Gallerias Precidiados in Madrid and Barcelona, Spain, on the Continent.

Truly global, Liz Claiborne Inc. conducts business in countries all over the world, sourcing here, selling there. But overall, the needs and wants of the Liz Claiborne clientele are of paramount importance and that is why Jerome Chazen is truly "a girl's best friend."

Based on Nancy Hass, "Like a Rock," *Financial World*, February 4, 1992, pp. 22–24; Thomas Ciampi, "Claiborne's 1991 Sales Up for Most Segments," *Women's Wear Daily*, March 30, 1992, p. 14; "Lean and Debt-Free," *Forbes*, January 6, 1992, p. 127; "The Economist Intelligence Unit," *Textile Outlook*, September, 1991, pp. 51–56. "Eclectic Harmony," *Fashion Weekly, UK*, March 14, 1991, p. 8.

tance, and they are worn initially by only fashion pacesetters. After a period of testing, the new fashion will either be rejected by consumers—as miniskirts were initially in the mid-1980s—or accepted. Because so many risks are attached to introducing a new fashion, it usually appears first in high-priced lines, and production is relatively limited.

RISE STAGE If it is accepted, the fashion moves to the next level, which is the **rise stage.** Now, the new fashion will be mass-produced, often in a line-for-line copy or a **knockoff.** These are versions of the original designer style duplicated by manufacturers. These copies look exactly like the original except that they have been mass-produced in less expensive fabrics. Because production of the merchandise is now on a larger scale, prices of the knockoffs are generally lower.

Adaptations also appear in the rise stage, as the new fashion is modified for even wider acceptance. If a jacket was originally made with four zippered pockets and the zipper handles were bold brass rings, it may now be adapted with lighter weight, silver-tone zippers—and only two pockets. These

changes supply the customer with the same "look" for less money.

CULMINATION STAGE Once a fashion has moved successfully through the rise stage, it enters the **culmination stage.** This is when it reaches the height of its popularity and is mass-produced in prices that make it affordable to most customers.

From the producer's point of view, one of two new strategies is needed at this stage. First, the new fashion may settle into that category known as a **classic,** a garment that is always in style, although not necessarily high style. Blazers are an example of a fashion classic—for both men and women. If this happens, production will be reduced from the rise stage but will settle into steady, predictable levels.

Second, a garment may be modified to extend its life. Jeans are a perfect example of modification. Each year, jeans are modified by enlarging or slimming the legs, making the waist band higher or lower, or modifying the fabric finish. In this strategy, production levels may bounce up and down with each modification.

Once a fashion is considered a classic (i.e., always in style), production achieves a steady, predictable level with little alteration in basic design. *Courtesy of Ralph Lauren.*

DECLINE STAGE   After the culmination stage, which may be prolonged for years, comes the **decline stage,** a period when the fashion begins to fade. It is worn by fewer consumers, and consumers will no longer pay regular prices for the garment. Stores reduce their orders; high-fashion stores no longer order the item at all. Markdowns and sales begin to move the remaining stock out of the store.

OBSOLESCENCE STAGE   Finally, when consumers develop a distaste for a particular style, it enters the **obsolescence stage.** It can no longer be found in stores because no one is willing to buy it.

GLOBAL VARIATIONS IN THE FASHION CYCLE

The fashion cycle applies to all fashion products, but the cycle is not the same around the world. This is because consumers around the world have different approaches to fashion. French women may gobble up new fashion, and in some regions of the United States, most notably, New York and California, women are known for consuming new styles. But in Scandinavia, where classic fashion is favored, the

market of women willing to try out a new style may be very small.

How long people keep their clothes affects the fashion cycle. In some countries, people may keep their clothes a long time, and that will slow down the decline stage. Conversely, if a country is rich and fashion hungry, as the United States was in the late 1980s, people may "use up" clothing in a very short time. In some very high-fashion circles, women do not like to be seen wearing the same garments over and over. Under these circumstances, fashion manufacturers may shorten the introduction cycle and move quickly into the rise stage. Alternately, if a country is poor, like Poland, the introduction stage may be skipped entirely, and the culmination stage will be very long.

Business cycles around the world also may disrupt the fashion cycle. Consumers will buy less high fashion, for example, during a recession, and business slowdowns do not occur at the same time in all countries. War also disrupts the fashion cycle. In 1991, during the Gulf War, American consumers stopped buying clothes.

Finally, the fashion cycle is affected by many variables that make fashion more difficult to sell in the international marketplace. Fashion varies far more than other products in terms of what must be done to make a product acceptable and popular. A computer manufacturer, for example, has only to wire its machine for another country's electrical system and change the keyboard to another language to sell computers in other countries. But fashion producers must cope with many, and far more subtle, variables at every level of production to sell their products abroad.

Many forces—cultural, social, economic, psychological, design, and business—work to keep the fashion industry dynamic in a way that no other industry is. These forces must be weighed and analyzed by any U.S. marketer planning to expand into the global marketplace.

THE IMPACT OF CONSUMER DEMAND ON INTERNATIONAL FASHION: MARKET ANALYSIS

Any international marketing strategy must also take into account consumer demand, something that would not have been a factor even two decades ago. Then, fashion makers dictated what customers wore. An active consumer movement that began in the 1970s has changed all that.

TECH TALK

INTERNATIONAL SHOW DIRECTORY

Eurofair, a database of international expositions in Europe, is now available on computer diskette through Exhibitor magazine and its European partner, Eurofair AsP Ltd. The directory provides up-to-date listings on 1500 European exhibitions. You can search by country, industry, and date in four languages. The diskettes are available in 3¹/₂ or 5¹/₄ inches. The cost is $98, with a full refund guarantee. It is available from Exhibitor magazine, 745 Marquette Bank Bldg., Rochester, Minnesota 55904.

Customer opinion has not only become more important than ever before, but as consumers have become more knowledgeable, sophisticated, and individual in their tastes, designers and manufacturers have learned to look to them as design sources. Fashion is now a two-way street, and what consumers are wearing influences designers as much as designers influence what customers buy.

Consumer demand is important in any industry but especially so in the fashion business where consumers may reject a product outright, as they did with trapeze dresses in early 1990s. In the international marketplace, the possibility of wide-scale rejection—and the margin for costly error—is magnified if one has not done the necessary market research.

Consumers affect the fashion cycle in international markets differently from the way they affect it at home. Factors that ordinarily accelerate the U.S. fashion cycle—buying power, leisure time, educational levels, the status of women, and seasonal change—may either accelerate or decelerate it in the international market.

BUYING POWER

Because fashion is about wants rather than needs, fashion consumers must have a certain amount of discretionary income to buy clothing. Citizens of developed countries are more likely to have that buying power than those who live in less developed countries, and this added buying power will accelerate the fashion cycle in a foreign market just as it does in the domestic market. In contrast, consumers in less developed countries will have less discretionary income, and this will serve to decelerate the fashion cycle. People will buy fewer clothes and wear them longer.

LEISURE TIME

Despite the perception that we are busier than ever, leisure time has in fact increased over the past fifty years in the industrialized nations. It has created among these consumers a demand for leisurewear and active sportswear that does not exist in less developed countries, where leisure time has not increased.

EDUCATIONAL LEVELS

The more education a consumer has, the greater his or her wants. Education leads to expanded horizons, and that has generally been viewed as good for the fashion industry in developed nations. In less developed nations, the lack of education slows down the fashion cycle in the same way that a lack of income does.

STATUS OF WOMEN

As the status of women has improved around the world (although not everywhere), women have become more independent. Many earn their own incomes and have a greater need for career wear. The market for fashion varies greatly from country to country, depending on the status of women.

SEASONAL CHANGE

Seasonal variation affects the market for clothing. Fashion producers must take account of the fact that it is summer in the Southern Hemisphere when it is winter in the Northern Hemisphere. Furthermore, customers living in year-round warm or chilly climates will have fewer clothing needs than will those living places with changing seasons. Changing seasons accelerate the fashion cycle.

RELIGION AND CUSTOM

Two other factors—religion and custom—also slow down the fashion cycle anywhere in the world.

For decades, the influence of religion on fashion had been waning. In the United States, for example,

GLOBAL GLIMPSES

INTELLIGENCE—FROM CAMPUS TO GOVERNMENT—AND BACK

In December 1991, President Bush signed the National Security Education Act of 1991, which aims to improve the country's poor track record in foreign studies and enlarge the pool of Americans fit to work in government intelligence programs.

In today's new, more multicultural world order, there is anxiety within the intelligence community: the fear that America's mostly monolingual society does not have enough people versed in other languages or customs to protect the nation from foreign threats.

In this case, campus intelligence will be the benefitter of government intelligence needs. The new act provides scholarships for college and graduate students to learn languages and to study abroad in countries deemed to be potentially crucial allies . . . or enemies. It also bestows grants to universities to improve their international programs. Senator David L. Boren, Oklahoma Democrat who heads the Senate Select Committee on Intelligence says, "We can no longer define our national security in military terms alone. Our ignorance of world cultures and world languages represents a threat to our ability to remain a world leader."

This thought also impacts on our future as a world leader in international trade. Without adequately educated future business leaders in the languages and cultural ways of the world, we will not be able to be world-class competitors.

Today, fewer than one fourth of American colleges and universities require students to take foreign languages to graduate, and only 7.8 percent of all college students are enrolled in foreign language courses. The new education act more than triples the amount for scholarships for undergraduates to study abroad, increases by 40 percent the amount for graduate fellowships for the study of foreign languages, and marks the first program donated solely to providing grants to colleges and universities to create and to improve foreign language and area studies programs.

Intelligence needs—whether governmental or educational—will be better met by this support, and international trade will be the recipient of better educated and trained personnel who will be truly part of the global marketplace.

Based on "U.S. Plans Scholarship to Push Foreign Studies," *New York Times*, December, 1991—special to the New York Times, no author, p. 22.

---

the fact that women were no longer required to cover their heads during religious services changed the market for hats. This, combined with the fact that it was no longer customary for women to wear hats on certain social occasions, led to a serious decline from which the hat industry has never fully recuperated.

Beginning in the late 1970s, however, a worldwide rise in religious conservatism changed the demand for certain kinds of fashion among some consumers. After years of gradually adopting Western dress, Mideastern Muslim women once again donned **purdah**—the ultraconservative, head-to-toe, black garment dictated by their religious leaders. In the United States, a similar return to orthodoxy has led to more conservative dress among evangelical Christian women and Orthodox Jewish women.

Consumer demand causes customers to desire or denigrate any individual product or mode of dress—and their reactions to fashion will vary greatly depending on where and how they live. Only careful research and strategy enables a fashion producer to predict his or her success with foreign-market consumers with any assurance.

DEVELOPING AN INTERNATIONAL PERSPECTIVE AND GENERAL STRATEGIES

Before U.S. entrepreneurs can begin to develop the kinds of specific strategies that are necessary for success in foreign markets, they must, many experts believe, develop a more **international orientation,** a perspective that encompasses an overview as well as specific strategies required to perform well in the international marketplace.[2]

Producers who hope to sell their products in the international marketplace must first of all be willing to learn about their foreign customers. They must be willing to learn the different customs and traditions as well as the procedures and regulations that will

DOING BUSINESS IN...
INTERNATIONAL AUDIO GUIDES

This unique series has been created by International Cultural Enterprises in association with leading experts from SRI International, one of the world's top business consulting firms. Now you can profit from their professional advice.

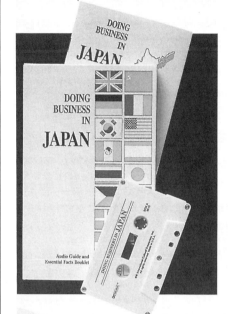

" A WEALTH OF TIMELY RESEARCH AND COORDINATED INFORMATION IS JAM-PACKED INTO THIS BARGAIN-PRICED SOURCE. **"**
—*Library Journal*

"INFORMATION THAT THE TRAVELLING BUSINESS PERSON NEEDS BEFORE LANDING IN THE HOST COUNTRY AND PROCEEDING TO DO BUSINESS THERE. **"**
—Philip Kotler, S.C. Johnson & Son Professor of International Marketing J.L. Kellogg Graduate School of Management

Each audio tape from the series, packaged with a booklet of essential facts about the country is delivered in an upbeat, easy to understand style and contains clear, concise information on:

How to get things started	Connections
How to get things done	The perception of space
Reaching an agreement	Social contact and entertainment
How to facilitate mutual understanding	The first meeting
Women in business	Decision makers and decision making
Dress	Image enhancers and taboos
Initial contact	Manners
Negotiating	Titles

The convenient audio format maximizes learning flexibility at home, in the office, while driving or commuting, or even enroute to your new market.

Business aids, such as audio tapes, providing essential information on interacting with other cultures, are often extremely helpful to U.S. fashion exporters. *Courtesy of International Cultural Enterprises, Inc.*

affect them when they move their goods across international borders and through various trade regions. Knowing other people's languages is important as well, even though the argument could be made that English is becoming the international business language. It is because U.S. business people have not been motivated to learn much about other nations that they have lagged behind other nations in international commerce.

The market research that prospective entrepreneurs must undertake before entering an international market will depend entirely on their individual needs. But even before this research can begin, entrepreneurs must be familiar with some general strategies that apply to anyone who is contemplating entry into the international arena. Such issues as allocation of resources, limitations of the markets, and the need to obtain outside assistance are principles of international marketing that no entrepreneur can ignore.

ALLOCATION OF RESOURCES

Few business owners would tackle any other kind of expansion without allocating the appropriate resources to ensure success, yet would-be international entrepreneurs often leap into the global arena on a whim. Fashion producers must assign enough money and time to ensure a thorough exploration of all the elements they will confront in a foreign market.

GLOBETROTTING **Gaffes**
PLAYING HOST IN JAPAN

You want to play host in Japan? Not right away! Be aware that the Japanese will insist on hosting the first time out. The Japanese regard evening dining and entertainment as a normal component of every business relationship. They will judge you by your reactions at dinner. Can you adjust to new situations? Are you predictable? Can they trust you to meet them halfway if a problem arises? Their basic approach to these questions is "let's eat." However, when it is time for you to play host there are a few guidelines for you to follow. Dine early—business dinners begin as early as 6:00 and seldom go past 9:00 p.m. Think continental—you are more likely to shine in a Western setting and the Japanese enjoy Western food, if you suggest food that everyone can order. Seafood and steak are always appropriate. Stay away from exotic suggestions like brains and sweetbreads or sauces with pungent cheese. Go solo—when you are invited for an evening, assume that the invitation is only for you unless your Japanese hosts specifically include your spouse—and you should do the honors alone when your turn comes to host.

LIMITATIONS OF THE MARKET

Too many variables go into any international marketing strategy for an entrepreneur to take on the entire world or even a significantly sized region of the world all at once. No one has successfully done this. Successful fashion producers target a small market or region of the world, take it on, and when they are successful there, use that experience to build on for the next market. Most international marketers must carefully research several markets before determining which one is best for them.

OBTAINING ASSISTANCE

The fashion industry is made up of small to mid-sized businesses, run primarily by independent-minded entrepreneurs. An entry into the global arena, however, is one time when independence does not serve an owner well. To operate successfully in this milieu, one needs assistance. Fortunately, a variety of organizations and agencies, some private, some public, stand ready to offer import/export assistance to U.S. fashion producers. Many are described in Chapters 4 and 5 of this book.

Most successful international businesspersons report using expert advice to develop their global strategy. In a recent survey, 100 percent said they used consultants, 64 percent used research reports, and the same number also relied on other managers' experiences and the recommendations of dealers in various markets.[3]

PREPARATION OF A BUSINESS PLAN

No business can hope to successfully market itself without a business plan, and the same is true when entering the international arena. An international business plan helps an entrepreneur determine when new factors must be considered and when old ones must be rethought in a new light. The same elements that make up a domestic marketing strategy—target marketing, market segmentation, and market mix—must also be considered in an international strategy. The difference is that each of these elements must be applied to the region or country where one plans to introduce one's goods.

DEVELOPING ADAPTABILITY

Generally speaking, two approaches are used by international marketers: They either market new products or they adapt old ones. Of these two, the most difficult by far for U.S. manufacturers has been to adapt old products to new foreign markets. American fashion producers have been slow to realize that sizes, colors, and styles differ dramatically from country to country, and that they must adapt their manufacturing methods to these variations if they hope to market their fashion lines successfully in foreign markets.

Even so seemingly simple a product as a woman's handbag may vary with national or regional tastes, as one entrepreneur discovered when she sought to take her classic handbag into the French market. During her initial market research, she had met with French agents, producers, and marketers, all of whom offered general advice about breaking into the French market. But it was not until she sat at an outdoor cafe on a fashionable Parisian street and carefully studied the handbags that French women were carrying that she saw the changes she needed to make to accommodate her product to the foreign market.

VAN DER MAAL / BRADY INTERNATIONAL, INC.

333 West Indian School Road
Phoenix, Arizona 85013
(602) 351-8565
Fax (602) 351-8566

Foreign Trade Consultants
- Product Distribution -
- Technology Licensing -
- Technology Sales -
- Joint Ventures -

Associates In:
Japan, Korea, Taiwan, & Hong Kong

Our Mission
To assist small to medium sized U.S. manufacturers in the export of their products and technology through our worldwide contacts and with a special emphasis on environmentally friendly products.

Product Distribution
- Obtain access for your company to overseas distribution networks
- Assist you in negotiating the distribution agreement

Technology Licensing & Sales
- Identify potential licensees or purchasers
- Arrange for foreign legal counsel, if necessary
- Assist you in negotiating the business terms of the agreement

Joint Ventures
- Target joint venture partners
- Evaluate the benefits of the joint venture
- Assist you in negotiating the joint venture agreement

We can also provide informational assistance as to tax and export incentive programs that are available, arrange the formation of offshore tax incentive corporations (FSC), and perform other services.

Foreign trade consultants provide expert advice to international businesspersons seeking to develop their global strategy. *Courtesy of Van der Maal/Brady International, Inc.*

French women, she observed, tended to favor brown for their basic, everyday bags, whereas her American customers bought more black. American women opted for practicality and comfort, which meant a wider shoulder strap. French women, less practical about their dress and more concerned with looking traditionally feminine, would want a daintier shoulder strap.

The entrepreneur came home and delayed production while she incorporated the changes she had observed firsthand in Paris. When she finally brought her American classic into the French market, it was a success.

In another equally telling example, a small U.S. t-shirt producer was encouraged by an exporting consultant he had hired to rethink his price list to sell his shirts in Taiwan. He resisted changing his price, even though the consultant pointed out that certain domestic expenses, such as advertising, promotion, and brokers, would be borne by overseas distributors. The would-be exporter simply could not understand that he could have a different price structure and still pull in the same profit. Unwilling or unable to adapt, this manufacturer took his t-shirts into the foreign market with his U.S. price and failed.

Hard as adapting to new conditions may be, this is absolutely necessary to survive in a foreign market. Adaptability will involve a review of every aspect of one's product, from such basics as color, fabric, and shape to other production details such as sizing and labeling to even such promotion details as store display.

Experienced international entrepreneurs warn the U.S. fashion industry that it has a choice: It can either adapt or it can give up the idea of global trading. Because most American fashion producers have an enormous amount to gain from participating in the international market, most will learn to adapt to new customs and traditions, languages, and ways of doing business.

IMPLICATIONS FOR THE INDUSTRY PROFESSIONAL

The world of the international fashion business is a glamorous one, filled with travel, exciting new sights, and what amounts to an insider's view of other cultures. As the international fashion market opens up, new jobs will be created. Two of the more promising new areas will be (1) consulting jobs helping manufacturers and retailers enter the international market, and (2) staff jobs in new retail operations that U.S. producers will operate overseas.

More important for those who elect to work in the international sector will be their leadership role. The new generation of industry professionals, now being trained, will be pioneers. They will be the ones who will open their industry to the vast possibilities and potential of the global marketplace.

GLOBAL *Goodies*

THE RENT IS WHAT!?!

If only the best will do, the Ginza in Tokyo is the place for the enterprising international businessperson to open up shop . . . if "bragging rights" to paying the highest rent is important.

The top ten international most expensive price per square foot are:

1.	The Ginza (Tokyo)	$625
2.	Nathan Road/Queens Road (Hong Kong)	$500
3.	Fifth Ave. (New York)	$400
4.	East 57th St. (New York)	$375
5.	Place Vendôme (Paris)	$325
6.	Madison Ave. (New York)	$300
7.	Bond St. (London)	$250
8.	Rue de Rhône (Geneva)	$225
9.	Via Condotti (Rome)	$175
10.	Rodeo Drive (Beverly Hills)	$175

Based on "Most Expensive Feet," *North American International Business*, April, 1991.

ENDNOTES

1. *International Business Magazine*, "Survey, Global Marketing," August, 1991, p. 95.
2. Dun & Bradstreet, no author, March 4, 1988, page 34.
3. *International Business Magazine*, op. cit.

VOCABULARY

classic _____

culmination stage _____

decline stage _____

fashion cycle _____

international orientation _____

introductory stage _____

_____

_____

knockoff _____

_____

_____

obsolescence stage _____

_____

_____

purdah _____

_____

_____

rise stage _____

_____

_____

GLOBAL REVIEW

1. The fashion cycle follows an orderly pattern. Name the five stages of the fashion cycle in the order that they occur.

   _____

   _____

   _____

   _____

2. Give an example of a fashion product and explain how and when it fits into the five stages of the fashion cycle.

   _____

   _____

   _____

   _____

3. Explain how businesses and economic cycles around the world may disrupt the fashion cycle.

   _____

   _____

   _____

   _____

4. Give three examples of global variations in the fashion cycle.

   _____

   _____

   _____

   _____

5. The status of women around the world differs greatly. How can it help fashion products expand in a global perspective?

   _____

   _____

   _____

   _____

6. What is meant by an international orientation?

   _____

   _____

   _____

   _____

7. Why is consumer demand so important in fashion? Why particularly in your international fashion market analysis?

   _____

   _____

   _____

   _____

8. Learning about your international customers is very important. Explain why we have been lagging behind in this area.

   _____

   _____

   _____

   _____

9. Give examples of adaptability that might be needed by the U.S. manufacturer of women's sportswear in the European market and in the Asian market.

   _____

   _____

   _____

10. What are some of the implications for the fashion professional in the international marketplace?

_____

_____

_____

_____

GLOBAL DIGEST

1. Analyzing a foreign market is difficult in the fashion business for many reasons. List three factors that make the fashion business different and explain why they are deterrents to fashion success in the global marketplace.

_____

_____

_____

_____

_____

_____

_____

_____

2. There are accelerating and decelerating factors that affect the fashion cycle. Choose four factors and explain how each of these can be used as either an accelerating or a decelerating factor.

_____

_____

_____

_____

_____

_____

_____

3. Allocation of resources, limitations of the market, and the need to obtain outside assistance are principles of international marketing. Design marketing effort for a fashion product using the three principles.

_____

_____

_____

_____

_____

_____

UNIT 1 READING
REAMS OF CHANGE FOR TEXTILES & APPAREL

By Julie Ritzer Ross

Importers have long seen frequent changes in the design and color displayed by textiles and apparel purchased abroad. Yet, the market for such items is slowly experiencing an even greater "revolution" outside the fashion realm.

Myriad legislative and nonlegislative developments are presently altering or will soon impact the sourcing of both commodities, narrowing some trade routes while opening others and giving rise to new transportation modes.

Fewer goods falling into the textile and apparel categories should be shipped from the Far East in the near future, sources told *Global Trade* recently. They attribute the change partially to the fact that the Multi-Fibre Arrangement (MFA), which governs the bulk of world fabrics and clothing commerce via a quota system, was extended this past July 31 through Dec. 31, 1992.

Talks had been underway to phase out the MFA and incorporate textile trade into the General Agreement on Tariffs and Trade (GATT) rules that control most other global merchandise exchange. However, temporary MFA renewal halted the discussions.

"China was experiencing an inability to move large-scale imports before the recent MFA decision because it had entered a peak repayment period on overseas loans," said Jones, president, United States Association of Importers of Textiles and Apparel (USA-ITA), New York City. "Quotas put forth under the now-stretched agreement will obviously remain in effect," she added, thereby forcing buyers to find materials elsewhere.

Transshipment-related actions are also drying up Chinese import pipelines and could likely have a similar effect on neighboring nations, pointed out attorney Gail T. Cumins, senior partner of New York City and Washington, D.C.-based Sharretts, Paley, Carter & Blauvelt, P.C. Cumins, whose firm serves as a counsel to the Textile and Apparel Group of the New York City-based American Association of Exporters and Importers (AAEI), said all charges for textiles and apparel made in China and shipped through Makao or other third-party countries in 1991 will be subtracted from 1991 quotas, as will charges for 1990 commodities deemed above unused 1990 quotas. Consequently, certain heavily shipped classifications could be embargoed by year-end.

"The U.S. government wants to ban transshipment entirely, so it has begun monitoring similar alleged activity by India, Pakistan and Taiwan," Cumins reported. "Countries found culpable will face retroactive quota charges, likely changing carriers' plans."

Just as significantly, although Most Favored Nation (MFN) status currently allows China to remit the lowest possible general import duties, a bill that would strip it of such a privilege and impose higher Column II rates is presently pending in Congress and the House of Representatives. "Should this happen, duties will skyrocket," stated Steven S. Weiser, a senior partner in the customs/tariff law firm of Siegel, Mandell & Davidson, P.C., based in New York City and Washington, D.C. For example, he claims, rates of duty on woven shirts would rise from 21 percent ad valorem to 45 percent; those on 100 percent acrylic sweaters, from 34.2 percent to 90 percent.

"President Bush claims he intends to veto the bill, but if it passes, the prospect of paying stiff duties could shift allegiances elsewhere," Weiser asserted.

In a related vein, the Office of the U.S Trade Representative has announced that Hong Kong will slash its textile imports to the United States by 27 square meter equivalents, or, in layperson's terms, quantities equaling some 16 million shirts, 81 million brassieres or 112 million pairs of cotton mittens. The cuts were made so that "Washington could compensate Turkey for its Gulf War contributions with double apparel exports," Jones explained. She believes additional restraints of Far Eastern trade, and consequent limitations on the viability of trade routes there, are in the offing.

What's more, China—along with Taiwan and Hong Kong—is shifting away from textile/apparel production, gravitating instead toward electronics manufacture and petroleum exports. The Third World has grown increasingly sophisticated technology-wise; access to better machinery and a natural movement up the learning curve means laborers and factory owners alike are far less interested in turning out the most time-intensive, least lucrative items, purported Steven M. Kott, director of membership services, AAEI and former manager of foreign merchandising services, Kmart Corp. "Even clothing still being created for import here—coats are a prime example—is produced when work on other items is at a standstill. However, since buyers order goods months before they need them, demand from the United States at these times is always peaking and must be fulfilled in other corners of the world."

NEW ROUTES OPENING

But just as the Far East is closing ranks where textiles and apparel are concerned, opportunities for establishment of alternate trade routes abound. Notably, despite unsuccessful communist attempts to overthrow the Soviet government two months ago, President Bush will probably send the U.S.-Soviet Trade Agreement to Congress for consideration shortly, sources predicted. Once approved, the agreement would grant the Soviets MFN standing, thus increasing importers' interest in and ability to procure goods from its states.

"Latvia and Estonia have actually enjoyed MFN for many years," Cumins observed. "There, it's merely a matter of restoring privilege, which shouldn't prove overly difficult."

Jones added that the House Ways and Means Trade Subcommittee has, meanwhile, submitted for complete committee action resolutions yielding Mongolia and Bulgaria MFN status. Both countries have already been granted 1991 Jackson-Vanik waivers of Column II duties, meaning that only a few steps remain before requirements are suspended permanently.

"After the resolutions have gone through the Ways and Means Committee and full House, Congress will have 90 legislative days to act on them," Jones elaborated. "The Mongolian and Bulgarian legislatures must then accept their trade agreements with the United States and give us reciprocal notes acknowledging reciprocal MFN."

As the resolutions are thought to be non-controversial, Mongolian and Bulgarian products should commence receiving MFN treatment by press time or shortly thereafter, Jones said.

In addition, experts anticipate continued heightened demand for transport of textiles and apparel from Czechoslovakia and Hungary by year-end based on the Bush Administration's plans to cease requiring that either nation apply for MFN annually. H.R.1724 and S.1468, legislation containing such provisos, have been received for review by the House Ways and Means Committee and Senate, respectively. That the administration also intends to re-negotiate more liberal bilateral textile quotas for Czechoslovakia, Hungary and Poland by year-end will render extra Eastern European trade routes an even greater necessity, sources insisted.

Textile/apparel movement between the United States and Caribbean, South American and Central American nations is escalating as well, Cumins stated.

REAMS OF CHANGE FOR TEXTILES & APPAREL
CONTINUED

"All three regions are progressing upward on the learning curve from simplistic industry into the clothing and fabrics areas," she claimed. "And since larger volumes of (investors) are promoting textile/apparel manufacture as an alternative to illicit drug trade, the trend is taking tighter hold at a rapid rate."

INVESTMENTS REACH THAILAND

Meanwhile, Chinese laborers' tendency toward eschewing garment production in favor of manufacturing electronics and similar items is spurring entrepreneurs from that country to establish factories in Thailand, Malaysia and the Indian Subcontinent. Noted Steven Ferreira, marketing manager, emerging markets, SeaLand Service, Inc., "This most certainly means companies like our own will need to look at stepping up service from these areas." Bangladesh is experiencing a particularly marked textile/apparel growth spurt. Ten years ago, its annual garment exports were valued at $3.7 million at current exchange; 1991 exports are projected to exceed $750 million. Clothing is consequently the nation's largest export, surpassing jute and tea for the first time.

"Movement into Thailand, Malaysia and the Subcontinent isn't something that will abate at any (juncture) in the foreseeable future," Ferreira remarked.

Further, the next three to five years should bring a flurry of activity originating in the African market, contended Jonathan Fink, manager, government affairs, AAEI. He sees Kenya, Zimbabwe and Botswana as particularly ripe for penetration by carriers. "Governments there no longer think farming and cattle raising are the answers to the development they so badly want to (spark)," Fink explained. "They know, though, that they have sufficient labor resources to begin making textiles and apparel. Carriers that want to protect their income and

use tonnage wisely will recognize this and act on it."

TRANSPORT MODES SHIFTING

Not surprisingly, external factors are also influencing the manner and conditions under which apparel and textiles are being shipped to the United States from new and old sources alike. For instance, Kott states, a general softening of the American economy is restricting consumer spending, thereby compelling importers to price wares reasonably. To enable them to do so, such firms are working harder at negotiating lower shipping rates.

"With economic conditions as they are, savvier companies are urging the formation of shippers' associations that ensure fair contracts and allow for the pooling of volumes to obtain better rates," Kott reported. He anticipates that as more importers learn about the benefits of association membership, they will commence clamoring for the right to save money on shipping by pooling commodities with each other.

"(Carriers) should not be surprised to find companies combining, say, sweaters and hard goods on a vessel," he elaborated.

Similarly, importers' increased tendency toward adapting "just-in-time" ordering methodologies means more prevalent shipment of textiles and apparel by air, rather than by sea, Cumins pointed out. However, she asserted, importers' awareness that materials may be compacted to render shipment more cost efficient will incite requests for "fairer," significantly lower air transportation tariffs.

Finally, the advent of EC '92, coupled with legislative moves to facilitate movement of merchandise from the Soviet Union, Eastern Bloc and other nations, will incite demand for carrier introduction of intermodal services.

"Some countries, with which we anticipate dealing, have air and seaport facilities that are far far inland," Fink concluded. "To compete for textile/apparel accounts, carrying concerns will need to help manufacturers move product from origination point to the port."

Global Sourcing for an International Fashion Mix

CHAPTER 4

Who Exports and Why

If the store shelves of the United States were filled with fashion imports throughout the 1980s, the same could not be said for the rest of the world's shelves. They were not filled with American fashion exports. Even though the United States maintains the world's largest textile industry, it did not participate in the worldwide fashion boom of the 1980s. During this period, in fact, U.S. fashion exports declined. In 1963, the United States was the eighth-largest exporter of apparel, and the eighth-largest exporter of textiles. By the end of the 1980s, the United States was not even in the top fifteen exporting nations for apparel and had slipped to twelfth place as a textile exporter. In contrast, Italy and Germany, with their much smaller fashion industries, remained in the top five apparel-exporting nations.[1]

The fashion industry has been criticized for not being more export oriented, but this is about to change. Many industry analysts believe that the U.S. fashion industry stands on the brink of a fashion-exporting boom. Economists predict that during the 1990s, exports will assume a greater role than imports.[2]

In this chapter, you will explore the expanding world of U.S. exports. Discussion will focus on who exports and why as well as the advantages and disadvantages of taking fashion into the larger international arena. Special programs and services available to exporters will also be described.

ADVANTAGES OF EXPORTING

There are benefits and drawbacks to exporting.

The single most important reason to export is to increase sales. Even if Americans continue to buy imports, American fashion producers can boost flagging sales at home by selling their goods around the world.

Exporting enables a fashion producer to spread costs over a wider base. With a wider base of customers, producers can lower costs and fund expansion, thus making themselves even more competitive.

Exporting gives American fashion producers a valuable bird's-eye view of the competition. In recent years, foreign competitors have introduced new products and made technological innovations of their own. When American producers locate plants outside the United States, they can observe these new

Country	Total	O.E.C.D.		Soviet Union and Eastern Europe	China: Mainland, Vietnam, North Korea	O.P.E.C.	Other developing countries	Africa	America	Middle East	Far East
		Total	E.E.C.								
EXPORTS											
United States	363.8	232.0	86.6	5.3	5.8	13.2	107.0	7.7	49.1	11.1	57.0
Austria	32.4	26.4	20.7	2.9	0.2	0.9	2.1	0.6	0.2	0.7	0.9
Belgium	100.0	87.1	73.7	1.2	0.4	1.7	8.9	2.5	0.8	2.7	4.5
Canada	116.2	105.7	9.8	0.8	1.0	1.6	7.1	0.9	2.2	1.0	5.5
Denmark	28.0	24.3	14.2	0.7	0.1	0.7	2.3	0.5	0.6	0.7	0.9
France	172.8	136.8	105.8	3.5	1.7	6.5	24.3	12.8	5.2	4.2	8.2
Italy	149.2	118.8	84.3	4.6	1.3	7.1	16.8	7.1	3.3	5.0	6.7
Japan	275.2	166.3	56.6	3.8	8.9	10.8	85.5	5.2	8.9	7.5	82.4
Netherlands	107.8	95.9	81.3	1.8	0.3	2.2	6.8	2.6	1.2	1.8	3.1
Spain	44.4	36.1	29.6	0.7	0.2	1.7	4.8	2.0	1.8	1.2	1.2
Sweden	51.5	44.9	27.5	1.1	0.2	1.0	4.2	0.9	0.9	0.9	2.5
Switzerland	51.5	40.7	29.2	1.7	0.4	1.6	7.1	1.1	1.4	2.1	4.1
United Kingdom	152.6	120.5	77.3	2.2	0.7	8.3	19.4	5.5	2.6	8.6	10.6
West Germany	341.4	284.9	188.2	13.0	2.5	8.7	31.6	9.1	6.2	7.4	15.7
Percent distribution:											
United States	100.0	63.8	23.8	1.5	1.6	3.6	29.4	2.1	13.5	3.1	15.7
Austria	100.0	81.4	63.8	9.0	0.6	2.6	6.4	1.8	0.7	2.0	2.8
Belgium	100.0	87.1	73.7	1.2	0.4	1.7	8.9	2.5	0.8	2.7	4.5
Canada	100.0	91.0	8.4	0.7	0.8	1.4	6.1	0.8	1.9	0.9	4.7
Denmark	100.0	86.5	50.6	2.5	0.3	2.3	8.2	1.9	2.2	2.5	3.3
France	100.0	79.1	61.2	2.0	1.0	3.8	14.1	7.4	3.0	2.4	4.8
Italy	100.0	79.6	56.5	3.1	0.9	4.8	11.3	4.8	2.2	3.4	4.5
Japan	100.0	60.4	20.6	1.4	3.2	3.9	31.1	1.9	3.2	2.7	29.9
Netherlands	100.0	89.0	75.4	1.6	0.2	2.1	6.3	2.5	1.2	1.7	2.8
Spain	100.0	81.4	66.8	1.5	0.5	3.9	10.9	4.6	4.0	2.8	2.7
Sweden	100.0	87.1	53.4	2.2	0.4	2.0	8.2	1.8	1.7	1.7	4.8
Switzerland	100.0	79.1	56.6	3.2	0.8	3.1	13.8	2.1	2.7	4.1	8.0
United Kingdom ..	100.0	79.0	50.7	1.5	0.5	5.5	12.7	3.6	1.7	5.6	7.0
West Germany	100.0	83.5	55.1	3.8	0.7	2.6	9.3	2.7	1.8	2.2	4.6

Foreign Trade of Selected Countries—Destination of Exports in Billions of Dollars: 1989. *Courtesy of Organization for Economic Cooperation and Development, Paris, France. Data derived from* Monthly Statistics of Foreign Trade, *series A, May 1990.*

techniques and study foreign production methods in much the same way that foreign business people come to the United States to study its production methods.

Exporting provides much needed flexibility in the face of economic change. Fashion producers with customers and production centers around the world will feel economic crunches like recession and inflation less than will those with all their eggs in one basket, so to speak.

Another kind of economic flexibility, one tied to the value of the dollar, helps exporters. When the dollar is weak, as it was throughout much of the late 1980s, American fashion producers have a competitive edge. Their goods look cheap to the rest of the world. When the dollar is strong, U.S. producers have the option of relying more heavily on those foreign sources of production that are less expensive, thus holding down their costs in a tight market.

DISADVANTAGES OF EXPORTING

Business is more complicated on every level when one begins to sell to other countries. Under the best of circumstances, fashion is a complex undertaking.

GLOBAL *Goodies*

FOOTBALL

Although baseball has long been the team sport of choice among Japanese, football's popularity is increasing. Two Japanese magazines, *Touchdown* and *American Football*, focus on National Football League (NFL) games. The NFL puts on an annual exhibition game, the "American Bowl," each August at Tokyo Dome. San Francisco 49ers quarterback Joe Montana appears in Mitsubishi Electric commercials. Satellite television beams 100 NFL games a season into over 3 million Japanese homes. Employees of 79 Japanese companies participate in a nationwide amateur football league.

The popularity of the game has generated a consumer demand for football "lifestyle" products, including t-shirts, sweatshirts, and jackets, all bearing the names of America's professional football teams at the Official NFL Shop in Tokyo's Harajuku district. Large-screen television blasts out a taped football game, but the visitors' attention is focused on a big table piled high with NFL-licensed fashion merchandise.

Although the $3.5 billion Japanese sporting-apparel market is dominated by local producers, American-made products enjoy a unique status. U.S. sporting goods and sports apparel have a very good reputation in Japan and make up about an estimated 5 percent of all sporting goods sold in Japan. U.S. based suppliers of NFL-licensed goods are pleased to take advantage of the cordial reception.

Based on "Touchdown!," Jean Downey, *Business Tokyo*, March, 1992, p. 34.

When you sell toothpaste, you need only to make a product that cleans teeth and helps to fight dental decay. When fashion is the product, you are selling image, an idea people have about how they should look. And that image can vary dramatically from culture to culture.

In one culture, for example, black may be considered a sophisticated color, favored mostly by young, chic women. In another, it may still be the color of mourning or a stodgy, old-woman's uniform. What is acceptably low-cut in a dress in one culture may be considered shockingly immodest in another.

Even clothing sizes vary from culture to culture. A typical Italian woman's body is not shaped like the typical American's or a typical Zambian's body. Although the world is eager to wear American styles, fashion producers must accommodate them to other cultures. This may mean creating new patterns, adjusting markers, or using a different weight fabric to adapt to their new customers.

A price that is right for one market may not work in another. Even as big a name as Ralph Lauren, for example, has not sold as well as was expected in French department stores, mostly because his prices are too expensive for European consumers. At $800, a Lauren jacket is about twice the price of a domestic designer jacket in France.[3]

Virtually every aspect of production and promotion must be reassessed for the export market. Successful fashion producers ask themselves the same questions about their market. When the market is a foreign one, the questions not only must be asked all over again, but they must be aimed specifically at the potential foreign market: Is the price right for the foreign market? Is the style right for this particular country? Do people in this country wear these colors? Whatever the answers have been for the U.S. market, they may be very different for each foreign market.

However advantageous global sourcing is for a producer who wants to be able to shop the world for the best-priced sources, pulling together all those sources to create a garment can be a difficult and time-consuming task.

Exporting also involves extensive paperwork. Documents vary from country to country. A bill of sale may be called by a different name or may not even exist in another country. In addition, most countries have regulations regarding who may export and how much may be exported. These regulations add another layer of paperwork beyond what is required to do business domestically.

Finally, U.S. fashion producers must deal with a long-standing prejudice against them that is largely of their own making. The United States has tended to export fashion when business was bad at home. And then it tried to unload American rejects or shoddy products on the rest of the world. Not surprisingly, U.S. fashion is viewed by many around the world as an inferior product.

As soon as business improved, American producers stopped exporting and concentrated on the

When selling image, exporters must take into account that fashions viewed as chic in one culture may be viewed as inappropriate for public appearance in another. In addition, an image that is current and fashionable today may be thoroughly dated and unsaleable a year from now. *Courtesy of Donna Karan.*

EXPORTING BY MANUFACTURERS

Both manufacturers and retailers export, but until recently, manufacturers have been the dominant force in exporting. For example, the United States is the world's leading supplier of cotton and synthetic yarns. Its active sportswear is known around the world and exported into many markets.

Manufacturers, who make both the raw materials and the finished garments, typically enter the export arena by one of three routes.

INDIRECT EXPORTING

In **indirect exporting,** manufacturers use a management company, a trading company, or a broker to market their products. These foreign agents, who work on commission, are responsible for the selling and promotion of the exporters' products.

The risk to a manufacturer of such an arrangement is minimal. Goods are not even shipped until orders are taken. The agent takes all or most of the responsibility for shaping the product to the foreign market.

DIRECT EXPORTING

In **direct exporting,** manufacturers take complete responsibility for all aspects of marketing their products in a foreign market. They sell their product directly to a wholesaler or a consumer.

Direct exporting is the riskiest method of foreign sales because the manufacturer assumes all the costs connected with producing the product and marketing it in a foreign market without knowing either how or if the product will be received. The possibility of making bigger profits by direct exporting because of fewer middle-man costs, however, balances the risky nature of direct exporting.

JOINT VENTURES

Although the United States permits complete ownership by foreign investors, most countries limit the amount of foreign investment to partnerships and other joint ventures. In a **joint venture,** a manufacturer is part owner of a trading operation. Sometimes the foreign government is the trading partner; sometimes the partner is another business.

The disadvantage of a joint venture in the fashion industry is the same as for foreign investment. War and political upheaval can cause the investor to lose his money. In addition, government regulations

domestic market again. This has caused other countries to view American fashion exports with suspicion, a prejudice that can be overcome by showing the world that American fashion is in the international marketplace to stay.

GLOBETROTTING Gaffes

OFFICE HOURS

There is nothing more frustrating for good business relations than to keep missing your intended business partner when making a call. It is a sign of either ignorance or noninterest if you make your calls when the office is not open. Whether it is a telephone call or an in-person business call, arriving at the wrong time is frustrating . . . for both you and your international partner or customer.

Because of the difference in time zones, it is important for savvy global traders to be aware of these time differences and to schedule their telephone calls to occur when the foreign office is open. Even though your work time may be very brief, it is considered poor business practice to ask your foreign associate to work at times that the office would not normally be open. This is particularly true if you are in the country and ask them to work on Sundays or other times that are not scheduled as office hours. Remember, you would not be pleased if your global associate came here and wanted you to work on Sunday or any of our national holidays. Remember, do unto others as you would have them do unto you!

may also favor the trading partner who has citizenship.

The advantage of a joint venture is that the U.S. manufacturer can expect genuine assistance, with everything from cultural practices to technology, from the foreign partner. The risk is midrange, not so great as direct exporting, not so little as indirect exporting.

EXPORTING BY RETAILERS

For many years, retailers were not in the exporting business. With the fashion boom of the 1980s, however, they began to try their hands at direct exporting. These days, most large cities' shopping streets have an increasingly international look. Valentino, Furla, and Agnes B. have stores on Madison Avenue, and it is not unheard of to spot a Gap store in a European city. Thus far, the balance has swung in favor of European imports coming into the United States, but that is beginning to turn around as U.S. retailers discover they have successful markets in Europe and other parts of the world. Increasingly, retailers are learning to think international from the moment they open their doors. The most common methods of doing business internationally are licensing agreements, franchises, and nonfranchise stores.

METHODS USED TO EXPORT BY RETAILERS

Before a retailer can take his or her business abroad, though, he or she must build an image and product that the world wants to buy. American producers have successfully saturated the world market with American pop icons such as Mickey Mouse, Miss

Piggy, Kermit the Frog, and Superman, but t-shirts with logos are also popular worldwide, and in the fashion industry, perfumes, scarves, and other small fashion products are good candidates for licensing.

Producers who license or franchise internationally must comply with an array of regulations in the country where their licenses or franchised products will be sold. Some of these regulations may not even be in their favor, but then again, licensing and franchising may be the only way to do business in a country that severely restricts imports.

LICENSING ARRANGEMENTS Most foreign retailers first penetrated the U.S. market through licensing arrangements, and U.S. retailers have discovered the value of this same route for introducing their products into foreign markets. Retailers tend to use franchising, whereas licensing is used by both retailers and wholesalers.

Licensing is an agreement between a producer in one country and a foreign producer to manufacture goods, using the former's trademark. In exchange for allowing the product to be licensed, a producer receives a royalty for each item that is sold. The foreign producer, in turn, often provides technical assistance in manufacturing the product, sometimes actually overseeing production. Some fashion producers prefer to keep a very tight rein on their licensing operations; others easily relinquish control.

The advantage of licensing is that it provides another source of profit for producers. The earnings potential in licensing is enormous, especially for products with true international appeal.

Its primary disadvantage is that manufacturers risk losing some control over their products. Although in theory the original producer still has con-

Today, retailers look beyond the boundaries of their own countries and engage in the direct export of their products. American designers and retailers such as Ralph Lauren are now found in European markets while European retailers now have their own stores in the United States. *Courtesy of Ralph Lauren.*

GLOBAL GLIMPSES
PRODUCING UNDER LICENSE

Global licensing is trickier than domestic licensing. Each country has laws regulating licensing, and those laws define the rocky road a licensor must follow. Step one toward licensing is registering the trademark. Registration protects the licensor from anyone else using the "mark." This simple-sounding process often is not. Registration procedures differ from country to country.

In the United States, the first to use or to file intent to use a trademark gets it, whereas overseas, many countries give the trademark to the first person to register it. For example, if Anne Klein wants to register in Hong Kong or Korea and someone else has already registered that trademark, that is the end of it. Because a trademark can be so valuable, companies should register their marks in as many countries as possible.

Licensees are advised not to just hope for the best. "Key man insurance," not only for the licensee but for a celebrity spokesperson, is important. Licensees have an insurable interest to protect. For solid business reasons, companies represented by Magic Johnson asked him to remain their pitchman after he was found HIV-positive: they are protected if he becomes too sick to finish his contract. At the moment they can afford to be generous.

Based on the article "On the Mark," no author, *World Trade*, Jan/Feb, 1992 p. 64.

trol over the product once it is licensed, in practice this is not always the case, particularly when the licensee is halfway around the world. Quality standards and production methods can vary in ways so that the product is different, usually inferior, rather than superior, to the original.

Another drawback to licensing is that earnings may be limited. Some countries, most notably Latin America and other developing countries, limit the amount of the royalty that may be earned, usually to 1 to 3 percent. They may also limit the duration of the license, usually to one year. This usually hinders the licensing process, as most products need time to build a following.

FRANCHISING ARRANGEMENTS Franchising is an agreement between a producer (franchisor) and distributor or dealer (franchisee) to sell the franchisor's products in a store that bears the original producer's name and image. The franchisor receives a share of the profits and, in return, supplies products, managerial advice, and most important, an image. Rive Gauche and Bennetton are two of the more successful franchise operations in recent years. Recently, Au Printemps opened a franchise in Denver, Colorado, that was not successful.

A franchise's great strength is its uniformity. Americans eat at McDonald's restaurants because they know what to expect; they know exactly what the food and service will be like in every McDonald's outlet.

A franchisee is obligated to run a franchise according to standards set by the franchisor. If the franchisee does not meet the franchisor's standards, the franchisor can take back the franchise. Generally, in retail operations, the franchisor maintains control over the store's layout, fixtures, price points, and kinds of merchandise.

But such uniformity can work against a fashion franchise in a foreign market. Franchises can and often do run into difficulties because of national differences in taste. What sells in the United States won't necessarily sell in France, and vice versa.[4] For example, the French display shoes in glass cases, where Americans display them in easily reached shelves. Conversely, Americans display costume jewelry in revolving counter-top cases, whereas the French display it in glass cases under the counter. Perhaps American women are wearing scarves this year and Italian women are not interested in them.

One popular Italian franchise, Bennetton, attempted to deal with this problem by allowing its franchisees to select their own merchandise from a wide array it manufactured. As a result, merchandise varied from outlet to outlet. Even the target customer

differed. Some Bennetton stores were geared to the youth market; others catered to the young working man and woman. The franchisor sought uniformity in store design and presentation of the product.

Although this innovative sales approach was lauded, it did not entirely solve the problem of how to franchise in so many different markets. Bennetton has been more successful in some markets than in others.

Regardless of the problems, more and more U.S. producers are turning to franchises as a means of selling their products in an international market. It especially makes sense to do so if one is a major name in fashion and has an image to both cultivate and protect.

THE SUCCESS OF AMERICAN LABELS ABROAD

Some apparel makers who do not want to license or franchise their products are exporting their fashion products by opening stores bearing their names in foreign cities or selling their labels to European department stores. Among those who have successfully marketed their names in Europe are Liz Claiborne, Silks, Donna Karan, and Ralph Lauren. The potential to expand such operations around the world exists.

U.S. SUPPORT PROGRAMS FOR EXPORTING

The United States is too rich to be the recipient of preferential programs from other nations, but the federal government and many state governments have developed several programs to help exporters. On the federal level, export-service programs are typically administered through the Department of Commerce's International Trade Administration (ITA), the Small Business Administration (SBA), and Export-Import Bank (EXIMBANK).

FEDERAL PROGRAMS FOR EXPORTERS

The International Trade Administration (ITA) is the primary agency within the Department of Commerce handling export programs. ITA provides market research to help prospective exporters decide whether, when, and how to enter the global market, counseling by trade specialists who share information on potential markets and customers, and it sponsors matchmaker and trade mission programs.

GLOBAL *GO-GETTERS*

ATHLETE'S FOOT: MARCHING TO A GLOBAL BEAT

The Athlete's Foot Group opened the first of its stores in Indonesia in 1991. The store is selling in excess of 500 pairs of athletic shoes per week.

The Athlete's Foot Group, which is headquartered in Atlanta, Georgia, is the originator of the athletic footwear specialty-store concept. Founded in 1972, the Athlete's Foot Group operates over 200 company-owned stores in the United States and over 300 stores franchised in the United States and licensed in 13 foreign countries (including Hong Kong, Malaysia, Singapore, and Indonesia).

The Athlete's Foot Group licensed its concept to the Matahari Group, the largest department store chain in Indonesia. The store currently offers traditional sports shoe brands including Nike, Reebok, and Avia, as well as several local-brand products. The stores also offer sports apparel including a variety of licensed products from various U.S. professional sports associations.

A second store opened in Bali and a third store in Jakarta in Spring, 1992. The Athlete's Foot Indonesia plans to aggressively expand the concept throughout the country in the next several years.

The Athlete's Foot Group is planning to develop its retail concept in Japan, Thailand, Taiwan, and Korea in the near future. It is obvious that their global outlook on expanding their business makes their shoes, including those that are made for walking, famous all over the world.

Excerpted from *Interco World*, Vol. 3, No. 1, "Athlete's Foot Opens in Indonesia," no author, Spring, 1992, p. 1.

Courtesy of IMTEC World.

MATCHMAKER PROGRAMS. Matchmaker programs provide an opportunity for small business trade delegations to travel to foreign markets specifically for the purpose of meeting with persons with whom they might conduct business. The trips are designed to establish and promote international trade. At each stop along the trip, exporters are matched to potential distributors, agents, and licensing and joint venture partners. Matchmaker programs are sponsored by the Department of Commerce and the Small Business Administration.

TRADE MISSIONS During a **trade mission,** a group of businesspersons travels abroad for the pur-

---

Matchmakers
TO PROMOTE YOUR PRODUCTS

Matchmaker Trade Delegations pave your way to new export markets.

Matchmaker Trade Delegations "match" you with potential agents, distributors, and joint venture or licensing partners. We do the background work — evaluating your product's potential, finding and screening contacts, and handling logistics. You follow up with an intensive trip filled with face-to-face meetings with prospective clients and in-depth briefings on the economic and business climate of the countries visited. We offer:

✓ **prescreened prospects interested in your product or service**

✓ **in-country publicity**

✓ **convenient sales avenues**

✓ **business appointments scheduled for you through the U.S. embassy or consulate**

✓ **thorough briefings on market requirements and business practices**

✓ **interpreter services**

Matchmakers help small and medium-sized companies meet export sales objectives efficiently and economically. We generally target major markets in two countries and limit trips to a week or less so you can interview the maximum number of good candidates with a minimum of time away from the office. You also have the advantage of group-rate hotels and airfare, as well as on-the-spot U.S. embassy support.

" It is hard to imagine a better program for small to mid-sized companies to be involved in than Matchmaker!"

John G. Richardson
General Manager
James Alexander Corp.
Blairstown, New Jersey

If your firm is new to export or new to market in the countries scheduled for visits, and if U.S. content represents 51 percent of the finished value of your products, Matchmakers could be your answer. Contact your nearest U.S. Department of Commerce district office for details.

Let Matchmakers pave your way to profits!

U. S. DEPARTMENT OF COMMERCE ★ INTERNATIONAL TRADE ADMINISTRATION ★ U.S. AND FOREIGN COMMERCIAL SERVICE 7/89

The International Trade Administration's Matchmaker program helps small and medium-sized American exporters connect with potential agents, distributors, and joint venture or licensing partners. *Courtesy of the U.S. Dept. of Commerce*

pose of exploring and developing foreign markets. Trips are usually coordinated by various U.S. agencies, states, and trade associations. The purpose is to meet as many business contacts as possible for purposes of exploring the possibility of doing business together.

THE U.S. AND FOREIGN COMMERCIAL SERVICE The U.S. and Foreign Commercial Service (US&FCS) was established in 1982 to help exporters compete in the global market. Trade specialists located in 67 U.S. cities and 126 sites in foreign markets are available to counsel exporters. US&FCS's services range from counseling assistance to establishing contacts. The agency also represents U.S. companies seeking to change trade barriers that affect them adversely.

The International Economic Policy (IEP) works with the US&FCS to provide information on trade potential in foreign countries.

TRADE DEVELOPMENT PROGRAM Trade Development (TD) is oriented toward industry sectors, including textiles and apparel. It works with representatives from industry and trade associations to smooth out obstacles to trade and identify trade opportunities. It provides economic analysis, industry statistics, and investment studies.

BUREAU OF EXPORT ADMINISTRATION The Bureau of Export Administration (BXA), the newest agency within the Commerce Department, monitors exporters' applications for licenses and investigates breaches of U.S. export control laws. (Licenses, or permits to export, should not be confused with the licensing agreements involving products, which were discussed earlier in this chapter.)

The Center for International Research (CIR), which operates out of the Bureau of the Census, is a source of worldwide demographic studies and also provides exporters with a data base.

SMALL BUSINESS ADMINISTRATION PROGRAMS (SBA) The Office of International Trade is the primary agency within SBA that works to promote U.S. exports. It offers counseling to exporters, export training, legal advice, market information, and it sponsors matchmaker events. SBA also sponsors the Exporters Revolving Line of Credit (ERLC), which provides exporters with a line of credit for up to eighteen months.

EXPORT-IMPORT BANK (EXIMBANK) Eximbank is an independent U.S. government agency with the primary purpose of facilitating the export of U.S. goods and services. Eximbank meets this objective by providing loans, guarantees, and insurance coverage to U.S. exporters and foreign buyers, normally on market-related credit terms. It maintains an advisory service on the availablilty and use of its programs.

TAX ASSISTANCE FOR EXPORTERS

Since 1984, special tax assistance has been available to promote U.S. exports. Exporters who qualify can register as Foreign Services Corporations or Small Foreign Services Corporations or as Interest Charge Domestic International Sales Corporations (IC-DISC). Under these forms of corporate organization, part of the company's income from exports is exempt from corporate taxes.

CARTELS In an effort to boost international trade among small and mid-sized companies, the Commerce Department has turned to the inventive idea of cartels. A **cartel** is a group of similar businesses that work together to regulate production, promotion, and pricing. Although cartels are usually illegal on grounds that they are unfair competition, in this case, the Department of Commerce has issued certificates providing antitrust immunity to cartel members. So long as their actions do not affect competition in the United States, the cartels are permitted to trade market data and prices to bolster foreign trade.

Cartel members reduce expenses by sharing costs. They are eligible, for example, to apply for foreign export licenses and permits as a unit. Members typically share profits as well. Along with catfish farmers and flour millers, textile manufacturers have been among those to take advantage of the cartels.[5]

STATE PROGRAMS TO SUPPORT EXPORTING

In addition to offering an array of services similar to those offered by the federal agencies to exporters, state programs sometimes provide financial assistance, most typically in the form of bank referrals and loan guarantees. States also sponsor trade missions and matchmaker programs, provide language banks, and sponsor trade shows.

UNIVERSITY EXPORT SUPPORT SERVICES

Export support services have begun to spring up in universities around the country. One of the oldest programs, which is geared specifically to the textile and apparel industry, is the Fashion Institute of Technology's Export Advisory Service Extension (EASE).

EASE counsels fashion manufacturers on possibilities and options in exporting and also sponsors seminars, conferences, and workshops that promote exporting.

Although it does not service the fashion industry directly, another typical program is Bryant College's Rhode Island Export Assistance Center. It matches small businesses in Rhode Island with trade leads and has also formed a trading block of New England firms.[6]

EXPORT-IMPORT TENSIONS

Exports and imports are often linked in an attempt to resolve the tension that has arisen in the garment industry as manufacturers have watched whole chunks of their businesses being taken over by importers. Ideally, domestic manufacturers would like to keep imports entirely out of the U.S. marketplace on grounds that they would find it easier to thrive in an already tough market without the competition from international marketers. Failing this, they seek protective legislation to limit the number of imports.

Exporters oppose such legislation because they know that it will affect their ability to export. Exporting will thrive only if the United States continues to allow imports to enter the country.

Most unbiased experts agree that the United States does not need to keep others out as much as it needs to learn to sell its fashion abroad. They usually observe that there is a need for the United States to establish guidelines that promote both importing and exporting and also protect the domestic fashion industry to some extent.

Among the guidelines that are most often put forth is one stressing the need for the United States to insist that countries it imports from also buy U.S. exports.

The United States might also negotiate reciprocal trade agreements that allow for imports and exports of equivalent value. Many of the U.S. current trade agreements limit products by category rather than by value. This means that if a foreign producer's sweater exports to the United States are cut from 10,000 to 5,000, he or she will attempt to make up the loss by exporting more expensive sweaters and will thus not suffer any overall loss of import income. This trade imbalance could be eased by negotiating trade agreements that impose dollar-equivalent values on imports and exports.

GLOBAL PATTERNS OF CONSUMPTION

Ultimately, how much exporting will be done and where it will be done depends on global patterns of consumption. Exporters must take account of who is buying in the global market and what they are buying.

Global patterns in consumption, which are always in a state of flux, are affected by broad economic trends. The consumption of fabric declined, for example, during the two most recent recessions, in 1982–1983 and the early 1990s. The lessened demand for fiber hurt exporters who were not able to take the reduced demand into account.

Future global consumption is generally predicted through two measures, which are used together to predict future fashion needs. The first measure is **fiber consumption**, that is, how much fiber was used during a given period. The second is **consumer expenditures**, that is, how much people are spending on fashion products.

In measuring fiber consumption, it is important to break down fiber usage by country and/or region. Poor countries buy less fiber than rich countries, but as the developing nations of the world become richer, they become larger consumers of fiber.

Similarly, consumer expenditures are higher in rich countries. People in affluent countries have more money to spend on fashion, although as people's income goes up, they spend a relatively smaller percentage of it on clothing. This trend is counteracted by people's tendency to "trade up," that is, as their income goes up, so does their taste for more expensive goods.

At present the industrialized nations in Europe and the United States consume 36 percent of the world's fiber, despite having only 13 percent of the world's population.[7] This is about to change, however, because the world's population is shifting from the Northern Hemisphere to the Southern Hemisphere.

As the population shifts from north to south, greater numbers of people will consume fiber, but because many countries in the Southern Hemisphere are still less developed nations, consumer expenditure per person may go down. In the developed

Export-import tensions caused by importers thriving at the expense of domestic manufacturers has resulted in cries for protective legislation to limit the number of imports allowed into the U.S. market. *Courtesy of the International Ladies Garment Workers Union.*

countries, by contrast, there are fewer consumers of fiber, but consumer expenditures are higher.

What does this mean for the fabric manufacturer who wants to expand into international markets in the 1990s? He or she might explore previously untapped markets in the Southern Hemisphere, but because consumer expenditures will not be high, the

manufacturer might decide to target his or her product to low and midrange markets.

Government agencies and export service centers track these changing demographics so they can help exporters predict where the best future markets will be.

The swing toward international marketing is both inevitable and permanent, and American pro-

TECH TALK

EXPORT TO WIN

A business software package simulates the difficult day-to-day decisions (and their consequences) that companies often face when entering the international trade arena for the first time.

Known as "EXPORT TO WIN," the package is extremely easy to use and is currently an educational tool in both large and small corporations, in educational institutions, and in general trade associations.

"Export to Win" puts the user in the role of the International Marketing Manager for Xebec Company. The user must perform in that role over a simulated five-year period, making more complex decisions as each year evolves.

This highly interactive program can involve the user in up to 17 key events . . . all based on challenging decisions like those that must be faced in the real world day-to-day operation of any export department.

Specifically, the user will be able to develop a marketing plan, finance the export operation, analyze distribution options, keep track of global business trends, and plan for new product development.

Technical specifications:

"Export to Win" is available for use with the IBM PC and compatibles and requires 640K RAM memory. A color monitor is preferred. It is not necessary to use a graphics adapter.

Based on "Export to Win," John Otis, *Nasbite News*, Summer, 1991, p. 9.

ducers will have no choice in the coming years but to join the ranks of exporters.

It will help that European fashion buyers have once again become very interested in American labels. Just as New York department store Henri Bendel led the way in promoting European designers in the 1970s, major European department stores are now interested in promoting American design. What remains to be seen is whether American manufacturers will seize the moment.

If they do, they will encounter problems of the type that have just been described, but they will also discover exciting, hitherto untapped markets—and the profits those markets can generate.

ENDNOTES

1. *GATT International Trade* (annual), 1988.
2. Kevin McDermott, "What It Takes To Make It Overseas," Dun & Bradstreet Reports, March/April 1988, p. 6.
3. *Crain's*, June 24, 1991.
4. *Crain's*, Phyllis Furman, "Fashion Houses Invading Europe," June 24, 1991.
5. *Wall Street Journal*, "Marketplace," June 26, 1991.
6. *Wall Street Journal*, "Marketplace," June 26, 1991.
7. *US Global Competitiveness: The US Textile Mill Industry*, U.S. International Trade Commission, December 1987.

VOCABULARY   cartel   _____

_____

_____

consumer expenditures   _____

_____

_____

direct exporting   _____

_____

_____

fiber consumption   _____

_____

_____

franchising   _____

_____

_____

indirect exporting   _____

_____

_____

joint venture   _____

_____

_____

licensing   _____

_____

_____

matchmaker programs   _____

_____

_____

trade missions   _____

_____

_____

GLOBAL REVIEW   1.   What is the most important reason for exporting?

_____

_____

_____

_____

2. Exporting provides needed flexibility for fashion producers. What is the most important flexibility and how can it help a company prosper?

    _____

    _____

    _____

    _____

3. What has been the prevailing prejudice against American fashion exporters?

    _____

    _____

    _____

    _____

4. How does indirect exporting differ from direct exporting?

    _____

    _____

    _____

    _____

5. Joint ventures can be very complicated and risky. Name two of the major risks associated with joint ventures.

    _____

    _____

    _____

    _____

6. List the services available for exporters that are directed through the U.S. Department of Commerce.

    _____

    _____

    _____

    _____

    _____

7. What are the advantages of cartels and how do they help exporters succeed?

    _____

    _____

    _____

    _____

    _____

8. What is the difference between "matchmaker" programs and "trade missions"? Which do you think might be more beneficial for a first-time fashion exporter?

_____

_____

_____

_____

9. How are colleges and universities responding to the need of U.S. fashion exporters?

_____

_____

_____

_____

10. Why do you think that the American label is wanted by international consumers?

_____

_____

_____

_____

GLOBAL DIGEST

1. What are the major differences between licensing and franchising in the global marketplace? Give examples of each and discuss which one would be better for a fashion business of your choice.

_____

_____

_____

_____

_____

_____

_____

2. The text states, "unbiased experts agree that the United States does not need to keep others out as much as it needs to learn to sell its fashion abroad." What are some of the guidelines being suggested and how will they affect our trade balance?

_____

_____

_____

_____

_____

_____

_____

_____

3. How do global patterns of consumption affect the decision to export a fashion product? What must be considered for future market entry?

_____

_____

_____

_____

_____

_____

_____

_____

CHAPTER 5

Who Imports and Why

A walk through a major department store in the United States today is like a walk through an international bazaar. One counter is stacked with expensive Italian leather purses; another displays inexpensive Swiss watches; another, Scottish cashmere sweaters. Brazilian shoes fill a display case, and still another displays silk robes from China.

The United States is in the middle of the largest import boom in its history. Imports are a multibillion dollar market. In 1980, imported fashion accounted for $5.1 billion in sales annually. By 1989, Americans were buying $32.4 billion worth of imported fashions—six times more![1] The influx of imported goods into the U.S. market has been the single most important event in retailing in the past decade.

To understand what this import boom means to the fashion industry, it is necessary to examine, as you will in this chapter, why the importing boom has happened, who imports and why, as well as the benefits and drawbacks importing poses for the international fashion business as well as the domestic fashion industry.

ADVANTAGES OF IMPORTING

There are many reasons to import, but the most important is to satisfy customer demand. High-fashion imports have status, and low-end imported goods offer consumers a price advantage. For both reasons, imported goods appeal to the customers. The fashion industry needs satisfied customers, and it cannot afford not to sell imported goods.

Sales of imported goods also help to maintain the U.S. balance of trade. If Americans want to sell their goods to other countries, then they must let others sell to them.

Initially, imports were attractive to retailers and manufacturers because of their low cost, which, in turn, was largely due to lower wages outside the United States. Cost is still a factor in the purchasing of imported goods, even though many imported goods are expensive luxury items. Today, retailers can stock their stores with low-end, inexpensive imports, on which they can expect a larger profit margin than they would make on similar domestic

Country	Total	O.E.C.D.		Soviet Union and Eastern Europe	China: Mainland, Vietnam, North Korea	O.P.E.C.	Other developing countries	Africa	America	Middle East	Far East
		Total	E.E.C.								
IMPORTS											
United States	473.4	287.7	85.1	2.1	12.0	30.6	141.0	14.0	57.4	15.1	96.0
Austria	38.9	32.9	26.4	2.4	0.2	0.7	2.7	0.9	0.5	0.3	1.5
Belgium	98.5	84.4	70.3	1.8	0.3	2.9	9.0	4.6	1.8	2.6	3.0
Canada	114.1	98.8	12.6	0.4	1.0	1.6	10.8	1.0	4.1	0.6	7.8
Denmark	26.6	22.5	13.3	0.8	0.3	0.6	2.4	0.2	0.9	0.5	1.4
France	190.6	153.8	114.3	4.7	1.8	8.0	19.2	9.3	4.5	5.2	8.8
Italy	162.3	123.2	92.1	6.6	1.8	10.3	20.1	12.9	4.7	4.7	6.8
Japan	210.8	105.6	28.3	3.7	11.8	31.9	57.8	4.2	8.7	22.8	64.7
Netherlands	104.2	86.2	65.8	2.4	0.5	6.0	9.0	2.7	2.8	4.5	5.2
Spain	71.5	45.0	40.8	1.8	0.5	5.3	8.1	4.6	3.5	2.5	3.1
Sweden	48.9	42.9	26.9	1.7	0.3	0.5	3.4	0.2	1.1	0.5	2.3
Switzerland	58.2	52.3	41.2	0.7	0.2	0.3	4.6	1.0	1.3	0.5	2.2
United Kingdom	197.6	167.3	104.0	2.9	0.9	3.2	22.3	4.2	3.6	3.0	14.6
West Germany	269.8	217.8	137.9	10.1	3.1	6.6	31.9	8.2	8.2	3.4	17.6
Percent distribution:											
United States	100.0	60.8	18.0	0.4	2.5	6.5	29.8	3.0	12.1	3.2	20.3
Austria	100.0	84.6	67.9	6.0	0.6	1.8	7.0	2.2	1.3	0.8	3.9
Belgium	100.0	85.7	71.4	1.8	0.3	3.0	9.2	4.7	1.8	2.7	3.1
Canada	100.0	86.5	11.0	0.4	0.9	1.4	9.5	0.9	3.6	0.5	6.8
Denmark	100.0	84.7	50.0	2.9	1.2	2.1	9.1	0.9	3.5	1.9	5.4
France	100.0	80.7	60.0	2.4	0.9	4.2	10.1	4.9	2.4	2.7	4.6
Italy	100.0	75.9	56.7	4.1	1.1	6.4	12.4	7.9	2.9	2.9	4.2
Japan	100.0	50.1	13.4	1.8	5.6	15.1	27.4	2.0	4.1	10.8	30.7
Netherlands	100.0	82.8	63.2	2.3	0.5	5.8	8.7	2.6	2.7	4.3	5.0
Spain	100.0	62.9	57.1	2.5	0.8	7.4	11.3	6.4	4.8	3.5	4.4
Sweden	100.0	87.8	55.0	3.5	0.7	1.1	6.9	0.4	2.2	1.0	4.7
Switzerland	100.0	89.9	70.8	1.2	0.4	0.6	7.9	1.8	2.2	0.9	3.8
United Kingdom ..	100.0	84.6	52.6	1.4	0.4	1.8	11.3	2.1	1.8	1.5	7.4
West Germany	100.0	80.8	51.1	3.8	1.2	2.5	11.8	3.1	3.0	1.3	6.5

Foreign Trade of Selected Countries—Source of Imports in Billions of Dollars: 1989.
Courtesy of Organization for Economic Cooperation and Development, Paris, France. Data derived from Monthly Statistics of Foreign Trade, *series A, May 1990.*

goods, or they buy high-end goods and may expect better quality than the domestic market can supply.

Another appeal of imported goods is their uniqueness, which also gives them snob appeal. In a label-conscious era, foreign goods have cachet that domestic goods often lack.

Finally, these days, imported goods are attractive because of the quality they offer. Although American industrial standards were slipping over the past decade, the rest of the world's standards were improving. A customer who once would have scorned the inferior quality of a coat made in many Asian countries, now sees quality that is equal to, if not better than, that found in many domestic products. Foreign fashion products, once considered inferior, are now viewed as superior to many American-made products.

DISADVANTAGES OF IMPORTING

Despite their advantages, imported goods are not without their drawbacks. Their quality is generally good, but it is often unpredictable, especially in low-end goods produced in countries with relatively new fashion industries.

Buying imported goods also increases the **lead time**, the amount of time between ordering goods

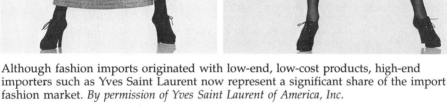

Although fashion imports originated with low-end, low-cost products, high-end importers such as Yves Saint Laurent now represent a significant share of the import fashion market. *By permission of Yves Saint Laurent of America, Inc.*

and receiving them in a store. Ordering foreign fabric adds several weeks to the lead time; using foreign production adds several months. This poses problems for importers, who must ask themselves, Will this garment still be fashionable by the time it arrives on my store shelves? Is it worthwhile to tie up my money on imported goods, which, unlike domestic products, typically must be paid for when an order is placed rather than when the goods are delivered?

Delivery may be slow or unpredictable. Not all cultures have the same sense of time, and a foreign plant that promises quick delivery on goods may not be operating on the same schedule that its fast-paced American counterpart is. Inadequate transportation may slow delivery.

Communication can be another problem for a buyer and seller who do not speak the same language, especially in an industry as technical as the fashion industry has become.

Political instability—wars, coups, even elections—have been known to hold up orders.

Even government regulations can throw off a production schedule. One American producer spent five extra months trying to get 2000 summer skirts out of a warehouse, where they were held up while a government decided how best to enforce a new cus-

toms regulation. By the time the skirts arrived, it was the dead of winter, and the prospects for sales were dead, too.

THE SPREAD OF IMPORTING

For many years, most nations' clothing industries were self-sufficient. People were interested in what others made, but they did not necessarily buy it. American women, for example, had long looked to France for high-style clothing, but little of this clothing was actually imported into the United States. Instead, the U.S. fashion industry copied (and modified) French couturier fashions, produced them, and sold them in its own domestic market. Some U.S. fashion producers specialized in imported clothing, but these were mostly cheap, low-end garments that never accounted for any sizeable portion of the overall apparel market.

GLOBAL RETAILING

Starting in the late 1970s, however, imports began to flow into the United States in great volume, or rather,

GLOBAL *GO-GETTERS*
DEN FUJITA: JAPAN'S MASTER IMPORTER

A master importer, Den Fujita is the man who made the hamburger a Japanese passion. In fact, many young Japanese believe that the "Big Mac" or Bi-gu Ma-ku was born on the Ginza.

This entrepreneur also fought the idea that Japan is and should remain a nation of small shopkeepers. He took on the Japanese government and had it ease laws that had made it next to impossible to build large-scale stores. This cleared the way for the entry of Toys "R" Us, a large U.S. retail chain, into Japan . . . and Mr. Fujita owns a 20-percent stake in this new venture.

He has imported beef patties and french fries to people who were said to prefer rice. He introduced large-scale discounting to people who supposedly wanted only cozy but high-priced neighborhood shops. In a nation whose economic vigor comes from its exporting prowess, Mr. Fujita is a master importer. He is probably the most sought after joint-venture partner for American and European companies trying to make their way in this complex market. His latest joint venture is a deal with Blockbuster Video to develop a chain of 15 rental stores. Three of them opened in early 1992.

His start in importing was focused in the fashion business. In the late 1950s and early 1960s he imported Christian Dior handbags and other accessories into an economy where almost everything was rationed and imports were severly restricted.

Because it has become increasingly difficult to find good sites for new McDonald's restaurants, Mr. Fujita is now constructing McDonald's at many of the new shopping centers where the Toys "R" Us stores will be located. Each will feed off the traffic created by the other.

Based on "Den Fujita, Japan's Mr. Joint Venture" by James Sterngold, *New York Times*, Business Section, March 3, 1992, pp. 1–6.

---

it would be more accurate to say that imports started to flow around the world in ways that they had not previously done. When retail fashion operations in many countries began to expand into other countries, **global retailing** was born. In a dramatic shift from two decades ago, many retailers, both large and small, are now international; their markets and profits are heavily tied to their operations around the world.

The United States has attracted many of the world's global retailers, mostly because it has a large population, many of whom are rich, educated, and eager to consume. The United States is the world's leading consumer-oriented country.

IMPORT PENETRATION

Imports are usually measured in terms of their dollar volume, but another way of measuring their impact is to examine **import penetration,** or the degree to which imports have saturated a market. In 1980, imports averaged 31 percent of the overall U.S. fashion market. By 1989, imports were 55 percent of the market. They are expected to comprise 65 percent of the market within the next few years.[2]

This means that for every 100 garments that will be sold in the United States, 65 will be imported goods. In some categories, imports already exceed domestic goods. For example, three quarters of the sweaters sold in the United States are imported.[3] Import penetration is most widespread in low- and high-end merchandise. The midrange market is still met by U.S. manufacturers.

Such extensive import penetration has left its imprint on the domestic fashion industry. To understand how importing has changed the face of American fashion, one must understand who imports and why.

IMPORTING BY RETAILERS

Retailers are a major force in fashion importing. **Global sourcing,** the term used to describe the process of purchasing imported goods from markets around the world, is now such an important part of retailing that consumers would consider it odd not to find imported goods in department stores, boutiques, and other retail outlets when they shop. In many large department stores, whole departments are given over to imported goods, and some boutiques specialize in imported goods. Bloomingdales stages storewide festivals with international themes.

TECH TALK

E.T. CALL HOME

A hodge-podge of faxes, overnight mail, and conference calls kept international executives in touch with each other, but it was slow, costly, and guaranteed to disturb someone's sleep in the middle of the night.

All that changed when global networking came onto the international scene. Until the late 1980s, global networking, linking far-flung corporate offices by moving voice, data, and images over telephone lines was out of reach of small and mid-sized companies.

However, thanks to technological advances and a boom in international business, many of the world's leading long-distance carriers, AT&T, MCI, Sprint, British Telecom, Cable & Wireless, France Telecom, Deutsche-bundespost Telekom, and Kokusai Denshin Denwa of Japan, are providing quality networking services at prices many mid-size companies are finding acceptable. By joining a network, U.S. companies that rack up $3000 a month in international and domestic communications charges can save as much as 40 percent on their telephone bills.

Global networks typically give the biggest discounts to companies that use them the most. Therefore, the more a company uses the network, the more money it saves.

Beside the price savings, global networks give international companies better quality service than they could get by transacting business over local public telephone lines or by piecing together a network on their own. And they can receive telephone bills in a single currency instead of half a dozen.

Despite their many advantages, global networks are by no means right for everyone. It does not pay for an exporter or importer who has an office in Paris that he or she calls two or three times a day to set up a global network.

Even high-volume telecommunications users may stay away, and perhaps for good reason. With a system linking telephones and computers, companies risk losing time and data in a systemwide "crash" should the network temporarily go "down."

Even so, smaller and mid-size companies can agree on one thing: With a network, communicating has never been cheaper or easier for those who like to call home often.

Based on "The Calls Heard 'Round the World," Rosalind Resnick, *International Business*, March, 1992, pp. 72–73.

Sales from these import festivals are estimated to double the store's annual profits.

SOURCING OPTIONS FOR RETAILERS

Retailers usually buy garments ready-made, that is, ready for the ultimate user. Less often, they buy all or part of their raw materials abroad and bring them home for domestic production. More and more often these days, retailers are also using **offshore production,** having garments entirely made in another part of the world.

However they get their imports, retailers have several options available to aid them in their continuous search for unique and interesting imported products. The six major options include foreign fashion markets, direct assistance from importers, store-owned buying offices, commissionaires and independent agents, import fairs, and import companies.

FOREIGN FASHION MARKETS Twice a year buyers gather at fashion markets to preview the new fashion lines. Paris used to be the buyers' only stop, but in the late 1960s, other market centers developed, and buyers now literally shop the world, scouring all parts of Asia, South and North America, and Europe for whatever is trendy and exciting. Fashion fairs, or "market weeks," as they are called are held twice a year in such European fashion capitals as Paris, London, and Milan. Buyers routinely make two or three buying trips a year to the Far East, and increas-

YOU DON'T MAKE THE FORTUNE 500®
BY MAKING BAD MOVES.

AMP Incorporated
Abbott Laboratories
Air Products and Chemicals, Inc.
Alberto-Culver Company
American Cyanamid Company
American Home Products Corp.
Avon Products, Inc.
C.R. Bard, Inc.
Baxter International, Inc.
Becton Dickinson and Company
Bell & Howell
Borden, Inc.
Bristol-Myers Squibb Company
CPC International Inc.
Campbell Soup Co.
Central Soya Company, Inc.
The Clorox Company
The Coca-Cola Company
Colgate-Palmolive Company
ConAgra, Inc.
Crown Cork & Seal Co., Inc.
Digital Equipment Corp.
Dixie Yarns, Inc.
Du Pont (E.I.) De Nemours & Co., Inc.
Echlin Inc.
Emerson Electric Co.
Figgie International Inc.
Ford Motor Co.
H.B. Fuller
General Electric Company
General Instrument Corp.
General Signal Corporation
The Gillette Co.
Gould Inc.
W.R. Grace & Co.
H.J. Heinz Co.
Hewlett-Packard
Hubbell, Inc.
ITT Corp.
Insilco Corporation
Intel Corp.
Johnson & Johnson
Eli Lilly and Company
Medtronic, Inc.
Merck & Co., Inc.
Millipore Corp.
Motorola, Inc.
National Service Industries, Inc.
North American Philips Corporation
Ohio Mattress Company
Owens-Illinois, Inc.
Parker Hannifin Corporation
Pepsico, Inc.
Perkin-Elmer Corp.
Pfizer Inc.
Phillips-Van Heusen Corp.
Pittway Corp.
Prime Computer, Inc.
Procter & Gamble Company
RJR Nabisco Inc.
Raychem Corp.
Reynolds Metals Co.
Rorer Group, Inc.
Sara Lee Corporation
Schering-Plough Corp.
Sonoco Products Company
Sterling Drug Inc.
Storage Technology Corporation
Teledyne, Inc.
Union Carbide Corp.
Unisys
The Upjohn Company
Wang Laboratories, Inc.
Warner-Lambert Company
Western Digital Corporation
Westinghouse Electric Corp.
Worthington Industries, Inc.

Fact: These companies have over 200 manufacturing facilities in Puerto Rico. Surprising? Not to those driven by a healthy bottom line. Because for many compelling reasons, Puerto Rico is a thriving profit center for a diverse range of businesses.

Take our work force. Well-educated, highly skilled bilingual U.S. citizens whose output per dollar of production wages is double that of the U.S. mainland. And whose managerial abilities are reflected by the fact that 98% of all plant managers in Puerto Rico are Puerto Ricans. Consider the 100% U.S. federal tax credit. As well as the 90% Puerto Rico tax exemption. Our communications systems are state-of-the-art. And our highly developed shipping and air cargo networks provide easy access to U.S. and overseas markets. For a plant location that can make you a fortune, make the right move. To Puerto Rico.

© July 1990 Commonwealth of Puerto Rico

PUERTO RICO
Profits are our biggest export.

Please send me specific information on the advantages of Puerto Rico.
Mail to: Commonwealth of Puerto Rico Economic Development Administration
1290 Avenue of the Americas
New York, NY 10104-0092
Or call (212) 245-1200 ext. 427
(800) 223-0699

Name_____ Title_____
Company_____
Address_____
City_____ State_____ Zip_____
Telephone (____)_____ Product_____
☐ Current expansion project ☐ Future expansion project

Offshore production allows retailers to avoid most of the burden of paying taxes while enjoying the benefits of low-cost labor abroad. *Courtesy of Saatchi and Saatchi Advertising.*

ingly often these days, they also travel to South America and Canada.

International buying trips, which invariably coincide with market weeks, ensure that buyers will see the newest and most interesting products that are available. Such expeditions also serve as sources of inspiration and creativity to buyers, keeping them informed about other cultures' trends and new ideas, some of which will be translated, either directly or indirectly, into products to sell at home.

ASSISTANCE FROM FOREIGN SOURCES

Most major importing countries make some attempt to promote and expand their market share of imports to the world. Embassies often maintain offices to act as liaisons between domestic manufacturers and various countries' buyers.

Some trade groups have formed to facilitate and promote fashion importing. In France, for example, French fashion producers belong to the Federation Francaise des Industries de l'Habillement, a group similar to the American Apparel Manufacturers Association. The organization helps French producers find U.S. agents, works with department stores on promotions, and engages in other activities that promote French fashion imports. Other major fashion importing countries provide similar services.

In addition, many fashion designers maintain offices in New York and other fashion capitals around the world to handle their import business. Major designers from around the world—Valentino, Yves St. Laurent, and Matsuhiro Matsuda, to name but a few—have also begun to open retail stores, usually boutiques, in New York and other major U.S. fashion centers.

STORE-OWNED FOREIGN BUYING OF-FICES Stores that do a lot of importing often maintain their own **foreign buying offices,** specialized departments located in foreign markets whose purpose is to facilitate importing in that trade region for the store. The buyers who work in these offices are able, because of their foreign locations, constantly to survey their markets for new products. International buyers advise domestic buyers on international trends originating within their areas.

Foreign fashion fairs, such as those that are held in March and September at the world's largest exhibition—Igedo Düsseldorf—are valuable sources of information on unique and interesting imported products. *Courtesy of Igedo Düsseldorf.*

GLOBETROTTING Gaffes

MESSAGES RECEIVED . . . WRONG!

Familiarization with cultural expectations and their accompanying nonverbal cues is an important step for an international executive before making contact with people in other countries. An example of poor intercultural communication would be when a fashion producer from the United States visits a Saudi business partner to convince him to expedite permits for his merchandise. The Saudi partner offers the American coffee, which he politely refuses because he had drunk too much coffee at the hotel while planning this meeting. The American sits down and crosses his legs, exposing the soles of his shoes, passes documents to the Saudi partner with his left hand, inquires about the Saudi's wife, and emphasizes the urgency of the needed permits. Thus, in a short time, the international executive from the United States has unwittingly offended the Saudi partner five times.

He refused his host's hospitality, showed disrespect by displaying the soles of his shoes, used his left hand (which is considered rude), implied an unintended familial familiarity, and displayed impatience with his host. The international executive certainly had no intention of offending his host and probably was not aware of the rudeness of his behavior. The Saudi might forgive his American guest for being ignorant of local customs, but the forgiven international executive is in a weakened position for business negotiations and deals.

Based on "Inconsistent Messages," Franklin B. Krohn and Zafar U. Ahmed, *Hospitality and Tourism*, November, 1991, Vol. 4, No. 1, pp. 40–43.

Buyers in buying offices usually have the same authority to purchase items that domestic buyers do. Buying offices are located in major import capitals such as Beijing, Paris, Hong Kong, London, and Tokyo.

COMMISSIONAIRES AND INDEPENDENT AGENTS   Stores that are not large enough to maintain their own foreign buying offices often rely on **commissionaires** or **independent agents,** specialists who act as agents for their clients. Commissionaires or independent agents' offices are often smaller than stores' foreign buying offices, and commissionaires and agents represent both retailers and manufacturers.

These agents provide many of the same services that stores' foreign buying offices do, but unlike these offices, they do not buy without special authorization. They are paid by commission.

FOREIGN IMPORT FAIRS   As the export business to the United States has boomed, importers have begun to hold special import fairs in key cities in the United States, usually New York, Chicago, Los Angeles, and Dallas. The New York *Pret* is the largest and most prestigious of the import fairs.

These fairs do for foreign exporters what fashion week does for U.S. buyers abroad, that is, give them a chance to observe our culture, including our styles and trends, first-hand. The fairs are invaluable, too, in establishing and building contacts with small and mid-sized retailers who would not ordinarily travel to international fashion markets.

IMPORT COMPANIES   American-owned import companies are another important form of foreign sourcing. These firms shop in the international markets, put together their own product lines, and then sell them to U.S. retailers and wholesalers. Import companies have always existed, but with the onset of the import boom, they have taken on added importance. Like import fairs, they provide small and mid-sized firms access to imports.

SPECIFICATION AND PRIVATE LABEL BUYING

The boom in importing has led many retailers to engage in **specification buying,** in which retailers create and manufacture lines to their own standards rather than manufacturer's standards. For years, manufacturers set the industry's standards, declining to deviate from those standards to customize work for individual retailers.

In the past, manufacturers' standards played an important role in building up the U.S. fashion industry by making it more streamlined and efficient. With the advent of global marketing, however, what was once an advantage has become a disadvantage. Many importers, especially those who are eager to

Import fairs in cities such as Dallas, Texas, provide importers with valuable opportunities to showcase new styles and trends to retailers who ordinarily do not travel to international fashion markets. *Courtesy of the Dallas Apparel Mart.*

build their own fashion businesses, are willing to work to retailers' specifications.

Success in specification buying led retailers to experiment, with even greater success, with **private labels,** in which stores design and produce their own lines under their own labels. Major department stores have been able to create genuine personas for these labels, so much so that many customers are unaware that they are buying store brands rather than a designer label. Bloomingdale's Express and Macy's Aerospostale are two examples of successful private labels. Because private labels compete with national brands, retailers often can maintain profit margins only by turning to offshore sources for all or part of their products.

IMPORTING BY MANUFACTURERS

Manufacturers, who import raw materials as well as finished products, are the other major segment of the textile and apparel industry involved in importing.

GLOBAL *Goodies*
BUSINESS CARD

(212) 760-7662

ELAINE STONE
PROFESSOR OF
MERCHANDISING AND MARKETING

FASHION INSTITUTE OF TECHNOLOGY
STATE UNIVERSITY OF NEW YORK
227 WEST 27 STREET
NEW YORK, NEW YORK 10001

In international business, the real passport to success can be your business card. To a foreigner, your name is foreign and therefore easier to absorb in writing, but particularly because rank and profession are taken much more seriously abroad than in the United States.

On the card, include your company name and your position, plus any titles such as vice-president, manager, director. Do not use abbreviations. Overseas, a bachelor's degree entitles you to put a Dr. in front of your name. Professor is also used much more loosely than in the United States.

If you go to a country where English is not widely spoken, take your cards to a printer and have the reverse side printed in the local language. (It is helpful to have this checked by someone who is fluent in the language.) Remember—you *are* what your card presents you to be!

Macy's Aerospostale is one example of a successful private label produced by an American retailer. *Courtesy of Macy's.*

Their goal is to make the product in the least expensive and highest quality way, and for most manufacturers today, that goal could not be achieved without global sourcing.

Domestic production with domestic materials is still the standard against which all other production methods are measured. This method offers the most control over the product, including everything from lead time to quality. But with the advent of importing, several other, newer options for producing garments have emerged.

DOMESTIC PRODUCTION, FOREIGN FABRIC

Fashion products may be produced domestically using foreign raw materials. This method is favored by manufacturers who specialize in using unique or unusual fabrics. One advantage is that foreign fabric exporters often are willing to cut smaller yardages than most U.S. fabric manufacturers allow. This enables producers to create a line with a wider range of fabrics than they would use if they were buying the fabric domestically. Producers can also experiment with unusual fabrics in small runs. This method adds four- to six-weeks lead time to a production schedule.

FOREIGN CONTRACTOR, FOREIGN FABRIC

Another option involves complete foreign production, with all its attendant advantages and difficulties. Foreign production adds five to six months to a production schedule but often allows for smaller, more specified runs, an advantage to small and mid-sized manufacturers.

FOREIGN CONTRACTOR, DOMESTIC FABRIC

A third option gives manufacturers control over their raw materials and also may save money when fabrics are cut in large yardages. A disadvantage is the amount of time that is lost sending the fabric to a foreign contractor. Three- to four-months extra lead time is required with this production method.

MANUFACTURER-OWNED OVERSEAS PRODUCTION

Long popular in Europe, manufacturer-owned overseas production is the least used to date among American manufacturers. When it is used, production facilities may be manufacturer-owned or joint ventures. The advantage of manufacturer-owned overseas production is that, depending on the culture, almost as much—and sometimes as much—control can be exercised as over domestic production. Labor may be cheaper than in the United States. The disadvantages are that money must be tied up in the foreign investment and there is added risk in doing business in another country.

9802 PRODUCTION

9802 production, formerly called 807 production, is an option for manufacturers that permit some stage of production, usually assembly, to be done outside the United States and brought into the country with tariff paid on the **value-added** portion of the garment only. This means that on a garment cut in the United States and assembled in Costa Rica or some other Caribbean nation, the manufacturer pays a tariff only on the assembly, not on the entire garment. (Most 9802 productions are done with Caribbean nations.) The remainder of the production is done domestically; the fabric may be domestic or foreign. Some manufacturers own or co-own the foreign plants. The primary reason to use 9802 production is to take advantage of lower labor costs outside the United States. Because of the added shipping costs, however, large quantity runs are required.

Drawbacks to 9802 production are the fluctuations in quality and added shipping time.

TENSIONS BETWEEN RETAILERS AND MANUFACTURERS

Importing has contributed to growing tensions between manufacturers and retailers within the fashion sector. In the interest of promoting their own private labels and specification buying, retailers have sometimes offered help, including technical assistance, to foreign sources.

Manufacturers, along with labor unions, charge that actions like this, along with the purchasing of cheap imports, have served to undermine the U.S. fashion industry at a time when it is already in a weakened position due to the import boom.

Retailers respond by pointing out that the exchange of information and technical know-how will help everyone grow. They also observe that they only turned to foreign sourcing when domestic manufacturers refused to make lines to their specifications.

IMPORTING: TWO VIEWS

In fact, the issue of whether or not—or how much—to import is a subject of ongoing and often heated debate in the fashion industry as well as in Congress.

Some people believe that imports should be severely limited so as not to hurt American businesses making the same products. Advocates of limited trade, who consist largely of domestic manufacturers and labor unions, are called **isolationists.**

They argue that many foreign countries can produce goods more cheaply than can the United States and thus have an unfair advantage in selling their goods here. The U.S. textile/apparel industry, unlike that of most nations of the world, is heavily regulated by Congress and by restrictions imposed by labor unions. Thus, U.S. labor is expensive when compared with other countries.

Another group, called **free traders,** supports trade with no or few limitations. They believe that U.S. businesses should learn to compete with foreign businesses. If domestic manufacturers cannot make a product more cheaply, free traders argue, then perhaps they should let other countries make it and concentrate on producing the goods at which they excel.

GLOBAL GLIMPSES

QUOTAS

Do fashion trends beget quotas or do quotas beget fashion trends? That's a question government officials administering the U.S. Textile Quota Program and importers subject to the program's restraints have pondered many times over the last thirty or so years.

The newest product to enter the quota classification fray is tights. It happened because of the exercise craze of the 1980s (and perhaps because of the use of exercise clubs and spas as a meeting place for singles), which brought about a fashion focus on exercise wear.

The problem is that the fashion of wearing tights, often topped with long shirts or thigh-length sweaters began making a debut on city streets. Retailers, spotting a hot trend, began to stock these stretch, form-fitting bottoms in their sportswear departments while continuing to market the exercise wear in their hosiery departments. The hot new question of those imported "sportswear" products was—did they enter the United States as tights, under the easy to obtain and not-too-quickly-to-fill basket quotas, or were they entered as pants, an often expensive and highly competitive quota category?

People involved in the fashion-importing business could go on forever with stories of "quota engineering," that is, the designing of products to either avoid or fit into certain quota categories. For example, in the early 1980s, ski vests were the rage, but many believe the only reason the vest fashion was created was to get around the quota on man-made fiber coats. Without sleeves, the products could not be labeled coats and came in under the less used vest quota. More recently, battles have been waged over "big shirts" and men's swim trunks. The big shirts were imported as sleepwear, but because women were wearing them as streetwear, the U.S. Customs service asked that they be entered under shirt quotas. A court reviewed the evidence and the goods were ultimately classified as nightwear.

With respect to swim trunks, the U.S. Government contended that the imports were really intended to be worn as shorts, a much more competitive quota category. The courts ultimately set up a list of criteria for determining whether a product was shorts or swimwear, including whether it was lined and closed with the use of a drawstring.

The Committee for the Implementation of Textile Agreements (CITA), the interagency committee charged with administration of the U.S. quota program, must, many times, deliver the decision of King Solomon.

Based on "New Guidelines Puts Importers in Tight Spot," Brenda A. Jacobs, *Bobbin,* January, 1992, pp. 12–16.

SPECIAL-INTEREST ORGANIZATIONS

Within the fashion industry some groups have formed for the purpose of protecting the special interests of textile and apparel importers. The U.S. Apparel Industry Council (USAIC), a small group formed in 1985, concerns itself primarily with 9802 productions.

The American Association of Exporters and Importers (AAEI), a coalition of importers and exporters in all industrial sectors, works against all protective legislation. The Textile and Apparel Group within AAEI is especially active.

The U.S. Association of Importers of Textiles and Apparel (USA-ITA) broke off from AAEI in 1989 when some AAEI members felt that not enough at-

Special interest organizations, such as the American Association of Exporters and Importers, function within the fashion industry as protectors of the interests of textile and apparel importers and exporters. *Courtesy of the American Association of Exporters and Importers.*

tention was focused on the fashion industry. USA-ITA lobbies against protective legislation and also works on U.S. Customs problems.

U.S. REGULATION OF THE TEXTILE AND APPAREL INDUSTRY

Both isolationists and free traders have valid points, and Congress, which makes laws regarding imports, often walks a tightrope in its attempts to satisfy both groups.

Throughout the 1980s, several attempts were made to pass protectionist legislation limiting imports, specifically in some cases, of textile and apparel. Any bills that managed to pass through both houses were vetoed by Presidents Ronald Reagan and George Bush. Manufacturers and labor unions have vowed, however, not to give up the fight, and they say they will propose a compromise bill that will be acceptable to Congress and the President.

In 1988, Congress passed an omnibus, or general purpose, trade bill. It contained no specific provision for the fashion industry. The bill strengthened the process of trade regulation and gave the President new discretionary powers to act against nations that engaged in unfair trade practices. Critics of the bill say it lets the Administration decide unilaterally what is fair regarding imports. They also claim that the bill is heavily balanced in favor of exporting.

FUTURE REGULATORY TRENDS

As for future regulatory trends, some experts say that U.S. fashion producers will need special protection from high- and low-end imports to get back on their feet and compete efficiently in the world market.

Opponents of future legislation worry about the effects of protectionism. They warn that other nations could retaliate by refusing to permit U.S. exports.

PREFERENTIAL PROGRAMS

From time to time, the United States enacts preferential programs that exempt certain nations with whom it trades from tariffs and quotas. Such programs are intended to stimulate trade between the nations involved. The 9802 production is an example of a preferential program designed to bolster trade between the Caribbean nations and the United States.

The **Caribbean Basin Initiative (CBI),** the parent organization to 9802 production that is described in Chapter 2, is another example of a preferential program. It is designed to eliminate quota restrictions on manufactured and semimanufactured goods that come into the United States from certain Caribbean nations.

The **Generalized System of Preferences (GSP)** is an agreement to remove quotas and tariffs on certain imports from developing countries, particularly in industrial areas where they are weak. Each nation has the right to set limitations and restrictions on the amount of special treatment given. Domestic manufacturers and labor unions have fought lifting restrictions on textiles and apparel, and as a result, in the United States, these areas are excluded from special preferential treatment most of the time. This has had little effect, however, on the flow of textile and apparel imports from developing nations into the United States.

THE VALUE OF FASHION IMPORTS IN THE FUTURE

Most industry experts believe the kinds of growth and new forms of competition generated by importing will ultimately prove to be valuable to both the manufacturing and retailing segments of the fashion industry. U.S. fashion manufacturers will be forced by competition from imports to adapt in new ways by doing more work to specification, by finding innovative ways to shorten lead times, and by becoming more flexible and efficient in general. Retailers who have already discovered innovative ways to use imports to bolster their profits will continue to do so.

The impact of global importing, whether it is done by retailers or manufacturers, also benefits the global market. More international business means more markets for everyone—and that always helps business both at home and in the increasingly interlinked global market.

ENDNOTES

1. U.S. Industrial Outlook
2. "Import Penetration of the Apparel Industry," Fiber, Fabric, and Apparel Coalition, September, 1989, unpaged flyer.

3. "Industry Surveys, Textile, Apparel and Home Furnishing," Standard and Poors, 1990, p. 2.

VOCABULARY

commissionaire

_____

_____

_____

foreign buying office

_____

_____

_____

free trader

_____

_____

_____

generalized system of
preferences (GSP)

_____

_____

_____

global retailing

_____

_____

_____

global sourcing

_____

_____

_____

import penetration

_____

_____

_____

independent agents

_____

_____

_____

isolationist

_____

_____

_____

lead time

_____

_____

_____

9802 production

_____

_____

_____

offshore production

_____

_____

_____

private label

_____

_____

_____

specification buying

_____

_____

_____

value-added

_____

_____

_____

GLOBAL REVIEW

1. Name three advantages of importing for a fashion producer.

_____

_____

_____

_____

2. Name three disadvantages of importing for a fashion producer.

_____

_____

_____

_____

_____

3. Why do you think that import penetration is most widespread in low- and high-end fashion merchandise?

_____

_____

_____

_____

_____

4. What are six major options available to retailers who want to import?

_____

_____

_____

_____

5. Stores that are not large enough to maintain their own foreign buying office rely on "commissionaires." How do these people or offices differ from a store-owned buying office?

_____

_____

_____

_____

6. Name three foreign import fairs that are presented in the United States and explain their importance to the fashion industry here.

_____

_____

_____

_____

7. What is specification buying? How does it differ from other buying methods?

_____

_____

_____

_____

8. 9802 is an option for manufacturers that permits certain regulations to be used for easier entry into the United States. What is the major reason manufacturers take advantage of 9802?

_____

_____

_____

_____

9. What is the major difference between "isolationists" and "free traders"?

_____

_____

_____

_____

_____

10. Explain what a preferential program is and give an example other than the 9802 operation.

_____

_____

_____

_____

GLOBAL DIGEST

1. What will be the new forms of competition generated by importing? How do you think it can prove to be valuable to both the retailing and manufacturing sectors of the fashion industry?

_____

_____

_____

_____

_____

_____

_____

2. There are many special interest organizations within the fashion industry that are organized to protect the special interests of textile, apparel, and retail groups. Explain and discuss the major differences that these special interest groups lobby the government about and how they affect the ultimate global consumer.

_____

_____

_____

_____

_____

_____

_____

3. What will be the impact of global marketing on both retailers and fashion product manufacturers? Discuss the effect global marketing will have on the fashion industry in the coming decade.

_____

_____

_____

_____

_____

_____

_____

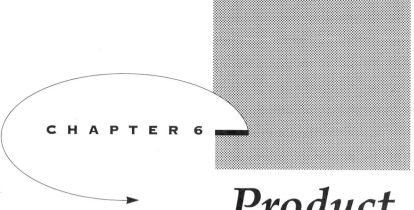

CHAPTER 6

Product Development for International Trade

George S. Parker, founder of Parker Pens, loved to tell people: "Our pens write in any language." He was lucky to be right. His product *was* one of the rare ones that could be used—with no changes—anywhere in the world. Few products are like that. Fashion, which thrives on what is new and trendy, is certainly not one of the world's timeless products. No one expects it to be, and no one would like it if it were.

Indeed, fashion would lose much of its allure if it were not constantly new and exciting. But fashion's trendy nature also poses special problems for importers and exporters, who must take products that are current and popular and quickly translate them into something they can sell around the world to many different kinds of people in many different places.

The development of products that can be traded in the global market is one of the most stimulating and exhilarating aspects of international business. It is also one of the riskiest and is best not undertaken without considerable forethought and planning.

Global product development, the subject of this chapter, is the process of screening and judging products to make sure they suit the international market for which they are intended, meet the legal requirements of the importing country or countries, and can be developed and delivered in a timely fashion. Al-

though this is a lengthy definition, it boils down to one question, Will this product be profitable in a foreign market? If it will not be, it may be better not to take it into a global market or it may need a variety of changes before it can successfully compete in this market.

There are reasons not to take a product into an international market at all. If a product does not suit the market, it will not sell. If it does not meet the legal requirements, it probably cannot be imported. If it cannot be developed with existing or easily adapted resources, it may be too costly to produce. In all these situations, the importer and exporter risk being robbed of their profits.

The process of global product development enables importers and exporters to figure out, with some certainty, whether they can sell a product internationally and what they can expect from a product in the global market.

THE ORIGINS OF PRODUCT DEVELOPMENT

A few years ago, businesses typically designed a product and then set about convincing people they needed it. Today, market research and analysis is a much more sophisticated process. Companies have reversed the process: They have learned to look for a need and then try to fill it. Most of the products developed in this manner are technological—appliances, improvements on cars, and gadgetry.

The fashion industry awakened to the possibilities of doing its own product development only when importing took off in the late 1970s. Big department stores like Bloomingdale's and Macy's and innovative specialty stores, such as Ann Taylor, The Gap, and The Limited, led the way in developing their own product lines. Staff specialists, called **product developers,** create products, test them on store buyers, and eventually follow through on all aspects of their production.

Attracted by cheap foreign labor and production costs, these fashion retailers produce most of their new products offshore. This has led other importers and exporters, even those who work independently, to think about developing their own products so they can take advantage of the new, exciting global market.

Today, fashion importers tend to fall into one of two categories: traditionalists and innovators. Traditionalists operate the way importers have for years.

Fashion retailers such as Anne Klein have become successful by developing and marketing their own product lines. *Courtesy of Anne Klein; collection by Louis Dell'olio.*

They buy fashion products designed and produced by foreign manufacturers and bring them into the United States to sell.

Innovators, however, often act as the product developer, developing a new product idea, finding an overseas manufacturer who makes it to their specifications, and following the product through all stages of distribution and sales promotion.

Both the stores and the independent importer–product developer create individual products as well as complete product lines, although the latter tend to be more the domain of the stores, with their large staffs and foreign and domestic support services.

MARKET RESEARCH AND ANALYSIS

Market research and analysis is the important first step in developing a product for the international market. It is basically a process of testing a product prior to production to see whether or not marketing it is feasible and then writing a strategy plan for how the product will be produced and merchandised.

William Leiva and James Obermayer, authors of "Commonsense Product Development," emphasized the importance of a systematic approach to product development when they wrote: "A product that reaches the market and fails usually results from a company's failure to understand (or to heed) market dynamics. Don't assume people will love your idea just because you do, and don't pull assumptions out of thin air. Get out there and find out what's going on before diving in."[1]

Market research and analysis is used to figure out how much it will cost to make a product, what price it can be sold for, how much competition to expect, and what modifications will be required to sell it, among other factors. With market research and analysis, importers and exporters can uncover all these facts prior to sending their products into the global marketplace—and the products can be appropriately revised for the new market if necessary.

Market research and analysis is a process of discovery. Does a line of cotton sweaters have to be produced in bright colors rather than pastels to sell in Latin America? Must the labels on fur coats be changed to show country of origin or some other product information required by law? Will different sales techniques be required to sell prepackaged sheet sets in France?

Four steps are involved in creating a solid, workable market strategy for a fashion product. These are:

WHO NEEDS AMERICAN PRODUCTS? THE FAMED DEPAATOS IN JAPAN

Depaato (rhymes with "You say tomahto") are modeled on Western department stores, but they have become cultural institutions as much as retailers in Japan. They are so influential that the success of any new product is almost 60 percent guaranteed, provided the product fits in with the depaato image. That image is cosmopolitan. The department stores helped create and satisfy Japan's demand for Western styles.

The first depaato, Matsuzakaya, started as a kimono couturier in 1611, followed by Mitsukoshi and Takashimaya in the mid-1800s. Department stores are irresistible markets for American products, and the United States has long wanted to weaken the Large-Scale Retail Store Law, the descendent of a Depression-era law restricting the growth of department stores to protect mom-and-pop stores. In 1949, the American Occupation administration and the Japanese Cabinet decided that big retailers could help stop inflation and stabilize the economy.

Japanese department store buyers rarely talk business with newcomers. As defenders of the depaato creed—"The customer is God, the depaato his humble servant"—they are duty-bound to make their stores the safest places to shop, where quality and flawless service are taken for granted.

Selling in department stores instead of mom-and-pop stores made Estee Lauder's Clinique line a household word in Japan. The hottest American name at Isetan, a department store in Tokyo's Shinjuku district, is Donna Karan, and Takasimaya has long nurtured a relationship with Geoffrey Beene, who, in 1978, became one of the first American designers to sell under his own name in Japan.

Spend a day in the Ginza district or Tokyo's Fifth Avenue and you will find something special going on. Recent offerings were a European wine-and-cheese fair at Matsuzakaya and a Jasper Johns exhibit at Isetan. At Seibu, Norma Kamali, Converse sneakers, and Guess jeans are available for lovers of the American casual look, but the prices are far from casual. The same pair of straight-leg Guess jeans that retails for $56 in the United States costs $110 at Seibu.

The department stores have become cradle-to-grave providers of infant clothes, toys, wedding kimonos, honeymoon trips, furniture, life insurance, and funeral kimonos. No matter what happens to the economy in Japan, if the customer is God, the depaato will always be heaven.

Based on Kaori Shoji, "The Glitz and Glamour of the Depaato," *Business Tokyo*, July, 1990, pp. 32–36.

1. Preparation of a customer profile.
2. Preparation of a competitor profile.
3. Preparation of a market strategy report.
4. Creation of a merchandise plan.

PREPARING A CUSTOMER PROFILE

The purpose of a customer profile is to identify a **target market.** This is a group of potential customers, identified according to their needs and buying habits, that a business is attempting to turn into regular customers. Prospective importers must consider how potential customers will perceive and use the product.

By identifying specific target markets, it is possible to write a **customer profile** of each one. A customer profile for a fashion product is a written description that is derived from studying the variables of demographic studies that address such salient sales facts as the customer's gender, age, education, family size, occupation, income, and geographic location.

Apart from these physical demographics, a customer profile also addresses the psychographics of potential customers. These studies develop fuller, more personal traits of potential customers and their lifestyles.[2] A fashion product may—and often does—appeal to such psychological needs as a customer's sense of self-esteem, convenience, safety, and security. Importers and exporters, like domestic fashion producers, need to identify these needs to know how to sell their product.

Customers' motives drive them to satisfy their needs. A target group may have several motives for making any individual purchase. Customers in one target group, for example, might be motivated to buy

Comparison Shopping Service
TO FIND & ASSESS YOUR MARKETS

Will your product sell in Germany? Kenya? Brazil? Find out with our Comparison Shopping Service.

Our Comparison Shopping Service (CSS) offers you a quick, accurate assessment of how your product will sell in a given market. For a very reasonable fee, you get a concise report answering these critical questions:

- ❑ **Does your product have sales potential in the market?**
- ❑ **Who is supplying a comparable product locally?**
- ❑ **What is the usual sales channel for getting this product into the market?**
- ❑ **What is the going price for a comparable product?**
- ❑ **Are purchasers of such products primarily influenced by price, or by other competitive factors, such as credit, quality, delivery, service, promotion, or brand?**
- ❑ **What is the best way to get sales exposure in the market?**
- ❑ **Are there any impediments to selling the product, such as quotas, duties, or local regulations?**
- ❑ **Who might be interested and qualified to represent or purchase your product in this market?**
- ❑ **Who might be an interested, qualified licensing or joint venture partner for your company?**

To provide you with answers, one of our research specialists in your target country interviews importers, distributors, retailers, wholesalers, end-users, and local producers of comparable products and inspects similar products on the market. Your customized report usually is completed and in your hands within 45 days.

Especially valuable for small and first-time exporters with few foreign contacts and limited overseas sales expertise, CSS provides you with on-the-spot, current data you need to make marketing decisions — without the large travel, investigative, and other expenses associated with overseas product research.

Contact your nearest U.S. Department of Commerce district office to find out whether a survey of your product's marketability can be conducted in the country you've targeted for export sales. Please note that products manufactured outside the United States must be marketed using the name of the U.S. firm, and the content must represent 51 percent of the value of the finished goods.

Our Comparison Shopping Service puts your product on target!

U. S. DEPARTMENT OF COMMERCE ★ INTERNATIONAL TRADE ADMINISTRATION ★ U.S. AND FOREIGN COMMERCIAL SERVICE   7/89

The International Trade Administration helps American export businesses locate and assess their overseas sales potential through its Comparison Shopping Service. *Courtesy of the U.S. Dept. of Commerce.*

---

a fur coat by a need to impress others or themselves or a desire to appeal to the opposite sex (self-esteem), whereas those in another target group might be motivated by a desire to keep warm (convenience).

Customers' perceptions about a product also affect their buying patterns. **Perceptions** are a customer's immediate intuitive feelings about a purchase. Depending on the product, the customer uses hear-ing, touch, taste, smell, and sight to form an immediate reaction to the product. The reaction will be based on the product's size, color, shape, and design.

Attitudes are the customer's basic opinions and emotions about the product—how much status the producer's name carries, how much service can be expected when buying the product, whether the product is worthy of the consumer or not. Attitudes are difficult to change or influence, but they must be identified as much to rule out a target group as to cater to one.

CUSTOMERS' LIFE STAGE   Another psychographic involves the customers' **life stage.**[3] A life stage is a psychological profile based on the customer's psychological age, which may or may not match the chronological age. These days, for example, a woman may spend fifteen or twenty years building a career and may undertake motherhood only in her mid-thirties. While one group of women is career-building, another group is following a more traditional lifestyle. Thus, two women of the same chronological age can be at very different life stages. A person's life stage is very significant in shaping his or her buying patterns.

Every kind of fashion need—from a customer's wardrobe to home furnishings to the use of cosmetics—varies with the life stage. A traditional at-home mother will spend more time and money on her home and may require a wardrobe of casual, sturdy clothing. She will have few dressy outfits, especially when compared with a working mother. She will have more time for her home—specifically, to shop for home furnishings. The photos below show customer profiles for men and women at three different stages of their lives.

To further complicate international marketing, life stages vary from country to country. U.S. mothers

As individuals move through their life stages, their fashion needs change as well as their psychological needs. *Courtesy of Mary M. Langenfeld, photographer.*

were still at home when European mothers had entered the work force.

GATHERING INFORMATION ON POTENTIAL CUSTOMERS

The kinds of information required to write a customer profile are available from several sources. Importers and exporters rely on foreign agents and suppliers, foreign buying offices, sales staffs, and outside consultants to supply them with information about prospective customers.

Information can also be gathered from the trade press and journalists, industry analysts, competition, distributors, and reports from foreign fashion shows. Trade shows are another excellent source of informa-

tion, and prospective importers and exporters will also gather information on trade missions and other visitors to countries where they hope to conduct business.

PREPARING A COMPETITOR'S PROFILE

A market strategy cannot be developed without a solid working knowledge of one's competitors, which is compiled in a report called a **competitor's profile.** To compete well, importers and exporters need to know each competition's market share, profitability, industry position, and likely future activities. Armed with this information, you can

GLOBAL *GO-GETTERS*

MARTIN TRUST: IN MARTIN WE TRUST

Courtesy of Mast Industries, Inc.

In 1970, Martin Trust, founder of Mast Industries, Inc., managed its growth into a major internationally based manufacturer of women's apparel, with headquarters in Andover, Massachusetts, and offices in Hong Kong, Italy, Korea, Taiwan, and New York City.

With his mechanical engineering degree from Cooper Union in New York City and his master's degree in industrial management from the Sloan School at Massachusetts Institute of Technology, Martin Trust has the educational background as well as the entrepreneurial spirit to be a premier leader in an industry full of leaders.

In addition to leading Mast's sourcing into an international network of approximately 300 factories, Trust is the moving force behind the company's joint venture activities in Israel, Sri Lanka, Singapore, and Costa Rica.

In 1978, Mast was acquired by The Limited, Inc. and Trust became a member of the Board of Directors of The Limited, Inc. Mast keeps the Limited buying and management teams involved from sewing machines on up. Mast helps Limited marketing people track and predict trends, locates countries and manufacturers, and will even set up a promising entrepreneur into business or buy machinery for a small, undercapitalized manufacturer.

Mast has full-time quota specialists that try to stay ahead of the international protectionist game by buying up production "options." Mast is an international manufacturing organization that gives Limited a critical edge over the competition in supply, pricing, and timing. A significant percentage of Mast's output goes to outsiders in the industry; some are Limited's competitors. This helps keep Mast up-to-date on the rest of the industry.

Martin Trust seems almost fixated on giving the customers what they want *when* they want it. The reason for his fixation on speed relates directly to changes going on in the world and the speed with which these changes are disseminated by technology and communication. How fast is fast? The definition of fast is continually changing. In 1970, when Mast was formed, the response time was six to nine months. In 1983, sixteen weeks; 1989, thirty to fifty days and the present target for the 1990s is 500 hours! Whether the production is produced in Israel, Taiwan, Latin America, or Italy, Martin Trust truly believes in a global environment where everything is accomplished to benefit the customer.

Based on "MAST: The Limited's Fast Gun," *Apparel Industry Magazine*, March, 1990 pp. 40–46; Biography of Martin Trust 1992 FIT-Speech introduction for Center for Global Enterprise, Fashion Institute of Technology, March 25, 1992.

determine whether you will be able to compete effectively—or perhaps even enjoy competitive superiority.

A competitor's profile should describe specific competitors, the size of each one's market, how their product is similar or dissimilar to yours, their resources, and their sales and marketing capabilities. It should project their customer loyalty.

Competitors' products should be examined in terms of quality, design, price, use, service, advertising, and customer support—all with an eye for seeing where and how you can do better.

Information on competitors can be obtained from the trade press, trade shows, suppliers, and the competitors themselves, that is, from speeches and seminars they may sponsor and from their sales and advertising materials.

Only by writing a comprehensive competitor's profile can a prospective importer or exporter identify competitors' strengths and weaknesses—and figure out how to avoid the latter.[4]

PREPARING A MARKET STRATEGY REPORT

Once the customer and competitor profiles have been prepared, it is time to think about a market strategy. A **market strategy report** uses all the information that has been gathered to outline the product's prospects for success. It summarizes the size, structure, and dynamics of the overall market, as well as your target markets. Most important, it describes the characteristics that distinguish this product from the competition—from the customers' point of view.

It weighs, for example, whether price will be the primary selling point, or perhaps quality, or maybe style. It considers how many market segments will be targeted. It evaluates potential outlets, that is, whether the product will be sold through discount outlets, department stores, or specialty stores.

Ultimately, in its most comprehensive sense, a market strategy is designed to ask and answer the question, why should a customer buy from you and not someone else?

PORTFOLIO FIT If you are introducing a new product into an established product line, a market strategy report will also consider **portfolio fit.** Portfolio fit describes how well any new product will work within an established product line. A coat manufacturer, for example, would do better to add a jacket, which extends its present line, rather than a hat, which is not a natural extension and also requires entirely different production methods.

ASSESSING RESOURCES As a final important step, the marketing strategy report should assess the resources that can and must be used to sell the product internationally. These involve financial and human resources.

Financial resources involve what equipment, material, and technology will be used, versus what will have to be purchased to create the product for a specific foreign market.

Human resources involve the talent in design, production, marketing, and management that will be required to make the product. It is up to the importers and exporters to decide whether and how these resources are best used in taking a product into a new, international market. The bottom line is that importers and exporters must ask themselves whether their companies have the resources to produce and sell the proposed products successfully.

CREATING A MERCHANDISE PLAN

Once a market strategy has been devised for a product, the next step is to set production in motion. This is accomplished through the use of a **merchandise plan.** While the market strategy report sets forth what must be done to sell the product successfully, the merchandise plan sets about showing how—or whether—these goals can be achieved. This action-oriented plan describes what must be done to create an acceptable finished product delivered to its ultimate destination.

The process begins when the importer or exporter meets with the manufacturers to discuss whether the garment or other fashion product can be made according to the specifications.

To test the product, one or more **samples,** or prototypes, will be made up. Changes ordered as a result of examining and testing the samples are noted in the merchandise plan.

Once a sample has been modified to specification—or accepted as is, a relatively rare occurrence in the world of fashion—**models** will be made. These are the primary sales tools. Models are shown to fashion buyers, who add their input (which, in turn, leads to still more changes) and also place orders for the garment based on the changes they have indicated. By this time, the importer knows the producers' capabilities well enough to know that they will be able to handle the additional changes, which are typically minor.

Once orders are taken, the importer rewrites the merchandise plan to include the latest round of specifications and takes them to the producer, who begins production. A production schedule is established.

Importers and exporters often oversee all or several stages of production; at the same time, they attend to other details—shipping and transportation, preparing labels, sales training, checking inventory.

This is the basic process of researching and analyzing a product for the international trade arena. Much more, however, goes into creating the market strategy.

FACTORS AFFECTING INTERNATIONAL MARKET STRATEGY

Rare is the product that is not changed or adjusted in some way so that it can be sold in international markets. Adjustments may have to be made for every single foreign market—and occasionally, for every target market within the foreign market.

The changes that are made to adapt a product to the foreign market are called **modifications.** For any one market, modifications may involve a product's basic design, its quality, its cost, and ultimately, its price.

REASONS FOR PRODUCT MODIFICATION

A variety of reasons—government or trade association regulations, culture, economic development, and climate and geography—inspire importers and exporters to modify their products.

GOVERNMENT REGULATION   Governments and, as often these days, free trade regions like the EEC and ASEAN establish laws regarding what may and may not be imported into their territories, as well as the circumstances under which products can be imported. A quota, you will recall, limits the quantity and sometimes the quality of a garment for a specified time period.

Importers and exporters have no choice but to comply with these laws if they want to bring products into the country or trade region. The United States, for example, requires that fabrics be labeled with content and care instructions. Other nations and free trade regions have their own regulations.

Sometimes the importer and exporter have some choices about compliance. Consider, for example, the import of a mohair sweater with gold buttons. The materials, especially the buttons, garner the product a luxury-tax tariff. But if the importer and exporter choose to use plastic instead of gold buttons, they can bring the garment in—at considerable savings—

The difference between an outfit with gilt buttons, such as the one pictured here, and one with gold buttons can be considerable when the luxury taxes placed on high-end goods is factored in. *Courtesy of the Hong Kong Trade Development Council.*

without paying the luxury tax. Importers and exporters are always on the lookout for modifications that reduce the cost of their product.

CULTURE   The most important reason to modify a product for international trade is the culture of the country or region into which it is being imported. A low-cut jersey top will not appeal to Arab women, for example, unless it is redesigned to suit their standards for modesty. Similarly, the Japanese do not consider purple an appropriate color for clothing, and many other cultures have other color taboos.

Cultural taboos are extremely difficult to buck, but they do change with time. The trend is increasingly toward one-world fashion, with a decidedly Western emphasis—but this is still many years away. Until then, importers and exporters must modify their garments based on cultural considerations.

ECONOMIC DEVELOPMENT   You cannot sell French haute couture to a developing nation that has no money to buy it and no place to wear it. Because most fashion is a luxury item—people don't need it; they want it—most of the world's trade in fashion is

GLOBETROTTING Gaffes

GREETINGS!

There are many different ways by which people greet one another. In the United States, it is customary to give a firm handshake. Greetings in other countries may vary between the firm handshake in French Canada to the light, quick handshake in France and Belgium. In some Arab nations, people of the same sex sometimes greet each other with embraces. In Finland, both hands are often used in shaking hands. Men do not shake hands with women in India as a mark of respect to their privacy.

Although the handshake is nearly a universal greeting despite variations in its use, some cultures use different greetings. Oriental cultures, among many others, commonly use the bow, but there are rigid rules as to who bows to whom, when, and how low. In Taiwan a slight bow is appropriate, whereas kneeling down before the elderly and social superiors is the norm in Zambia.

The problem of culturally appropriate nonverbal communication is compounded in that many countries have variations within their borders. For instance, differences exist between the French Canadians and other Canadians, Israeli Jews and Israeli Arabs, Indian Muslims and Indian Hindus, Belgium's north and south, American-style openness and British reserve in New Zealand.

As you can see, the simple act of greeting a business associate can be frought with danger. Remember, your greeting is the first impression you make on people. Make sure it's not "Hey yo, babe!"

Based on Franklin B. Krohn and Zafar U. Ahmed, "Communication Encounters," *Hospitality & Tourism Educator*, November, 1991, Vol. 4, No. 1, p. 40–43.

done in First and Second World countries. Third World countries tend to make their own clothing and household products, often on a small, nonindustrial scale.

CLIMATE AND GEOGRAPHY You cannot sell raincoats in the Sahara or sandals in northern climes or heavy coats in southern climes. Sometimes, a fine-tuned modification is enough, though, to turn a product suited to one climate into a product equally well suited for another. One importer relined a winter coat with a heavier lining and found he could sell it in Scandinavia as well as the East Coast of the United States. Another importer made a raincoat of a lighter weight fabric and found a new market in South America, where the style and color were popular.

Importers and exporters should constantly be on the lookout for changes that can result in an expanded market or major savings in production costs.

PRODUCT DESIGN

The need to modify a product to suit its market means that virtually everything about it—the style, the color, the fabric, and method of production—may have to be rethought once the product is a candidate for the import/export market.

STYLE Style can build on previous styles or be fashion forward by creating new styles. Product development by retailers typically involves the creation of new styles, but product development for the international market often breaks this rule and builds on previously successful styles.

Two kinds of style changes can be made in a garment. The first involves its outside line, or **silhouette**; the second, its inside line, or the **details** of the garment. Changes can occur alone or in both simultaneously.

Shopping the target foreign market is an excellent way to discover the style changes that will be necessary to bring a product into a foreign market. Importers and exporters should not only survey stores and attend fashion shows in a foreign market, but should also take time to watch potential customers as they go about their daily activities—attending theater, eating in restaurants, sitting in parks and sidewalk cafes—to see what does and does not work for them.

In seeking ideas for modification, study the details. You may be developing a "new" garment, but in reality, fashion creators have increasingly come to accept that there is little that is truly new in the world of fashion today. Every conceivable silhouette, line, and color has been mined at one time or another. Designer Georgio Armani recently observed of this phenomenon: "In fashion, everything has been done. The only challenge now is new associations of the same elements—ties, stretch pants, the jackets."[5]

The implications of this for importers and exporters are enormous. A more studied, sophisticated eye is needed to figure out which products will be successful imports or exports. Many kinds of subtle changes may be what is necessary to make a garment successful in many markets.

COLOR   Color trends are often trickier than style changes in foreign markets. Persons in warm climates around the world favor bright colors, while Northerners—and city dwellers—wear dark colors, but apart from this, many cultures have color taboos. Black is the color of mourning in many parts of the world, but in some parts, notably the tropics, it is white. Some colors are taboo in some cultures. On top of this, color is trendy, and what is fashionable one year may look outdated the next.

In the United States, product developers rely on forecasting services and color houses to keep them informed, but importers and exporters must look to comparable foreign resources to determine color trends. As is the case with style, the best way to research color trends is through firsthand observation—at fashion shows, trade shows, and of course, on the street.

FABRIC   The next step is to select the fabric. In foreign markets, as at home, you buy from either a mill or a converter. Many considerations go into the decision to choose one fabric over another: its color and brand, its price, its availability, import quotas, ability to control quality or modify the fabric for a specific market or a small run, and delivery times.

METHOD OF PRODUCTION   Depending on the degree of individuality required, it possible to purchase the components of a fashion product "ready-made" rather than pulling them together individually. Fabric can be purchased from a mill, for example, rather than working with the mill to create a fabric. "Ready-made" production is less costly. It is also less exclusive, and products are priced accordingly.

COST, QUALITY, AND PRICE

Cost and quality are inextricably interwoven and largely responsible for determining price. Pricing is perhaps the most difficult concept to test at home and doubly so in a foreign market.[6]

But price never occurs in a vacuum. You have a target market, so even before beginning production, you have some idea of what they will pay—a target

Fashion showcases offer product developers the best way to research trends in color and style. *Courtesy of the Hong Kong Trade Development Council.*

price, in other words. The next step is to determine the cost of making the product.

No one has unlimited funds to spend, and even if the goal is to produce a unique and expensive dress, for example, the importer and exporter still want to earn a profit. That can be harder to do with an expensive, custom-made garment than a ready-made.

Cost is generally tied to several elements of production. It depends on whether a garment is measured by each individual item or, as is more common in the fashion industry, per **assortment.**

ASSORTMENTS Assortments describe the number of styles, number of fabrics per style, number of colors per fabric, number of sizes, and number of units that will be shipped.

In the United States, many fashion products are sold by the dozen. Some countries and some products ship individually, however, and some countries will have other standardized assortments—half dozen, or gross, for example. Importers and exporters must learn what assortments are expected by the target market and base their costs on this number.

CUT, MAKE, AND TRIM (CMT) Cost is also determined by cut, make, and trim. **Cut** is the cost of the use of the materials used to make a garment. It costs more to waste, and less to use every inch of fabric and lining. If adding several tucks to a blouse would cause the producer to cut into another yard of fabric, for example, then costs can be reduced by foregoing the extra tucks or reducing their number.

The **make** is the cost of labor and production. Not surprisingly, quality influences make dramatically. A producer can use skimpy seams or generous seams, can sew seams once or twice. Costs escalate with detail. The greater the number of darts, collars, smocking, pleating and other tailoring effects, the higher the cost.

Trim—the number, size, and expense of buttons, zippers, appliques, and other "extras"—all add to the cost of the garment. These extras, if not controlled, can eat up profits, especially because these "extras" can be called ornamentation and thus become subject to higher custom duties.

LOCATION Because products destined for the international market can also be produced in foreign

TECH TALK
LABELS

Apparel manufacturers who want their lines to present a polished, consistent image globally are turning to label manufacturers for help.

This consistency and uniformity applies to an entire product identification package, including labels, tags, stickers, and specialty trim products. There is an increased interest in new uses for labels, new concepts, and new colors.

To meet these demands, label makers are concentrating on new technology. In addition to its U.S. facility, a U.S. label maker has a "technology advanced" factory in Hong Kong that sells to the Far Eastern market. Together, the two facilities can offer consistency to a manufacturer who has label needs in both the United States and the Far East.

The ongoing importance of labels has prompted newer technology and faster delivery. For example, computer-aided design/computer-aided manufacturing (CAD/CAM) is used for producing exciting new woven labels. New adhesive is now nonsticky and labels can be carrier mounted for problem-for processing through a computer printer. Also, label manufacturers are experimenting with dimensional stability in labels to complement automatic sewing and feeding equipment. The market for labels is being driven by the same factors that drive apparel producers—fashion, service, and technology.

Based on Susan S. Block, "Labels: A Coordinated Appeal," *Bobbin*, December, 1991, p. 66.

GLOBAL *Goodies*
HONG KONG

When the British occupied sparsely populated Hong Kong island more than 150 years ago, it was an inconspicuous dot off the south coast of Imperial China. During the last half of the nineteenth century, it expanded as a British colony by treaty (Kowloon Peninsula and additional islands) and by lease (the so-called New Territories, which spread inland from Kowloon). The city is now one of the world's most important financial centers.

Population today is about 6 million, of which more than 98 percent is Chinese. Of this number, 2.2 million live in the largely agricultural New Territories. The whole of Hong Kong is a vibrant mix of East and West, old and new.

Let's assume that you have finished your business and still have time to spare. Now you're ready to discover Hong Kong, a Hong Kong you were aware of only as a shopping mecca . . . but it is also a most impressive sightseeing city . . . one of the best in the world.

The magnificent harbor is Hong Kong's crowning glory. Take the celebrated STAR ferry, a seven-minute ride between Hong Kong Island and the mainland, one of the world's best sight-seeing bargains. It costs about 12 cents U.S. (lower deck) and 15 cents U.S. (upper deck) and enjoy the harbor view.

For another impressive view, stroll the promenade along Kowloon's Tsim Sha Tsui waterfront. And do not fail to see the breathtaking view from The Peak. It is possible to reach the peak by taxi, but more fun to ascend via the wonderful funicular, the Peak Tram—a steep, eight-minute ride that's a sight-seeing marvel in itself.

Across the bay from Hong Kong is the Kowloon Peninsula, which incorporates the Kowloon section of Hong Kong and the New Territories. Here you will find the famous Jade Market and the wonderful narrow, winding commercial lanes of Kowloon between Nathan Road and Chatham Road.

Another day-long sightseeing option is a visit to the New Territories, which sprawls from metropolitan Hong Kong to the borders of the People's Republic of China. You can reach this area by tour bus, private car and driver, or by the Kowloon-Canton Railway, which you can board in downtown Kowloon.

At the reconstructed Sung Dynasty Village, you will get a glimpse of life in an ancient Chinese village. A typical wedding procession and ceremony are presented at published times. Visit a woodcarver's stall, an herb shop, a calligraphy pavillion, and a small, but elaborate shrine, where you can tap the huge bell seven times for good luck.

There are many more delights that can be explored: cuisine, sports, the Outer Islands, arts, and antiquities. Learning more about the island and customs can help you become a more astute businessperson, and better equipped to negotiate your international buying and marketing plans.

Based on "Rediscover Hong Kong," a Supplement to *Travel & Leisure*, April, 1992.

markets, location is an important factor in cost. Location affects the cost of production, the logistics of moving garment from manufacturing site to shipping site, quotas and other legal requirements, the ability to manufacture, and perhaps most important to fashion producers, the ability to deliver in a timely manner. The cost to produce is less in less developed countries, but often, so is the quality and capacity to deliver a sophisticated garment.

Every product has an intrinsic value, and it will not sell if the price does not reflect this value. Furthermore, an imported fashion product must reflect the intrinsic value in the nation of import, perhaps even in specific target markets, and not just in the importer's or exporter's own domestic market.

IMPORTANCE OF OBJECTIVITY

The most important marketing tool prospective importers and exporters can bring to the research and analysis of a new product is objectivity. You must constantly ask yourself, Does this product have a market or do I just think it should? Is the need for this product currently being met by someone else or do I just not like the competition? Ultimately, of course, market research and analysis is designed to ask, and answer, the all-important question: Why would anyone buy this product?[7]

Smart importers and exporters also know that market research and analysis are only the beginning.

Once a market strategy has been developed, it must be maintained. Minor modifications may be needed to sell a fashion product in the county or province adjacent to one's initial target market, to keep a product alive in its target market, or simply to get the most out of a product. Importers and exporters, who choose the added challenge of working in foreign markets, must accept that more will be required of them to achieve their goals. Of course, the rewards can be far greater, too, as one discovers the thrill of successfully conducting business in other people's worlds.

ENDNOTES

1. William Leiva and James Obermayer, "Commonsense Product Development," *Business Marketing*, August, 1989, pp. 44–48.
2. "Product Positioning: A Crucial Marketing Strategy," no author, *Small Business Reporter*, April, 1988, pp. 18–21.
3. Andrea Dunham, "New Product Marketing in an Era of Transition," *Journal of Consumer Marketing*, Vol. 1, No. 4, 1984, pp. 5–16.
4. *Small Business Reporter*, op. cit., p. 20.
5. Tad Friend, "The Armani Edge," *Vogue*, March, 1983, pp. 316–323.
6. Tom Gorman, "What Will Our Customers Think of This Product Idea," *Business Marketing*, September, 1987, p. 80.
7. Ibid., p. 80.

VOCABULARY

assortments _____
_____
_____

competitor's profile _____
_____
_____

customer profile _____
_____

cut _____
_____
_____

details _____
_____
_____

global product development _____
_____

life stage

_____

_____

_____

make

_____

_____

_____

market strategy report

_____

_____

_____

merchandise plan

_____

_____

_____

models

_____

_____

_____

modifications

_____

_____

_____

portfolio fit

_____

_____

_____

product developers

_____

_____

_____

psychographics

_____

_____

_____

samples

_____

_____

_____

silhouette

_____

_____

_____

target market

_____

_____

_____

trim

_____

_____

_____

GLOBAL REVIEW

1. What was the origin of product development?

_____

_____

_____

_____

2. Describe how innovators often act as product developers.

_____

_____

_____

_____

3. Market research and analysis is used widely in product development. What are some of the steps that must be taken before a product is considered for development?

_____

_____

_____

_____

4. How are customer profiles used in a successful market strategy?

_____

_____

_____

_____

5. Explain how a person's life stage becomes a significant factor in shaping their buying patterns.

_____

_____

_____

_____

6. To compete successfully, an international trader must have knowledge about the competition. How do you compile a competitor's profile?

_____

_____

_____

_____

7. Why is it important to consider a portfolio fit?

_____

_____

_____

_____

8. What does a merchandise plan accomplish in the overall market strategy for product development?

_____

_____

_____

_____

9. There are many reasons for product modification. List six and explain how they affect the success of the final product.

_____

_____

_____

_____

10. Explain cut, make, and trim.

_____

_____

_____

_____

GLOBAL DIGEST
1. Discuss the importance of global product development. How does it help an importer or exporter successfully compete? Why is it particularly essential in fashion global marketing?

_____

_____

_____

_____

_____

_____

_____

2. What are the four steps in creating a market strategy for a fashion product? Discuss how each step is prepared and how they fit together to form the best marketing strategy.

_____

_____

_____

_____

_____

_____

_____

_____

3. The text says, "the most important marketing tool prospective importers and exporters can bring to the research and analysis of a new product is objectivity." Explain objectivity and give examples of how objectivity could be used in product development for international trade.

_____

_____

_____

_____

_____

_____

_____

_____

UNIT 2 READING
MAKING SENSE OUT OF THE NEW EUROPE
By Paul B. Finney

On the eve of its grand debut, the "United States of Europe" looks more like an unwieldy cluster of nations than anything resembling the federal union the Treaty of Rome envisioned nearly 35 years ago. In the final crunch, before the European Community's self-imposed Jan. 1, 1993, deadline for unity, politicians from London to Rome are backpedaling and bickering so bitterly that the underlying steps toward a common market of 340 million people that have already been taken are getting lost in the shuffle.

Some of the confusion is understandable. In one of history's most memorable series of surprises, Eastern Europe threw off the yoke of communism, East Germany merged with West Germany to create an economic Goliath and the Soviet empire disintegrated and then reconstituted itself as a commonwealth, a term that conjures up the somewhat mystical British Commonwealth of Nations.

It's an untidy series of upsets. EC supporters bewail the fact that the European Community lost a lot of momentum when it no longer faced an enemy to the east. But it did gain some back at the recent summit in Maastricht, a Dutch border town that hosted a meeting of Europe's leaders.

Down in the trenches, where American companies do business, the EC is making a lot more progress as it knocks down intercountry barriers, one after another.

In fact, U.S. companies, large or small, have long been treating the continent as a Euromarket, dealing with national differences in the way they design and sell products but aiming to put production and marketing on a multinational basis wherever possible. With little discussion and lots of action, companies such as General Motors and IBM and their smaller suppliers have been managing European operations as a single market or group of regional markets for decades. Even such newcomers as Compaq Computer have been selling to Europe as a whole since the mid-1980s.

Virtually all companies with a stake in the EC are scaling up to larger size, through acquisitions and mergers, to cope with Eurocompetition. Some signal examples:

⊕ As early as the mid-1980s, Sweden's Asea and Switzerland's Brown Boveri, both powerhouses in electrical generating equipment but EC outsiders, merged and shifted their headquarters to Zurich.

⊕ Not long ago, Spain's major banks went through a wave of mergers to ensure that they would bulk large enough to serve customers in the new, aggressive EC climate.

⊕ Right now Fiat, which once had some 90 percent of the Italian vehicle market in its pocket, is diversifying into food and beverages in a move somewhat akin to having Chrysler make and market breakfast cereals and soft drinks.

In fact, the politics of the New Europe, played out at the meeting in Maastricht, are playing catch-up with the economics of a New Europe that is already partly in place. Thanks to a long list of 282 single-market directives handed down by the EC executive branch in Brussels some five years ago, the nuts-and-bolts program of shaping Europe in to a unified trade zone is well underway.

Here's what the EC is doing to streamline business:

Customs: As of Jan. 1, 1993, goods and people within the EC should be able to cross borders with a minimum of red tape—in some cases, with no documents required at all.

That means, for example, that if you're taking a sample product from a trade show in Dusseldorf to one in Amsterdam, you shouldn't face any hassles at the border or in airports.

Competition: Though it has a long way to go, the EC is attempting to shake up Europe's cartel mentality by handing down rules of competition patterned after American antitrust law.

Many EC commercial regulations have already superseded those of individual countries. And liberalization, Europe's buzzword for deregulation, is picking up speed. But at the same time the Brussels bureaucracy is edging toward social and industrial policies that may promote subsidies for European industry and help create global companies such as the multination Airbus consortium.

Labor: The EC is encouraging the development of a communitywide labor pool.

But it's a hot issue partly sparked by the rush of Eastern European workers—usually skilled and willing to accept low wages—to Western Europe in search of jobs. Workers can move around the EC freely. But until the stormy issue of *gastarbeiter* (guest workers) and other emigrants is settled, individual countries can—and do—block any permanent stays by not issuing all-important residence permits.

Transportation: The EC market is spurring countries to coordinate construction of new expressways for trucking and modernize rail transport. "Bullet trains" such as France's TGV and Germany's IC expresses (to be followed in time by even faster magnetic-levitation rolling stock) are already racing down Europe's tracks, making the train a better option than the plane between many city pairs such as Paris and Lyon. When the "Chunnel" under the English Channel is open, London and Paris, two key business centers, will be only three hours apart by train. Containers and other cargo also will benefit from Europe's upgraded rail network.

Currency: A European Monetary System (EMS) is already operating—with a European Currency Unit (ECU) as its basis. There's no ECU coinage as yet and not likely to be before 1999. But there's an ECU that exists on paper and in computers, based on a basket of "weighted" currencies.

To avoid the nightmares of intramural accounting between European subsidiaries, some companies price their EC supplies and products in the ECU, thereby saving time and the cost of exchange transactions. Banks transfer funds in ECU denominations, and there's a growing market for ECU bond issues.

When it comes to the EC's loftier goals, debated at Maastricht, you have to read between the headlines. Few of the targets will be met—if they're attainable at all—before the year 2000.

Central Bank: The New Europe will have a central bank like our Federal Reserve, which will control money supplies and set interest rates—but again, not until 1999.

The bank is only a vague blueprint—with Germany the strongest contender to serve as headquarters and Britain the biggest opponent of a scheme that would force it to put pounds sterling and monetary policy under anyone else's control.

Business Centers: Two of Europe's heftiest business hubs will be familiar names—London and Paris—and they'll have that status because of new office clusters as well as their traditional roles in commerce.

East of The City, London's financial district, is the humongous Docklands Development, centered on Canary Wharf, with London City Airport nearby. And about a mile west of the Arc de Triomphe in Paris is La Defense, an enormous congeries of corporate skyscrapers, which business visitors liken to Rockefeller Center.

Even with the New Europe's birth pangs, so much that's happening to business in the EC is alluring that everyone wants in. Stung by the awareness that they're about to end up outside the coveted EC, the six members of the long-dormant European Free Trade Association have negotiated a pact to create a 19-country trading bloc.

MAKING SENSE OUT OF THE NEW EUROPE
CONTINUED

Though diluting the power of the founding EC nations, the expanding trade bloc raises the specter of a Fortress Europe with protectionist walls around it. That's why every savvy American company exporting or selling to European markets has been scrambling to climb over the wall and establish a sound base inside.

The EC-EFTA market is astonishing in its magnitude. It is roughly 125 million larger in population than the U.S. and the biggest, richest market in the world (*see charts, this page*).

Though a massive Euromarket in itself, the EC-EFTA area also serves as an efficient springboard for exporting European-made goods to other countries, including, of course, the U.S. Its manufacturing skills, from French and German to British and Swedish, are well known. The newest idea, which has attracted numerous Japanese companies (partly because of tight European restrictions on imports of their cars and electronics products), is to take advantage of the low-wage labor force in at least three of the four weakest EC countries: Ireland, Portugal and Spain.

Germany's foreign minister, Hans-Dietrich Genscher, neatly sized up the European Community in words any American multinational corporation or exporter can understand. "The train to European union is standing at the platform," he wrote in December before the Maastricht meeting. "It's about to leave. Anyone who does not climb on board won't stop it from going. They'll be left standing alone."

The Power Line-up: European Community . . .			
	GNP [U.S.$ billions]	Population [millions]	GNP per capita [U.S.$ millions]
Germany	1530.4	79.5	19,250.3
France	1190.0*	56.7	21,099.3
Italy	1077.6	57.7	18,675.9
Britain	981.1	57.5	17,152.1
Spain	487.1	39.0	12,362.9
Netherlands	278.2	15.0	18,671.1
Belgium	197.1	9.9	19,909.1
Denmark	125.5	5.1	24,607.8
Greece	67.3*	10.1	6,663.4
Portugal	59.8*	10.4	5,695.2
Ireland	34.6	3.5	9,885.7
Luxembourg	10.6	0.4	26,500.0

Note: Population is 1991; all others are 1990 figures
*Gross Domestic Product
SOURCES: IMF, POLITICAL RISK SERVICES, 1992 ALMANAC, EMBASSIES

. . . European Free Trade Association			
	GNP [U.S.$ billions]	Population [millions]	GNP per capita [U.S.$ millions]
Switzerland	228.0*	6.8	34,029.9
Sweden	220.0	8.6	25,581.4
Austria	157.9	7.7	20,506.5
Finland	137.3*	5.0	27,460.0
Norway	103.1	4.3	24,547.6
Iceland	5.6	0.3	22,400.0

Note: Population is 1991; all others are 1990 figures
*Gross Domestic Product
SOURCES: IMF, POLITICAL RISK SERVICES, 1992 ALMANAC, EMBASSIES

Courtesy of *International Business* (March 1992).

The Export Marketing Study

CHAPTER 7

Getting Into the Export Business

Businesses decide to export for a variety of reasons. An interest in exporting is sometimes prompted by external motives, such as a newly established demand from a foreign market or the fact that a company presently numbers among its customers several foreign buyers. Exporting may be prompted by internal motives, for example, by a chief executive who is interested in expanding the company's horizons to international markets. Whatever the reason, no company can hope to export successfully without considerable advance planning.

The development of an export strategy—the important first step that every business must take before entering the export market—is the subject of this chapter. Just as new businesses must write business plans before they begin operations, so, too, must new and old businesses produce an export strategy if they hope to be successful in their international endeavors. An **export strategy** is a business plan specifically slanted toward the selection and development of a particular international market.

STEPS TO DEVELOPING AN EXPORT STRATEGY

An export strategy consists of three basic steps. First, a company must research and analyze the product it wishes to export. Second, a company must do research and analysis on competitors here and abroad. Third, having determined that the product is viable and the competition is not too forbidding, a company must research and analyze several potential foreign markets, eventually narrowing its choice to the best one.

PRODUCT RESEARCH AND ANALYSIS

The first step is to identify the product you hope to export. The government assigns a classification number to all products and services that are exported each year from the United States into foreign markets. This number holds the key to a wealth of information about products and related markets.

PRODUCT CLASSIFICATION

In the United States, two systems of classification are used. The most widely used, the **Standard Industrial Classification** (SIC) is domestic and the **Standard Industrial Trade Classification** (SITC) is international. In 1989, the United States revised its classification system and put the **Harmonized System** (HS) into effect, but exporters still need to work with all three systems because the SIC and SITC systems contain all information prior to 1989. An exporter exploring a specific product, for example, would want to check sales records and other data over a period of several years. Under all three systems, each product is assigned a code, based on whether it is a service or a product, a manufactured good or an agricultural product. Clothing is classified as manufactured goods, but textiles in their raw state, cotton, for example, are often classified as an agricultural product. In both systems of classification, apparel is assigned to one broad category whereas textiles are assigned to another.

With one or, more often, both of the two codes, an exporter can learn, among other things, how much of a product was exported in past years, what regions or countries it was exported into, and whether a quota or duty is attached to the product.

With either of the older systems, two-digit numbers are required to begin doing research on any product category, but multiple-digit numbers are needed to pinpoint products specifically. For example, apparel is group 23 under the SIC, but women's, misses, and juniors blouses is 2331. The last two digits are the product identification number.

Product classifications are not always the same under SIC and SITC, so be sure to check categories under both systems. Also, keep in mind that different kinds of information are available under each of the systems. For example, two SIC schedules, Schedule B Commodity Number and Schedule E Classification Number, supply specialized product information.

To simplify the exporter's search, the HS eliminates Schedules B and E. In the future, all an exporter need know will be the one product number of the HS.

PRODUCT ANALYSIS

Product analysis begins by examining how well the product is currently doing at home. Its market at home is at least an indication of how it will do abroad.

Potential fashion exporters should next ask themselves what factors would make their product do well in a foreign market. Is the geography right for a company that sells bathing suits, for example? Is there an availability of cheap raw materials to produce the product in a foreign market? Must it be produced, even partially, in a foreign market, or can it be manufactured in the United States? How does that work to the exporter's advantage or disadvantage? Is there less regulation of the product in the United States or perhaps more? Exporters must take care to analyze what works against, as well as for, a product they plan to export.

The next step is to analyze how well the product can be expected to do abroad. Is it a product in hot demand, or will you have to educate the market to the need for your product? Is it identifiably American, and does this influence how well it can be expected to do, as was true for Levi's when the demand for American-made jeans soared.

As the fashion world becomes more homogeneous, identifiably "national" looks are diminishing in importance, but individual nations are becoming known for certain fashion specialties. For example, American-made products that appeal to foreign markets because they are made in the United States include hunting, fishing, and camping apparel, activewear, surfwear, military products, workwear, basic jeans, children's wear, sportswear, and sports shoes.[1]

Finally, product analysis is not complete until you begin to consider what, if any, specifications must be changed to accommodate the international market. Although this cannot be known definitely until a specific market is targeted, it is possible to begin gathering general information at this stage of research. If you are investigating, for example, Europe as a potential market, then it is possible to obtain a list of European sizes in various countries that are different from those in the United States as well as information about general style preferences in this part of the world. Changing even minor specifications often spells the difference between success and failure, as one fashion producer of shirts found out when he shortened the sleeves on one of his products and tripled his foreign sales as a result.[2]

Once you have determined with reasonable certainty that your product will translate into sales—and profit—in a foreign market, the next step is to analyze the competition for your product.

COMPETITOR RESEARCH AND ANALYSIS

No businessperson would open a business in the United States without first considering the strengths and weaknesses of the competition. The same is true for a foreign market.

Checking out the foreign competition is a much harder task than checking out the domestic competition if only because it is so far away. The questions you must ask, however, are the same whether the competition is domestic or international. How many competitors do you have? Where are they located? What is their market share? What are their prices? How do they promote and distribute their products? These questions must be answered on a country-by-country basis, because all these factors typically vary

A Pound of Prevention

An anorak and pair of wind pants are the most versatile, functional items you can carry on the trail—and they only weigh about a pound.

Compact and easy to pack, these wind shells can be pulled out at a moment's notice to prevent annoying "back chills" during rest stops, take the edge off a mountain breeze or help keep you comfortable in misty weather. Wind shells are also useful for coping with biting insects. They can't bite through the dense nylon fabric.

For a complete list of items to bring on a day hike, including helpful tips, call 1-800-221-4221 and ask for our Day Hiking Activity Sheet.

Bean's® Supplex®
Nylon Anorak and Windpants
(For Men and Women)

Designed for rugged, lightweight wind protection when backpacking, canoeing, hiking or mountain biking. Constructed from soft, durable 2-ply Supplex nylon. DuPont Teflon®(Zepel) fabric treatment repels wind and resists moisture in misty or drizzle conditions. Double-needle stitching for long wear. Packable. Made in USA. Machine wash.

Anorak Full, athletic cut can be layered over our Fleece Active Wear. Drawstring hood. Extra-large "kangaroo" pocket and separate tunnel pocket. Elasticized wrists and drawcord at waist and hips.

Colors: Teal Green. Coral. Purple. Bright Royal. Turquoise. Red. Fuchsia (Women's only).
E313PP Men's Regular $49.50
Men's Regular sizes: S(34-36), M(38-40), L(42-44), XL(46-48).
G547PP Men's Tall $54.00
Men's Tall sizes: M to XL.
E314PP Women's $49.50
Women's sizes: S(6-8), M(10-12), L(14-16), XL(18-20).

Windpants Offer a functional and comfortable fit with backpacking gear. Improved waist has a wide panel back with elasticized front on Men's model. Women's has yoke front and elasticized back. Adjustable Velcro® tab closures at sides. Storm flap backs full-length side zips. Tapered lower legs and adjustable, Velcro-closure cuffs.

Colors: Black. Teal Green. Bright Royal.
G272PP Men's Regular $49.00
Men's Regular waist sizes: S(28-30), M(32-34), L(36-38), XL(40-42).
G548PP Men's Tall $54.00
Men's Tall waist sizes: M to XL.
G290PP Women's $49.00
Women's sizes: S(6-8), M(10-12), L(14-16), XL(18-20).

Merchandise with a distinctly American-made flavor, such as camping apparel from L.L. Bean, has strong appeal outside of the U.S. market. *Courtesy of L.L. Bean, Inc.*

from country to country and sometimes from region to region within countries.

Analyzing the competition will also help you decide how to set up your export operation. What suppliers does a competitor use? Can you use the same ones? What is the competitor's production capacity? Must yours match his or can you initially mount a smaller scale operation? In a foreign market, producers must also ask themselves what, if any, preferential market arrangements competitors may have

made. Preferential market arrangements are not as closely regulated in most foreign countries as they are in the United States. In fact, in many countries, bribes are an accepted fact of business life. Finally, producers must learn about and weigh government regulations and ties that may help or hinder the sale of their products.

In addition to analyzing foreign competition, it is also helpful to take a look at domestic competitors who are exporting products like yours. If domestic

GLOBAL *GO-GETTERS*

STEPHEN WAYNE: OO LALA, SASSON!

Courtesy of Stephen Wayne & Associates.

From his office on the 38th floor of a Manhattan high rise, Stephen Wayne answers telephone calls, checks samples of t-shirts and undies, and directs Sasson, the multimillion-dollar international company he is credited with bringing back from near death.

When the people at Trust Company of the West Capital (TCW) bought the Sasson trademark—"oo la la, Sasson" and a hand with thumb and forefinger touching and three fingers extended—they bought it in bankruptcy court, for it had little of value except its image as a producer of moderately priced designer jeans.

Wayne quickly capitalized on that image. He rebuilt Sasson from four licensees to 42, and pushed the company into the profit side of the ledger. With nine employees, no inventory, no factory, and profits skyrocketing, Wayne had invented a money-making machine.

How did he do it? He found reputable licensees in the United States to produce the jeans and added new products—handbags, shoes, costume jewelry, children's sportswear, women's sleepwear, men's socks, bathing suits, men's athletic wear, underwear, and watches, to name a few. He also hired celebrities, singers, athletes, actors to appear in the "oo la la, Sasson" ads, and soon everyone wanted a Sasson product. Finally, Wayne built a team that developed honest and exciting relationships with every retailer in the United States.

Sure of his success in the United States, Wayne instituted a marketing strategy for international sales and has built an enviable business in Canada and Europe. Asia has been Sasson's hottest growth market and Wayne anticipates that Australia will be a big growth market, hungry as Australians are for American products.

So domestically and overseas, the Sasson list of licensees and products continues to grow. From a tainted trademark that TCW picked up at a bargain basement price in bankruptcy court and turned over to him, Wayne has built an empire founded on licensing and marketing.

Based on Marlene C. Piturro, "Oo lala, Sasson!," *World Trade*, January/February 1992, pp. 63–66.

---

producers have tapped into the same market you are considering, then take a look at what they are exporting and whether they are doing it successfully. If no domestic competitor has ventured into the export market with your product, then you must analyze why not. And you must realize that if you decide to go into a market where no other competitor has ventured, you will be a pioneer with the advantages and disadvantages of that role.

Once you have determined that the competition is not too forbidding, you are now ready to begin researching and analyzing potential foreign markets to find the one that is right for you. Actually, in the course of the research you have done on the product

and the competition, you have probably also developed some ideas about potential foreign markets.

FOREIGN MARKET RESEARCH AND ANALYSIS

The global market is huge, and no one could hope to succeed in every part of it. At best, you will target one country or even one region of a country; perhaps, you will target several countries or a region comprised of several countries.

In any event, the task is to find potential foreign markets that promise to be right for you. The big questions prospective exporters must ask themselves is, Is this a viable market? Will the product be able to show a profit in this market?

FINDING POTENTIAL MARKETS

A fashion producer should first seek to identify potential target markets in a general way. Let us assume, for example, that you are planning to sell wool coats to a foreign market. You do not know exactly where you should sell them, but your preference is Europe because you have traveled there and are familiar with at least some aspects of the culture. You know that you would like to locate your market in this specific area. But where? What country or countries have a large enough market to support your product?

Your domestic market research shows that your coats sell better in the cold climates, places such as Wisconsin, Minnesota, Montana, and the Dakotas, than in states with more moderate weather. This is an example of the way that a domestic market can lead the way into an export market. With this information, you can conclude that you need to look for a European market area with cold winters.

Preliminary research reveals that the Scandinavian countries have the ideal climate to serve as a market area for your coat. But the next question you must resolve is whether their populations, their buying public, in other words, is large enough to support your product. Preliminary research shows that this is a relatively small potential market, especially when compared with your U.S. market, but that if you also sell to some more southerly countries, you will have a large enough market to make exporting your product worthwhile.

The next step is to identify one or more additional potential markets in other countries. Perhaps they exist; perhaps they do not. That is the point of doing general research on potential markets. At this stage of research, you must be prepared to acknowledge that there may be no market, little market, or, indeed, a large, viable market for your product. The market

GLOBAL GLIMPSES

BOTTOM OF THE NINTH INNING . . . WHO'S WINNING?

The "World Competitiveness Report" is an annual comparative study of 34 countries focusing on the attractiveness of their environment for investment and the aggressiveness of their enterprises in world competition. It is sponsored by the management school IMD in Lausanne, Switzerland, and the World Economic Forum, a Swiss foundation.

The "World Competitiveness Report" ranks countries based on two kinds of data. Hard data describe the factual elements of competitiveness as recorded by international organizations. Survey data, compiled from questionnaires sent to 10,000 executives worldwide, describe countries' perceived competitiveness among the international business community. The eight factors of a country's competitiveness are domestic economic strength, internationalization, government, finance, infrastructure, management, science and technology, and people.

Countries are split into two groups. Group I consists of Organization for Economic Cooperation and Development (OECD) members (excluding Iceland) and Hungary. Group II comprises the newly industrialized economies (NIEs)—Brazil, Hong Kong, India, Indonesia, Malaysia, Mexico, Singapore, South Korea, Taiwan, and Thailand.

Ranking first in six of the eight factors of competitiveness, Japan remains the top position in Group I. The United States remains in second position. Germany is third, Switzerland is fourth, Canada is fifth, and Austria has moved from eleventh to sixth.

Singapore maintains a good lead in Group II, with Hong Kong and South Korea following. Taiwan has dropped from second to fourth place. Business executives evaluate South Korea, Thailand, and Malaysia as increasingly competitive countries, and Indonesia and Mexico are seen as high potential countries for business development.

Based on this competitiveness report, the United States is certainly in the ball game. It leads the world's nations in terms of infrastructure, including natural resources, transportation, and information systems. It presently ranks second in science and technology and in the quality of its work force. Now is the time for the United States to strengthen its quality controls and to better train the work force. Coupled with international education and the natural competititive spirit of Americans, we can look forward to becoming Number One.

Based on "The Most Competitive Countries," *World Press Review*, November 11, 1991, p. 44.

you assumed was right for you at the outset of your research may not, in fact, be the right one for you.

In addition to studying market data, it is useful at this stage of research to make every effort to obtain first-hand knowledge of the potential markets, either by making contacts among foreign businesspersons who travel to the United States or by traveling to potential foreign markets for the specific purpose of testing the viability of your market. Trade missions, as trips organized for this purpose are called, are often organized by the government or trade associations. Again, you must be prepared after visiting potential markets to come to the realization that none of them is right for your product. In such a case, you return to the drawing board, or as is more likely the case, to the computer data base, and begin your search for a target market all over again.

ANALYZING FOREIGN MARKETS

In the second level of foreign market research and analysis, the questions—and the answers—become much more specific. Out of several potential markets, the fashion producer must screen to find the one best market in which to initiate exporting. Using data about each target market, it is important to examine specific economic, political, and social conditions that will help or hinder exporting in the potential target market you have selected.

Is there a duty or quota imposed on wool coats that would make them too expensive to sell in the target market? Is the target market politically stable and economically viable? If the country is in the midst of its worst recession in twenty years and has recently imposed new duties on clothing in an effort to stave off imports it believes are slowing down its lumbering economy, then this may not be the best market for you.

Do customers look as if they would be receptive to wool coats, or is this a part of the world where people take perverse pleasure in wearing lightweight coats in freezing weather?

With data in hand and the target markets considerably narrowed, it is a good idea to pay another visit to a target market—or this may be your first visit. Perhaps the trade mission trip did not take you to any of the markets you are now considering.

Matchmaker programs organized by the government and by trade associations are designed to help potential exporters make specific contacts within a target market. During the trip, you can observe first hand the state of the economy, talk with experts and even people on the street about your product, check out what people are wearing and using in their homes, meet potential manufacturers, competitors, and agents or other representatives with whom you might work. If all goes well, you may even find yourself negotiating a contract for someone to manufacture or represent your product.

A new aspect of global marketing is **market segmentation**, or the division of markets into specialized niches.[3] In recent years, niche marketing has achieved great success in the United States, to the point where whole stores are devoted to specialized size categories, petite and large sizes for women and tall and large sizes for men. Retailers are currently exploring the development of ethnic markets, the newest concept in niche marketing. For many years, however, marketers believed that niche marketing would not work in most foreign markets because they were viewed as so much more homogenous than the United States.

Fashion marketers have now begun to realize that even a culture as homogeneous as Japan does, indeed, have market segments. Formerly, even the Japanese did not believe their markets could be segmented, but after watching market segmentation at work in the United States, they have adopted this market theory. Marketing experts now acknowledge that variations exist among the Japanese in income, values, and lifestyles, to name but a few of the differentiating factors. Foreign market indicators will be different from those for a domestic market, but they are now increasingly being identified and used by fashion exporters.

In addition to segmenting markets within countries, international marketers are also learning to segment market across national borders. In other words, parts of several countries may be clustered into one market segment. To some extent, the idea for regional market clusters that ignore national boundaries was suggested by the formation of free trade regions among similar nations. International markets are segmented on the basis of the sociological, traditional, and behavioral factors that were discussed in detail in Chapter 2.

SOURCES OF EXPORT INFORMATION

An overwhelming amount of information is available to anyone who is considering exporting, but would-be exporters must know what information they need and where to find it. In the first part of this chapter, discussion is centered on the information that is needed; in the second half, discussion centers on where the information is.

Sample Outline for an Export Plan

Table of Contents

Executive Summary (one or two pages maximum)

Introduction: Why This Company Should Export

Part I—Export Policy Commitment Statement

Part II—Situation/Background Analysis

- Product or Service
- Operations
- Personnel and Export Organization
- Resources of the Firm
- Industry Structure, Competition, and Demand

Part III—Marketing Component

- Identifying, Evaluating, and Selecting Target Markets
- Product Selection and Pricing
- Distribution Methods
- Terms and Conditions
- Internal Organization and Procedures
- Sales Goals: Profit and Loss Forecasts

Part IV—Tactics: Action Steps

- Primary Target Countries
- Secondary Target Countries
- Indirect Marketing Efforts

Part V—Export Budget

- Pro Forma Financial Statements

Part VI—Implementation Schedule

- Follow-up
- Periodic Operational and Management Review (Measuring Results Against Plan)

Addenda: Background Data on Target Countries and Market

- Basic Market Statistics: Historical and Projected
- Background Facts
- Competitive Environment

One essential element in creating an effective export plan is identifying potential markets. *Courtesy of the U.S. Dept. of Commerce.*

PRIVATE SOURCES OF INFORMATION

Private sources of information about exporting come from Chambers of Commerce, both federal and state trade associations, and world trade clubs, commercial banks, and various private consultants. Of these, the latter two will charge for their services, and are expensive to use. Chambers of Commerce, world trade clubs, and trade associations are less expensive to use, usually requiring only a membership fee and possibly a small research fee.

GLOBETROTTING Gaffes

A ROSE BY ANY OTHER NAME . . .

Perhaps Boris Yeltsin should hold a contest for the best name for the new entity created from the old Soviet Union. CIS and Commonwealth of Independent States are just not catching on . . . CIS sounds like "sis" and Great Britain owns the trademark for "Commonwealth."

During the 1992 Winter Olympics, commentators referred to the "Unified Team"; others speak constantly of the "former Soviet Union" and "what used to be the Soviet Union."

To make it easier for all of us, here is a list of the "former Soviet Republics."

- ⊕ Russia
- ⊕ Western Region (including the Ukraine, Belarus, and Moldova)
- ⊕ The Baltics (including Estonia, Latvia, and Lithuania)
- ⊕ Trans-Caucasia (including Georgia, Armenia, and Azerbaijan)
- ⊕ Central Asia (including Uzebekistan, Kirghistan, Tajikhistan, Turkmenistan, and Kazakhstan)

All 11 countries in the Commonwealth of Independent States (CIS), the Baltics, and Georgia (the only former Soviet republic that has declined to join the CIS) are potential markets for export. First-time exporters should target the western republics of Russia, Ukraine, Belarus, Moldova, and the Baltics (Latvia, Lithuania, Estonia) where there is an established infrastructure and a more sophisticated business community.

Even though Georgia has declined to join, some suggestions for new names might be: Russia and Friends, Republics 'R' Us, Eurasia, Rusasia, and Greater Sarmatia (that's what the Romans called it 2000 years ago). Any other ideas?????

Based on J.D. Howard, "Boris & Co.?," *International Business*, April 1992, p. 94; Gretchen A. Burkle," Faraway Places with Strange-Sounding Names Offer Rare Opportunities," *Export Today*, April 1992, pp. 24–31.

CHAMBERS OF COMMERCE AND TRADE ASSOCIATIONS Chambers of Commerce and trade associations promote international business among members through a variety of programs. They are an invaluable source of contacts, often referring exporters to other specialists, including distributors and agents. Occasionally, they point the way to foreign customers as well. They host trade missions, matchmaker programs, and domestic events designed to introduce exporters to useful foreign contacts.

These two groups typically promote foreign trade by sponsoring educational seminars and workshops geared to specific industries.

They also offer concrete support providing documentation, assistance at foreign fashion fairs, and even aid with ongoing operations. For example, they sometimes help an exporter work out transportation routes or consolidate shipments with other exporters.

The organizations maintain files of information on market demand, trends, and new government research, and also provide a U.S. presence at international trade shows.

Both the U.S. and many state Chambers of Commerce also operate offices abroad, where their task is to provide exporters with up-to-date market information. They will answer inquiries from any business and will provide more specific information to members.

WORLD TRADE CLUBS World trade clubs organized by local or regional businesses engaged in exporting are another important source of information and service. The clubs' primary goal is educational, and to that end, they frequently sponsor seminars and workshops for exporters. They also organize promotional visits to foreign countries.

Trade clubs are a valuable source of information, contacts, and advice, with the advice often coming from other exporters. Clubs also often have affiliate branches that provide exporters with a home away from home as well as current market information.

COMMERCIAL BANKS Many commercial banks have sophisticated international banking departments. Some large banks, mostly those located in

Banks such as the MTB Banking Corporation now provide sophisticated international banking departments to satisfy the trade service requirements of American exporters. *Courtesy of the MTB Banking Corporation.*

cities, maintain correspondent relations with a foreign branch to facilitate export trade. Other U.S. banks support overseas branches.

Banks' experts are generally well informed, even about areas of exporting outside the financial sector. Some banks publish materials of special interest to exporters.

Among the regular international banking services provided by commercial banks are advice on export regulations and currency exchanges, financing assistance, transfers of funds, letters of introduction and credit, credit information on potential customers, and credit assistance to exporters' foreign customers.

CONSULTANTS Many kinds of consultants specialize in helping exporters. They can advise and assist an exporter on any aspect of business. According to one study, the most typical ways in which consultants aid exporters are by locating and qualifying joint venture partners, conducting feasibility studies, providing market survey information, establishing foreign branches of an exporter's business, and negotiating sales agreements.[4]

Consultants usually specialize by product and global region. For example, a consultant might deal only in helping shoe exporters or exporters of misses dresses to Scandinavia.

Large accounting, law, and public relations firms also offer consulting services to exporters; they, too, are often specialized.

Private consultants are expensive, so it pays to use them only after availing yourself of public advice, which is discussed in the next section, and only after deciding on your product and target market. Trade associations, world trade clubs, and other exporters are the best resource for finding private consultants.

PUBLIC SOURCES OF INFORMATION

An array of government sources are available at low or no cost to potential exporters, but three are especially useful to a fashion business in the process of developing an export strategy. These are the Custom Statistical Service, the Comparison Shopping Service, and the Country Consumer Market Research.

CUSTOM STATISTICAL SERVICE The Custom Statistical Service operates under ITA within the Department of Commerce and provides information on thousands of products in over 200 markets. The information includes dollar values, quantities sold, unit values, and market share percentages. This service helps exporters with product research and analysis.

Foreign trade consultants can be hired by fashion exporters to identify markets, potential customers, and distribution channels for their products. *Courtesy of Trade Partners International.*

COMPARISON SHOPPING SERVICE Another service designed to aid in product and market analysis, the Comparison Shopping Service provides exporters with specific data on products in specific markets. The service is customized, that is, a special report is prepared for each individual exporter who uses the service. The data supplied cover sales potential in various markets, a survey of comparable markets, distribution channels, competition,

TECH TALK

THE ECONOMIC BULLETIN BOARD

The Economic Bulletin Board (EBB) is a personal computer-based electronic bulletin board operated by the U.S. Department of Commerce.

The EBB is your on-line source for trade leads as well as for the latest statistical releases from the Bureau of Economic Analysis, the Bureau of the Census, the Bureau of Labor Statistics, the Federal Reserve Board,

Department of the Treasury, and other Federal agencies. A free, limited access service is available to those who would like to get acquainted with the EBB before subscribing.

Information can be had from the U.S. Department of Commerce; Office of Bureau Analysis; HCHB Room 4885; Washington, D.C. 20230: Telephone: (202) 377-1986.

GLOBAL *Goodies*

OPIC—OVERSEAS PRIVATE INVESTMENT CORPORATION

From Argentina to Poland to Zimbabwe, the Overseas Private Investment Corporation (OPIC) offers valuable assistance to U.S. firms planning projects around the world.

OPIC is just one of many federal programs designed to promote U.S. private investment in over 100 developing countries. The organization was established by Congress in 1969 and began operating in 1971 as a self-sustaining government agency. Starting with seed funding of $106 million, OPIC's reserves have grown to more than $1.5 billion, which it uses primarily for two purposes: to provide financing for U.S. investments and projects through direct loans, loan guarantees, and equity investments; and to provide U.S. firms with investment insurance against political risks.

OPIC's direct loan and guarantee programs provide medium- and long-term funding and permanent capital to projects involving significant equity and management participation by U.S. companies. Through direct loans, U.S. investors may obtain financing for smaller projects. Loans for such projects typically range from $500,000 up to a maximum of $6 million. Direct loans may be used only to finance projects sponsored by or significantly involving U.S. small business.

OPIC provides insurance to U.S. sponsors for qualified projects to protect the investments against loss due to: inability to convert local currency into dollars; expropriation, nationalization, or confiscation by a foreign government; political violence (war, revolution, civil strife, or insurrection).

OPIC policies can cover up to 90 percent of the investment in an eligible project. It is OPIC's policy to offer insurance only for new investments involving the expansion or modernization of an existing plant or equipment, or involving the acquisition of additional working capital to expand an existing enterprise.

Eligible investors are citizens of the United States; corporations, partnerships, or other organizations founded under U.S. laws, substantially owned by U.S. citizens; any state or territory of the United States; or a foreign business at least 95 percent owned by sponsors eligible under the above requirements.

Other programs offered by OPIC are: investment missions to developing countries so that U.S. businesspeople can meet with key business and government officials from foreign countries; the Opportunity Bank, which is a computer data system that matches U.S. companies' interests with specific international investments and projects; the Investor Information Service, which provides U.S. companies with country-specific and region-specific kits containing business, political, and economic information from over 100 developing countries and 16 geographical regions.

Based on William A. Delphos, "OPIC's Programs Assist Small U.S. Businesses," *Global Trade*, November 1991, p. 34.

and lists of qualified customers. Information is obtained through interviews with local businesses and business contacts by US&FCS staff.

COUNTRY CONSUMER MARKET RESEARCH Helpful to exporters who are researching foreign markets, this service, conducted by the Center for International Research, Bureau of the Census, provides up-to-date worldwide demographic statistics for foreign markets. The information is comparable with what may be found for domestic markets in the U.S. Census. It includes such statistics as population, marital status, education, literacy, household size, and household income. This service is also referred to as the International Data Base.

PUBLISHED INFORMATION

A wealth of information exists in books, specialized encyclopedias, and data bases, to name only a few sources. Much of it is available at low cost from the Small Business Administration and the Department of Commerce. Published export information is typically divided into broad categories: worldwide data, industry statistics, and country statistics.

Some important resources, published by nongovernment sources, are available from the library. For example, the *American Export Register*, which tells potential exporters about international competitors, is an important research tool. *FINDEX: The Directory of Market Research Reports and Surveys*, a source of market studies on countries and products, is another valuable reference.

EXPORT INFORMATION IN THE FASHION INDUSTRY

Like many industries just beginning to awaken to the potential of exporting, the fashion industry is in the early stages of forming specialized groups devoted to the promotion of exporting. The development of such groups—world trade centers dedicated to fashion and export trade associations specifically for the industry—will be the task of the next generation of fashion professionals, who will be the first to work in a world where fashion exporting is the rule rather than the exception.

ENDNOTES

1. Michael Spiewak, "Export Start Up (Aggressive Patience)," in Irving Vigdor, *Exporting: Get Into It!*, Merrick, NY: Redwood Associates, 1989, pp. 23–25.
2. *Ibid.*, p. 24.
3. *International Business*, pp. 506–508.
4. "The First Steps in Exporting," *Business America*, March 27, 1987, pp. 31–38.

VOCABULARY

export strategy _____

_____

_____

Harmonized System _____

_____

_____

market segmentation _____

_____

_____

Standard Industrial Classification _____

_____

_____

Standard Industrial Trade Classification _____

_____

_____

GLOBAL REVIEW

1. What is the main purpose of an export strategy?

_____

_____

_____

_____

2. Name the three basic steps in developing an export strategy.

_____

_____

_____

_____

3. SIC and SITC are two classification systems. What are they and how do they differ?

_____

_____

_____

_____

4. What is the name of the revised classification system put into effect in 1989 in the United States?

_____

_____

_____

_____

5. How can first-time exporters find a potential international market and then determine if that market is a viable market for their products?

_____

_____

_____

_____

6. What are the two broad categories of sources of information for U.S. exporters?

_____

_____

_____

_____

7. Name three sources under each of the two broad categories of sources of information.

_____

_____

_____

_____

8. Market segmentation has been very successful in the United States. Why did most of the U.S. marketers think it would not be successful in most foreign markets?

_____

_____

_____

_____

9. What are the broad categories that published export information divided into?

_____

_____

_____

_____

10. Explain the kind of information that is available from FINDEX: The Directory of Market Research Reports and Surveys.

_____

_____

_____

_____

GLOBAL DIGEST

1. What information should you research and analyze about your domestic competitors so that you can be better prepared to determine the possible success of your fashion product as an export?

_____

_____

_____

_____

_____

_____

_____

2. Once you have finished your preliminary research into possible markets for your chosen product, list the next steps that must be taken and give examples of where you would have to research to become more country specific for your product.

_____

_____

_____

_____

_____

_____

_____

_____

3. Describe the benefits of "matchmaker programs" that are organized by government and trade associations. How can these programs aid the first time exporter and how can market segmentation become an easier task because of participating in these programs?

_____

_____

_____

_____

_____

_____

_____

_____

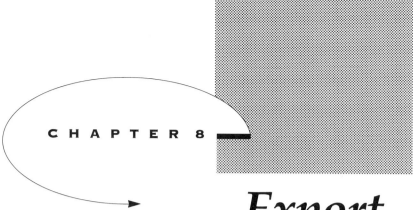

CHAPTER 8

Export Distribution, Promotion, and Pricing Strategy

You aren't really in business, some fashion sage must surely have said at one time or another, until the product reaches the customer and the customer knows it is there, waiting to be purchased. The process of getting the fashion product to the customer is called **distribution;** the process of letting the customer know the product is available to purchase is **promotion.** These two important operations, the twin subjects of this chapter, go hand in hand, no matter where in the world you are selling a product.

U.S. producers are part of a domestic channel of distribution and promotion that serves them well, putting their product within reach of their customers in a timely manner. The fashion producer who is planning to export a product line, however, must start all over with new distribution channels and promotion strategies, some of which will echo those used at home and some of which will involve entirely new ways of conducting business.

AGENTS FOR DISTRIBUTION AND PROMOTION

Figuring out how to distribute and promote a product is probably the biggest challenge any exporter faces. The job must be done and done well. According to a report in *Business America*, distribution and promotion are key factors in a product's success in the international arena.[1] How a product is distributed and promoted depends largely on how it is sold. Exported goods may be sold, as was noted in Chapter 4, either directly or indirectly.

Exporters who want to become involved in direct sales usually must open their own export offices and staff them with personnel whose purpose it is to distribute and promote the products. The time, energy, expense, and expertise involved is considerable, more, in fact, than most small and medium-sized fashion producers are able to afford.

Exporters who sell indirectly, in contrast, hire a company that specializes in exporting to sell their fashion products for them. Far less time and expense are required because the exporter needs no staff or foreign office, and the specialist may pick up many of the expenses associated with distribution and promotion.

Even when a product is sold directly, however, most exporters rely on the services of some kind of intermediary or agent to distribute and promote their product. Unlike selling in the United States, where an intermediary may not be necessary, it is highly unusual—to say nothing of impractical—to conduct

GLOBAL *GO-GETTERS*

R.R. DONNELLEY & SONS COMPANY: IT'S IN THE MAIL

At the suggestion of a big Chicago printer, the R.R. Donnelley & Sons Company, a dozen mail-order merchants, collaborated on a catalog designed to sell slices of America to Japanese consumers.

Land's End, Tweeds, L.L. Bean, Orvis, and eight other mail-order merchants each have two pages in the catalog. Using the catalog, Japanese shoppers can order a complete catalog from any of the merchants.

Although L.L. Bean has already been sending its own catalog to Japan, the idea for the group effort came from R.R. Donnelley, which prints and mails catalogs for many of the nation's largest mail-order retailers and picked up the cost of the Japanese experiment.

Although mail-order retailing has been slow to catch on in Japan, the American merchants are banking on the popularity of name-brand American products among fashionable Japanese. With the help of a Japanese advertising firm, the first catalog was carefully tailored to the Japanese market. Retailers were told to emphasize fashionable apparel and to avoid including electronics products or products that were labeled "Made in Korea." Japan and Korea are trade rivals.

Because Japan is a nation of golf buffs, the first mailing included a golf-ball personalizer and personalized gold tees from Austad's golf catalog. There were also a lot of denim and items like silver-plated bolo ties for the well-dressed Eastern Westerner. The Sheplers Western Wear section of the group catalog offered, in addition to $850 cowboy boots, a $1400 lamb blazer.

The cover of the catalog featured a photograph of a woman with blond hair and blue eyes peering over a Japanese-style hand fan emblazoned with an American Flag. The catalog, called American Showcase, is printed in Japanese.

Donnelley research found that Japanese were more comfortable dealing with a venture based in Japan. As a result, Japanese shoppers send their orders to an R.R. Donnelley facility in Japan, which faxes the orders each day to the various retailers in the United States. The orders are filled immediately and are promptly on their way back to the Japanese customer.

Based on Eben Shapiro, "U.S. Mail-Order Merchants Try Japanese Market," *The New York Times*, November 5, 1991, p. D5; Art Garcia, "It's In the Mail," *World Trade*, April 1992, pp. 56–62.

business this way in the vast majority of foreign markets. Most exporters seek out this expert advice at some stage of their export venture.

THE VALUE OF INTERMEDIARIES

Intermediaries serve as a bridge between exporters and the culture they are exporting into. An **intermediary** is a middleperson who helps an exporter communicate—literally, socially, and psychologically—with foreign customers. An intermediary may be a independent export agent who works for a few clients or an export trading company that represents many different clients and products. Exporters can choose from several different kinds of agents, each offering a variety of services.

The benefits of using an intermediary range from such operational savings as bulk orders, streamlined shipping, reduced handling costs, and centralized distribution to less tangible benefits such as advice about business practices, dress, and behavior when conducting business in a foreign climate.

Intermediaries speak the language of the country where the export is being sold, but they also serve as a translator of local customs and business practices, something all exporters need, never more so than when they are starting out. An intermediary knows, for example, when to sweeten a deal or push for a sale and when to play a sale in a low-key manner. In some countries, it is acceptable business practice to use a certain amount of pressure to persuade someone to buy a product; in other cultures, such behavior would be considered rude. In some parts of the world, it is an insult to expect anyone to pay the listed price; in other parts, it is expected that everyone will pay the asking price. Intermediaries are well versed in all of these local practices in ways that the average exporter cannot possibly be.

Intermediaries are well-informed about local laws and regulations involving merchandise imported into the country where they operate. In France, for example, door-to-door selling is illegal, something the average exporter might not know but an intermediary should. Intermediaries will also know

Courtesy of R.R. Donnelly and Sons Company.

whether exclusive distribution is illegal, as it is in many countries.²

Equally helpful to exporters is an intermediary's sense of what will sell in a foreign market, what will not, and why. Consider, for example, the American jewelry manufacturer who discovered some beautiful beads being made in a small factory in Togo. Eager to expand into a foreign market, he decided to try to sell some bead necklaces to the Togoese.

He barged ahead without any help from an intermediary. The country was small, after all, and he was a sophisticated traveler who had been to Togo several times, so he saw no need to seek outside advice. His first ads were prepared using American models dressed in breezy chiffon dresses and heavily laden with the bead necklaces. Imagine the exporter's surprise when people literally fell down laughing at his ads.

Consultation with an export agent would have uncovered the fact that the Togoese wore beads only around their waists, for the sole purpose of holding up their underwear. Investing in the services of an intermediary beforehand could have saved this exporter a great deal of time, money, and embarrassment.

Perhaps the most important reason to use an intermediary, however, is to satisfy demand. Throughout the world, businesspeople prefer to do business with their own compatriots rather than with foreign nationals who are sent in merely to sell them something.

AGENTS FOR DIRECT DISTRIBUTION AND PROMOTION

In direct distribution and promotion, the product is sold to an end user, most typically a wholesaler, distributor, manufacturer, or occasionally, to a retailer.

WHOLESALERS A foreign wholesaler, like a domestic wholesaler, operates as a customer, per-

Intermediaries provide expert advice when serving as middlepersons between exporters and their customers. Services provided range from determining export feasibility to handling business arrangements with foreign retailers. *Courtesy of John E. Cleek.*

---

haps a steady one, perhaps one who places one order and never buys again. The exporter has no contract with a wholesaler and must court this customer like any other.

Whether or not an exporter sells to a wholesaler depends entirely on the market and local custom. In some foreign markets, an agent is used even when dealing with a wholesaler.

DISTRIBUTORS In contrast to a wholesaler, a distributor typically works under a long-term contract with the exporter. Unlike a wholesaler, who rarely has a vested interest in preserving the product's identity, distributors keep the producer's name and image.

Distributors sell products on commission or buy them outright for resale. They typically assume the cost of warehousing the products. Distributors also often handle the marketing of a product, including advertising and promotion, although they sometimes work closely with the exporter on this. Foreign distributors may also extend credit to end users.

Distributors work best for products, such as cars and computers, that require service or support. In the fashion industry, distributors are seldom used for apparel or houseware, but they are used in the interna-tional marketing of cosmetics, for example, and some lines of jewelry.

MANUFACTURERS Exporters of raw materials sell their products directly to manufacturers. For example, the United States is a leading exporter of cotton. Its mills routinely sell cotton to foreign manufacturers, who then make it into garments and such domestic products as towels and sheets. As is the case with wholesalers, an agent is often used in foreign markets to smooth the path and increase direct sales.

RETAILERS Selling directly to a retailer is not impossible, but it is time-consuming and often proves to be more expensive than any other form of direct selling. Retailers expect the exporter to be on hand to service the accounts, something an exporter, especially a small or medium-sized one, may not be prepared or able to do. Orders from retailers will also be smaller than those from other direct selling agents and more complicated to process because each must be handled separately.

Selling directly to retailers works best for large exporters. Not only does it involve a major commitment on the part of the exporter, but an exporter who sells directly to retailers also loses the expert advice of intermediaries who provide valuable information on export practices and customs.

LOCATING DIRECT CUSTOMERS

A number of services are available to help exporters who are interested in distributing their products directly. Private consultants will locate direct customers for exporters, for a fee, of course. The Commerce Department provides regular sales leads, either in print or electronically, in *Trade Opportunities Programs* (TOP), a listing of foreign firms that want to buy U.S. products.[3]

Some exporters list themselves in *Commercial News USA,* a Commerce Department publication that promotes U.S. products abroad. Listings are inexpensive and often quite productive. One small manufacturer with a limited promotion budget said of his listing, "It's the best $150 I've ever spent. We're getting a ton of inquiries from all over the world."[4]

In an attempt to help develop business, many states have begun to operate programs similar to those run by the Commerce Department and other federal agencies.

Networks are a newer and increasingly popular way to find direct customers. World Trade Centers, located in New York City, is an international organization of 160 world trade centers. Among its other services for members, it provides an on-line data base where exporters can advertise their products and search for customers around the world.[5]

AGENTS FOR INDIRECT DISTRIBUTION AND PROMOTION

Indirect foreign sales are typically handled by export management companies, export trading companies, export merchants, and export agents.

EXPORTS MANAGEMENT COMPANIES AND EXPORT TRADING COMPANIES Export management companies (EMCs) and export trading companies (ETCs) are the quickest—and least costly—way for an exporter to distribute and promote fashion products, at least for the short term. Some fashion producers begin working with these companies and then open their own offices after they have carved out a profitable niche in the market.

ETCs and EMCs help the exporter avoid, at least initially, building a costly overseas operation. They resemble the foreign buying offices operated by large department stores and retail chains who are heavily involved in importing, but EMCs and ETCs always operate independently when a buying office is an extension of its parent company.

An **export management company** handles exports for foreign producers who, in turn, are its clients. EMCs are specialized within the industry. An EMC may sell only men's accessories, for example. Many EMCs also carve out geographic turfs, doing business only in specific countries or regions of the world. Agreements with EMCs are usually exclusive, that is, an exporter works with only one EMC at a time.

Export management companies work on commission, salaries, and retainers, or some combination of all three. The companies assume the credit risks of the customer to whom they sell and also take responsibility for billing customers. Some EMCs will arrange for financing and shipping.

An **export trading company** functions almost identically to an export management company except that it takes title to the product, whereas an EMC does not. This offers the exporter the considerable convenience of having only one export account in the United States in contrast to having to maintain an export account for each foreign customer.

Whereas export management companies work with related product lines and are highly specialized, export trading companies tend to work with a variety of products, of which yours will be but one. ETCs tend to be larger than EMCs, and an exporter's products may not be given the same priority, time, and attention they would receive from an EMC.

It is still an advantage, however, for exporters to be able to sell their products outright, especially when starting out in the export business with limited capital.

EXPORT AGENTS A **foreign sales agent,** sometimes also referred to as a broker, operates much as a domestic sales representative does. Agents work on commission and may represent only one exporter or several exporters with similar products. Like EMCs, agents specialize in segments of the fashion industry and sometimes handle only a specific product, such as women's dresses or bed linens.

Agents' responsibilities depend on the type of contract they have with an exporter. Before negotiating any contract, an exporter should learn what legal rights an agent has in his or her country to avoid getting stuck with an agent who does not perform as promised. Agents usually have the authority to commit an exporter to sales.

Agents develop market strategies, make contacts, and take and place orders. Although agents do

The World Trade Center Association provides exporters with such services as instant access to current offers to buy and sell products. *Courtesy of the World Trade Center Association.*

occasionally provide consulting services on packaging, labels, sizing, and documentation, they do not, except in the most peripheral way, become involved in shipping or financing. Foreign agents are often more respected abroad than in the United States.

EXPORT MERCHANTS An **export merchant** buys goods outright and sells them in foreign markets. From an exporter's view, selling to an export merchant resembles selling to a wholesaler.

LOCATING INDIRECT SALES AGENTS

Export consultants can help prospective exporters locate agents for indirect selling. The US&FCS operates an Agent/Distributor Service, a customized computer search program to help exporters locate the right agent. The program identifies up to six prospects who have examined the exporter's literature and have indicated a willingness to work with her or him.

TECH TALK

THE EXPORT HOTLINE

A.T.& T., The Journal of Commerce, Cahners Publishing, and others have established a fax-back information retrieval system designed to provide up-to-date information on 50 key industries of all major trading partners of the United States. The service was developed by International Strategies, a Boston consulting firm. By calling 1-800-USA-XPORT (toll free), the caller will be directed to a designated telephone number, which will fax back within minutes the information requested. The only cost for the service is fax time. Reports average 5 to 10 pages. For further information call A.T.& T.; 277 West Monroe Street, floor 20th North; Chicago, IL 60606; Telephone: (312) 230-4889.

Reprinted from ASSIST International, Vol.I: Issue 5, March 2, 1992, pp. 2–3.

Two publications provide comprehensive listings of export management and export trading companies: *Partners in Export Trade,* published by the Commerce Department, and *Directory of Leading Export Management Companies,* published by Bergano Book Company. Libraries often have copies of both books. Both directories list firms by industry and product area.[6]

STEPS TO FINDING A REPUTABLE AGENT

Because you will be signing a contract with an export company or foreign agent to conduct business in a country where you do not know the law or business practices, it is important to find a reliable representative, as well as someone who understands how to market your image and your product. To find an agent that best suits your needs, you should follow a five-step process.

1. *The first step is to actively solicit and locate several leads on trading partners.*
2. *The list of potential candidates should be screened.* To screen candidates, write to each one expressing an interest in his or her services. Request additional information if you feel you need it. Check references by talking to past and present clients, trade associations and clubs, and other consultants to see what they know about the agents.
3. *Narrow the list to two or three prospects.* At this stage, an exporter should make every effort to visit prospective agents to observe their operations firsthand.
4. *Appoint the agent and negotiate a contract with him or her.* You and the agent whom you have selected will work out a contract together, either in person or through your lawyers.
5. *Exporters must do everything possible to keep their new representative motivated to sell their products.* Exporters sometimes think they can ignore this final step once an agent has been chosen. An intermediary's interest will be at a peak when he or she agrees to represent your fashion product, but it is up to you, as the exporter, to make sure that this enthusiasm is sustained by constant contact and by providing a quality product.

DEVELOPING A PRICING STRATEGY

Pricing and promotion go hand in hand. Before a product can be promoted, it must be priced to sell. To determine how they will set their prices, exporters develop pricing strategies.

A **pricing strategy** is the process of evaluating and setting the price of a product, taking into account such factors as cost, competition, and other elements of the marketing factors.

Rarely can fashion exporters price their products exactly the same in a domestic and a foreign market, nor would they want to do so. There may be room for larger profits, or if the costs are less or some expenses are picked up by the exporter's agent, a lower price may result in the same profit.

Most exporters also find they must develop a different pricing strategy for each foreign market they target. Prices may vary by region, country, or even regions within countries. Bathroom towels sell

GLOBAL *Goodies*

THE AGENT/DISTRIBUTOR SERVICE HELPS EXPORTERS FIND HELP

The cost and time required for small and medium-sized companies to locate foreign agents and distributors is often prohibitive. For both experienced and inexperienced exporters, the necessary research and travel are both time-consuming and expensive.

Recognizing the quandry of small and medium-sized companies, the Department of Commerce established the Agent/Distributor Service (ADS) some years ago. The service helps U.S. firms find product representatives overseas with a minimum of time and expenditure. It will locate, screen, and help evaluate agents, distributors, representatives, and other foreign partners for U.S. businesses.

To start the search, the U.S. firm must provide the district office trade specialist with several sets of product literature, an export price, and a general letter to potential agents and distributors detailing the criteria for a representative. The firm must also let the trade specialist know if it already has other agents or distributors in the area.

Once the company, with the help of research by the trade specialist, has targeted the countries where it wishes to find representatives, the district office sends the company's product information to the appropriate foreign posts.

One follow-up service that particularly complements ADS is the World Traders Data Report (WTDR), which provides thorough, confidential background reports on potential foreign trading partners, including agents and distributors, on request. Sometimes, companies combine their final overseas agent/distributor interviews with participation in trade shows.

Numerous firms have reported successful outcomes to their ADS searches. They represent a cross section of companies—first time exporters, experienced exporters that may be dissatisfied with their press agents, export management companies researching new product markets, and entrepreneurs.

Although there have been many successes in the ADS program, the Department of Commerce does not guarantee that its trade specialists can find an agent or distributor in a particular country. However, many companies find that even when a search is unsuccessful, they feel more experienced from being involved in the process.

Based on Katherine Glover, "Agent/Distributor Service," *Business America*, November 6, 1989, pp. 2–5.

---

for more in a Paris department store, for example, than they do in a small provincial shop.

Exporters may also find that they have to set lower prices because consumers in a foreign market will not buy at U.S. prices. Or perhaps the reverse is true, and foreign consumers expect to pay far more for a product than U.S. consumers do. All these considerations must be taken into account when devising a pricing strategy.

Pricing also has a psychological component that consists of the exporter taking the measure of a market and the product and simply deciding how much someone will pay for it. The only problem with such intuitive or "psychological" judgments is that they are much riskier in a foreign culture than in one's own familiar world.

COST FACTORS

Of all the elements that go into a pricing strategy for a foreign market, cost is the most important determinant of price. The elements in cost that are likely to influence pricing strategy in a foreign market are the product itself, marketing and advertising, and the life cycle of the product.

THE PRODUCT Few products can successfully enter a foreign market without any modifications. Modifications, in turn, add more to the cost of a product than any other factor. Different markets require varying degrees of product modification, ranging from no modifications to minimal to major ones. A dress manufacturer may have to modify dresses for every single market. An exporter must always weigh the cost of the modifications against the profit to be made from any one market.

If no modifications are required, the cost of getting the product ready for market is minimal. But exporters who send fashion products abroad without any modifications are often only unloading their surpluses, not a particularly rejuvenating long-term pricing strategy.

The following checklist should be tailored by each company to its own needs. Key factors vary significantly with the products and countries involved.

Size of sales force

⊕ How many field sales personnel does the representative or distributor have?

⊕ What are its short- and long-range expansion plans, if any?

⊕ Would it need to expand to accommodate your account properly? If so, would it be willing to do so?

Sales record

⊕ Has its sales growth been consistent? If not, why not? Try to determine sales volume for the past five years.

⊕ What is its sales volume per outside salesperson?

⊕ What are its sales objectives for next year? How were they determined?

Territorial analysis

⊕ What territory does it now cover?

⊕ Is it consistent with the coverage you desire? If not, is it able and willing to expand?

⊕ Does it have any branch offices in the territory to be covered?

⊕ If so, are they located where your sales prospects are greatest?

⊕ Does it have any plans to open additional offices?

Product mix

⊕ How many product lines does it represent?

⊕ Are these product lines compatible with yours?

⊕ Would there be any conflict of interest?

⊕ Does it represent any other U.S. firms? If so, which ones?

⊕ If necessary, would it be willing to alter its present product mix to accommodate yours?

⊕ What would be the minimum sales volume needed to justify its handling your lines? Do its sales projections reflect this minimum figure? From what you know of the territory and the prospective representative or distributor, is its projection realistic?

Facilities and equipment

⊕ Does it have adequate warehouse facilities?

⊕ What is its method of stock control?

⊕ Does it use computers? Are they compatible with yours?

⊕ What communications facilities does it have (fax, modem, telex, etc.)?

⊕ If your product requires servicing, is it equipped and qualified to do so? If not, is it willing to acquire the needed equipment and arrange for necessaary training? To what extent will you have to share the training cost?

⊕ If necessary and customary, is it willing to inventory repair parts and replacement items?

Marketing policies

⊕ How is its sales staff compensated?

⊕ Does it have special incentive or motivation programs?

⊕ Does it use product managers to coordinate sales efforts for specific product lines?

⊕ How does it monitor sales performance?

⊕ How does it train its sales staff?

⊕ Would it share expenses for sales personnel to attend factory-sponsored seminars?

(Continued)

Factors to consider when choosing a foreign representative or distributor.

Customer profile

⊕ What kinds of customers is it currently contacting?

⊕ Are its interests compatible with your product line?

⊕ Who are its key accounts?

⊕ What percentage of its total gross receipts do these key accounts represent?

Principals represented

⊕ How many principals is it currently representing?

⊕ Would you be its primary supplier?

⊕ If not, what percentage of its total business would you represent? How does this percentage compare with other suppliers?

Promotional thrust

⊕ Can it help you compile market research information to be used in making forecasts?

⊕ What media does it use, if any, to promote sales?

⊕ How much of its budget is allocated to advertising? How is it distributed among various principals?

⊕ Will you be expected to contribute funds for promotional purposes? How will the amount be determined?

⊕ If it uses direct mail, how many prospects are on its mailing list?

⊕ What type of brochure does it use to describe its company and the products that it represents?

⊕ If necessary, can it translate your advertising copy?

Factors to consider when choosing a foreign representative or distributor. *Courtesy of the U.S. Dept. of Commerce.*

If minor modifications are necessary, limited time and money can be committed with good results. An exporter committed to making only minor modifications may decide to forgo a particular market if too many substantial modifications are required.

Major modifications to a product require a major commitment of time and money and may entail the establishment of separate production facilities.

Exporters must understand that their target market dictates the modifications that are required and not the other way around. Allen-Edmonds, which made high-quality men's shoes, discovered, in the words of its CEO John Stollenwerk, that having "a high-quality product wasn't enough." Allen-Edmonds realized that its shoes had to be tailored to each target market. "For instance," Stollenwerk observed, "double-soled wingtip shoes in black will sell well in Italy and Germany, but not in other countries."[7]

MARKETING AND ADVERTISING Marketing and advertising are also factors in cost. Most U.S. marketing and advertising programs do not translate well into foreign cultures, and entirely new ones must be devised.

Taking cultural differences into account was especially crucial during the late 1980s when Commu-

nism crumbled, and many new, hitherto closed markets were suddenly open to the West. Special sensitivity was called for, however, in devising marketing programs for eastern European nations. One advertising executive with accounts in that part of the world observed, "In the old days, Communist propaganda bombarded the people with hyperbole, so when you write an ad today, you can't use too many superlatives. You just won't be believed."[8]

Some costs of marketing and advertising are unique to a particular market. For example, some countries ban contests; others ban competitive advertising. One country may regulate advertising much more than the United States does, thus restricting what may be said or shown in an advertisement. In general, advertising is more tightly regulated, either legally or by self-regulation, in most other countries than it is in the United States.

One additional cost must also be included in marketing and advertising in foreign markets, and that is the sometimes considerable expense of translating materials into another language. Marketing materials and advertisements must be especially well translated. No exporter can risk diluting or entirely losing the impact of his or her message because a word—or a gesture—means something different in another language.

GLOBETROTTING **Gaffes**

TRADE SHOW SALES STRATEGIES

American companies are awakening to the need to attend foreign trade fairs. Any trade show, especially those held abroad, is too important to treat lightly. One of the factors that can affect your success is your exhibit space.

Pacific Rim nations in particular tend to look at the exhibit itself as one more representation of the company on the selling floor. On average, foreign companies spend 22 percent of their media budgets on trade shows. American companies usually allot 1 percent to 5 percent of their media budget on trade shows. Also, trade shows tend to run longer than the fairs in the United States. Therefore, there is greater emphasis on taking the time to develop relationships on the show floor, on sitting down and relaxing, and maybe concluding a sale over several visits. Here, we want to do as much as we can in as short a time period as possible at a trade show.

In most foreign countries, exhibition halls usually run trade shows, not trade show companies, which essentially just sublet space to exhibitors. Because of this, the show operators are a lot more flexible, a lot more oriented to making a show a profitable experience for everybody.

Americans have to learn what European and Pacific Rim exhibitors already know. The important thing at the show booth is sales and marketing, not fittings or special sound systems or video walls.

Based on Richard Szathmary, "Over There for Fun and Profit," *Sales Marketing and Management*, September 1991, pp. 161–162; Gregory Sandler, "Asian Trade Shows: 10 Steps to Success," *Export Today*, April 1992, pp. 12–16.

One American exporter decided, on his own, to promote his knapsacks by showing a young man hitchhiking. What he didn't know was that the standard American gesture for a hitchhiker—thumb pointed out away from the body—was an obscene gesture in many of the countries where he chose to advertise.[9]

LIFE CYCLE   Finally, the life cycle of a fashion product is also a factor in its cost. Will you be introducing a mature product, in which case you will already have taken your profit at home and may even be selling the surplus? Will you be selling fashion in the introductory stage, in which case your costs will be higher and your runs smaller, just as they would be with a domestic introductory product? These factors will be figured into the pricing strategy.

OTHER FACTORS   There may be added costs when selling in a foreign market, duties and taxes being the most obvious ones. Shipping will cost more, as will the paperwork required to process foreign sales.

On the other hand, there may also be unexpected savings, as when an agent or export company assumes the cost of promotion, shipping, or some of the paperwork.

Because elements like these will also affect the price of the product, exporters need to obtain as

much information as possible about selling in their target markets before developing a pricing strategy.

APPROACHES TO PRICING STRATEGIES

Experts have devised many approaches to pricing strategy, but two are especially helpful to the exporter. The most widely used strategy for pricing products involves dividing the product by price range, that is, by whether the price should be high, low, or medium. The other approach considers where the product is being sold and whether and to what degree price should be affected by country or region.

STRATEGIES BASED ON PRICE RANGE   A high price can be used when the product is unique or new or has a high-quality image. A high price usually, but not always, leads to high profit margins, but it can also limit the market, and as is the case with anything new or unusual, it may draw competition, which in turn, usually serves to bring the price down.

A low price, in sharp contrast, works best with a basic, minimal product. For exporters, low pricing is usually a short-term strategy, the best way to get in and out of a market quickly. Low prices work for the long term at home, but basic, cheap products do not have much appeal when they are imports. This is

GLOBAL GLIMPSES
SHOW AND SELL

You're off to another international trade show. Jet lag has just hit . . . so has an upset stomach. Your display set-up has wilted. You finally reach the trade show floor and discover that sellers are selling to one another. What an agony. However, help is on the way; it is called USA Catalog Exhibits and Infocentrum.

The idea is simple: Participating manufacturers ship their catalogs to Bob Heller, of USA Catalog Exhibits. He and his crew take the literature and set up "reading rooms" in hotels in places like Latin America, Australia, South Africa, New Zealand, and the Philippines. Staffers supervise the entire exhibit—in effect, representing your product—and register all visitors who express an interest in your products or services. The information is sent via courier to Georgia where it is processed by computer. Within a few days, you, the manufacturer, receives a comprehensive report—in English—detailing these leads.

However, this service should not substitute for attendance at international trade shows. In fact, USA Catalog Exhibits and Infocentrum had its trade premier at the International Trade Rand Show in South Africa in April 1992, and plans are underway to bring this operation to many established major trade shows.

Based on Farzin Toussi, "Go to Heller," *World Trade*, March 1992, p. 10.

where the psychological appeal of imports comes into play; consumers who buy imports are looking for something unusual, and that typically is not your basic, low-priced product.

Some experts also argue that cheap imports have hurt the U.S. image in the past, signalling only a short-term interest in a foreign market. Cheap exports, some believe, perpetuate an image the United States has been trying to overcome as it persuades the world to accept its exports.

A moderate price is a good alternative to the other two strategies when an exporter is unsure or unable to determine where a fashion product fits into a foreign market. A moderate price, which allows the exporter to compete and retain a healthy profit margin, is also a good long-term position in a market.

ETHNOCENTRIC, POLYCENTRIC, AND GEOCENTRIC PRICING STRATEGIES Three other approaches to pricing strategy are frequently used by multinational corporations. The distinction among these approaches are of somewhat limited value to fashion producers, because one is clearly the most applicable to the industry. They are, however, worth examining for how they play up the differences between fashion products and other products.

In **ethnocentric pricing,** exporters assume that their products are the same everywhere and do not take national or regional differences into account. This strategy works only when a product truly is the same in every market, and relatively few products, especially fashion goods, fall into this category. Computers, for example, are marketed the same all over the world, and with the exception of duties and taxes, they are priced the same worldwide.

Virtually no fashion products can be marketed with ethnocentric pricing because fashion is unique. Even in the domestic market, pricing strategies vary with the region or locale where the product is sold.

In **polycentric pricing,** national and regional differences are taken into account in setting price. This is the most flexible form of pricing, the one most suitable to fashion products. It is most responsive to the market.

In **geocentric pricing,** the local intermediaries set the price in their regions independently of the exporter's other markets. This method is more rigid than polycentric pricing but less rigid than ethnocentric pricing. The problem with geocentric pricing, for the fashion industry, is that most fashion producers are not multinational corporations. Thus, they are too small to have regional corporate offices with personnel skilled enough to establish and monitor prices.

THE ELUSIVENESS OF UNIFORMITY IN DISTRIBUTION AND PROMOTION

In summary, one of the few things that can be said for certain about distribution and promotion in foreign markets is that uniformity is probably impossible to achieve, given the unique and highly individual nature of fashion products. Distribution and promotion usually must be adjusted, if not continually fine-tuned, from market to market on a continuing basis.

ENDNOTES

1. "The First Steps in Exporting," *Business America*, March 2, 1987, pp. 31–38.
2. Parviz Asheghian and Bahman Ebrahimi, *International Business*, New York: Harper & Row, 1990, p. 238.
3. William A. Delphos, *The World Is Your Market: An Export Guide for Small Businesses*, Washington, DC: Braddock Communications, 1990, p. 28.
4. *Ibid.*, p. 28.
5. *Ibid.*, p. 167.
6. *Ibid.*, p. 23.
7. *Small Business Reports*, no author, May 1989, p. 29.
8. Jerry Ferry, "Global Business," *Pan Am Clipper*, August 1991, p. 46.
9. Roger E. Axtell, Ed., *Do's and Taboos Around the World*, New York: John Wiley and Sons, 1985, p. 37.

VOCABULARY

distribution

_____

_____

_____

ethnocentric pricing

_____

_____

_____

export management
company

_____

_____

_____

export merchant

_____

_____

_____

export trading
company

_____

_____

foreign sales agent

_____

_____

geocentric pricing

_____

_____

intermediary

_____

_____

_____

polycentric pricing

_____

_____

_____

pricing strategy

_____

_____

_____

promotion

_____

_____

_____

GLOBAL REVIEW

1. Why are the important keys to success in both domestic and foreign selling . . . distribution and selling?

_____

_____

_____

_____

2. Intermediaries serve as an important function in bridging the differences between domestic producers and foreign sales. What is the main purpose for using an intermediary?

_____

_____

_____

_____

3. Name the four major types of agents used in direct distribution and promotion for international sales.

_____

_____

_____

_____

4. Describe the services of each of the four types of agents used in direct distribution and promotion for international sales.

_____

_____

_____

_____

5. TOP is the acronym which U.S. Department of Commerce service?

_____

_____

_____

_____

6. What is the name of the U.S. Department of Commerce publication that promotes U.S. products abroad?

_____

_____

_____

_____

7. What is the main major difference between an export management company
and an export trading company to an exporter?

_____

_____

_____

_____

8. List the five steps in the process needed to find a reputable agent.

_____

_____

_____

_____

9. What is a pricing strategy?

_____

_____

_____

_____

10. Name and explain the three pricing strategies mentioned in this chapter.

_____

_____

_____

_____

GLOBAL DIGEST

1. Why are distribution and promotion such important factors in successful exporting? Describe how each of these strategies must be used for a fashion product of your choice.

_____

_____

_____

_____

_____

_____

_____

2. In developing a price strategy, cost is the most important determinant of price. What are the elements in cost that are likely to influence pricing strategy for a foreign market for your fashion product?

_____

_____

_____

_____

_____

_____

_____

3. Explain how the high, low, or medium price range theory can be used to help you determine some of the pricing strategies needed for success in the international marketplace.

_____

_____

_____

_____

_____

_____

_____

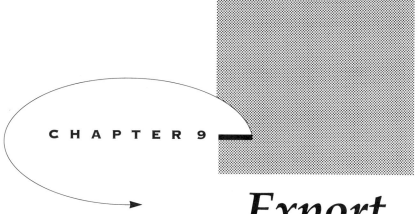

CHAPTER 9

Export Procedures

At first glance, the paperwork, or documentation, involved in processing the international sale seems overwhelming. Writing up a domestic sale takes a few minutes of your time. Arranging an international sale can eat up days, and until you know what you are doing, it is like working your way through a maze. But after you have worked your way through a few times, you will begin to see that the process, if not exactly simple, is decidedly logical. But why, you may still be asking yourself, do you have to go through all this paperwork?

Extensive documentation is required in part because governments want to keep track of what is coming into and going out of their countries. At minimum, they need to know who the buyers and sellers are, what is being exchanged, and its value. As added motivation, failure to comply also brings civil and criminal penalties in many countries.

But more important, the export process also works to protect the exporter. Some documents, for example, insure that the exporter gets paid. Others guarantee that damaged goods can be replaced. Still others detail the transfer of title.

All in all, the paperwork serves an important function for all involved and makes the whole process smoother and safer.

GATHERING DOCUMENTATION FOR EXPORTING

One of the most important tasks for an exporter is to prepare the documents associated with an export purchase. For purposes of this discussion, we shall divide these documents into five general categories:

1. Export licenses.
2. Transportation documents.
3. Packing and handling documents.
4. Legal documents.
5. Payment documents.

Many nations require one or more licenses before they will permit the importation of goods. Transportation documents facilitate the transportation of goods exported from one country to another. Packing and handling documents describe the goods, often to an array of handlers who speak many different languages, and give special instructions regarding their care during transport. Legal documents insure that ownership of the goods is correctly transferred, a process that is always more complex when the goods are crossing national boundaries. Payment documents are used to make sure that payment is ren-

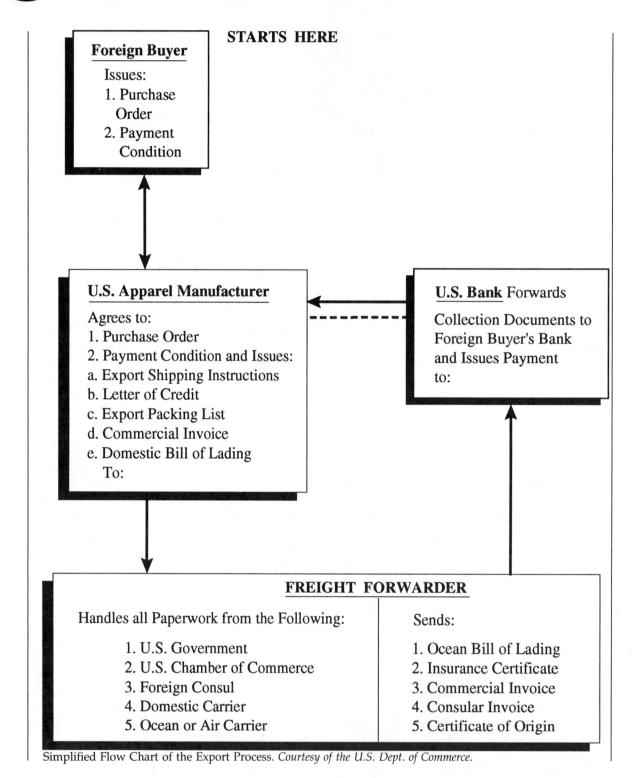

STARTS HERE

Foreign Buyer

Issues:
1. Purchase
Order
2. Payment
Condition

U.S. Apparel Manufacturer

Agrees to:
1. Purchase Order
2. Payment Condition and Issues:
a. Export Shipping Instructions
b. Letter of Credit
c. Export Packing List
d. Commercial Invoice
e. Domestic Bill of Lading
To:

U.S. Bank Forwards

Collection Documents to
Foreign Buyer's Bank
and Issues Payment
to:

FREIGHT FORWARDER

Handles all Paperwork from the Following:

1. U.S. Government
2. U.S. Chamber of Commerce
3. Foreign Consul
4. Domestic Carrier
5. Ocean or Air Carrier

Sends:

1. Ocean Bill of Lading
2. Insurance Certificate
3. Commercial Invoice
4. Consular Invoice
5. Certificate of Origin

Simplified Flow Chart of the Export Process. *Courtesy of the U.S. Dept. of Commerce.*

dered in a manner acceptable to both the importer-buyer and the exporter-seller.

EXPORT LICENSES

Export licenses are designed to control shortages, protect public safety and national security, and en-force foreign policy. To protect public safety, for ex-ample, the United States, like most other nations, does not permit certain plants and foods to be brought into the country. As a matter of foreign poli-cy, it does not permit its citizens to trade with Cuba.

Even if these reasons vanished tomorrow, gov-ernment officials would still track goods entering and leaving their countries if only for economic reasons. To track goods coming into the country, the United States requires import licenses. Before exporting goods to any part of the world, a U.S. exporter must make sure that this country permits trade with the country or region under consideration. To do this, the exporter must ask and answer three questions:

1. What is the destination of the goods?
2. What is the product or service being exported?
3. Do any special restrictions apply?

After answering these questions, the exporter knows whether the goods can be exported at all, as well as whether they are subject to any special conditions.[1]

Generally, two kinds of export licenses are required by the United States. An **export license** is a general decree permitting the export of general categories of goods to specific destinations. A **validated license** is issued to individuals on a case by case basis for a single transaction or a specific time period. You may think of an export license as being a sort of passport for merchandise and a validated license as being like a visa.

The Department of Commerce assists exporters in determining which kind of license applies to their export operation. If goods can be exported under a general export license, the exporter need do nothing else to export goods. If a validated license is required, the exporter must apply for it to the Department of Commerce.

In addition to a validated license, supporting documents also are sometimes required. The most common supporting document is a Statement of Ultimate Consignor and Purchaser, certifying that the importer will not resell the goods except as permitted under the export license. The exporter is responsible for the accuracy of this and any other supporting documents.

Apart from the export documents required by the United States, exporters must also comply with requirements for documents by other countries, specifically, the country they are exporting into.

TRANSPORTATION DOCUMENTS

Transportation documents are used to identify the importer and exporter, name the carrier on which the exported goods travel, and show the freight costs, which in turn, will add to the overall cost of the exported merchandise.

Three kinds of transportation documents are used, depending on the mode of transportation.

They are generally referred to as bills of lading, *lading* being a word that means "cargo" or "freight." An **air waybill** is used for air transport, the most common method of moving fashion products, and an **ocean bill of lading** is used when cargo is moved by ship. An **inland bill of lading** is a receipt for imported goods transported from a port of entry to a destination somewhere within a country.

A bill of lading is also the contract between the exporter and the carrier. It specifies such details as the exporter, the importer, the loading port, the unloading port, freight cost, vessel name (if sent by ship), and kind of cargo.

A bill of lading is always signed after the goods are loaded onto the carrier. This is one of the steps that initiates the payment process. An unsigned bill of lading can never be used to claim payment because the buyer would have no proof that the exporter had actually begun to transport the goods.

Ocean and inland bills of lading transfer title to the goods from the exporter to the importer. An air waybill is never used to transfer title because air freight travels faster than the original bill, so it would not be received in time to be used for the title transfer.

PACKING AND HANDLING DOCUMENTS

Apart from any personal interest exporters have in carefully packing goods and marking their exported products so they arrive in good shape, exporters must also comply with a system of labeling and handling instructions that help to move products successfully around the world.

To understand why these rules must be used, just consider what is involved when a company called Uncommon Scents decides to move a shipment of perfume from southern France to Chicago, Illinois. What needs to be written on the outside so that the perfume bottles are not crushed and broken? How many crates of perfume should Uncommon Scents be expecting? How do cargo loaders know how many crates there are in any one shipment so they can keep the shipment together? How do cargo handlers know where to move the perfume, as it travels through several countries, ports, and across thousands of miles inland? All this information is answered by the packing and handling documents.

Before packing can begin, the exporter must decide on the safest and most secure way to move the products. Clothing can be shipped on hangers, for example, and importers consider this a benefit, but the garments shipped this way will take up more space and cost more to transport. Exporters can save freight costs by shipping clothes folded, and even

Form 35-643 Printed and Sold by *UNZ&CO* 190 Baldwin Ave., Jersey City, NJ 07306 • (800) 631-3098 • (201) 795-5400

STRAIGHT BILL OF LADING—SHORT FORM—ORIGINAL—NOT NEGOTIABLE

RECEIVED, subject to the classifications and tariffs in effect on the date of the issue of this Bill of Lading, the property described above in apparent good order, except as noted (contents and condition of contents of packages unknown), marked, consigned, and destined as indicated above which said carrier (the word carrier being understood throughout this contract as meaning any person or corporation in possession of the property under the contract) agrees to carry to its usual place of delivery at said destination, if on its route, otherwise to deliver to another carrier on the route to said destination. It is mutually agreed as to each carrier of all or any of said property over all or any portion of said route to destination and as to each party at any time interested in all or any said property, that every service to be performed hereunder shall be subject to all the bill of lading terms and conditions in the governing classification on the date of shipment.

Shipper hereby certifies that he is familiar with all the bill of lading terms and conditions in the governing classification and the said terms and conditions are hereby agreed to by the shipper and accepted for himself and his assigns.

From _____

At _____ 19 ___ DESIGNATE WITH AN (X) BY TRUCK ☐ FREIGHT ☐ Shipper's No. _____

Carrier _____ Agent's No. _____

(Mail or street address of consignee—For purposes of notification only.)

Consigned to _____

Destination _____ State of _____ County of _____

Route _____

Delivering Carrier _____ Vehicle or Car Initial _____ No. _____

No. Packages	Kind of Package, Description of Articles, Special Marks, and Exceptions	*Weight (Sub. to Cor.)	Class or Rate	Check Column	
					Subject to Section 7 of conditions of applicable bill of lading, if this shipment is to be delivered to the consignee without recourse on the consignor, the consignor shall sign the following statement:
					The carrier shall not make delivery of this shipment without payment of freight and all other lawful charges.
					Per _____ (Signature of Consignor.)
					If charges are to be prepaid, write or stamp here, "To be Prepaid."
					Received $ _____ to apply in prepayment of the charges on the property described hereon.
					Agent or Cashier
					Per _____ (The signature here acknowledges only the amount prepaid.)
					Charges Advanced:

C.O.D. SHIPMENT

Prepaid ☐
Collect ☐ $ _____
Collection Fee _____
Total Charges _____

*If the shipment moves between two ports by a carrier by water, the law requires that the bill of lading shall state whether it is "Carrier's or Shipper's weight."

†Shipper's imprint in lieu of stamp; not a part of bill of lading approved by the Department of Transportation.

NOTE—Where the rate is dependent on value, shippers are required to state specifically in writing the agreed or declared value of the property.

THIS SHIPMENT IS CORRECTLY DESCRIBED. CORRECT WEIGHT IS

_____ LBS.

Subject to verification by the Respective Weighing and Inspection Bureau According to Agreement.

Per _____

TOTAL PIECES |

†"The fibre containers used for this shipment conform to the specifications set forth in the box maker's certificate thereon, and all other requirements of Rule 41 of the Uniform Freight Classification and Rule 5 of the National Motor Freight Classification." †Shipper's imprint in lieu of stamp, not a part of bill of lading approved by the Interstate Commerce Commission.

If lower charges result, the agreed or declared value of the within described containers is hereby specifically stated to be not exceeding 50 cents per pound per article.

_____ Shipper, Per _____

_____ Agent, Per _____

Permanent post-office address of shipper

This is to certify that the above-named materials are properly classified, described, packaged, marked and labeled and are in proper condition for transportation according to the applicable regulations of the Department of Transportation.

_____ SIGNATURE

Reprinted by permission of Unz & Co., 190 Baldwin Avenue, Jersey City, NJ 07306.

Copyright © 1989 UNZ & CO.

House Air Waybill Number

Shipper's Name and Address | Shipper's account Number

Not negotiable
Air Waybill
(Air Consignment note)
Issued by

Copies 1, 2 and 3 of this Air Waybill are originals and have the same validity.

Consignee's Name and Address | Consignee's account Number

It is agreed that the goods described herein are accepted in apparent good order and condition (except as noted) for carriage SUBJECT TO THE CONDITIONS OF CONTRACT ON THE REVERSE HEREOF. THE SHIPPER'S ATTENTION IS DRAWN TO THE NOTICE CONCERNING CARRIERS' LIMITATION OF LIABILITY. Shipper may increase such limitation of liability by declaring a higher value for carriage and paying a supplemental charge if required.

These commodities licensed by the United States for ultimate destination

Diversion contrary to

United States law prohibited.

Airport of Departure (Addr. of first Carrier) and requested Routing

to | By first Carrier | Routing and Destination | Air Waybill Number | Currency | CHGS Code | WT/VAL PPD COLL | Other PPD COLL | Declared Value for Carriage | Declared Value for Customs

Airport of Destination | Flight/Date | For Carrier Use only | Flight Date | Amount of Insurance | INSURANCE: If Carrier offers insurance and such insurance is requested in accordance with conditions on reverse hereof, indicate amount to be insured in figures in box marked 'amount of insurance'

Handling Information

No. of Pieces RCP	Gross Weight	kg lb	Rate Class / Commodity Item No.	Chargeable Weight	Rate / Charge	Total	Nature and Quantity of Goods (incl. Dimensions or Volume)

Prepaid | Weight Charge | Collect | Other Charges

Valuation Charge

Tax

Total other Charges Due Agent

Total other Charges Due Carrier

Shipper certifies that the particulars on the face hereof are correct and that insofar as any part of the consignment contains dangerous goods such part is properly described by name and is in proper condition for carriage by air according to the applicable Dangerous Goods Regulations.

Signature of Shipper or his Agent

Total prepaid | Total collect

Currency Conversion Rates | cc charges in Dest. Currency

Executed on (Date) at (Place) Signature of Issuing Carrier or its Agent

House Air Waybill Number

Form 16-810 Printed and Sold by UNZ&CO 190 Baldwin Ave., Jersey City, NJ 07306 • (800) 631-3098 • (201) 795-5400

GLOBAL *GO-GETTERS*

PATRICIA UNDERWOOD: YOU GO TO MY HEAD

Photo: Rick Gillette.

Patricia Underwood manufactures high-fashion hats from her workroom in Manhattan's garment center. It is a small business, producing about 10,000 hats a year. For Ms. Underwood, breaking into Europe is easy. A foreign buyer shopping the U.S. market saw her hats and gave her an order. That was about ten years ago, and today, foreign sales account for 15 percent of her $1 million-plus annual sales.

Twice a year, Underwood goes to the Fashion Accessories Show in Paris, spending one week on each trip. The show, known as the "Premiere Classe" show is sponsored by a private company that sells booth space to exhibitors; among the amenities it provides are translators for those who need them. The show is attended by buyers from around the world and exhibitors are as likely to make a sale to a Tokyo buyer as a buyer from West Germany.

Underwood's business is seasonal, so much of her effort in filling foreign orders is limited to the two weeks she ships abroad. She is very insistent that all orders are shipped on time and to the exact specification of the foreign orders that she received. In the course of a year, she makes several brief trips to Europe to stay in touch with her foreign clients, to shop the foreign competition, to observe first-hand how and why her hats are selling; spending a total of three to four weeks a year on the Continent.

Patricia Underwood's hats sell for $200 to $1300 in better stores in the United States, and, now in the past ten years, in Europe. She finds that sometimes she will have to adjust colorations for her foreign clients, but basically, it is the finest materials and workmanship that she puts into her hats that make them a wanted "finishing touch" by women on both sides of the Atlantic.

Underwood finds that many of her customers are now willing to prepay for their merchandise. This has eliminated the need for a letter of credit. She fills the orders for $2000 to $3000 at a time and it would be very costly to have to pay for a letter of credit for such small amounts. This is a wonderful example of how through interest, perseverance, top-quality merchandise, and personal attention, a very small business can indeed become a "world-class" global business.

Based on Anita Hussey, "Go Global The World is My Oyster," *Executive Female*, September/October 1990, pp. 35–38.

offering a discount to the importer to rehanger them.[2]

Fashion items like perfume, cosmetics, and costume jewelry are traditionally sold in boxes, but an exporter may find it is cheaper to ship the boxes knocked down, that is, folded flat and then put together when received. Because international freight is calculated based on volume as well as weight, all these factors must be evaluated.

Fashion products are also subject to certain kinds of damage that must be considered when transportation is being arranged. Clothing, for example, can be crushed so badly that it is unwearable. Similarly, it can arrive dirty or torn if it is not properly protected in transit, all of which is the exporter's responsibility.

International transport undergoes much more handling than domestic transport does. Most experts suggest that exporters should spend a little extra to pack garments in sealed polyvinyl bags. But even then, an exporter must know a few tricks of the trade to avoid adding unnecessarily to the freight costs. To cite just one example, poly bags should be taped not only to protect the garments but also because the carrier will measure volume from the greatest distance, that is, the full length of an untaped bag. Untaped bags can add 10 to 15 percent to shipping costs.[3]

Once arrangements have been made to ship the fashion products the cheapest and most efficient way, the packing and handling documents that will travel with them must be prepared. The most important document is the **packing list**, an itemized index of the contents of the shipment.

This list is used to find the last package shipped (because it tells how many packages are in the total shipment), to collect insurance for damaged or lost items, and to facilitate the goods' passage through customs.

A customs official can read the packing list, see if the contents match it in one package, and then pass through the remaining boxes. Without properly detailed information, customs inspectors are much more likely to do a full-scale, time-consuming inspection.

Careful labeling is used to back up the packing list. Typically, labeling is done in at least two languages (the language of the importing country and the language of the exporting country), as well as several international signs that are easily read and understood by cargo handlers around the world. Instructions should be written at least four-inches high with a heavy, black waterproof pen.

At minimum, every crate should be labeled with the shipper's mark, the country of origin, the weight (in kilograms and pounds), the number of packages ("one of three" or "two of five," for example), the size of the crates (in inches and centimeters), the ports of exit and entry, and any special instructions for handling. The figure on this page shows the international symbols that are used in international shipping for special handling.

The packing list will be signed at appropriate points along the way—when the goods are loaded, when they are unloaded, when they are transferred from one carrier to another, and before the list is passed along to the buyer, with a copy going to the exporter as well.

LEGAL DOCUMENTS

For legal purposes, several specialized documents are required when goods travel between countries. The first is the **commercial invoice**, a document detailing the terms of sale. Like the domestic invoice, a commercial invoice is a bill for the goods, as well as a description of the order, and it is prepared by the exporter for the importer, who needs it to begin to arrange for payment.

A **consular invoice** may be required by the country to which the goods are being shipped. A means of identifying and controlling goods, it is also sometimes used to determine what the duty will be on the goods.

A consular invoice can be purchased from the consulate of the country involved and must be written in that country's language. Sometimes the commercial invoice is presented to the consular official in charge, who simply stamps it and returns it to the exporter-shipper.

Some nations also require a **certificate of origin.** This document describes where the goods come from. Like the consular invoice, it is used to determine what duty will be due on the goods.

The last legal document is the **shipper's export declaration** (SED), which is a U.S. export document. (Some other countries have comparable documents; others do not.) The SED is used by the Census Bureau to compile trade statistics. Statistics from SEDs are used, for example, to show how many women's scarves are exported from the United States each year.

INSURANCE DOCUMENT

Finally, an insurance document may be required as proof that insurance has been purchased to cover the goods in transit. The purchase of insurance is usually a point to be negotiated between exporter and importer. One document—the insurance certificate—states the type and amount of insurance that has been provided.

Reprinted by permission of Unz & Co., 190 Baldwin Avenue, Jersey City, NJ 07306.

All of the documents previously described are typical of those used to process exported goods. Of great importance to the exporter, this package of papers, when taken together and presented to the proper authorities, initiates the payment process.

GETTING PAID FOR YOUR EXPORTS

Exporters are always eager for timely payment. To trace a typical payment process, from the exporter's point of view, assume that Uncommon Scents, the perfume company discussed earlier, arranged payment through a letter of credit, as is often the case in an international exchange.

Once Uncommon Scents's bank has prepared the letter of credit, it sends this document to a correspondent bank or any bank that La Belle Air Exports designates for confirmation. The letter of credit is next sent, usually by mail, to the exporter, who must review it carefully.

On receiving the letter of credit, La Belle Air Exports will initiate the shipping process. At every step, the exporter will save the documents associated with the shipping process. A signed bill of lading, for example, will be mailed to the exporter after the goods are loaded. When La Belle Air has collected the required documents—typically, the commercial (and sometimes the consular) invoice, the bill of lading, the packing list, the certificate of origin, and the insurance certificate—it will present them to the bank holding the letter of credit for Uncommon Scents. This, in turn, will cause the letter of credit to be executed.

Uncommon Scents's bank will review the documents and if they are in order, issue a check to La Belle Air Exports; but the process is not over yet. The documents are then forwarded to Uncommon Scents, who will use them to claim their imported goods.

TECH TALK

INTERNATIONAL FAXING: YOU'VE COME A LONG WAY, BABY!

Today, fax machines are powerful business tools that can do far more than transmit copies of documents quickly.

Beside the usual features to look for—look for features that are especially good for faxing internationally. These features could include:

1. ACTIVITY REPORTS: Written log of calls made and verification of successful overseas transmission. Because international telecommunications still is not perfect, this feature lets you know if the message was received.
2. BROADCASTING: This feature allows you to send copies of a document to many recipients at one time.
3. DELAYED TRANSMISSION: This allows you to delay transmission until telephone calls are lowest—a big money-saver for international calls.
4. ERROR CORRECTION: This built-in feature retransmits data that may be garbled by a poor telephone connection.
5. MAILBOX RECEPTION: Maintains a mailbox in the fax's memory to store a document for transmission or reception. Only people with the correct address code can have the document printed out. This feature is great to keep designs or measurement documents secret.
6. PORTABILITY: This feature allows you to take the fax with you wherever you travel.
7. VOICE REQUEST: This feature indicates that the operator at the remote fax location wants to talk to you. It saves the cost of a telephone call if you need to fax and speak with someone.

Based on Eric J. Adams, "Must-Have Features for International Faxing," *World Trade*, April 1992, p. 42.

EXECUTING A LETTER OF CREDIT

Although the process sounds simple, a **letter of credit** (L/C), which is a written guarantee that the goods will be paid for, can be troublesome to execute. If the terms of the L/C are not met precisely, right down to correct spellings of names, the bank may be reluctant to honor it. A delay in presenting a letter of credit can result in an invalid L/C. Some banks will not pay if the delivery is made other than on the date specified in the L/C. Furthermore, most banks will pay only if they have received a "clean" bill of lading, which means there must be no irregularities in the shipment (as described in detail in the L/C) or damage to the goods at the time of shipment.

PRODUCT DEVIATIONS IN LETTERS OF CREDIT

Obtaining a "clean" bill of lading is more difficult in the fashion business than in many other businesses because fashion goods, more than other products, do not necessarily arrive in the exact specified colors or quantities. Textiles, in particular, are subject to deviations that simply cannot be avoided.

Generally, banks have learned to expect some deviations from specifications in textiles and apparel and to make some allowances for them. A letter of credit for a fashion purchase often specifies that quantities will vary, therefore, by 2 to 4 percent. Some L/Cs use the term "approximate" to describe expected variations, with "approximate" being interpreted to mean a 10 percent, plus or minus, deviation allowance.

TERMS OF SALE

The difficulty in executing a letter of credit points to the need to use careful sales terms in preparing an invoice, or bill of sale. Sales terms are not to be confused with credit terms. **Credit terms** outline the responsibilities of the buyer to the seller, that is, how payment will be rendered, whether it will be thirty, sixty, or ninety days, net or no discount. In contrast, **sales terms** describe the responsibilities of the seller to the buyer. The terms of sale also specify when, from a legal standpoint, title to the goods changes hands.[4]

In international trade, confusion often arises over where the seller's responsibility for paying for the delivery of the goods ends and the buyer's begins. In the United States, the expression **FOB,** meaning "free on board" or "free to the point of loading," is used when sellers are relieved of responsibility for the cost of transporting goods at their warehouses or factory loading docks.

In the rest of the world, however, the term **EX,** as in *EX mill* or *EX factory,* is used to convey the end of the seller's responsibility at his or her warehouse, mill, or whatever point is specified. Outside the United States, however, FOB is used to indicate that the seller will pay for the delivery of the goods on board a ship or airplane or to an inland point or a port.

Other sales terms that will be new to exporters are **C.I.F.,** which means the seller pays cost, insurance, and freight to a port named by the seller. **C. & F.,** means the seller pays only cost and freight, and the buyer pays for the insurance.

The U.S. Government publishes a booklet *Revised American Foreign Trade Definitions* that describes commonly used sales terms in international trade. However, it was written in 1941, and since then, as might be expected, some terms have evolved into new meanings. The best solution is for those involved in a foreign sale to be sure they understand what each party means by any sales terms that are used to describe their specific transaction.

TERMS OF CREDIT: THE EXPORTER'S VIEW

The no-risk way for a seller to get paid is to demand cash in advance. The next least risky method of payment collection is a letter of credit, followed, in ascending order of risk, by documentary drafts, open account, and consignment.

CASH IN ADVANCE

Sellers would always like to insist on cash in advance because there are no collection problems, but few buyers can afford to accept this term of credit beyond the initial sale. The buyer is left unprotected should the seller not deliver and, more important, will almost certainly find his or her cash flow affected by a demand for cash in advance. However, partial payment in advance may be required, especially for new customers.

LETTERS OF CREDIT

A letter of credit also carries with it certain risks, some of which exporters can lessen further by taking a few extra steps to protect themselves. For one thing, a L/C should always be irrevocable so the

© Copyright 1990 UNZ & CO.

Date: _____

TO

LETTER OF CREDIT INSTRUCTIONS

FROM

NAME		
COMPANY		
ADDRESS		
CITY	STATE	ZIP CODE
TELEPHONE	TELEX	

GENTLEMEN:

Following are the particular details we wish to have included in your documentary Letter of Credit, issued in reply to our Pro Forma invoice number _____ dated _____.

Please instruct your bank to open and issue this credit, by telecommunication or by mail, in accordance with the following terms and subject to the Uniform Customs and Practices for Documentary Credits, International Chamber of Commerce Publication 400 (revision currently in force).

We have made every effort in these instructions to provide you with terms which can be easily accommodated. If you or your bank are unable to comply with these terms and conditions, please consult with our offices prior to the issuance of the credit to avoid delay or non-shipment. Thank you for your cooperation.

1. The Letter of Credit shall be irrevocable.

2. The credit shall be ☐ advised by _____
   ☐ confirmed by _____

3. The credit shall be payable at the counters of _____

4. The credit shall show as the beneficiary _____

5. The credit shall be payable in _____, in the amount ☐ not to exceed _____.
   (currency) ☐ exactly _____.
   ☐ about _____.

6. The credit shall be payable ☐ at sight
   ☐ _____ days sight   upon presentation at the counters of the bank stated in item #3 above.
   ☐ _____ days from _____ Date

7. The Letter of Credit ☐ shall / ☐ shall not be transferrable.

8. The credit shall show that all banking charges incurred ☐ inside / ☐ outside the beneficiary's country are for the account of the applicant.

9. The credit shall show that all charges for amendments to the credit, including related communications expenses, are for the account of ☐ applicant. / ☐ beneficiary.

10. Partial shipments ☐ shall be allowed. / ☐ shall not be allowed.

11. Transshipments ☐ shall be allowed. / ☐ shall not be allowed.

12. The credit shall allow for required transport documents dated
    ☐ No later than _____.
    ☐ No later than _____ days from the advising bank's issuance of written notice to the beneficiary.

13. The credit shall allow for a minimum of _____ days after the required transport document date for presentation of documents at the counters of the bank stated in item #3.

14. The required documents should include:
    ☐ Commercial Invoice Totaled ☐ F.O.B. ☐ C. & F. _____
    ☐ F.A.S. ☐ C.I.F. (named point)
    ☐ Commercial invoice shall cover ☐ Pro Forma invoice # _____ or
    ☐ the following:

    ☐ Packing list for above
    ☐ Insurance certificate showing insurance/policy provided by seller in the amount of _____.
    ☐ Ocean Bill of Lading
    ☐ The credit ☐ shall / ☐ shall not allow for NVOCC bills of lading.
    ☐ The Bill of Lading shall be consigned ☐ to _____.
    ☐ to the order of _____.
    ☐ The Bill of Lading ☐ shall / ☐ need not be marked on board.
    ☐ Air Waybill consigned to _____
    _____
    ☐ The credit ☐ shall / ☐ shall not allow for air consolidators Airway Bills.
    ☐ The transport document shall be marked freight ☐ prepaid / ☐ collect
    ☐ Inland straight bill of lading consigned to _____
    ☐ Any shipping documents required shall show as the origin _____ and as the destination _____
    ☐ Other required documents: _____

15. If designated, the forwarder shall be shown as _____

16. If designated, the carrier shall be shown as _____

17. Special instructions:

Form 10-015 Printed and Sold by *UNZCO* 190 Baldwin Ave., Jersey City, NJ 07306 • (800) 631-3098 • (201) 795-5400

A Letter of Credit insurance form. *Reprinted by permission of Unz. & Co., 190 Baldwin Avenue, Jersey City, NJ 07306.*

importer cannot have a change of mind and stop payment.

CONFIRMED LETTER OF CREDIT Another question that always comes up with a letter of credit is whether it should be confirmed. One problem with letters of credit is that they are only as reliable as the bank on which they are written. If a country is going through political instability, its banks may not be able to make good on letters of credit.

Exporters can avoid this problem by requesting a **confirmed letter of credit**, which means that a bank in the exporter's country guarantees payment. An unconfirmed letter of credit is guaranteed only by the issuing bank. Confirmed letters of credit involve an extra expense, and the exporter who insists on one usually has to pay for it.

Finally, exporters can protect themselves against some of the predictable problems associated with executing a letter of credit by building in a longer delivery schedule than they might otherwise want.

DOCUMENTARY DRAFTS

In the United States, the usual terms of credit are COD or open account. A variety of drafts, or bills of exchange, are used in place of these terms in international trade.

SIGHT DRAFT A **sight draft** is a bill for immediate payment, the equivalent of a COD in the United States. The seller retains title until the goods reach their destination. To execute a sight draft, the docu-

mentation is sent to the buyer's bank, along with the sight draft. The bank informs the buyer of its receipt, pays the sight draft, and forwards the documents to the buyer so the goods can be claimed.

A sight draft is risky if the buyer changes his or her mind or if the policies of a country regarding imports change while the goods are in transit. The buyer cannot or will not take custody and will not want to pay for the goods, either. Shipping them back to their point of origin may be too costly to be worthwhile to the exporter. Often, such goods are destroyed, and the seller-exporter is out the money spent on shipping.[5]

TIME DRAFT A **time draft** is a bill of exchange that specifies a number of days within which payment is due. It is most like a bill for an open account. Once a buyer signs a time draft, he or she is obligated to pay on time. A time draft is a way for an exporter to extend credit to an importer. It is also negotiable. Exporters often sell them to international factors for immediate payment. When a time draft is used, the exporter officially holds title until the bill is paid.[6]

NOTE DRAFT A **note draft** is the third commonly used bill of exchange. This note designates a specific date on which payment is due. The exporter holds title until the bill is paid.[7]

OPEN ACCOUNT

Open account, a widespread practice among U.S. fashion producers, is used less often internationally,

GLOBAL GLIMPSES
UNTYING TIED AID

If some U.S. exporters are losing sales to a foreign competitor whose government is giving out economic aid tied to purchases from the donor country . . . the Export-Import Bank wants to know. Congress has given EXIM a $500 million war chest to match such offers and help U.S. goods win the sales.

Under the auspices of the Organization for Economic Cooperation and Development (OECD), the developed nations recently agreed to new limits on so-called tied aid. The arrangement does not apply to outright grants for a whole project but comes into play when a developed country offers loans at below market rate (or a package of grants and subsidized loans) and "ties" the assistance to buying from the donor country. Such deals are forbidden to countries with a per capita over $2465, measured in 1990 dollars.

However, the OECD agreement allows developed countries below the cut-off to tie cheap loans to purchases, but only on projects that look strong enough to generate the income to cover their own operating costs and pay off the loans.

EXIM says that it will get notice of loans planned by other countries and challenge those where the project's economic viability is doubtful. If the donor country will not back off, EXIM will tap the war chest to match the offer; but policing the agreement depends on help from U.S. exporters. EXIM hopes to hear from exporters who face problems in Third World markets because their competitors suggest their governments can provide concessional financing. "We want them to come to us as soon as they hear rumors that a competitor is using tied aid," says the head of EXIM.

You can report lost sales to Executive Vice-President, EXIM, 811 Vermont Avenue, N.W., Washington DC 20571.

Based on "Washington Report," *International Business*, March 1992, p. 78.

largely because it ties up the exporter's money for too long a time. Considering that time already must be added to the payment schedule to compensate for shipping and that international mail takes still more time, most exporters are disinclined to further stretch out the payment schedule with an open account.

When an open account is used, it is invariably reserved for an old and trusted customer. Few exporters would risk one with a new, unknown client. As with a documentary draft, title changes hands when the bill is paid.

CONSIGNMENT

Consignment works the same way in international trade as in the United States. The goods are shipped by the exporter to the importer. The exporter holds title on the goods until they are sold, and in turn, the importer does not have to pay the exporter until then.

This is perhaps the riskiest method of payment because the goods are usually thousands of miles away from the exporter, who cannot see if they are well displayed or allowed to gather dust in a back room. Also, because the goods are held for a relatively long time and payment is drawn out, the risk is greater than in other exchanges that a political up-

heaval may intervene before a sale is completed. At minimum, an exporter should never offer consignment as a term of credit without thoroughly checking the credit of the importer.

TARIFF AND NONTARIFF BARRIERS TO EXPORTING

Exporters must also concern themselves with tariffs levied by any country into which they plan to import goods. A **tariff,** also called a duty, is in essence a barrier to trade that the exporter must constantly take under consideration. Tariffs pit one country's products against those of another, and for the individual exporter, a tariff can make it unprofitable to import into certain countries.

Although negotiations have been under way among various nations to reduce tariffs, many of the world's nations still impose them on fashion imports. Tariffs are widely applied to fibers, fabrics, yarns, cosmetics, and clothing. In most countries, clothing tariffs are higher than textile tariffs. Tariffs should not be confused with quotas, which block the importation of certain items altogether or severely limit their numbers.

In recent years, the U.S. fashion industry has repeatedly applied pressure on Congress and international trade groups to maintain tariffs on fashion imports. They have generally been successful in their efforts, for although tariffs have been reduced on many products, they have been reduced to only a limited extent on textiles and apparel.[8] U.S. clothing tariffs are generally high when compared with those of other nations.[9]

Tariffs do make prices on imported goods more competitive with prices for domestic goods. Consider this example: China, observing that baseball caps have become popular fashion accessories in the United States, may decide to flood the United States with hundreds of thousands of its cheap caps, made and sold for far less than U.S.-made caps. Undoubtedly, this would cause U.S. cap manufacturers to protest the admission of so many cheap hats on grounds that they hurt the American hat industry. So, if the government wants to protect U.S. hat manufacturers and keep its domestic profits high, one way to do so is to impose a trade barrier—such as a tariff—on the Chinese hats. A tariff will bring the price of the Chinese caps more in line with those of the U.S. manufacturers and, often, make it even higher than domestic goods.

Despite their widespread use, tariffs have not generally deterred imports anywhere in the world. When customers want to buy imported goods, they do not seem to care when they must sometimes pay more for them.

KINDS OF TARIFFS

Exporters generally encounter two kinds of tariffs. **Specific tariffs** involve a per-unit charge. These are intended to raise revenues for governments. **Ad valorem** tariffs are a percentage of the purchase price, and they are intended to protect domestic products from cheap imports.

NONTARIFF BARRIERS

Some nontariff barriers impede fashion trade, although this is not always the intent of the governments when they establish these regulations. For example, labeling requirements, anticounterfeiting restrictions, and flammability regulations all work to keep many exporters from selling their products in the United States.

Another example of a nontariff barrier occurs when some national governments demand that some part of a product be made in their country before the goods will be accepted for importation.

Other nontariff barriers are impossible to measure but their effects are widely felt. Exporting to Japan, for example, is hard because Japanese-run cartels control distribution of many products. These cartels make importation a trying if not impossible process. Social, cultural, and even economic factors may act as unwitting restrictive barriers. However, eager U.S. exporters in 1992 were to take their fashion products to Russia, for example, where they were

GLOBAL *Goodies*

THE NEW TIGER CUBS

By now, most American companies are aware of the economic success of the Asia-Pacific's Four Tigers—Hong Kong, Singapore, South Korea, and Taiwan. In many industries, they are approaching the industrial sophistication of Japan, Western Europe, and the United States. At the same time, the achievements of a new group of up-and-coming Asia-Pacific nations mirror the way the Four Tigers took over Japan's heavy industries in the 1970s and 1980s. Just as Japan built offshore manufacturing sites in the Four Tigers to sidestep the high domestic wages created by its industrial successes, so too are the Taiwanese and Korean companies relocating labor-and-capital-intensive operations to the region's less developed countries, Indonesia, Malaysia, the Philippines, and Thailand.

The primary reasons for migration are that, as in Japan, wages and living standards in the Four Tigers have risen to such a level that countries are losing their competitive edge. In Hong Kong and Singapore, there is simply too little land and infrastructure to accommodate more heavy manufacturing facilities.

Aside from solo trade and investment opportunities, U.S. companies are likely to get involved with Japanese and Four Tigers firms in manufacturing joint ventures located in the LDCs. And as the standard of living in these countries rises, they will become insatiable consumer markets for products made worldwide.

Based on "Asia Pacific's New Tigers," Special Report, *Export Today*, November/December 1991, p. 18.

much in demand. The dire straits of the economy there, as it switched from a centrally planned to a market-oriented economy, made this a largely impossible task, at least for the smaller exporter who could not afford such a high-risk venture.

Conversely, of course, high consumer demand sometimes works to break down nontariff—and even tariff—barriers. For example, the Japanese may not want to buy American cars, but they are intensely interested in "antique" blue jeans, often spending as much as $2000 per pair for jeans with original pre-1970 rivets. So far, no cultural, social, or economic barrier has been enough to stop this craving.

FREIGHT FORWARDERS

If everything involved in carrying out an international sale still seems mind-boggling, there is a two-word solution to this, too, and the solution is called a **freight forwarder.** This is an expert who assists exporters with all the details of processing their goods.

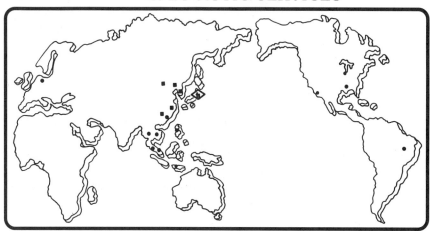

Although freight forwarders may handle many aspects of the exporting process, their primary expertise is in shipping. *Courtesy of Sankyu USA, Inc.*

Freight forwarders help with the documentation and can provide advice on payment terms and financing. International freight forwarders' real expertise, however, is shipping. They know the customs, duties, and procedures for the world's two-hundred-plus nations. Just buying the books that are required to locate ocean and air schedules would cost an exporter several hundred dollars annually. Freight forwarders not only have the books, but they are experts in tracking down the best and least expensive routes. In short, freight forwarders save time, money, and red tape.

One of the biggest advantages of using a freight forwarder, however, is that person's expertise in languages. Most of the documents that must be filled out during the export process must be in the language of the importing country, and as you can well imagine, a misspelling can spell disaster as can a misunderstanding about trade terms. Freight forwarders know the languages of the countries in which they work, and they serve as valuable cultural and social interpreters, as well, in matters regarding financing and shipping.

Many forwarders specialize in either air or ocean travel. Regardless of the specialty, an exporter can expect a freight forwarder to perform the following tasks:[10]

1. All phases of shipping, including transferring, documenting, and dispatching goods.
2. Detailing of best travel routes.
3. Meeting conditions for ports of entry around the world plus execution of consular documents.
4. Assisting in packing and labeling.
5. Assisting in arranging inland transportation.
6. Assisting with customs clearance.
7. Consolidating of the small shipments that are common in the fashion industry.

Freight forwarders shop for the most competitive prices for their clients. They charge a handling fee for their services. In short, like travel agents, they handle the trip from door to door and make sure it all goes smoothly.

Finally, just because an exporter can turn over many of the export-processing functions to an expert freight forwarder does not mean that the exporter does not need to understand the process. Without a basic understanding of the process, as presented in this chapter, the exporter, even one with the world's best freight forwarder, will always be operating at a disadvantage.

ENDNOTES

1. *A Basic Guide to Exporting*, U.S. Department of Commerce, International Trade Administration, U.S. and Foreign Commercial Service, September 1986, p. 52.
2. Irving Vigdor, *Exporting: Get Into It*, Merrick, NY: Redwood Associates, p. 149.
3. *Ibid.*, p. 150.
4. *Ibid.*, p. 87.
5. *Basic Guide to Exporting*, p. 72.
6. *Ibid.*, p. 52.
7. *Ibid.*, p. 52.
8. *Ibid.*, p. 57.
9. R. Dardis and K. Cooke, "The Impact of Trade Restrictions on U.S. Apparel Consumers," *Journal of Consumer Policy*, 7, 1–12, 1984.
10. FIT, *Import Buying*, unpublished pamphlet, p. 3.

VOCABULARY   ad valorem tariff   _____

_____

_____

air waybill

_____

_____

_____

C. & F.

_____

_____

_____

certificate of origin

_____

_____

_____

C.I.F.

_____

_____

_____

commercial invoice

_____

_____

_____

confirmed letter of
credit

_____

_____

_____

consignment

_____

_____

_____

consular invoice

_____

_____

_____

credit terms

_____

_____

_____

EX

_____

_____

_____

export license

_____

_____

_____

FOB

_____

_____

_____

freight forwarder

_____

_____

_____

inland bill of lading

_____

_____

_____

letter of credit (L/C)

_____

_____

_____

note draft

_____

_____

_____

ocean bill of lading

_____

_____

_____

packing list

_____

_____

_____

sales terms

_____

_____

_____

shipper's export
declaration

_____

_____

_____

sight draft

_____

_____

_____

specific tariff   _____

_____

_____

tariff   _____

_____

_____

time draft   _____

_____

_____

validated license   _____

_____

_____

GLOBAL REVIEW

1. Name some of the reasons why the extensive documentation and paperwork involved in export sales are helpful to exporters.

2. What are the five general categories of documentation for exporting?

3. Explain the need for export licenses and name the two types of export licenses.

4. What are the three kinds of transportation documents used as bills of lading?

_____

_____

_____

5. Both packing and handling documents are very important. What is the *major* benefit of the packing list?

_____

_____

_____

_____

6. What are the legal ramifications of the shipping export declaration (SED)?

_____

_____

_____

_____

7. Explain the pluses and minuses of a letter of credit to a small fashion exporter.

_____

_____

_____

_____

8. Trade barriers are used by many governments to limit imports into their countries. What are the two kinds of tariffs used as trade barriers?

_____

_____

_____

_____

9. Explain the duties of a freight forwarder.

_____

_____

_____

_____

10. Why should exporters understand all the steps needed to process an order even though they use a freight forwarder?

_____

_____

_____

_____

GLOBAL DIGEST

1. Extensive documentation is required in processing international sales. Prepare the information that might be required to process packing and handling documents for an order of two-piece ladies dresses that are to be shipped on hangers.

_____

_____

_____

_____

_____

_____

_____

2. Nontariff barriers are used worldwide. Name ten (10) such types of nontariff barriers and explain how each would affect the chances of a fashion product becoming a successful international item.

_____

_____

_____

_____

_____

_____

_____

3. What are the factors to be considered when making the decision about how to ship? Give reasons and types of products that are best shipped by either . . . air, land, sea.

_____

_____

_____

_____

_____

_____

CHAPTER 10

The World is Your Market

The U.S. exporters who rode the coattails of the export bóom in the 1970s and 1980s mostly operated by the seat of their pants. Many had started domestic businesses without any thought that they would ever compete in an international market. But then, suddenly, they had no choice. The world was becoming a global market, and those who wanted to survive were forced to try to sell their products in it. They did the best they could.

There is a difference, however, between surviving and thriving. The next generation can—and will be expected to—operate with more substance and more style than past exporters have. For one thing, the coming generation of exporters will be the first to have actually trained to work in the international marketplace.

PREPARING YOURSELF FOR INTERNATIONAL BUSINESS

Even today, many people who should be participating in the global market avoid it because they do not feel prepared to cope with it or, worse still, they plunge ahead in a blundering fashion that leaves everyone—themselves and their customers—feeling a little bruised and alienated. This is a situation that can, with a little work and special preparation, be avoided. It is possible to prepare yourself for entering the international marketplace in such as way as to ensure that you will begin the new endeavor feeling confident and self-assured.

Three of the most important ways to prepare yourself to conduct business in another country are taking courses to learn about the people, the culture, and the business practices; studying the language; and reading on your own.

TAKING COURSES IN INTERNATIONAL BUSINESS

Even people who have studied their own domestic business need to learn how to conduct business in a new culture. It goes without saying that you should also know a lot about your own business, because you may find yourself teaching it to someone from another country and culture, who speaks a different language.

The best way to learn about business practices in other cultures is to take specialized courses designed to teach you this. The Fashion Institute of Tech-

GLOBAL *GO-GETTERS*

GREG BARDIN AND JOHN GOLDSBERRY: BULA WEAR

Some people call it the American disease, the SITS syndrome: "Stay in the States." However, this mindset is changing and on the eve of the twenty-first century, U.S. manufacturers need new customers and exports are building.

This new thinking is uppermost in the minds of the owners of Bula Wear, a Colorado-based maker of colorful t-shirts, headgear, and beach bags selling under the brand name Bula Wear . . . whose products are marketed almost everywhere around the world.

Bula Wear, started in 1983, happened almost by accident. The owners, Greg Bardin and John Goldsberry, were members of the 1983 U.S. ski team training group. Their destination was New Zealand for winter skiing during the Northern Hemisphere summer, but there was no snow there; they decided to vacation in Fiji, and the rest is history.

"Made in the U.S.A." is the compelling effort for Bula Wear, because to their customers "Made in the U.S.A." implies a quality standard that is helping them to sell overseas. They are staking their future expansions on export sales.

Bardin and Goldsberry believe that you must maintain your sensitivity toward each market and monitor the distribution network constantly. They also emphasize the importance of recognizing the cultural differences between countries.

Bula Wear was conceived with a global approach because it targets the upper reaches of the sportswear market. It intends to remain a niche player. As they strive toward their goal of remaining a top-of-the-line marketer, Bardin and Goldsberry want to place their products in upscale specialty shops all over the world.

Based on Daniel J. McConville, "Growing Global," *World Trade*, October 1991, pp. 40–48.

Courtesy of Greg Bardin and John Goldsberry.

nology, part of the State University of New York, runs seminars on conducting business with the Japanese, as do Asian institutes around the country. Trade associations and the Chamber of Commerce have become increasingly attuned to the need to teach Americans about other cultures and now offer courses and seminars of the type needed to enter the international arena.

STUDYING THE LANGUAGE

Do you have to know a foreign language to operate a business in a foreign country? This question has been debated since the 1970s when Americans stepped up their exporting and found themselves in the midst of an import boom, both of which increased their contact with foreigners by several hundred percent.

Many experts will tell would-be international entrepreneurs that they do not have to speak the language—and technically, they are right. You can certainly buy the services of an interpreter anywhere in the world. And around the world, many people speak English, which is truly the language of international business.

But think for a moment about a trip that President George Bush made to Japan in early 1992. The purpose of the trip was to round up business, and to this end, the president was accompanied by about twenty U.S. business leaders. The most striking images from that trip were the exchanges between the Japanese and American businesspeople, which made it blatantly clear to the world that, between two countries that desperately needed to do business with each other and were having trouble doing so, there was no common language. When an interpreter was not needed, almost without exception, it was because the Japanese spoke English. And the person who speaks another's language always has an edge.

So the question is not whether you can start a business in another part of the world without speaking a foreign language, but whether you would really want to. In the 1990s, Americans will be honing their skills so they can compete more effectively in new foreign markets, and one of the skills that the new generation of exporters should bring to the job is an ability to speak the other languages.

READING ABOUT OTHER CULTURES

Much can be learned about other cultures from reading about them, and you can do a considerable amount of this kind of study on your own. Many books are now published about how other people live, how they conduct business, their social customs, their taboos.

Although speaking a foreign language can be a real asset in the global fashion market, companies such as Wordnet provide translation services that allow businesses to compete internationally with the ability to deal with any country in practically any language. *Courtesy of Lee Chadeayne, Wordnet, Inc.*

Don't overlook the most popular category of reading—travel books. They contain a wealth of facts and specialized data for anyone planning to visit another country. When your host and potential business partner mentions a mountain range, a shrine, or

GLOBAL *Goodies*
GLOBAL TOASTS

Here are some common global toasts that will please your foreign hosts.

RUSSIA: "Gomar Jost" (bottoms up) or "Na Zdorovye" (to your health).

JAPAN: "Kampai" (to your health and happiness).

AUSTRALIA: "Cheers, mate" is a well-accepted toast.

ENGLAND: A good toast for the British is "Gentlemen, the Queen."

FRANCE: "A votre santé" (to your health) is a toast of choice.

ITALY: Informal toasts include "cin-cin" (clink clink) and "salute" (to your health).

---

a well-known waterfall, it is nice—and flattering—to be able to say, "Oh, yes, I read about that. It sounds fantastic."

We are flattered when people take the time to find out things about us, and this kind of flattery can also take us a long way when we are trying to build business around the world.

COMMUNICATING IN INTERNATIONAL BUSINESS

We learn about other cultures for one important reason, so we can communicate with them. Before we can communicate with someone socially, we must be able to communicate with them physically.

In years past, one of the biggest problems in conducting business abroad was the inability to communicate quickly and clearly. Fifteen years ago, it was impossible to telephone some parts of the world. Modern communications systems have vastly improved to the point where, today, you can fire off an order for children's clothing from Kewanee, Illinois, to Siena, Italy, and obtain confirmation of your order within minutes. A sample could be airfreighted to you within a day. All this has been made possible, in large part, by advances in modern communications.

COMMUNICATING BY TELEPHONE

It is now possible to direct-dial almost any place in the world. In larger countries, cities have area codes, and all countries have been assigned country codes. Information on dialing internationally is available in the telephone directory. If further assistance is needed, including information about a telephone number, call an overseas operator who can also put you through to information in any part of the world.

COMMUNICATING BY TELEX

Telex is a communication method that has been around for several decades. Because of the way it operates, it is often called "written telephone." You can send a message and get a response back immediately if you need to. Telex machines also have a feature that lets the users know whether they have gotten through to the right number.

When using a telex, the sender types a message on a special tape, which can be previewed before sending. The tape is then sent to the recipient, who answers in the same way. Telex provides both parties with a written record of all transmissions, something the telephone does not do.

Telex equipment can be purchased or leased from any major communications company—Western Union or RCA Communications, for example.

COMMUNICATING BY FAX

A **FAX** (short for facsimile) machine makes a copy of your transmission and sends the copy electronically over the telephone wires into another FAX machine. A FAX machine also provides a record that a message was sent and received.

FAX machines are replacing telexes in large offices, as well as making their way into small offices—as they are smaller and less expensive than telex machines.

To FAX a message, input the FAX telephone number of the recipient on the telephone part of your equipment. Then insert the page or pages with your message into the FAX machine. The copy will pass through the machine and be returned to you with the information that the message was transmitted. A response message is received in written form.

With telephone calls the primary means of conducting business in a global economy, communications companies such as Sprint frequently offer deep discounts to businesses willing to commit to the use of their services. *Courtesy of Sprint, L.P.*

COMMUNICATING BY COURIER SERVICE

Because everything moves quickly in the fashion industry, courier services are often used when more than words are being transmitted. Color samples, textiles, even clothing samples are often sent by courier services like Federal Express and United Parcel Service.

Make sure any courier service you use delivers directly to the recipient and does not leave the package with anyone else or, worse, deliver it to an overseas terminal where your client will have to go to claim it. A courier service is one of the more expensive ways to communicate, and you should be sure you get first-rate service.

Most fashion producers maintain an open account with a courier service, so that it will always be on call when needed.

Fax services have made business communications in the fashion industry faster and easier than ever before. Important documents and designs as well as routine correspondence can now be transported across the country or across the world in less time than it takes to fill out a postal receipt. *Courtesy of AT&T and Young & Rubicam.*

COMMUNICATING BY MAIL

Because it takes so long, the international fashion business rarely communicates by regular mail unless an importer specifically requests that something be sent this way. When time is not of the essence, fashion producers do occasionally use the mail. The U.S. mail is one of the least expensive ways to ship. Private mail services charge 20 to 50 percent more than the U.S. mail service.

SOCIAL COMMUNICATION IN INTERNATIONAL BUSINESS

Physical communication is not the only kind of connection that matters. It is also important to be able to communicate with others by understanding their culture and customs. This is called **social communication.**

TECH TALK

CAT-CAN: WE CAN DO IT WITH COMPUTER-AIDED TRANSLATION

An increasing number of companies faced with a growing need for translation have moved toward computer-aided translation. This machine translation has been available for a number of years but has had some severe problems and was only available on a mainframe.

Now common on PCs, computer-aided translation programs are currently being used by many international companies. The programs are best used when integrated as part of the translation process. Although translation computers do not always get "the hang" of the correct or elegant use of the language, for technical and industry-specific documentation, the results are good.

Finding the right software program is the difficult part. The catchall phrase "computer-aided translation" includes everything from entry-level programs under $100 to powerful mainframe-only programs costing thousands a month to run. Even professional translators are jumping on the bandwagon and using software to speed their work. Consider that human translation can cost up to $75 a page compared with the cost of human postediting a computer-aided translation at about $10 a page.

Translation software has come a long way from even a few years ago. There is good reason to believe that it will get better. The total market for language translation is currently $100 billion and growing at a 20 percent compound annual rate, according to the European Community. A scarcity of translators qualified to translate more technical and industry-specific documents has companies looking for other solutions. Having hurdled some severe problems, translation software is winning converts—even among professional translators.

Based on Eric J. Adams, "Come Again?," *World Trade*, April 1992, pp. 44–46.

Around the world, people have different social customs and habits. If you have ever watched tourists struggling to get along in the United States, you will understand the nature of the problem. The tourists may not know that people in your community line up to buy groceries or board a bus, and so they may step in line ahead of others and thus appear rude. They may be louder than Americans or so quiet they cannot make their needs known. They may wear the wrong clothes, for example, or use offensive table manners without realizing it.

Just as we often do not show much sympathy when people come here and try to move through our world without understanding it, we cannot expect to receive much sympathy when we try to move in someone else's world without first acquainting ourselves with it. International entrepreneurs have no choice—and some would say, no excuse—but to try to fit in as much as is possible in whatever culture they are visiting.

The old adage "When in Rome, do as the Romans do" is true for any exporter, but is especially true for a fashion exporter. After all, how can you hope to sell a product as highly individualized as American fashion if you yourself are not a good representative of the product?

Finally, it may be of some consolation for all the work that is involved in learning how others live to realize that the reverse is also true: When foreigners come to the United States, they must learn our ways if they hope to sell us their products and services.

There is hardly an area of our lives that does not vary from culture to culture. For example:

- Our dining customs, even the foods we eat. Breakfast around the world ranges from soup to nuts, quite literally. Eating utensils vary, too. Even where the same utensils are used, they may be handled differently; in Europe, one typically holds the fork—face down—in the left hand and uses the knife, in the right hand, to cut the food. It is especially important to understand and adapt to others' foods and eating customs, for this is where conviviality begins.

- Our greeting customs. Some of the world's people bow, others assume a prayerful pose, many shake hands, some kiss when they greet one another. In some cultures, you must return the greeting or risk giving offense; in others, you need not return the greeting.

- Our dress, which varies around the world, and also between urban and nonurban areas. In some cities, men must wear dark suits to be taken seriously by their business counterparts; in other parts of the world, such attire would seem highly overdressed.

- Our social customs. Will you be entertained in people's homes, or even at all? Must you entertain prospective clients?

These are just a few of the differences that come into play when we conduct business internationally.

CENTER FOR
INTERNATIONAL
TRADE
DEVELOPMENT

We Coach You Over the Hurdles

The track to international markets is laden with hurdles . . . market research, licensing, regulations, financing, distribution, foreign culture awareness, and numerous other challenges. A company must be poised, ready to jump the hurdles if they want to effectively penetrate an international market.

At the Center for International Trade Development, we see ourselves as part of the coaching staff, training the team how to jump the hurdles so they can get on with the race and cross the finish line!

The Center for International Trade Development offers comprehensive services to help you prepare for any international hurdle you encounter. Our primary areas of assistance include:

- ♦ Business and Trade Consulting
- ♦ Seminars and Workshops
- ♦ Culture and Language Resource Center
- ♦ International Consulting

Call us at (405) 744-7693 for further information. One of our trade specialists will be happy to talk with you and send you further information about CITD and its services.

 CENTER FOR INTERNATIONAL TRADE DEVELOPMENT ♦ OKLAHOMA STATE UNIVERSITY
Hall of Fame & Washington ♦ Stillwater, Oklahoma 74078 ♦ USA ♦ (405)744-7693 ♦ FAX: (405)744-8973

Organizations such as the Center for International Trade Development offer comprehensive services to American exporters eager to penetrate the international marketplace. *Courtesy of the Center for International Trade Development.*

EXTROVERTED VERSUS INTROVERTED CULTURES

The world's cultures can even be divided, although not too neatly, into extroverted and introverted cultures. In every culture, however, there are exceptions. Some people fit the mold; others do not.

In an **extroverted culture**, the people are outgoing and direct in their communications. Body posture and language are lively and vibrant. Among the extroverted cultures are most Americans, Canadians, Latin Americans, and some but not all Europeans.

In an **introverted culture**, people are more inward-looking and contemplative. Their body language is often reserved and harder to read, especially for someone from an extroverted culture. Among the introverted cultures are much of the Asian world and many parts of Africa.

What does this mean in actual practice to the exporter? It means that in Singapore, a hotel staffer may not be able to tell you directly that a conference room cannot be arranged. She will be too shy to say "no" to you directly and will instead often leave you with the impression she can provide what you have requested. You will believe you are all set for your 10 a.m. teleconference if you do not understand that you were given a very shy "no" with body language even if the person verbally said "yes."

In an African country, where direct communication is often considered rude, a businesswoman may not tell you directly that she will not buy your product. She may even spend hours listening to your sales pitch, waiting for you to get the message from her body language and only a few very slight verbal signals.

Universally, when people do not understand the language you are speaking, they are more likely to say "yes" than "no," rather than embarrass themselves by admitting they do not have the faintest idea what you have requested.

CELEBRATING OUR DIFFERENCES

Even though we describe cultures in terms of whether they are introverted or extroverted, it is important that we not let our ability to read another culture be hindered by stereotypes.

The first step in educating yourself about other cultures is to forget all the stereotypes you may have heard or been taught. People rarely live up—or down—to them anyway. Stereotypes are based on our perceptions rather than reality.

The purpose of stereotypes is to make us feel superior to others and to make others seem inferior to us, and this never makes for a good sales climate.

Equality is what you want when you are seeking international customers.

A SAMPLING OF OUR SOCIAL DIFFERENCES Perhaps the most important reason to learn about other cultures is so we do not unintentionally give offense to the very people whom we hope to have as customers. The brief entries that follow, for example, show just a few of the ways that a person could unknowingly offend someone in another culture:

- A nod means "no" in some parts of the world, "yes" in others. Shaking the head back and forth, our way of saying "no," means "yes" to some people.[1]
- Never pat the head of a Thai person or pass anything over it. It is considered sacred.[2]
- Red is a positive color in Denmark and the color of witchcraft and death in some African countries.[3]
- Triangular shapes in Hong Kong and Taiwan are negative shapes, never to be used in clothing or to decorate packages.[4]
- It is rude to sit with the soles of your feet facing another person in most Arab countries and in many other countries as well.[5]
- Forming a circle with one's thumb and forefinger, a common gesture for "OK" in the United States means "zero" in France, "money" in Japan, and is vulgar in Brazil. Similarly, the "V" sign we use to spell victory is vulgar in some parts of the world, especially when the palm of the hand is turned outward.

A SAMPLING OF OUR BUSINESS DIFFERENCES Apart from the social differences that separate us, people also have different ways of conducting business. These customs are something the international businessperson cannot afford not to know. They are too extensive to be covered in complete detail here, but there are excellent books available on this subject. The following discussion covers only the most major areas of difference.

NEGOTIATING STYLE One of the most salient features of the way that people conduct business is their negotiating style. In some countries, a very direct negotiating style is acceptable. The United States is particularly known for this rough-and-tumble kind of negotiating as are some European countries. In other parts of the world—much of Asia, Africa, and the Arab world—the negotiating style is so indirect as to seem almost ambivalent. Sellers have to read body language very carefully to understand whether their potential buyers are interested.

Apart from this, there are also a few idiosyncratic differences: The Japanese, for example, do not like to negotiate one-on-one. They consider this disloyal. Americans, in contrast, often try to break a negotiating team apart and bargain in this fashion.[6]

PUNCTUALITY   Around the world people run on different social clocks. In some countries you are expected to arrive on the dot, if not early, for an appointment. In others, if you are prompt, you will spend the next fifteen minutes twiddling your thumbs—alone.

Promptness is valued in Europe and in Japan, but it is usual for business meetings to run as much as thirty minutes late in Latin America without anyone taking offense.

The United States is so large that the customs vary regarding time. In New York and Los Angeles, for example, people routinely arrive ten or fifteen minutes late for meetings without apology, a tardiness, paradoxically, that New Yorkers manage to blame on the mass transit system and Los Angelenos on their freeways. In between these two places, however, the rest of the country is quite prompt, and apologies are made for even five minutes of lateness.

On the subject of time, keep in mind that business hours are not the same all over the world, to say nothing of the hours that people are actually in their offices. In some countries, people work on Saturdays, usually a half day only. In Latin countries around the world, businesses often close for a two-hour-long

GLOBETROTTING **Gaffes**
GLOBAL BEHAVIOR

Be a welcome guest abroad by learning in advance the social customs of your foreign clients. Here are some examples from around the world of appropriate and inappropriate behavior.

AUSTRALIA: When invited to your host's home, bring wine or flowers.

BULGARIA: A shake of the head means "yes," a nod means "no."

CZECHOSLOVAKIA: When traveling by taxi, always insist that the meter be turned on and demand a receipt. The authorities, for the time being, deal very harshly with black marketeering. Foreigners can be fined or even imprisoned.

DENMARK: Tipping is not customary in restaurants or hotels. The northern Europeans love their summers, so keep summer business meetings short and to the point.

ENGLAND: Showing interest in your food is considered rude by the British, as is setting down your knife when eating with a knife and fork.

FRANCE: At restaurants, "Service compris" means tip is included. Leave 8 to 12 percent when the bill reads "Service non compris."

GERMANY: If you read "Bedienung," in a restaurant, that means tip is included. Otherwise, include 10 to 15 percent as a gratuity.

HONG KONG: A gift will be expected if your arrival is during Chinese New Year in February.

HUNGARY: Don't take photographs outside normal tourist areas . . . you may arouse suspicion. Err on the formal side in dress and business etiquette. Avoid bright or flashy clothing, which is regarded in poor taste.

INDIA: The cow is sacred to the Hindus and not to be eaten. Muslims do not eat pork.

IVORY COAST (Côte d'Ivoire): The official language is French, but English is spoken widely in hotels and business offices.

SINGAPORE: Singaporeans take littering and spitting in public very seriously; the fine is about $500.

lunch and then stay open until 6 or 7 p.m. In Japan, people work from 8 a.m. to 6 p.m., but Japanese workers also often stay late, and American exporters have learned to use their late hours to make sales calls.

In some countries, everyone settles down to work the minute the parties to a negotiation or meeting are present, but in other countries, it would be rude to begin conducting business without first exchanging some polite conversation or even having a cup of coffee or tea.

GREETING CUSTOMS Even handshakes, perhaps the most common form of greeting, vary from place to place. Americans shake hands longer than Europeans do. In some places, it is considered too intimate to grasp someone else's hands with both of yours, a gesture Americans use to show they are really pleased to meet you.

In recent years, the Japanese custom of bowing has posed a problem for many American exporters. Do you bow, and if so, how low? In Japan, an inferior must bow lower than a superior, and not much thought is required to figure out that worldwide, the seller is considered subordinate to the buyer.

If you can bow with dignity, do so, but if you feel awkward bowing, then skip it. One welcome sign of just how global our world is becoming is the fact that Japanese and American businesspeople have begun to combine the bow with the handshake—a truly international custom.

DECIDING HOW MUCH TO BLEND IN

Some people find it easier than others do to slip into the skin of another culture. You must make your own decisions about how far you want to go, or comfortably can go, to fit into another world. But we can all develop a sense of what is appropriate when visiting others. That way, assuming that we respect others, even if we break a rule, advertently or inadvertently, no offense will be taken.[7] Here are some general guidelines to help you get along anywhere in the world:

DO WHAT OTHERS DO If you watch for clues, you can see what is expected of you. For example, it is more polite to take off your shoes in a Japanese restaurant than to leave them on, and visitors are given a lot of clues that this is the case.

WATCH HOW AND WHAT OTHERS EAT AND FOLLOW SUIT Don't take seconds unless they are offered. Let your host serve you. Remember that the American bent for self-sufficiency can go against another cultural grain.

FOLLOW THE LEADS OF PEOPLE'S BODY LANGUAGE If everyone is quieter than you are, tone down your natural American spontaneity. If people are more outgoing, you had better adjust to that, too, or you may never get on a bus, train, or subway in rush hour. If people stand and sit formally, do the same. If they sit informally, feel free to do so as well, although never exaggerate an informal posture—lest you show the soles of your feet to the wrong culture. Everywhere in the world, in even the most informal culture, it is always better to err a little bit on the side of formality.

Finally, although it is not necessary to rewrite your entire personality to conduct business with others, it does help to be a little chameleon-like.

COUNTRIES COMMUNICATING WITH ONE ANOTHER

On a much larger scale, exporting countries have been learning to communicate with one another their concerns about the problems and difficulties that inevitably arise in the one-world market that is emerging. Several international organizations work to improve conditions and communications among exporters.

GATT AND THE FASHION INDUSTRY

Every few years, the group comprising the General Agreement on Tariffs and Trade (GATT) meets to negotiate a new trade agreement among its member nations. There have been seven rounds, and round eight, a particularly rocky one, is now underway. Talks broke off once and were resumed again in early 1992.

One of GATT's primary goals is to reduce trade barriers, and it has been successful in doing this. Since GATT was established in 1947, tariffs on thousands of industrial products have fallen from 40 percent to under 5 percent. World trade has grown enormously. According to a *Wall Street Journal* report on the most recent round of GATT negotiations, GATT dispute-resolution panels have settled conflicts that might have exploded into trade wars, if not actual wars.[8]

The fashion industry has been a particularly sensitive area for GATT to deal with, so much so that conflict has been resolved only by excluding textiles and apparel from many of the GATT guidelines.

The primary source of contention is trade barriers that were initially set high to combat cheap im-

GLOBAL GLIMPSES

FREEDOM OF CHOICE

While politicians and bureaucrats in eastern Europe debate over how to push their governments into creating free economies, Western advertising agencies are already helping them do the work. These agencies are setting up offices in Budapest, Prague, and Warsaw—hiring and training local people and taking the first crucial steps in introducing Western products to eastern European consumers. They are also introducing this new market to the fundamental principle of capitalism: freedom of choice.

American advertising agencies, such as McCann-Erikson and J. Walter Thompson, have begun to develop name-brand recognition for many American products, including Coke and Levi jeans. Transportation Displays Inc. is the largest outdoor media specialist in the United States and through joint ventures with public transport systems in Hungary and the Commonwealth of Independent States (the former Soviet Union) has built up a massive network of advertising space on buses and trams.

D'Arcy Masius Benton and Bowles, a large U.S. advertising company discovered that in eastern Europe, it is widely assumed that if a product is advertised, there must be something wrong with it because authorities once used to help unload goods that were overproduced or of poor quality. Subtleties like this have caused many Western agencies to move slowly in the East.

For all the frustrations and (to date) difficulties of profits in eastern European markets (profits in zlotys or rubles are not quite the same as profits in dollars), many advertising executives say they are gratified by helping to bring freedom and prosperity to the region and, most of all, to bring them freedom of choice!

Based on Jeffrey Ferry, "Global Business," *Pan Am Clipper*, August 1991, pp. 12, 46.

ports and were never lowered. Adding to the problem is the fact that, in the United States at least, the fashion business is dominated by powerful lobbying and political interest groups, forces that generally work against GATT's goal of reducing world trade barriers. Although some barriers have come down, textile and apparel trade at best must still be described as managed rather than truly free trade.

To cope with the problems of the textile and apparel industry, GATT has established several internal structures, most notably the Textiles Committee, the Textiles Surveillance Body, and the Negotiating Group on Textiles and Clothing.

TEXTILES COMMITTEE   This is a political forum that meets once or twice a year to assess and study global trade patterns within the textile industry. Because many of the textile facilities are located in less developed countries, this committee seeks ways to accommodate and equalize the trade status of these countries.

TEXTILE SURVEILLANCE BODY   This group polices bilateral agreements. It cannot enforce any action, but it often works to negotiate compromises.

The TSB also provides another forum for the continuing north-south dialogue described in Chapter 2.

NEGOTIATING GROUP ON TEXTILES AND CLOTHING   This group is charged with exploring ways to bring fashion back under the GATT regulations. Established in 1987, it has not been in existence long enough to have affected any major changes.

SPECIAL PROJECTS DIVISION   This group, often referred to as the textile secretariat, services the three other committees devoted to the fashion industry and also coordinates activities between GATT and the Multi-Fiber and Textile Agreement.

MULTI-FIBER AND TEXTILE AGREEMENT (MFA)   The Multi-Fiber and Textile Agreement, composed of 54 fashion-producing nations, was established to set guidelines for bilateral trade agreements between fashion-producing countries. Established in 1974, the agreement has been renewed several times, but each time, the tensions between less developed countries, who want reduced tariffs, and developed countries, who oppose tariff reduction on fashion imports, have been heightened, and the next round of MFA talks may prove as difficult as the current round of GATT talks.

Fashion exporters eagerly await the outcome of these negotiations, as they will very much affect their profit margins. U.S. fashion producers do not feel MFA has been as helpful to their cause as it might. They objected, for example, when the MFA enacted **unit quotas,** that is, a quota based on unit of clothing, rather than **cost-value quotas,** which are based on the cost of the items imported. To get around the unit quotas, Asian countries began importing higher priced merchandise so they made more per unit even though they were importing fewer items. This hurt the U.S. market as much, if not more, as cheap imports.

ONE-WORLD MARKETING AND THE FASHION INDUSTRY

Despite these conflicts, the fashion world, like the rest of the world, is moving closer and closer to becoming a one-world market. The course of future trade, however, will depend on the ability of fashion industries around the world to communicate with one another both individually and through groups like GATT and MFA. There is no reason why these groups working together will not be able to reduce price distortions and trade barriers in the coming years and, eventually, make the world truly one big marketplace.

ENDNOTES

1. "Understand and Heed Cultural Differences," *Business America,* Department of Commerce, special ed., Vol. 112, 1991, pp. 26–27.
2. *Ibid.,* p. 26.
3. *Ibid.,* p. 26.
4. *Ibid.,* p. 26
5. *Ibid.,* p. 26.
6. *Ibid.,* p. 26.
7. Franklin Krohn and Zafar Ahmed, "Teaching International Cross-Cultural Diversity to Hospitality and Tourism Students," *Hospitality and Tourism Educator,* November 1991, No. 4, Vol. 1, pp. 40–45.
8. Bob Davis, "Squeaky Wheels: GATT Talks Resume with France and India Calling Many of the Shots," *Wall Street Journal,* January 13, 1992, pp. 1, 9.

VOCABULARY

cost-value quotas _____

_____

_____

extroverted culture _____

_____

_____

FAX _____

_____

_____

introverted culture _____

_____

_____

social communication   _____

_____

_____

telex   _____

_____

_____

unit quotas   _____

_____

_____

GLOBAL REVIEW

1. What are the three important ways to prepare yourself for success in international trade?

_____

_____

_____

_____

2. Because communication is so important in conducting business, what methods have recently been adapted to make international communication more rapid?

_____

_____

_____

_____

3. Social communication has become a major factor in global business. What do we mean by social communication?

_____

_____

_____

_____

4. Give three examples that illustrate how common customs can differ from country to country and culture to culture.

_____

_____

_____

_____

5. How does a U.S. businessperson try to "blend in" when visiting a foreign country?

_____

_____
_____
_____

6. List the factors that can affect whether a culture is an extroverted or intro-verted culture.

_____
_____
_____
_____

7. What is meant by the word "stereotype"?

_____
_____
_____
_____

8. The negotiating style of Americans is considered to be very direct. What do we mean by direct?

_____
_____
_____
_____

9. List the internal structures that GATT has established to cope with the prob-lems of the textile and apparel industries.

_____
_____
_____
_____

10. What functions do these internal structures perform and how do they help textile and apparel global trade?

_____
_____
_____
_____

GLOBAL DIGEST   1. Research a GATT dispute-resolution that has had an impact on international trade in fashion products.

_____
_____

_____

_____

_____

_____

_____

_____

2. Choose a country and research the social customs and how they differ from the United States.

_____

_____

_____

_____

_____

_____

_____

3. Because so much can be learned about other cultures from reading about them, research and compile a list of books that you would give to a person interested in entering the global marketplace.

_____

_____

_____

_____

_____

_____

_____

UNIT 3 READING
CAN WE MAKE A DEAL?

By Kerry Pechter

When his Malaysian joint-venture partner suggested he hire an exorcist to drive the evil spirits out of a new factory as a gesture of respect toward the plant's Chinese workers, Ray Harder, the managing director of Taylor-Wharton International of Theodore, Ala., readily agreed.

When the Malaysian government called on him to provide men's and women's prayer rooms in the factory for Muslim workers, Mr. Harder agreed again. And, most important, when he and the venture partner, a manufacturing firm called Kumpulan Emas Bhd., decided how to split their costs, the two sides didn't haggle in the usual sense. They just laid the numbers on the table and adopted the fairest terms.

It soon paid off: After two months of talks, seven flights to Asia, exhaustive studies by the accountants and finally a personal visit from the president of Taylor-Wharton's parent, $1.8 billion Harsco Corp., Mr. Harder had forged a 70/30 partnership to fabricate storage tanks for liquid oxygen and nitrogen for the Asian and Middle Eastern markets.

In doing as the Romans do, Mr. Harder, a 30-year veteran of international negotiations, wasn't being a pushover. He was merely practicing the low-key, nonadversarial, win/win negotiating style that's now regarded as the most effective way for Americans to do business with people from other cultures. "I wouldn't even call it negotiations," he says. "It's just doing business."

As more American companies go global, their managers are discovering that negotiating abroad is tougher than dickering with other Americans. The language barrier is only the most obvious hurdle. History, religion and business etiquette differ from one country to another in subtle ways that American negotiators have a reputation for failing to appreciate.

But it doesn't have to be that way. Successful negotiators like Mr. Harder say that any American manager can learn to bargain more skillfully with non-Americans. The secret is to listen more closely, focus on mutual interests rather than petty differences and nurture long-term relationships. Doing so could make the difference between flying home from Asia or Europe with a fat deal or just a lot of expense receipts.

GETTING TO "YES"

Negotiations are always problematic, and when they involve people from opposite sides of the globe they're even more so. "Two people talking to each other—even two people from the same town—have difficulty communicating," says Elizabeth Gray, president of Conflict Management Inc., a Cambridge, Mass., spin-off of the highly regarded Harvard Negotiation Project, which produced the best-selling book on negotiations *Getting to Yes* (Penguin Books, 1983). "When you factor in differences in language, culture and geographical distance, and the general lack of familiarity, you compound the problem."

Take language differences. Americans usually rely either on the English-speaking abilities of their foreign partners or on translators. But fine shades of meaning can get lost in the translation, especially in Japan, where the same spoken word can have three different meanings and where blunt refusals are considered impolite. "When the Japanese say a word, it doesn't mean the same thing that it means to you or me," says Robert J. Boehlke, chief financial officer of San Jose's KLA Instruments, which sells imaging equipment in Japan. "When they say something is 'difficult,' or that 'it will take some study,' they mean 'no.'"

Nor does everyone speak the same body language. Americans may not know that when the Japanese audibly suck air through their teeth, they feel pressured, says Gary Wederspahn, director of program design and development for Moran Stahl & Boyer, a cross-cultural consulting firm. And while a hearty handshake may convey sincerity in Denver or Atlanta, it will make Asians uncomfortable. Even colors have unexpected significance. One consultant tells of an American agri-businessman who stuck a green baseball cap on a Chinese visitor's head. In China, green is the sign of a cuckold. A red hat, on the other hand, would have signified joy and prosperity.

In former communist countries, local negotiators simply may not speak the language of capitalism. Ken Schaffer, vice president of Belka International, a New York consulting firm, has negotiated successfully with former Soviet ministries to install satellite-telephone systems in Russia so that American oil companies drilling in Siberia can phone home. The Western concept of dealmaking is virtually unknown in Russia, he says.

"They're very intelligent people, but they have no understanding of the natural progression of business or entrepreneurship," Mr. Schaffer says. "It's happened more than once that, after we've signed all the papers, the Russians will say to me, 'Now, by the way, Kenny, what are the financial terms?' There's just no model there for business as we know it."

Different ideas about punctuality can also confound negotiations. "In parts of black Africa, negotiators might decide to defer action till next year. But Americans get upset if they can't close a deal in time to catch the 4 o'clock plane," says Roger Fisher, a Harvard professor who is a cofounder of the Harvard Negotiation Project and coauthor of *Getting to Yes*.

Differing attitudes toward contracts can cause even more confusion. For instance, the custom of *naniwabushi* allows the Japanese to request a change in a contract if the terms become onerous or unfair, says Australian consultant Robert M. March, author of *The Japanese*

THE BASICS

It's risky if not rude to generalize about the negotiation style of any given country's citizens. But international bargaining behavior can often be predicted, consultants say. Here's how to haggle with six peoples:

⊕GERMANS: Germans bargain like Americans. They stress clarity, precision and literal interpretation of contracts. They will pursue their self-interests, maximize their advantages, concede as little as possible and hide their hole card. It's OK to bring your lawyer with you. The above also applies to the Swiss.

⊕JAPANESE: The Japanese seek flexible relationships. Don't expect snap decisions; they must retreat, confer and reach a consensus. Nods don't necessarily signal agreement. Leave your lawyer at home.

⊕KOREANS: Today, the South Koreans negotiate with Americans from a position of strength. Compared to the Japanese, they have a straightforward, American negotiating style. Koreans respect status: In Seoul, hire a chauffeur and emphasize your links with Fortune 100 companies.

⊕LATIN AMERICANS: In Latin America, choosing the right restaurant or wine can speak louder than words. Latin Americans establish specific positions and bargain hard; but they communicate through hints, nonverbal cues and intermediaries. Pay close attention to the location and mood of a meeting.

⊕BRITISH: Americans and Britons both speak English; the similarity stops there. Citizens of the U.K. resent aggressive, direct demands. Sensitive issues should be broached over an informal dinner or through intermediaries. Don't "micro-negotiate." Get the big picture right, and the details will fall into place.

⊕RUSSIANS: History taught the Russians to be inscrutable, stolid and skeptical. Then communism crushed their entrepreneurial instincts. Basic concepts such as risk need to be explained. Capitalism remains slightly shameful, so stress the social benefits of a deal. Establish trust, and the deals will come.

CAN WE MAKE A DEAL?

CONTINUED

Negotiator (Kodansha International, 1988). In fact, a business contract in Japan is like a wedding vow: It means more in spirit than in substance. "When you disagree with your wife," explains Mr. Fisher, "you don't go back to the marriage vow to settle the argument. If the relationship isn't working, rereading the contract isn't going to help." (It's also well-known that the Japanese are insulted if you bring your lawyer to negotiations.)

Managers who have overcome these obstacles offer several pieces of advice about negotiating overseas. Robert Shillman, president and C.E.O. of Cognex Corp., a Needham, Mass., maker of microprocessors and software that enable robotic machine tools to "see," says that in Japan it's unwise to start out talking about prices.

He tells the story of his first sales call on Fuji Machine Manufacturing Co., one of his best customers. "The first thing their C.E.O. asked me was, 'Can you help us get our product to market faster?' If it had been two American companies, the first thing they'd have discussed would have been price." The two companies negotiated like partners with a common goal, rather than like adversaries angling for the best short-term profit. Half of Cognex's $31.5 million in sales now comes from Japan.

Leading with a discussion of money is equally unwise in Russia. "You have to lead with feelings," says Mr. Schaffer. When negotiating for a telecommunications license, he stressed the fact that an international phone hookup would help the whole country and played down the profits to be made selling telephone services to multinational oil companies. "I put the conceptual part first." With Russians, he says, you have to penetrate their uncommunicative *poka-zuka* mask, and get into their "kitchen," where they speak their minds.

Understanding the other side's constraints also can help speed negotiations. Reese Palley, a Philadelphia entrepreneur, discovered recently while trying to buy exclusive rights to advertising space on a thousand Romanian buses that Eastern Europeans have been burned by exclusive contracts and won't sign them. So he wrote an unprecedented agreement that gave him rights to 100 buses and first-refusal rights to the rest. "I try to find out what they want, and I give it to them," he says.

DOING AS THE ROMANS DO

While candor is important, subterfuge still has its place in negotiations— not least of all in Asia, where the ethic of trust is alloyed with an appreciation for shrewdness. Chin-Ning Chu, a San Francisco marketing consultant and author of *The Asian Mind Game* (Rawson Associates, 1991), once counseled an American company that was unable to market its grass seed in China. The problem: The Chinese regard grass with contempt. "When the Chinese want to insult you, they say that you have nothing but grass between your ears," says Ms. Chu.

Knowing China's need for hard currency, however, Ms. Chu advised her client to suggest building a seed factory in China for export to the U.S. The Chinese agreed. The factory failed, but not before the 1989 Asia Games, where the Chinese saw that green grass looks very attractive on a playing field. The ploy took five years, but the Chinese were finally hooked on grass. "In international negotiations, nothing happens overnight," says Ms. Chu. "If you don't have the budget to wait, don't bother going over."

Western Europeans have their own elegant, indirect style of negotiation. William Rosenberg, a technology-transfer expert and president of Pax Technologies in the Boston area, describes a cross-licensing deal between American and German auto part makers that almost fell through because of a culture clash. "The American C.E.O. had a loose, joking manner that the German C.E.O. looked on as disrespectful. Personality clashes can be more pronounced in a cross-cultural negotiation." In another case, a "very controlled, punctual" American C.E.O. arrived in Paris for negotiations and became furious when the meeting didn't start on time, lunch dragged on and the French C.E.O. stepped out to take phone calls. "I told my client that with Europeans you have to walk before you can run. They want to size you up first and create a context. Then they'll get on with the deal," he says.

Indeed, international negotiations can be quite delicate. Mark Sandler, an Asia expert at the University of Maryland, tells the story of an American firm that for years had sold raw materials to a family-run Japanese company. One year, a manager from the American company flew to Japan to negotiate a deal to market the Japanese company's products throughout Asia. At the first meeting, he began dictating prices, deadlines and quality standards, and showed none of the deference that the long-time partner expected.

"That totally turned off the Japanese," Mr. Sandler says. "They never said no, they just obfuscated and delayed. The American manager should have spoken of the two companies' mutual interests and shown a familiarity with their past dealings. He should have reassured them that while he was a new face and wore a different hat from his predecessors, relations between the two businesses would still be positive."

The first rule of negotiation, experts say, is to fathom the interests of the other side. "You should look at the other side's interests, and not their positions," says Mr. Fisher, who advises negotiators to sit beside, rather than opposite, each other at the bargaining table. "Try to see their concerns, their hopes, their fears and their needs. If I want to change your

(Courtesy of *International Business*)

CAN WE MAKE A DEAL?
CONTINUED

mind, I have to know what's on your mind." Another rule of thumb: Divide negotiations into three meetings, with the first devoted to inventing agreement scenarios, the second to evaluating them and the third to picking the best one.

DEVELOP AN ESCAPE HATCH

Negotiators also should pick their "BATNA," or "best alternative to a negotiated agreement," before they begin bargaining. The BATNA, a concept described in *Getting to Yes* is a negotiator's escape hatch, a viable option to exercise if talks fail. "If you don't know your BATNA," says Ms. Gray of Conflict Management, "you'll feel like you're on the edge of an abyss. You'll end up agreeing to a disadvantageous deal."

If you can afford their fees, which may reach $3,000 a day, consultants often can smooth out cross-cultural negotiations. Yearn Hong Choi, a professor at the University of the District of Columbia, recalls helping an American design firm that had had encouraging talks with the American managers of Lucky-Goldstar International Corp., the big Korean trading company, but got nowhere on a subsequent trip to Seoul. Mr. Choi contacted a former schoolmate at Lucky-Goldstar and vouched for his client. A $1 million design contract ensued.

Regardless of nationality, negotiators say that the fairer the deal, the longer it will last. "Don't cut too rich a deal for yourself," advises Mr. Palley. "They'll find out about it. You may not have done anything wrong, but if

the deal generated too much profit for you" it will hurt the relationship. "Nobody likes to be ripped off," agrees Mr. Fisher.

Learning more about foreign cultures would also help American negotiators, observers say. "I've witnessed dozens of interactions between American and Japanese negotiators, and I've seen virtually no effort among the Americans to understand the Japanese culture," says Leo Kim, vice president for research at Mycogen Corp., a San Diego biotechnology company. "They say they do, but they just go through the motions."

The most efficient way of all to negotiate overseas might be to choose the right partner in the first place. Taylor-Wharton's Mr. Harder researched at least eight or nine different manufacturing firms in three Southeast Asian countries before sitting down to the bargaining table with Kumpulan Emas in Malaysia. By then, the two companies knew that they'd be compatible.

These suggestions are easier said than done, of course. American firms that are new to international trade will surely commit their share of gaffes. "Small companies that are beginning to do business in Japan tend to make the same mistakes that large companies made 10 or 20 years ago, and the medium-size companies made five to seven years ago," says one consultant. "As each new wave goes in, they learn by trial and error."

But American firms might not have to endure quite so many trials or errors if they remember certain basic principles: Focus on interests rather than positions; remember your BATNA; prepare for every possible question; and if foreign nationals ask you to hire an exorcist to drive demons out of a new factory, by all means do so.

The Import Marketing Strategy

CHAPTER 11

Import Product Strategy

Exclusivity, status, uniqueness of design were some of the reasons for the early importation of fashion products into the United States. Price had no impact on why these types of imports were successful. As recently as twenty years ago, however, one of the main reasons to import some fashion products was price. It was inexpensive and could be sold for a tidy profit. Americans bought these imports only to save money, and importers imported them only to make a large profit. As a result, imports were only a small part of all the fashion goods sold each year.

Today, it is rare for a designer's line or a department store's private label line not to include some imports, and many lines rely heavily on them. Cost is certainly no longer the exclusive reason to import. Reliance on imports has grown for over two decades and is expected to continue to grow. All this makes fashion importing a much more complicated business than in the past—and one that a fashion importer does not enter without considerable forethought and planning.

A **fashion importer** is a specialist who assumes responsibility for bringing foreign fashion goods into the country. The fashion importer's job ranges from finding fashion products that will appeal to domestic consumers and arranging to have them physically transported from one country to another to overseeing the sales and promotion of the product.

The overall goal of an importer is to bring in a foreign product that will reach a clearly defined target market and produce a decent profit margin. To achieve this goal, the first task of an importer is to decide what to import. This is done by devising and using an import strategy to make decisions about which goods to import and how to go about importing them, the subject of this chapter.

ANALYSIS OF THE IMPORT PRODUCT

An import product is far more than its physical parts, even though these are obviously part of its appeal. An import product may be appealing for a variety of other reasons, among them its quality, design, aesthetics, or even its status.

Before choosing a product to import, a fashion importer must have reason to believe that it will do well in the United States. Several different elements influence the decision to import a product.

Imports of Selected Women's and Children's Garments (in thousands of units)

Product	Fiber	Year 1986	Year 1987	Year 1988	Year 1989	Year 1990	Jan-Nov 1990	Jan-Nov 1991
Coats, jackets, raincoats	Cotton	28,635	32,018	25,283	23,058	24,785	22,933	20,273
	Wool	N.C.	5,850	5,292	5,051	5,607	5,459	6,836
	Synthetic	N.C.	52,020	55,732	48,249	65,886	60,915	66,232
	Other	N.A.	2,772	2,706	2,809	2,671	2,260	4,204
	Total	N.C.	93,460	89,013	79,166	98,949	91,568	97,545
Suits	Wool	N.C.	580	452	693	681	657	966
	Synthetic	N.C.	2,757	2,923	3,818	3,158	2,853	4,293
	Other	N.A.	511	930	706	1,566	1,455	1,903
	Total	N.C.	3,848	4,305	5,216	5,405	4,965	7,161
Dresses	Cotton	20,889	25,324	28,007	29,712	32,644	30,256	23,619
	Wool	2,326	1,607	1,396	1,703	1,603	1,582	1,528
	Synthetic	37,133	37,370	37,905	40,976	41,882	38,272	38,424
	Other	N.A.	2,085	1,960	4,276	2,573	2,300	2,317
	Total	60,348	66,386	69,268	76,667	78,701	72,410	65,887
Blouses	Cotton	160,071	164,222	134,801	138,667	126,738	118,105	106,354
	Wool	3,075	2,593	2,315	1,315	1,182	1,136	615
	Synthetic	137,464	108,246	111,390	121,590	129,967	121,529	130,910
	Other	N.A.	10,709	11,388	10,955	8,401	7,313	7,132
	Total	300,610	285,770	259,894	272,527	266,288	248,082	245,010
Knit shirts	Cotton	162,825	200,883	214,884	242,538	268,374	250,732	238,974
	Wool*	10,087	8,838	9,141	7,331	6,346	6,270	7,448
	Synthetic	244,681	240,392	195,354	283,722	280,916	265,103	239,031
	Other	N.A.	1,421	3,107	2,233	856	809	263
	Total	417,593	451,534	422,485	535,825	556,492	522,914	485,716
Sweaters*	Cotton	24,324	25,538	24,392	26,726	23,500	21,943	19,693
	Wool	41,653	38,219	34,820	29,809	26,690	26,134	23,638
	Synthetic	149,623	145,475	127,110	138,336	79,107	78,359	56,478
	Silk	9,289	15,067	10,127	6,128	4,514	4,470	4,673
	Other	127,289	107,362	67,107	107,158	89,854	86,284	82,128
	Total	352,171	331,661	263,556	308,157	223,664	217,190	186,610
Skirts	Cotton	38,450	63,053	50,841	40,455	41,844	39,317	28,091
	Wool	N.C.	6,713	5,157	4,721	4,820	4,736	5,008
	Synthetic	N.C.	40,084	35,695	36,300	36,706	33,634	39,453
	Other	4,751	7,341	5,124	4,985	4,607	4,094	4,812
	Total	N.C.	117,195	96,816	86,462	87,977	81,781	77,364
Slacks & Shorts	Cotton	182,205	189,093	204,627	248,565	238,938	222,384	223,678
	Wool	N.C.	3,586	4,066	3,909	3,935	3,830	3,985
	Synthetic	N.C.	134,810	132,350	158,434	170,767	159,613	149,604
	Other	N.A.	24,963	22,335	36,711	33,916	29,948	33,165
	Total	N.C.	352,452	363,379	447,618	447,555	415,775	410,433
Playsuits*	Total	69,334	58,706	52,276	46,016	58,908	52,133	60,312
Dressing gowns & robes*	Cotton	9,389	9,383	9,805	12,638	12,986	11,842	13,469
	Synthetic	5,630	6,725	8,544	12,238	10,063	9,561	8,655
	Total**	15,018	16,245	18,432	24,909	23,065	21,418	22,134
Nightwear & Pajamas*	Cotton	34,815	33,885	36,502	46,534	51,570	49,065	49,081
	Synthetic	27,820	30,432	32,740	40,936	41,141	38,943	41,585
	Total**	62,635	64,427	69,312	87,498	92,726	88,021	90,669
Underwear*	Cotton	137,350	164,462	209,589	276,603	314,615	291,218	366,368
	Synthetic	134,828	139,886	157,636	174,082	193,770	178,269	186,939
	Total**	272,178	305,120	367,852	450,811	508,449	469,549	553,325
Brassieres & girdles	Total	179,558	196,194	218,286	220,001	213,333	196,760	227,319

*Includes male garments   **Includes other fibers   N.A. Not Available
N.C. Not comparable with data beginning 1987 because of classification changes stemming from the Harmonized System
Source: U.S. Bureau of the Census (General Imports)

SUPERIORITY OF PRODUCT

The product may be superior to anything that is being generated domestically. Gloves and small leather goods from Italy, for example, are a better quality and workmanship than those produced in the United States—or in any other country, for that matter. France has until recently been the country that was on the cutting edge of high fashion. England has long been known for the excellence of its wool plaids, Scottish tartans, and Harris tweeds. Because these products are superior to similar products produced in the United States, the imported version is deemed more valuable.

UNIQUENESS OF PRODUCT

Similar to superiority is the quality of uniqueness. If a product is the only one of its kind, it often has special appeal. Arche, a French shoe company, managed to capture an affluent target market a few years ago because of the uniqueness of its product. Its shoes were comfortable at a time when American women, who had finally gotten bored with wearing running shoes everywhere, were demanding comfort. The fact that Arche shoes were also highly styled in an unusual way made them unique—at least for a few years, until other shoe manufacturers began to copy their features.

PRODUCT STATUS

Products also may be imported because of their status. In the 1980s, almost any product bearing a foreign name had more status than comparable domestic goods. The imported products cost more and they were often better made. These two qualities combined to give imported goods new cachet.

GLOBAL *GO-GETTERS*

DIANE FREIS: LA BLOND—HONG KONG BOUND

Courtesy of Diane Freis.

Diane Freis is an American expatriate who designs and produces women's clothes that sell in over 30 countries. Her home base now is Hong Kong and her fashion trademark is gorgeously colored, loose-fitting dresses with intricate embroidery and beading.

This California girl started designing a collection of jeans jackets with antique fabrics sewn in after she graduated from college in the early 1970s. Her quest for fabrics in glorious colors and textures took her to Hong Kong where she found an abundance of these fabrics and fantastic tailors. In 1973, Diane Freis settled in Hong Kong permanently, and Hong Kong and Freis have made a great pair ever since.

Diane Freis' marketing strategy, like her designing, is a study in creativity meeting commercialism. She has achieved worldwide distribution, and the Diane Freis collections are available in 450 boutiques and better department stores in the United States.

Scheduling fashion shows in Paris, Italy, and New York, sourcing and designing fabrics, producing samples, and pricing the goods keep her on a perpetual merry-go-round. Her travel schedule follows this kind of merry-go-round ride. She goes to the United States and France a least twice a year. Japan also gets twice-yearly visits. Then she goes on promotional tours that take her from Taiwan to Australia.

On her trip home to California, she enjoys American space and greenery, which is a giant change from Hong Kong's overcrowded hustle and bustle. Some say that her fashions evolve from some mysterious mingling of East and West. Asked about the impending takeover of Hong Kong by mainland Chinese in 1997, Diane Freis is unperturbed but does speak of the trauma of being forced to think about relocation. Indonesia, Thailand, and even Vietnam are considerations with India following behind. But the mix of high-skill levels and abundant resources make Hong Kong the perfect place for Diane Freis.

Based on Marlene C. Piturro, "The Jewel in the Crown Colony," *World Trade*, May 1992, pp. 107–110.

Among the countless products that are imported because of their status are Italian leather goods with names like Gucci, Fendi, and Botega Veneta; Porthault sheets, a French product; Missoni fabrics from Italy; Scottish cashmere, Chinese silk, and pearls from Japan.

AUTHENTICITY OF PRODUCT

Sometimes, so-called "ethnic" products, which have a distinct look, color, or texture, have a special value as imports. True champagne cannot be made anywhere except in France, and the same can be said for certain fashion products, which must come from their country of origin to be considered authentic. Wool caps and intricately patterned sweaters from Scandinavia are products that come only from that part of the world, as are lederhosen from Germany. The popular Loden coats made in Germany are another example of a product that is authentic because of its origins.

ECONOMICS OF PRODUCT

In the 1960s, when imports generally were not as well made as domestic goods but cost far less, price was their appeal to consumers as well as importers. But price cuts both ways and, in the 1980s, high-priced imports were what caught the eye of the customer who liked paying more for imported goods. With renewed emphasis on cost and value in the 1990s, cheap imports may once again become a viable market, and economics will again be an important reason to import.

AVAILABILITY OF PRODUCT

In the future, the availability of a product will become an increasingly important factor in the decision to import. As the world becomes a global marketplace, various countries will specialize in certain products—to the point where other countries stop making the product because they cannot compete with the quality or price. Most of the world's beadwork is now done in Hong Kong, for example, and 80 percent of the shoes sold in the United States are now imported. Unable to compete in terms of quality, style, and price, U.S. manufacturers have made fewer and fewer shoes, to the point at which American retailers are now unable to buy enough U.S. shoes to fill their needs. This makes the imported shoe market even more important.[1]

Gloves are so time-consuming and labor-intensive a product that American producers no longer bother with them. Other countries, Italy and France for expensive gloves and Asia for inexpensive ones, have picked up the slack. Men's dress shirts of medium quality, another labor-intensive product with their yokes, collars, and plackets, have sent production scampering overseas. Even U.S. manufacturers have turned to offshore production.[2]

All of these factors that encourage a desire for imported products on the part of the American consumer inspire retail fashion buyers and importers to seek out foreign sources to supply the huge, fashion-hungry U.S. market.

LOCATING SOURCES OF IMPORTED PRODUCTS

Once an importer has decided what kind of product to import, the next step is to locate sources, or suppliers, of the product. Many of the same research sources used by exporters to locate new markets for their goods—the Commerce Department, printed and electronic materials, foreign consulates, commercial banks, Chambers of Commerce and other trade associations—are also available to importers who are seeking foreign products.

COMMERCE DEPARTMENT RESOURCES

The Commerce Department maintains a huge database of import products produced in over 200 markets around the world. Databases are also maintained by international Chambers of Commerce and trade associations. With them, prospective importers can search for suppliers of products that they hope to import.

FOREIGN CONSULATES

One of the most important functions of a foreign consulate is to promote business within its own country. To this aim, consulates often maintain foreign desks dedicated to helping importers find suppliers. Consulates match importers with suitable suppliers, arrange trips and introductions so the two can meet, and supply any additional information that the importers require. Consulates are a safe method of finding suppliers because they screen sales leads before recommending them.[3]

COMMERCIAL BANKS

Commercial banks, a helpful source for exporters, are equally willing to play matchmaker for importers.

Dear Friends,

From the dawn of history in Peru, textiles have served as a primary form of cultural expression. Millennia old graves have yielded fragments of tapestry unequalled in sophistication in either ancient or modern worlds.

Since my mother, Biddy, and I began the Peruvian Connection in 1977, our catalogue designs have been shaped by the beauty and complexity of the old Native textiles. The superbly patterned ponchos and mantas (women's shawls) have provided endless inspiration. Peru's luxury fibers, alpaca and pima cotton, have been the other source of inspiration.

These indigenous luxury fibers, the same soft alpaca and silky Peruvian pima cotton we use in our present day catalogue collection, are at the core of Peru's extraordinary textile tradition. Early Paracas tapestries, regarded by textile scholars as among the finest in the world, were woven of a native cotton ancestral to pima. And alpaca was so prized by the the Incas that better grades were reserved for use by nobility.

Available in limited supply and principally in Peru, alpaca fleece and Peruvian pima cotton command healthy prices on world luxury fiber markets. Our catalogue knitwear designs make every effort to treat these precious fibers accordingly. The rich, homespun effects of handknitting, embroidery and handcrochet that you'll see in the pages that follow can't be mass produced.

Such painstaking attention to detail is a holdover from old Andean ways when it was not uncommon for a Native Quechua woman to spend a year weaving a prized poncho or manta. This catalogue is for discriminating people like you who recognize the difference between unique handmade things and machine made merchandise.

Best wishes,

Annie Hurlbut

Annie Hurlbut

Increased consumer interest in authentic native crafts has led importers to specialize in these goods, as The Peruvian Connection has done with textiles from Peru. *Courtesy of The Peruvian Connection, Ltd.*

GLOBAL GLIMPSES

1997—WHAT WILL IT MEAN TO INTERNATIONAL TRADERS?

From a humble fishing port to one of Asia's most prosperous modern economies, Hong Kong has traveled far. But perhaps its most important role still lies ahead, the 1997 conversion from a British Crown colony to a Special Administrative Region of China.

American businesses are betting their capital on Hong Kong's continued prosperity. To them it remains the trade and financial center of the Pacific Rim. The approach of 1997, they reason, will only improve Hong Kong's role as a golden gateway into China's vast market.

There are 900 American companies in Hong Kong, and since 1985, U.S. investment in Hong Kong has grown by 98 percent to a cumulative total of $7 billion, following only Japan and China.

Many people believe that Hong Kong will prosper under Chinese rule because it is in China's best interest. More than 70 percent of China's trade travels through Hong Kong ports, and Hong Kong is the top investor in China, generating more than 40 percent of China's hard currency. Why kill the golden goose?

Hong Kong remains a growing market for American exports. Residents consume about $1300 worth of U.S. imports per person per year. These days, the biggest advantage of being in Hong Kong is that you can have your plants in China and oversee them from Hong Kong. With the growing integration of Hong Kong and southern China's Guangdong Province, an economic partnership is emerging that in the coming years may become a formidable force in Asia. Hong Kong is becoming the financial capital for southern China and it seems, sometimes, that Hong Kong is taking over China instead of the other way around.

However, this enthusiasm is far from universal, and the general improvement in the public mood, which was bleak after the bloody Tiananmen Square crackdown in 1989, may be fickle. Apprehension is certain to grow in the tense final years before the hand over of power from Britain to China. But for now, many seem to believe that the considerable political risks of integration may be matched by substantial economic benefits.

Yet, for all the opportunities created by integration with China, many Hong Kong residents remain wary and remember that the territory is largely populated by people whose parents have already fled Chinese Communism. But as of now, the Hong Kong fence is no barrier to commerce.

Based on Sara Khalli, "Market Opportunity: Hong Kong," *International Business*, February 1992, pp. 48–49; Sheryl WuDunn, "Hong Kong-China Fence: No Barrier to Commerce," *New York Times*, April 4, 1992, p. 20.

Most large commercial banks maintain correspondent branches to facilitate trade among their clients in various countries. For a more detailed description of the services provided by commercial banks, see Chapter 7.

CHAMBERS OF COMMERCE AND TRADE ASSOCIATIONS

Chambers of Commerce and trade associations, which have offices worldwide, are also willing to put importers together with suppliers. They host trade missions, matchmaker programs, and other activities designed to introduce importers to valuable business contacts.

IMPORT DIRECTORIES

Several directories are aimed at importers. The most well-known English language guides are *Principal In-* *ternational Businesses*, by Dun & Bradstreet International, U.S.A.; *Kelly's Manufacturers and Merchants Directory*, by Kelly's Directories, England.[4] Some of these directories, such as *Principal International Businesses* are already available on-line to personal-computer users.

CHOOSING THE RIGHT IMPORT SUPPLIER

Import sourcing, as the business of buying and processing imports is called, is a complex, fascinating business. Its goal is to find the best supplier of the product. As an importer, you should look for the same qualities in foreign suppliers that you seek in domestic sources: reliability, price breaks, assured quality, and timely delivery. But because riding herd on a supplier who is 7000 miles away can be difficult,

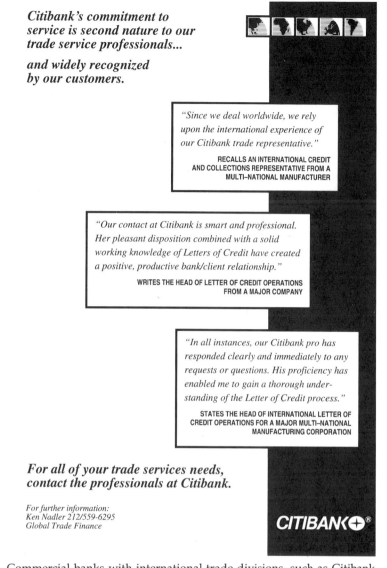

Citibank's commitment to service is second nature to our trade service professionals...

and widely recognized by our customers.

"Since we deal worldwide, we rely upon the international experience of our Citibank trade representative."
RECALLS AN INTERNATIONAL CREDIT AND COLLECTIONS REPRESENTATIVE FROM A MULTI–NATIONAL MANUFACTURER

"Our contact at Citibank is smart and professional. Her pleasant disposition combined with a solid working knowledge of Letters of Credit have created a positive, productive bank/client relationship."
WRITES THE HEAD OF LETTER OF CREDIT OPERATIONS FROM A MAJOR COMPANY

"In all instances, our Citibank pro has responded clearly and immediately to any requests or questions. His proficiency has enabled me to gain a thorough understanding of the Letter of Credit process."
STATES THE HEAD OF INTERNATIONAL LETTER OF CREDIT OPERATIONS FOR A MAJOR MULTI–NATIONAL MANUFACTURING CORPORATION

For all of your trade services needs, contact the professionals at Citibank.

For further information:
Ken Nadler 212/559-6295
Global Trade Finance

CITIBANK®

Commercial banks with international trade divisions, such as Citibank, offer their services to American exporters who want someone to handle their letters of credit from insurance to payment. *Courtesy of Citibank.*

prospective importers should go out of their way to check out their foreign sources before signing any contracts.

An importer should always conduct a credit check on any potential supplier. References should routinely be requested. This is not impolite in any country, and it is an important step in weeding out any unreliable sources. If a source suggests that the request for references is rude, the importer would do well to turn his or her attention elsewhere—just as would be the case with a U.S. supplier.

A **scouting trip** is another important step in locating suppliers; sometimes, even more than one trip is called for. In the early stages of research, an importer can often participate in a fact-finding or trade mission sponsored by a consulate or some other organization for purposes of scouting out potential products. This is a good way to view an array of products and also to test whether the country from which one is considering importing has the industrial capacity to meet the importer's standards. Manufacturing quality and consistency has risen throughout the world, but it still does not always meet U.S. standards, and this should weigh heavily in the importer's decision about where to buy a product. Later, importers should return to the countries that most interested them, often at their own expense, to meet more extensively with prospective suppliers to find out whether they personally can meet U.S. standards.

GLOBAL *Goodies*

YOUR FRIENDLY BANKER

In an effort to make it easier for companies to deal in international trade, several banks have branched into other related businesses and services. They have observed that more than 50 percent of the companies involved in getting into international trade do not know all the services of their bank and many times the best place to go to get started is a bank dealing in international finance.

Manufacturers Bank of Detroit, for example, owns a customs house brokerage and freight forwarder, John V. Carr & Son Inc. Combining a bank with a customs house brokerage and freight forwarder gives both the bank and Carr something their competitors don't have: the ability to speed the flow of international trade.

New York City-based Citibank offers *WorldLink*, a system that allows corporations and banks to make foreign currency payment in 65 different currencies from their offices by using a personal computer. The companies can make payments by check or wire transfer and can use the *WorldLink* system's on-line access to call up foreign exchange rates instantly. For drafts, companies are given check stock and can print checks, for instance, in Italian lira, Japanese yen, or in French francs and then mail the checks to the customer. The checks clear on a local Citibank account in that country much like a local check. In addition, *WorldLink* offers off-site check capability.

U.S. Bank of Portland, Oregon, owns an export trading company, U.S. World Trade Corp. This can be of particular assistance to undercapitalized firms who are unable to borrow from a bank to complete an overseas transaction because the trading company can take title to goods moving between buyer and seller and, therefore, issue any required letters of credit or provide any needed financing.

Based on John F. Carroll and Paul Eisenberg, "International Banking/Update '92," *International Business*, March 1992, pp. 93–94.

Finally, importers should request samples of any product before deciding to import. It is wise to keep in mind that although samples are one indication of quality, they are not the only one. Even sources who provide excellent samples may turn out shoddy shipments. That is why it is important to engage in a whole process—checking references, scouting trips—before settling on a supplier.

The importance of checking out foreign sources simply cannot be overestimated. Among other things, it is difficult—and often impossible—for importers to return unacceptable shipments. Some sources will not accept them, and even if they do, much valuable time has been wasted, to say nothing of money spent on freight and duties. The snafu that follows the poor selection of a foreign supplier can put an importer out of business before he or she even gets started.

ELEMENTS OF THE IMPORT-PRODUCT DECISIONS

Once an importer has decided what to import and has located potential suppliers, the next step is to work out a feasible strategy for importing the product. Sometimes, a product must be ruled out at this stage because it would be too complicated or too expensive to import it, but most of the time, if the importer has done solid preliminary research, he or she can develop a workable strategy for bringing in a foreign product. In devising an import strategy, four elements must be taken into consideration: (1) customs regulations and requirements, (2) product liability, (3) quality, and (4) added time.

CUSTOMS REGULATIONS AND REQUIREMENTS

Customs regulations are typically designed to encourage or discourage trade with specific countries. If the product has a quota or set limit that may be imported during a specified period of time (usually, one year), then importers must be sure that their shipments are under the quota's limits for the time period. If not, the importer will have to wait until a new quota period begins before bringing the product into the country. Similarly, a duty may increase in dollar value after a certain amount of a product has been imported, and an importer may want to find another source, one that is not subject to this annual restriction.

Not to be overlooked as a valuable source of imported goods are those from **preferred origin countries.** To encourage trade in certain parts of the world, the United States anoints some nations with preferred origin country status. Imports from these countries are favored over the imports of other countries.

An importer who has some leeway in choosing his product will find that preferred origin countries policies can work to his or her advantage. One importer, for example, wants to import scarves and loves the silk scarves he finds in Japan, but they are very expensive to import because of high duties. The United States wants to encourage the Japanese to buy more from us and is less interested in American consumers buying more from the Japanese.[5]

The United States does, however, have an interest in and a commitment to building up trade among its neighboring Caribbean basin nations. Because of this, scarves produced in this region may enter the United States duty free or at greatly reduced duties. (Mexico and Canada are two other nations with whom the United States has agreed or will shortly agree to reduce tariffs.) Our importer will always be able to move goods more cheaply through preferred origin countries than those that do not receive this favored treatment. Perhaps the scarves will be cotton instead of the silk for which Japan is known, but these are the kinds of trade-offs that importers often must make to ensure a profit—or even a smooth journey into the United States—with an imported product.

An importer also may encounter problems bringing in what appears to be a properly trademarked or licensed fashion product. In the past ten years, the number of trademarked and licensed fashion products has grown enormously and so has the number of **counterfeit**, or fake, versions of these products. It is illegal to import any product bearing the sign, packaging, or general makeup of a product owned by a U.S. manufacturer or citizen.

Over the past ten years importers have had to deal with an enormous increase in the amount of counterfeit goods flowing into the country from foreign suppliers. Cheap knockoffs of high-end fashions such as the outfit pictured here cost importers millions of dollars a year in lost sales. *Courtesy of Adrienne Vittidini.*

Sometimes importers unknowingly infringe a copyright when a counterfeiter assures them that it will be okay to bring a copy of the original into the United States, or the foreign manufacturer implies that the product is not protected by its trademark if it is produced outside the United States.

Under pressure from U.S. manufacturers, some of whom are swimming in a sea of counterfeits, customs officials have become stricter about confiscating counterfeit products. An importer who naively or knowingly buys a protected product may be unable to claim the product at customs and may be saddled with a huge fine as well.

Customs also enforces certain **product restrictions** on imported goods. For example, under the Textile Fiber Product Act, any textile or apparel brought into the United States (as well as products made domestically) must bear a label describing the manufacturer's name, the country of origin, and the fiber content. A similar act dictates labeling of furs of foreign and domestic origin. Customs will confiscate any imported products that are not properly labeled when they enter the United States, and getting them freed up again can entail considerable expense.

PRODUCT LIABILITY

To date, consumer safety has been a more important issue in the United States than in many foreign countries, and imported products must comply with U.S. regulations regarding the safety of a product. **Product liability** is the idea that someone, either the manufacturer or the importer, is legally obligated for any defects in a product. Importers can be and often are held responsible for the safe use and wear of any products they import.

For many years, the U.S. courts held a manufacturer or importer liable for product defects only when negligence could be proved. In recent years, however, the courts have begun to use a tougher standard called "strict liability," which the courts have interpreted to mean that an importer is responsible for faulty products regardless of any precautions that have been taken.

What does this mean in practical terms? If an importer is bringing in children's pajamas, which by law, must be flame-retardant, then the importer had better be very sure that the fiber content and treatment ensures that the pajamas are indeed inflammable. The importer can decide to trust the warranty of the manufacturer or, to be even safer, may insist on being present when flammability tests are conducted on the product. Safer still would be to conduct independent tests.

Some importers solve the problem by taking out liability insurance, but it is expensive and difficult to renew once an importer has been sued.

PRODUCT QUALITY

Importers generally struggle with the issue of quality. Although the existence of a global marketplace is serving to equalize standards of quality, it still varies radically in different countries around the world. Furthermore, U.S. consumers, more than any people on earth, are used to consistent quality. The need to meet American standards of quality when using a foreign supplier calls for a different strategy from the one applied to a domestic manufacturer. Where quality control might be left entirely in the hands of a domestic manufacturer, the importer must be prepared to check quality at every stage of the import process: during production, prior to shipment, and postshipment.

To the extent that they can, importers should exercise control over quality standards, not only checking them but often setting them as well.

TIME LAG

Put most simply, importing takes more time than buying domestically. This fact should surprise no one. An importer must add shipping time, time to process paperwork, time to deal with suppliers (and suppliers' banks) that are thousands of miles away, and even time to cope with a culture that may not operate at the same frenetic pace as the U.S. garment business.

Obviously, seasonal products like holiday fashion or bathing suits must arrive well before the season begins, but timeliness can be an issue with any fashion product. Imagine, for example, that a craving for red satin trench coats is a fad sweeping the United States. An importer believes he can import them for half the cost of making them domestically. In theory, that is how importers make money, but the importer will be successful only if he can get the coats into the country and into the stores while they are still a hot fashion.

Fashion, more than any other product except food, is perishable. Today's hot button is tomorrow's history, and the importer who cannot deliver in timely fashion pays a price, the price usually being a warehouse full of some fashion fad that was delivered too late for anyone to be interested in it.

The importer must take account of this and have a strategy that will insure that imported goods arrive in a timely manner. The obvious solution is to build

GLOBETROTTING Gaffes

COUNTRY OF ORIGIN OR WHERE DO YOU COME FROM?

Country of origin is the number one issue in the customs field now, and importers have to do their homework or they could face heavy losses. Although an importer may be completely innocent in accepting merchandise with a falsified country of origin, the Customs Service will go after the importer rather than the exporter. The exporter is out of the jurisdiction, whereas the importer is here where customs can get to him or her.

Recently, there has been a rush of transshipments from China through various countries, and the Customs Service has been busily blocking the sale of the merchandise and imposing penalties. Among the areas the Service has claimed are being used to transship goods from China are Macau, Panama, and the Philippines.

Even in dealing with reliable overseas manufacturers, the importer should obtain proof of where the apparel is being manufactured. The importer should visit the factories and take pictures or videotape the premises and the equipment to be used as evidence if Customs questions the origin of merchandise.

Some people compare the Customs Service with the Internal Revenue Service and some think that sometimes it can be worse. If the IRS finds intentional fraud, it will assess a fine of 80 percent of the unpaid tax. Customs will levy a fine of 200 percent of duties due for violations that are based on negligence rather than on intent to deceive. The fine for international deception in customs cases run from 800 to 1000 percent of the duties! So beware, check your country of origin, do not transship, and pay your taxes!

Based on Sidney Rutberg, "Warning to Importer: Eye Country of Origin," *Women's Wear Daily*, December 5, 1990, p. 20; *Daily News Record*, December 28, 1990, p. 6; Steve Farnsworth, "Customs at War vs. Import Violations," *Daily News Record*, November 14, 1991, p. 91.

---

extra time into the schedule, but even this must be done with care, given the rapidly changing state of American fashion.

UNFINISHED PRODUCTS

Unfinished products are another category of goods that may influence an importer's decision about what to buy and from where to import. **Unfinished products** are exactly what they sound like—goods whose production was begun somewhere outside the United States, usually in a favored country or region such as the Caribbean. The goods then travel in their unfinished state to the United States, where they are finished. Alternately, an unfinished product may use U.S. raw materials to produce garments assembled outside the United States. In either instance, the U.S. government offers reduced duties to producers who import with unfinished products.

Unfinished products are typically either brought home to sell domestically or they are returned to the United States postproduction and then moved out again to sell to other foreign buyers. An importer who buys unfinished products and then sells them to another foreign country is **reexporting** them.

Goods that are being reexported are held in a **free trade zone**, an enclosed or isolated area of a port of entry that provides shipping and loading facilities. Raw materials or unfinished goods may be stored, graded, sorted, and otherwise manipulated with a minimum of interference from customs.[6] A free trade zone, or FTZ, as it is commonly called, resembles a bonded warehouse.

These then are the basic influences that help to shape an importer's initial decision to import. Once production begins, still other decisions remain to be made.

SPECIFICATION DECISIONS REGARDING IMPORTS

The next important decision usually involves specification requirements. Products typically require some modification to be sold to various target markets within the United States, and the need is understandably even greater when a product is purchased in a foreign market and brought into the United States.

Product specifications are used for such tangible factors as the need to meet U.S. regulations regarding textiles and apparel and adjusting the sizes to U.S. standards as well as such intangible factors as accommodating differences in values and taste.

COMPLYING WITH GOVERNMENT REGULATIONS

Government regulations affect the specifications of imported fashion in several ways. For example, according to law, as noted earlier, certain fabrics must be made inflammable. Furs must be labeled with the country of origin, and textiles must bear content and care labels. If these products are brought in from a country that does not have the same requirements, then modifications must be made in the garments to accommodate U.S. laws.

Occasionally, specification changes are made in an attempt to reduce the duty that must be paid on a garment. If a government charges more for a luxury item than a basic one, then modifications in a garment might move it from the more expensive category to a less expensive one. One importer took elaborate gold buttons off a sweater and replaced them with plastic ones and thus put a shipment of sweaters into an entirely different (and lower) duty category. Similarly, another importer found that mixing a small amount of cashmere with cotton in a knit dress kept the garments out of the luxury-tax category that they would have fallen in had they been pure cashmere but kept them refined enough to promote as luxury products in the U.S. market.

PHYSICAL SPECIFICATIONS

Sizing is one of the more important ways in which garments must be modified to move easily from one foreign market to another. Most countries, by custom if not law, label their clothing with sizes that are familiar to their customers. For years, American women have expected to buy shoes in sizes 5 to 10, for example, whereas comparable European shoes vary from sizes 35 to 40.

Adding to the complications of sizing imports for specific markets is the fact that before importers can size-label their products, they must determine what those size equivalents are. This often varies, depending on the part of the world. A size 36 shoe made in an Italian factory may not be the same size as a size 36 shoe made in Sweden. Northern Europeans are like Americans in physical size, including the shape of their feet, whereas Italian women tend to have smaller feet.

Other physical specifications may be changed to accommodate competition, a target market, consumers' tastes or even their values, and geography and climate.

With some fashion imports, the product must be similar, if not identical, to the competition or there is no point in importing it. This is never more true than when a fad is sweeping the country. If customers are buying huge numbers of high-topped, black sneakers made by an American manufacturer, for example, there is no point in importing high-topped, orange sneakers—unless there is the realistic hope of breaking through to a new market. Any imports in black, high-topped sneakers should strive to imitate the current fad.

Target markets also affect the specification requirements for fashion products. A trench coat headed for the West Coast will do better in a lighter color than it will when headed for a large city on the East Coast. An importer often adopts the style of a foreign source but changes certain specifications to satisfy various target markets.

Similarly, imported goods must often be altered in slightly different ways to accommodate U.S. taste—and vice versa, of course. A classic example is European versus American upholstered furniture. Although high-end French, Italian, and Scandinavian soft goods often work well in any market, midrange priced goods often require certain modifications—in line or the use of color—for the same products to appeal to a U.S. market. No one's taste is right or wrong, but people definitely have different eyes for design in their furniture—and many other products as well.

Cultural values come into play in other ways that affect specifications. Midwesterners are believed to value durability and practicality over high style, for example, and in this they echo German taste. Italians and French, however, favor high style more than comfort on occasion, a value that is shared by U.S. women who live in New York and Los Angeles. Importers must adjust their products according to these cultural values if they want them to sell well.

Finally, geography and climate must be taken into account. A heavy wool coat that is just right for the Scandinavians who make it may have to be made in a lighter fabric to do well in Portland, Oregon, where the winters are mild and rain is more common than snow.

Surprisingly often these days, no specification changes are required to sell a foreign product in the United States. This is partly because of Americans' current infatuation with European styling, but it is also because of the global market, which now sends style fads whirling around the world instead of around one country. Just as style is becoming truly international, so too may other minor specifications such as size. Americans, for example, have begun to learn to read—and accept—European clothing sizes. In the future, fashion producers of the world may agree to one international set of sizes.

FACTORS AFFECTING IMPORT PRICE

Any import strategy must take into account additional costs that are present in imported goods. In these

Contrast of American and European Sizes

Ladies' Measurement Chart

European sizes:	32	34	36	38	40	42	44	46	48	50	52	54	56	58	60
Corresponding sizes:	6	8	10	12	14	16	18	20	22	24	26	28	30	32	34
1 cm								168							
ins								66¼							
2 cm	76	80	84	88	92	96	100	104	110	116	122	128	134	140	146
ins	30	31½	33	34¾	36¼	37¾	39½	41	43½	45¾	48	50½	52¾	55¼	57½
3 cm	58	62	66	70	74	78	82	86	92	98	104	110	116	122	128
ins	23	24½	26	27¾	29¼	30¾	32½	34	36¼	38¾	41	43½	45¾	48	50½
4 cm	82	86	90	94	98	102	106	110	116	122	128	134	140	146	152
ins	32½	34	35½	37	38¾	40¼	41¾	43½	45¾	48	50½	52¾	55¼	57½	60

Men's Measurement

European sizes:	44	46	48	50	52	54	56	58
Corresponding sizes:	34	36	38	40	42	44	46	48
1 cm	168	171	174	177	180	182	184	186
ins	66¼	67½	68½	69¾	71	71¾	72½	73¼
2 cm	76	88	92	96	100	104	110	116
ins	34¾	36¼	37¾	39½	41	42¼	44¼	45¾
3 cm	76	80	84	88	92	98	102	108
ins	30	31½	33	34¾	36¼	38¾	40¼	42½
4 cm	94	98	102	106	110	114	118	122
ins	37	38¾	40¼	41¾	43½	45	46½	48

Girls' Measurement Chart

Sizes	62	68	74	80	86	92	98	104	110	116	122	128	134	140	146	152	158	164	170	176
Approx. Age	3M	6M	9M	12M	18M	2	3	4	5	6	7	8	9	10	11	12	13jun	14jun	15jun	16jun
1 cm	62	68	74	80	86	92	98	104	110	116	122	128	134	140	146	152	158	164	170	176
ins	24½	26¾	29¼	31½	34	36¼	38¾	41	43½	45¾	48	50½	52¾	55¼	57½	59¾	62½	64¾	67	69¼
2 cm	47	49	51	53	55	56	57	58	59	60	62	64	66	68	72	76	80	84	88	92
ins	18½	19¼	20¼	21	21¾	22¼	22½	23	23¼	23¾	24½	25¼	26	26¾	28½	30	31½	33	34¾	36¼
3 cm	46	48	50	51	52	53	54	55	56	57	58	59	60	61	63	65	67	69	71	73
ins	18¼	19	19¾	20¼	20½	21	21¼	21¾	22¼	22½	23	23¼	23¾	24	24¾	25¾	26¼	27¼	28	28¾
4 cm	48	50	52	54	56	58	60	62	64	66	68	70	72	74	78	82	86	90	94	98
ins	19	19¾	20½	21¼	22¼	23	23¾	24½	25¼	26	26½	27¾	28½	29¼	30¾	32½	34	35½	37	38¾

Boys' Measurement Chart

Sizes	62	68	74	80	86	92	98	104	110	116	122	128	134	140	146	152	158	164	170	176
Approx. Age	3M	6M	9M	12M	18M	2	3	4	5	6	7	8	9	10	11	12	13	14	15	16
1 cm	62	68	74	80	86	92	98	104	110	116	122	128	134	140	146	152	158	164	170	176
ins	24½	26¾	29¼	31½	34	36¼	38¾	41	43½	45¾	48	50½	52¾	55¼	57½	59¾	62½	64¾	67	69¼
2 cm	47	49	51	53	55	56	57	58	59	60	63	66	69	72	75	78	81	84	87	90
ins	18½	19¼	20¼	21	21¾	22¼	22½	23	23¼	23¾	24¾	26	27¼	28½	29¾	30¾	32	33	34¼	35½
3 cm	47	48	50	51	52	53	54	55	56	57	58	60	62	64	66	68	70	72	74	78
ins	18¼	19	19¾	20¼	20½	21	21¼	21¾	22¼	22½	23	23¾	24½	25¼	26	26¾	27¾	28½	29¼	30¾
4 cm	48	50	52	54	56	58	60	62	64	66	68	70	72	75	78	81	84	87	90	94
ins	19	19¾	20½	21¼	22¼	23	23¾	24½	25¼	26	26¾	27¾	28½	29¾	30¾	32	33	34¼	35½	37

TECH TALK

THE ELECTRONIC OVERSEAS TRIP

Most major retailers and producers that run large foreign sourcing and manufacturing operations have their buyers, designers, merchandisers, and top management make about four trips a year, mostly to the Orient. When you allow for travel time, working time, loss of productivity, and recovery from jet lag, each trip costs each person about three weeks time. Multiply that by four trips a year, and almost 25 percent of these people's time is focused away from their home market.

Stepping into high technology, firms like Mast, Inc. and Liz Claiborne provide twenty-four-hour video conferencing over satellite communications lines. Combined with judicious scheduling to deal with the time differences, there can be constant contact with overseas offices. Sample development, garment fitting, and fashion conversations proceed by video conference, supplemented by modern electronic sampling techniques.

Mast is progressing even further with a high definition satellite transmission. The key feature of the high definition television is its sharp image and accurate color. Because there is great need for color accuracy and for sharp definition graphic images in the apparel industry, this type of technology is being investigated by many companies in the fashion industries. On the product side, the main technology includes CAD/CAM, electronic samples, color computers and digitized color, and automatic generation of specifications, patterns, and markers.

Using this kind of technology, the people at Mast and Liz Claiborne can view manufacturer's samples on the television tube without a long wait for shipping or the expense of air freight. Using this new technology will truly make this industry a one-world concept with global interface an everyday occurrence.

Based on "Mast: The Limited's Fast Gun," excerpt from Martin Trust Speech, *Apparel Industry Magazine*, March 1990, pp. 40–48; Eve Tahmincioglu, "Mast Test HDTV for Conferences With Its Offices," *Women's Wear Daily*, March 29, 1990, p. 9; "Lean and Debt Free," *Forbes*, January 6, 1992, p. 127.

days of expensive imports, these additional costs are typically added to the price of the product. For years, they were not. Fashion importers, in fact, did not examine the costs of imported goods too closely because foreign products were so much cheaper than U.S. products that, even with the added costs, importers could still sell them cheaply. Now with increased government regulations and a voracious American appetite for expensive imports, fashion importers are learning to look more carefully at the bottom line. Even though tariffs have been reduced or eradicated on many products, apparel and textiles have for the most part been excluded from international agreements to lower tariffs, so fashion importers still must struggle with the cost—and of course, ultimately, the price—of the goods they import.

PRICE ESCALATION

All imports involve some degree of price escalation as extra costs are added to the factory price, or **first**

cost, of goods. Shipping costs, duties, forwarding costs, and insurance charges are added to the first cost to determine the total, or **landed cost,** of bringing a product to its final destination. Tariffs and other taxes on fashion imports average 23 percent, and international shipping is three times that of domestic shipping, too much for the importer to absorb.[7] Therefore, the price charged by an importer is generally based on the landed, rather than first, costs.

There are other, less obvious costs attached to importing fashion products. Buying costs are higher, for example, because buyers travel farther to obtain foreign products. The fact that goods must travel many thousand miles more to reach their destinations means that longer lead time is involved. Longer travel time increases the risk of pilferage or of the product not arriving either on time or at all. Currency fluctuations over the longer shipping time also often add to the cost of foreign goods.

Even manufacturing schedules may add to the costs of buying imported goods, as many foreign manufacturers cannot produce goods as quickly as can domestic producers. **Quick response,** a U.S. industry strategy for delivering fashion products in timely fashion that has been highly successful domestically, has not taken hold in foreign markets.[8] Only 3 percent of all textile manufacturers worldwide were able to implement quick response as recently as 1990.[9]

GOVERNMENT REGULATIONS AND COST

Government regulations also affect the pricing of imported goods. The Tax Reform Act of 1986, a political-legal action designed to stem the tide of cheap imports that have undermined the U.S. fashion industry, mandates that the import-transfer price of a product cannot exceed the value claimed for it in customs. The **import-transfer price** is the price a foreign manufacturer charges the importer.[10]

Other government regulations that increase the cost of importing are the **antidumping duty** and **countervailing duty.** An antidumping duty is charged if the price of an imported good is lower than the price in its country of origin. If U.S. Customs finds that foreign goods are being dumped in this manner, it imposes the antidumping duty. The U.S. duty benefits domestic manufacturers of cheap products but is against GATT regulations. Most other governments do not impose antidumping duties.

Similar to antidumping duties are countervailing duties, which are imposed on foreign products that have been subsidized by their governments. Governments may have cost-reducing programs designed to encourage manufacturers to produce goods for ex-port. These programs enable manufacturers to sell products for less than they would if they were not subsidized.

The U.S. government, strongly influenced by the garment industry lobby, considers dumping and subsidized trade to be unfair competition and imposes the two duties in an attempt to equalize prices.[11] Importers who have to pay countervailing or antidumping duties must often pass along the added costs to the customer in the form of a higher price. In the future, the government could decide to reduce or eliminate these duties—or to impose new ones.

To stay in business, importers must know they will be able to make money on the products they import. These days, they can reasonably expect to do this only by keeping a careful eye on the bottom line, by choosing their assortments carefully—and occasionally, by deciding to forgo a foreign product entirely because, all things considered and all things being equal, it is too expensive to import.

In this chapter, we have discussed the basic elements that go into the import decision. They are not the only factors in an import decision nor are they unchanging. A country that once held favored-nation status may lose it, and duties will be imposed on its imports. A formerly stable country could suffer a coup, and an importer would have to add political instability to the list of items to consider when formulating an initial import strategy.

The best protection available to importers who want to ward off the numerous follies that can plague their business is to constantly stay on top of potential markets and to constantly reassess their market strategy to be sure it remains viable.

ENDNOTES

1. Kitty G. Dickerson, *Textiles and Apparel in the International Economy.* New York: Macmillan, 1991, p. 418.
2. *Ibid.,* p. 418.
3. Sandra L. Kruzel and Frank Reynolds, *Import/Export Procedures.* Cincinnati, OH: South-Western Publishing, 1992, p. 129.
4. *Ibid.,* p. 129.
5. *Ibid.,* pp. 129–30.
6. FIT, Small Business Center, Brochure No. 2, unpublished and undated, p. 1.
7. Dickerson, *Op. cit.,* p. 427.
8. Diane Elson, "Marketing Factors Affecting the Geovalisation [sic] of Textiles," *EIU Textile Outlook International,* March 1990, p. 55.
9. Robin Anson and Paul Simpson, "World Textile Trade and Production Trends," *EIU Textile Outlook International,* January 1991, p. 30.
10. Jerry Haar and Marta Ortiz-Buonafina, *Import Marketing: A Management Guide to Profitable Operations,* Lexington, MA: Lexington Books, 1989, p. 132.
11. Kruzel and Reynolds, *Op. cit.,* p. 151.

VOCABULARY

antidumping duty _____

_____

_____

counterfeit _____

_____

_____

countervailing duty _____

_____

_____

fashion importer _____

_____

_____

first cost _____

_____

_____

free trade zone _____

_____

_____

import sourcing _____

_____

_____

import-transfer price _____

_____

_____

landed cost _____

_____

_____

preferred origin countries _____

_____

_____

product liability _____

_____

_____

product restrictions _____

_____

_____

quick response _____

_____

_____

reexporting _____

_____

_____

scouting trip _____

_____

_____

unfinished products _____

_____

_____

GLOBAL REVIEW 1. What is the overall goal of an importer?

_____

_____

_____

_____

2. List the six factors that influence the decision to import a product.

_____

_____

_____

_____

_____

3. Name three agencies that can help you to locate sources or supplies for imported merchandise.

_____

_____

_____

4. Why is import sourcing so complex?

_____

_____

_____

_____

5. You should seek foreign suppliers with the same qualities you expect from domestic sources. Name three of these qualities and explain why they are so important.

_____

_____

_____

_____

6. What is a scouting trip?

_____

_____

_____

_____

7. What are the four elements that must be considered when you devise an import strategy?

_____

_____

_____

_____

8. Explain the difference between product liability and product quality.

_____

_____

_____

_____

9. Explain how a free trade zone helps an importer.

_____

_____

_____

_____

10. What is the difference between the first cost and the landed cost?

_____

_____

_____

_____

GLOBAL DIGEST   **1.** Choose a fashion product that you want to import and discuss the reasons you would import the product rather than produce it domestically.

_____

_____

_____

_____

_____

_____

_____

_____

2. Explain the various specification requirements and modifications that may be required when importing men's, children's, or women's apparel.

_____

_____

_____

_____

_____

_____

_____

_____

3. How do global political changes affect the decision to import by a U.S. importer?

_____

_____

_____

_____

_____

_____

_____

_____

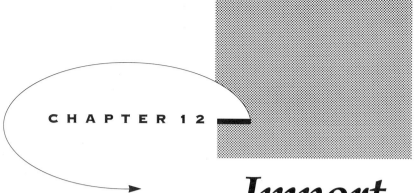

CHAPTER 12

Import Distribution and Promotion Strategy

If the imported fashion product does not reach the stores for which it is intended, and if the customer does not know it is there, it will languish on the shelves or on hangers, taking up store space and robbing the importer of profits after many months of effort. That is why the distribution and sales promotion of imported goods, the next stage of importing and the subject of this chapter, is such an important function of importing.

FACTORS IN IMPORT DISTRIBUTION

The importer is a crucial link in the channel of distribution. Whereas exporters use agents to move merchandise through the channel of distribution and often engage in indirect distribution, importers typically function as direct agents that move goods from the manufacturer to their point of purchase.

Importers usually establish a channel of distribution when they organize their businesses, and as long as all links are performing well, the channel does not vary. That is why it is important to give considerable thought to the kind of channel of distribution that will be most effective and to put it in place before it is needed.

Foreign producers are of little help in establishing or moving fashion imports though the channel of distribution because they know little about other countries' methods of distribution and promotion.

THE IMPORTER'S ROLE IN DISTRIBUTION

Importers typically function in one of three ways in the channel of distribution. They are either the wholesaler, the distributor, or the retailer.

IMPORTER AS WHOLESALER The importer-wholesaler buys products in bulk and sells them to other merchants, usually retailers. Importer-wholesalers operate much like domestic wholesalers. They arrange for the goods to move from one country to another. From the retailers' point of view, the advantage of using an importer-wholesaler is that the retailer can buy in small quantities from someone who has a large and ready supply on hand.

Importers can be either full-line wholesalers or limited-line wholesalers. A **full-line wholesaler** offers a full assortment of many different kinds of warehoused products, and a **limited-line wholesaler** offers only a few products, which are drop-shipped to customers.

IMPORTER AS DISTRIBUTOR An importer may also function as the distributor of a line of clothes or accessories or, as is often the case with distributorships, of furniture or other fashion products for the home. In this instance, an importer operates much like a wholesaler, but rather than buy on a per-shipment basis, he or she has an exclusive contract to control the merchandise for a specified period of time.

Like the wholesaler, the distributor assumes responsibility for shipping the goods, but unlike the wholesaler, the distributor is expected to be a source of market information and also of warranties and guarantees. (The wholesaler also provides information sometimes but rarely has the vested interest in doing so that a distributor does.)

IMPORTER AS MANUFACTURER-RETAILER Finally, importers function as manufacturer-retailers. They produce a fashion product or have it produced to their exact specifications, import it, and sell it, either through their own outlets or through other retailers.

The risks are greatest with this method, as are the potential profits. The importer who is also the manufacturer-retailer must assume responsibility for all aspects of production, from buying raw materials to quality control to shipping.

METHODS OF DISTRIBUTION AND CUSTOMER BUYING PATTERNS

Once an importer has determined whether to be a wholesaler, distributor, or retailer, the next step is to settle on a method of distribution. The method of distribution will depend on the goals of the importer and the type of product coverage that is sought.[1]

An importer who wants to maintain a great deal of control over the product will insist on **exclusive distribution** such as is found in such stores as the Body Shop and Bennetton. Their products are found only in their outlets. Exclusive distribution also permits centralized buying and warehousing as well as nationally coordinated sales promotion, if the importer desires it.

Alternately, an importer may opt for **selective distribution,** which means the imported goods will be sold through a limited number of outlets, usually all of a similar type in terms of quality and location. Escada, for example, is sold only through high-end department stores and women's specialty shops. The importer maintains some control over the product's image and may also oversee point-of-purchase display and sales techniques.

The last option, **extensive distribution,** puts imported goods into a large number of outlets and thereby dilutes the control that the importer can exercise over the product. Importers cannot control the image, display, or even the selection when they participate in extensive distribution. However, because of the possibility of greater volume, some importers are willing to relinquish control.

The kind of distribution an importer chooses depends to some extent on the customer's expectations. If a customer will not travel far to buy a product or spend much for it, then extensive distribution is the best way to sell the product. When the customer is willing to spend more money or relishes the exclusivity or status of the product, exclusive or selection distribution is not only warranted but may be necessary to maintain the elitist image of the product.

IMPORT CHANNELS OF DISTRIBUTION

Imports move through the same channels of distribution as domestic goods, that is, they are sold to **general merchandisers, specialty merchandisers,** or **chain organizations.**

GENERAL MERCHANDISE STORES General merchandisers include both department stores like Macy's, Marshall Field, L.S. Ayres, and Nordstrom's and such national department stores as J.C. Penney, Montgomery Ward, and Sears. Each, however, has a different approach to imports.

Department stores discovered the value of imports in the 1970s when they began to buy them in greater abundance than they ever had before. Today, department stores offer an array of imported fashion to their customers. In fact, these stores are perhaps most committed to—and have benefitted most from—foreign fashion imports. They offer their customers a variety of price ranges and quality in imported fashion. In return, imports have expanded their product mix and given them increasingly flexible profit margins.

Some retailers, for example, practice **price averaging,** a technique of mixing a range of imported garments from different suppliers on the same rack. Some garments cost more—or less—than others even though they are priced the same. The less costly goods are not necessarily inferior in quality, but rather, they are cheaper by virtue of their point of origin. Garments purchased from developing, labor-cheap

Stores such as Bennetton maintain control over their merchandise by retaining exclusive distribution of their products, selling only out of their own outlets. *Courtesy of The United Colors of Bennetton—store interior.*

countries inevitably cost less than those of the same quality purchased from more advanced countries with more highly organized apparel industries. The retailer sells all the imports for the same price, but enjoys higher markups on some than on others.

To facilitate foreign buying, department stores typically maintain their own staffs of foreign buyers and foreign buying offices, whose job is to scout for trendy, new styles. They fill out their product lines by buying from wholesale importers.

Department stores also have pioneered in **vertical marketing,** in which the retailer becomes both manufacturer and seller. Vertical marketing has led to the creation of **private label** lines, or store brands. These lines, which are produced almost exclusively offshore, now comprise about 20 percent of the apparel market. Despite costing an average of 20 percent less than **national brands,** that is, brands identified with a specific manufacturer, private label clothes support a higher markup, primarily because of their offshore origins.[2] Private labels that have done well for department stores include Bloomingdale's "Bloomie's Express" and Macy's "Charterhouse" label for men as well as their "Aeropostale" labels of sportswear.

In contrast to the department stores, the national chains, also sometimes called national department stores, were early importers several decades ago when they saw the value in buying cheap imports. Like the department stores, they benefitted from higher profit margins but unlike the department stores, they sought to pass on their savings to their customers. Their focus has changed little over time. The national chains still tend to buy low-end fashion imports in large quantities and sell them cheaply.

SPECIALTY MERCHANDISE STORES
Specialty merchandisers, small stores that carry a limited line of merchandise, are more likely than any other kind of store to carry imports exclusively. Imports often provide these small stores with the special cachet they need to make their mark in the world of fashion. Charivari, for example, a New York specialty store with several outlets throughout the city, made its name by selling high-end, imported fashion. They were among the first retailers to sell the stunning new fashions of the new Japanese designers in the 1980s.

Some specialty stores that sell imported goods have ventured into a new type of vertical marketing

GLOBAL *Goodies*
OH HOW I LOVE MY SISTERS

You may be surprised to learn that the National Sister Cities Program celebrated its 35th birthday in 1991. The program was originally established to promote educational and cultural exchanges between the continents, but it has long since outgrown that role. According to Sister Cities International, 902 U.S. cities are currently involved with 1441 Sister Cities in 98 countries.

Although the educational and cultural dimensions are no less important today, more and more communities and states are funding business-to-business angles of Sister City/Sister State programs and establishing bilateral trade links.

Of course, the more seasoned the relationship, the more tangible the likely economic gains. In the course of a twenty-year Sister City relationship between Coldwater, Michigan, and Soltau, Germany, three German manufacturing companies, employing over 140 people, have located in Coldwater.

A Sister Cities relationship begun in 1959 between Portland, Oregon, and Sapporo, Japan, produces hundreds of millions of dollars in trade annually.

Several U.S. states have also established profitable relationships with overseas jurisdictions. The state of Washington and Japan's Hyogo Prefecture have had close cultural and educational bonds since 1963. New Jersey has discovered the business-promotion aspects of the Sister State relationships. New Jersey signed its first Sister State agreement in 1981, and has since made four similar agreements. As a result of its relationship with Zhejiang, China, New Jersey companies are discussing joint ventures and direct sales to Chinese companies. Similar arrangements are underway with Japanese firms, and in December 1991, the New Jersey trade delegation visited its new sister, Israel, to establish business ties with Israeli companies and government agencies.

Although political turbulence sometimes dampens Sister City/Sister State relationships, these relationships are certain to have enduring economic benefits. Sister Cities International forecasts that by the year 2000 almost 90 percent of Sister City connections will include some degree of trade and business.

For more information, contact: Sister Cities International, 120 South Payne St., Alexandria, VA 22314, (707) 836–3535.

Based on Gretchen Birkle, "Sister City/Sister Statehood is Powerful," *Export Today*, November/December 1991, p. 43.

---

called **dispersion retailing**, a form of merchandising in which the retailer handles both the manufacturing and the selling functions. The appeal of dispersion retailing is that it allows tight control of the store's image as well as of the distribution channel and sales promotion. Another advantage is greater profits: The middleman-importer is eliminated.[3] The Body Shop, a British cosmetics chain; Laura Ashley, IKEA, and Bennetton are all examples of dispersion retailers.

CHAIN ORGANIZATIONS Chain organizations, which consist of a group of centrally owned stores, usually four or more, that carry similar goods and merchandise, also rely heavily on imports. Chains like the Gap, The Limited, and Lerner stores use imports to cut their costs and increase their profit margins. Because they buy centrally for all their outlets, they are able to reduce costs still more by purchasing in large quantities.

PHYSICAL DISTRIBUTION OF IMPORTS

The physical distribution of imports is not difficult because the United States is already highly efficient at moving goods across its 3000-mile girth. The choice of transportation will be affected by the cost, time, capacity, and customer needs. If products must move through the channel of distribution quickly, as is often the case with a fashion fad, then one method of transportation—air travel, for example—may be favored over another. Most imported fashion products come into the country by air. Once imports have arrived, they are usually trucked to their various domestic destinations.

The exporter, who is also the foreign manufacturer, or more likely, his agent, handles the extensive paperwork involved in moving goods from one

New Yorkers explore strange new lands.

WELCOME
NEW JERSEY
THE GARDEN STATE
First State to Ratify
the Bill of Rights

CHARIVARI
What is expected of New York is the unexpected.
Antony Price Women's Collection; Matsuda Men's Collection.

Specialty merchandisers, such as Charivari, carry a limited line of goods, often focusing exclusively on high-end fashion imports. *Advertising by Kirshenbaum & Bond.*

country to another, along with the transportation arrangements. Occasionally, an importer must make arrangements to ship a product after it reaches the United States, but most shipping companies arrange land as well as sea transportation.

Because of the size of the United States, many import shipments involve **intermodal** travel, a method involving two or more modes of transportation. Typically, as noted, this means plane and truck.

IMPORT PRODUCT PROMOTION STRATEGIES

Generally speaking, the importer is in a better position than the exporter-manufacturer to sell a product in his or her home country. Importers are more familiar with government regulations such as truth-in-advertising, marketing costs, and media suitability

GLOBAL *GO-GETTERS*

MALDEN MILLS—MADE IN AMERICA, REMAILED IN EUROPE

When the "poltermeisters" in Germany reach for meters of colorfast flocked velvet to upholster a setee, they think their supplier is European. After all, the order is filled in a week's time from Holland. However, six time zones away in Laurence, Massachusetts, it is the job of Malden Mills Inc. to keep up that illusion.

"European customers want local stock and they want fairly prompt service," observes the export manager for the upholstery division of the $250 million privately owned textile company. "Stateside shipping would take three weeks, while air freight costs would price the nylon velvet out of most upholsterer's budgets," he adds.

Instead, Malden Mills warehouses 150,000 yards of fabric in Arnheim, Netherlands, from a facility it leases from a unit of TNT Ltd., the Australian-based transportation conglomerate. When agents or customers place orders, Malden Mills notifies the TNT Fulfillment Division, which in turn communicates the order to the warehouse in Arnheim. There, the fabric is cut to order and then trucked to the customer, and TNT Fulfillment collects and deposits the payment for the delivered goods.

Fulfillment is the upper tier of a range of business reply services commonly known as "remail." Launched after the U.S. government deregulated a portion of the U.S. Postal Service in 1986, remail allows private carriers such as TNT, DHL, Federal Express, and Airborne Express to compete for the business of sending U.S.-based companies' mail to overseas destinations and bringing back replies. Because TNT is able to consolidate its own freight shipments, a customer can save between 30 and 50 percent below standard shipping rates if it decides to warehouse its products with TNT. These types of services—a far cry from the classic image of your local mail carrier on his or her daily rounds—are now available from most international carriers.

Well known today as a manufacturer of technically advanced high-performance upholstery fabrics as well as outerwear such as jackets made with the synthetic fiber known as Polarfleece, Malden Mills is one of the oldest operating mills remaining in the northeast, founded by Henry Feuerstein in 1906 in Malden, Massachusetts. Originally known as a major producer of wool sweaters and bathing suits in the early 1900s, the company has since become a major player in the production of velvet upholstery fabrics and synthetic clothing fibers. Today, at a time when imports threaten American mills and clothing manufacturers, Malden Mills exports its synthetic fiber, also known as Polartec, and woven velvet fabrics to both major domestic and European manufactuers and retailers. A global gogetter indeed!

Based on Helen-Chantal Pike, "Many Happy Returns," *International Business*, December 1991.

Courtesy of Malden Mills.

and availability. Even such finer points of selling, as the style and format of advertising, right down to the typefaces, often varies from one country to another. To cite just one example, in most of Europe, lingerie and cosmetic advertisements on television are far more explicit than would be acceptable in the United States. Importers who tried to import a European sales promotion might find themselves garnering more attention than they ever dreamed possible—more, perhaps, than would be good for their product. Most of the attention would amount to notoriety, which does not necessarily translate into sales.

Most of the time, the same sales tools can be used to promote an imported product as are used to promote domestic products. Samples, coupons, price packs, point of sale displays, and premiums all work equally well for both kinds of products.

Imported goods also go through the same product life cycle that domestic fashions do, and this will affect choices in advertising and promotion. Traditional sales theory dictates, for example, that more money will have to be spent to promote a new, unknown product than a familiar, mature one, if only to inform customers that the product exists and to minimalize any resistance they may have to its newness. In other words, it takes more money to get a new product off the ground. This is often, but not always, the case with fashion products.

Some customers may resist new fashion products simply because they are new or foreign, but the fashion industry also has a proportionally higher number of customers who will rush to buy new fashion imports and help to spread the word to other customers than most other businesses enjoy because of the unique nature of fashion.

In addition, imported fashion products must be targeted in the same way that domestic ones are. High-end, expensive products must reach the customer with the money to buy them. Conversely, low-end products cannot be sold in expensive outlets because they will not appeal to the customer.

Finally, importers not only need to understand the sales techniques and tools that are available to them in their own countries, but they should also explore how the product was promoted in its country of origin. This can provide valuable insight into promoting an import product in a new country.

SALES PROMOTION TOOLS

There are some differences—good and bad—in the way that imported and domestic products are promoted. For example, importers will lose the benefits of participating in the highly effective nationwide sales promotions that national manufacturers stage for their customers several times a year. They will not enjoy the benefits of co-op advertising.

The good news is that imports offer other opportunities for sales promotions that national brand manufacturers cannot avail themselves of. For example, as the global marketplace continues to evolve, an importer can increasingly use a product's uniqueness as a promotion tool. Some product features now available only in certain parts of the world—smocking, piping, beading, to name but a few—can be promoted as unique imported products.

Another sales tool that can be attributed almost exclusively to imports are the huge promotions and sales that stores now sponsor year-round. Higher markups on imported fashions are the reason that

GLOBETROTTING Gaffes

FORGET THE WOODEN SHOES

Many cities and countries conjure up specific images when people hear their names—New York-"The Big Apple," London-"Big Ben," Paris-"Eiffel Tower," Amsterdam-"Wooden Shoes"!

If Amsterdam Mayor Ed von Thijn had things his way, people would forget about wooden shoes and think of his city as a wonderful place for international trade.

As Mayor von Thijn is flying from Berlin to London and to Hungary, Japan, and North America, he insists his town is an urbanized, modern, twentieth-century city. "The canal and tulip image I don't mind, but the wooden shoes get to me."

However, as he heads off on another whirlwind round of business promotion for Amsterdam, the sensitive subject of wooden shoes comes up and the fact emerges that every time he goes on an investment promotion trip, he brings a pair of wooden shoes with him—for deep down, he knows it is what people want to see.

Based on Daniel R. Pruzen, "Against the Grain," *World Trade*, March 1992, pp. 76–78.

stores are able to offer these sales and stay in business. Sometimes, stores do not mention that the sales are related to import stock, and sometimes, they use the imports as a sales point. Either way, it is the higher initial markups seen in imports that make such sales promotions possible.

Alternately, as was mentioned earlier, some retailers take advantage of the lower costs of low-end imports by passing along the savings to their customers. This is another sales tool that is more widely available to sellers of imported goods than to those of domestic products.

Over the past decade, point-of-purchase displays became increasingly useful tools in selling imported apparel and accessories to the point where entire departments have been set up in stores to advertise these wares. High-end imports are sold this way, where low-end imports are more often blended with other products with little or no mention made of the fact that the products are foreign.

In any case, the importer must know how and when to tap into the import as a sales tool. Sometimes, the end user, or customer, cares that the fashion product is imported. At other times, the fact that a fashion product is imported would not be an important sales factor.

Consider, for example, a *Wall Street Journal* article about imported fashion. It described shoppers sifting their way through a stack of imported shirts in a New York department store. They compared fabric, price, style, and cut, but not one mentioned the fact that the shirts were imported.[4] If the fact that a garment or fashion product is imported does not matter to the consumer, then the importer may have no reason to use this knowledge as a sales tool. The product can be sold in the same way as any other garment similar of its type and style.

DEVISING THE BEST STRATEGY FOR THE PRODUCT

Whatever sales tools are used, they should all be part of a cohesive, overall strategy to promote the imported fashion product. A sales promotion strategy should be developed at the earliest possible time in the import process. It is the way the importer communicates with the customers. Four strategies are generally used to promote imported fashion products.[5]

PRODUCT INVENTION When the product is new, the importer's job is to introduce customers to this new idea. When rayon was first introduced several decades ago, customers had to learn what its properties were and how it could best be used to make attractive clothing.

Ironically, this most versatile of man-made fibers was eclipsed for several decades as customers demonstrated a preference for natural fibers. Rayon is now in the process of being invented, or rather, reinvented, largely through imported garments, in the minds of an entirely new generation of users.

PRODUCT ADAPTATION—COMMUNICATION EXTENSION This strategy is implemented when the imported product will be put to the same use as in the exporter's country but under different conditions. These different conditions must be conveyed to the potential new customer.

For example, lavish fur hats are worn by many Russian males who need them for warmth during the harsh Russian winters. When the hats were introduced to U.S. males some seasons ago, they could not be sold in the way as they had been in Russia. Instead they had to be adapted to new conditions. To achieve this, importers had to communicate to potential U.S. buyers the decorative rather than utilitarian qualities of the hats.

PRODUCT EXTENSION—COMMUNICATION ADAPTATION This strategy works best when the product will be put to a different use under similar conditions. The classic example is a racing bicycle. When these were introduced to the general American buying public a few years ago, the importer had to consider that although the bicycles were used the same way by all owners, they were used primarily for transportation in the rest of the world, whereas in the United States, they were purely recreational. This fact had to be taken under consideration in developing a sales strategy, because, obviously, a sales campaign that stressed the recreational use of a bicycle would differ from one that stressed the bicycle's use as a means of transportation.

In the world of fashion, floor pillows offer a comparable example. Used in parts of Asia as primary furniture, they are sold to U.S. consumers as an optional and alternate form of furniture. This fact affects the shape and flavor of any sales promotion of the pillows.

PRODUCT EXTENSION Finally, there is product extension, when a product is put to the same use in both the exporter's and the importer's countries. This is the easiest and cheapest kind of product to adapt to new markets, but it is not error-proof. For one thing, the customer must still be prepared to accept the product.

A few seasons ago, sueded silks were introduced as a new variation on an old fabric. Consumers were delighted with the new product, which was introduced across the country for summerwear. Unfortunately, the new silk was too heavy to be worn in hot U.S. climates during the summer when most consumers were used to wearing silk. Only when it was promoted as year-round fabric did the sueded silk catch on.

THE ROLE OF PRICE IN SALES STRATEGY

The price of an import also plays a role in the sales strategy. Products are not sold the same way in one price range as in another.

A simple and easily used strategy for selling imports is called **value-in-use,** which lets the customer save money by substituting an importer's product for one currently in use. The importer is simply offering the customer another option in a familiar product—one that is not radically different in price.

Psychological pricing is used to reach a target market. The importer takes a measure of his target customers, decides what they can and will pay for an imported product, and sets the price accordingly. Importers of expensive bed linens price their products high because of the status attached to these fine linens, whereas the importer who sells imported linens (admittedly of a far less fine quality) to a national department store like Montgomery Ward knows that these customers will expect the linens to be less than national brand linens.

Finally, **prestige pricing** took hold of the import market in the 1980s. When imports became status symbols, importers learned that customers would pay more for a product—regardless of its actual cost—simply because it was a foreign good. Their pricing strategy reflected this market trend as prices of certain fashion imports soared.

NEW TRENDS IN SALES STRATEGIES

New marketing trends come along regularly in the fashion industry, and for the most part, fashion importers must be prepared to pick up on them sooner than others in the fashion industry. The reason is that the trends often begin on one continent and travel to another. Unaware importers can be caught short with inappropriate sales strategies if they are not on top of trends on at least two continents—certainly in every country where they do business.

The two most current trends are the **green consumer** and the BUY-U.S.A. movements.

GREEN CONSUMERS

The green consumer is a new type of environmentally sophisticated and ethically motivated consumer. This buyer emerged—seemingly from nowhere—in 1989. (Actually, the green consumer is probably a logical extension of the growing interest in the environment.) Green consumer products refer to anything from nonaerosol cleaning products to unbleached, untreated bed linens.

One of the early signs of the green consumer movement occurred when the Body Shop, which does not test any of its products on animals, enjoyed great success in England and, later, in its many branches around the world by capitalizing on its ethics. In Europe, Habitat (or Conran's, as it is known in the United States) joined the bandwagon by putting together a "green consumer" room to illustrate the principles of this new breed of consumer.[6]

Green consumers' demands for unbleached, untreated, naturally colored fibers and fabrics have already begun to exert a strong pull on the U.S. textile and apparel market. To date, much of the demand exists in housewares, but marketers expect it to spill over to clothing as well. There is also a growing interest among cosmetics users.

Coming Home, a home-textiles division of Land's End, a mail-order clothing retailer, was one of the first American retailers to play to the green consumers. Their emphasis on untreated bed linens and undyed towels in their catalogs, and the subsequent popularity of these items with customers, has been strong enough to make domestic manufacturers take note. Several domestic manufacturers of bed linens and towels have either already introduced or are rushing to develop their own line of green consumer products.

Playing to green consumers, however, may not always be as easy as presenting them with a new line of products. One of the goals of green consumers is to use their purchasing power to make the world a better place. *New Consumer Magazine*, started in 1989, published an article in its second issue in which it expressed concern about exploitive labor practices and urged their readers, out of concern for the workers, to boycott a United Kingdom clothing company that took advantage of its foreign workers in Bataan.[7]

At present, the ethical concern regarding textiles does not rival concern for the Amazon rainforest and other environmental issues, but some experts in the

TECH TALK

COMPETITIVE COMPUTING

Each day more domestic apparel manufacturers are moving toward sourcing production overseas to supplement their domestic manufacturing.

An apparel company needs the ability to compare the full cost of domestic production with the landed cost of foreign goods. To manage both domestic and foreign product sourcing effectively, one must develop information systems that provide a view of plants and contractors.

A few domestic apparel manufacturers have developed custom systems to track overseas production, including unique cost accounting modules. Typically, these are completely separate systems from their domestic manufacturing and cost systems.

In developing information systems to support domestic and foreign production, it is important that the systems allow an apples-to-apples approach to comparison of each sourcing alternative. The systems should also evaluate quality, reliability, timeliness, cost, and flexibility.

The key information system components required to support foreign production and contracting should include:

Product cost estimates recognizing all costs, including foreign cost differentials.

A production plan helping select the best foreign plant based on available capacity, costs, quota, and location.

Product design/samples communicating design specifications to the contractor or the foreign-owned plant.

Raw material commitment identifying in advance raw material needs based on a high-level production plan.

Production status tracking the goods at the foreign plant.

In-transit goods tracking monitoring the status of the goods as they move from the foreign plant to the domestic distribution center.

Developing the information to support foreign production and contracting is not a quick or easy process. Once developed, however, these systems will manage a growing part of the business for many domestic apparel companies.

Based on Stephen Sprinkle, Paula Charles, Eva SooHoo, "Monitoring Overseas Manufacturing," *Apparel Industry Magazine*, July 1991, pp. 51–52.

---

garment industry predict it will. The European-based movement has already traveled to the United States, and both importers and exporters need to be aware of this potentially powerful trend so they can respond adequately to it.

BUY-U.S.A.

Importers may also soon find themselves coping with pro-U.S.A. sentiments in the marketplace. If consumers settled for cheap imports in the 1970s and relished buying expensive imports in the 1980s, the 1990s may well be a era when they turn away from imports—or try to anyway. (Turning away from im-

ports entirely will not be easy to do at this point in the development of world trade.)

BUY-U.S.A. sentiments have been growing for several years now, although they have only begun to crystalize in the public's imagination. Some retailers have already declined to participate in the import boom, and the next decade may well prove to be their heyday. Lord and Taylor, for example, emphasizes its ties to American designers, and Marks and Spencer, a British clothing chain with branches in Europe and Canada, has remained committed to British fashion. Wal-Mart, in the United States, has made a firm commitment to U.S.-made products. The "Buy America" program, developed in part by Wal-Mart's

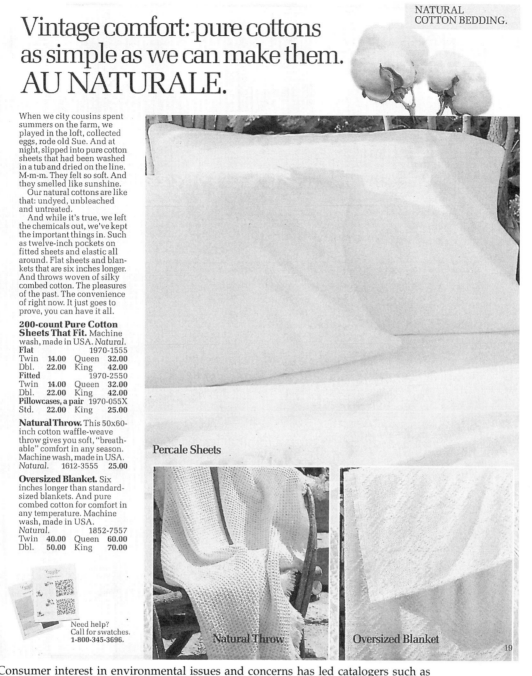

Vintage comfort: pure cottons as simple as we can make them. AU NATURALE.

NATURAL COTTON BEDDING.

When we city cousins spent summers on the farm, we played in the loft, collected eggs, rode old Sue. And at night, slipped into pure cotton sheets that had been washed in a tub and dried on the line. M-m-m. They felt so soft. And they smelled like sunshine.

Our natural cottons are like that: undyed, unbleached and untreated.

And while it's true, we left the chemicals out, we've kept the important things in. Such as twelve-inch pockets on fitted sheets and elastic all around. Flat sheets and blankets that are six inches longer. And throws woven of silky combed cotton. The pleasures of the past. The convenience of right now. It just goes to prove, you can have it all.

200-count Pure Cotton Sheets That Fit. Machine wash, made in USA. *Natural.*

Flat			1970-1555
Twin	14.00	Queen	32.00
Dbl.	22.00	King	42.00
Fitted			1970-2550
Twin	14.00	Queen	32.00
Dbl.	22.00	King	42.00
Pillowcases, a pair			1970-055X
Std.	22.00	King	25.00

Natural Throw. This 50x60-inch cotton waffle-weave throw gives you soft, "breathable" comfort in any season. Machine wash, made in USA. *Natural.* 1612-3555 25.00

Oversized Blanket. Six inches longer than standard-sized blankets. And pure combed cotton for comfort in any temperature. Machine wash, made in USA. *Natural.* 1852-7557

Twin	40.00	Queen	60.00
Dbl.	50.00	King	70.00

Need help? Call for swatches. 1-800-345-3696.

Percale Sheets

Natural Throw

Oversized Blanket

19

Consumer interest in environmental issues and concerns has led catalogers such as Coming Home to emphasize the unbleached and untreated nature of their products. *Courtesy of Land's End.*

former chairman Sam Walton, may enjoy renewed popularity in the 1990s.

To some extent, a case can be made for buying American: it puts Americans to work, and the customer must be working to buy anything—domestic or imported.

Importers may well have to cope with backlash against foreign goods over the next few years. One recent survey showed that although 32 percent of those interviewed actively sought out imports, 34 percent felt guilty about buying them.[8]

Fortunately for importers, the global market is too firmly established for consumers to reject all imports. Doing so would mean giving up certain products like leather gloves, altogether, not just giving up products made outside the United States.

BACKED BY POPULAR DEMAND.

Recent studies show that most Americans believe that American-made clothes and home fashions have the same, or better, quality than imports.

They also believe that they get more for their money when they buy American-made products.

And they're backing up their convictions at the cash register. Just ask Castner-Knott.

When they displayed and identified
Made in the U.S.A. clothes and home fashions
consumer response was inspiring. Dollar volume rose
a staggering 50% on featured merchandise
without a loss of volume on non-featured merchandise.

McAlpin's reports similar results with a 26% rise in dollar volume when they featured Made in the U.S.A. goods.

So source, promote and display Made in the U.S.A. clothing and home fashions. It's very smart business. Especially when millions of Americans think our star is rising.

Get with the program.

FOR MORE INFORMATION, WRITE OR PHONE:
Crafted with Pride in U.S.A. Council, Inc.,
1045 Avenue of the Americas, New York, NY 10018
(212)819-4397 Fax (212)819-4493.

The loss of job opportunities due to a rise in imported goods during the 1980s has led cotton growers and shippers, fabric distributors, labor organizers, and manufacturers of fiber, fiber apparel, and home fashions to promote Buy-U.S.A. sentiments through membership in organizations such as the Crafted With Pride in U.S.A. Council, Inc. *Courtesy of Crafted With Pride in U.S.A. Council, Inc.*

Importers may increasingly find, however, that they have to develop new and unique ways of distributing and selling their products over the next decade or two—methods that place less emphasis on the products as imports and far more emphasis on their other values, whether that be cost, design, or esthetics.

GLOBAL GLIMPSES

HERE'S HOW THE OTHER GUYS DO IT

The question has been asked, If the U.S. textile and apparel industry is shrinking, why is the same industry healthy and growing in many other nations?

One issue has to do with government attitudes. In those countries where the industry is healthy and thriving there is a strong governmental belief that the textile and apparel industry is good for their country's economic strength. Here are a few examples from around the world.

Japan—Funded by the Ministry of International Trade and Industry (MITI), Japan's Automated Sewing Systems project has spent more than $65 million to improve Japan's textile and apparel industry through automation and robotization of the manufacturing process.

European Community—The BRITE/EURAM program has targeted $700 million to research and development for manufacturing industries; a significant portion is slated for the textile and apparel industry "to strengthen the competitiveness of the European manufacturing industry, including small and medium-sized enterprises in world markets."

Hong Kong—The government funds vocational training, providing full-time and part-time courses for students to learn merchandising, industrial engineering, and clothing technology in government established and maintained training centers.

Singapore—Government encourages automation for apparel industry through very low-interest loans for investments in automation equipment. It also furnishes financial subsidies and manpower support for local research and development of automation equipment and complete software.

Turkey—Support for apparel industry through export-oriented government policies and selective investment incentives.

Britain—The British government offers grants for training and sponsors studies of technological improvements in the industry.

Australia—Has set aside $125 million to assist the industry in upgrading its manufacturing capabilities through purchases of automated manufacturing equipment.

Spain—Offers assistance to the industry in the form of tax benefits and monetary incentives for the purchase of capital equipments, buildings, and land, plus special incentives for research and development in manufacturing improvements.

The list goes on, but these few examples point to the fact that other governments around the world are active partners with their nations' textile and apparel industries.

Based on Frederic R. Rosen, "Has the U.S. Written Off Its Textile and Apparel Industry?," *Bobbin*, September 1991, pp. 18–28.

ENDNOTES

1. Jerry Haar and Marta Ortiz-Buonafina, *Import Buying: A Management Guide to Profitable Operations*. Lexington, MA: Southwestern. 1991, p. 96.
2. Kitty G. Dickerson, *Textiles and Apparel in the International Economy*. New York: Macmillan. 1991, p. 418.
3. M. Barry, C. Warfield, and R. Galbraith, "Dispersion Retailing: A Global Market Strategy," in *Textiles: Product Design and Marketing*. Paper presented at Annual World Conference, Como, Italy: The Textile Institute, May 4–7, 1987.
4. "Clothing Shoppers Talk Domestic But Look First for Style, Savings," *Wall Street Journal*, October 15, 1987, p. 31.
5. This section is adapted from Warren J. Keegan, "Multinational Product Planning: Strategic Alternatives," *Journal of Marketing*, Vol. 33, January 19, 1969, pp. 58–62.
6. Diane Elson, "Marketing Factors Affecting the Georalization [sic] of Textiles," *EIV Textile Outlook International*, March 1990, p. 58.
7. *Ibid.*, p. 60.
8. *RAB Instant Background: Imports*. Fall 1990, pp. 67–68.

VOCABULARY

chain organizations

_____

_____

_____

dispersion retailing

_____

_____

_____

exclusive distribution

_____

_____

_____

extensive distribution

_____

_____

_____

full-line wholesaler

_____

_____

_____

general merchandise

_____

_____

_____

green consumer

_____

_____

_____

intermodal

_____

_____

_____

limited-line wholesaler

_____

_____

_____

national brands

_____

_____

_____

prestige pricing

_____

_____

_____

price averaging

_____

_____

_____

private label

_____

_____

_____

psychological pricing

_____

_____

_____

selective distribution

_____

_____

_____

specialty merchandisers

_____

_____

_____

value-in-use

_____

_____

_____

vertical marketing

_____

_____

_____

GLOBAL REVIEW 1. The importer's role in distribution can be one of three channels. What are these channels?

_____

_____

_____

_____

2. What is the difference between a full-line wholesaler and a limited-line wholesaler?

_____

_____

_____

_____

_____

3. What is the difference between exclusive distribution, selective distribution, and extensive distribution?

_____

_____

_____

_____

_____

_____

_____

4. What is dispersion retailing and how does it differ from vertical marketing?

_____

_____

_____

_____

_____

_____

_____

5. Importers generally use four strategies to promote imported fashion products. What are these four strategies?

_____

_____

_____

_____

_____

6. Value-in-use, psychological pricing, and prestige pricing are different pricing strategies. Explain how each is used to promote sales of imports.

_____

_____

_____

_____

_____

_____

7. What is meant by the phrase "green consumers"?

_____

_____

_____

_____

8. Explain the long-range effect of "green consumers" marketing fashion-related products.

_____

_____

_____

_____

_____

9. Have American consumers been actively supporting the "Buy America" program? Support your answer.

_____

_____

_____

_____

_____

10. What are some factors that can be used to promote imports against the "Buy America" program?

_____

_____

_____

_____

_____

GLOBAL DIGEST

1. If you were an importer of mid-priced children's sportswear, which of the distribution methods would be best for your merchandise? Give reasons for your method.

_____

_____

_____

_____

_____

_____

2. Which of the promotion strategies would be best suited for selling expensive imported men's suits? What sales promotion tools should be used?

_____

_____

_____

_____

_____

_____

_____

3. What is the role of pricing in sales promotion strategies used for imported products? Which pricing strategy should be considered for expensive imported men's suits?

_____

_____

_____

_____

_____

_____

_____

CHAPTER 13

Processing the Import Product

Much of the early stages of importing are novel and sometimes even glamorous to the start-up international entrepreneur. As a prospective importer, you spend intensive but ultimately fulfilling months researching what kind of goods you will import and where they will come from. In search of product lines, you may travel to fascinating parts of the world to sample their wares. This may seem glamorous and exciting, but it is often tedious and hard work. However, now you have selected the products you plan to import, and it is time to move to the next step, processing the import. This is when you figure out exactly how you will get the imported goods from their place of purchase to your place of sale.

PROCESSING THE IMPORTED GOODS

Two important steps are involved in processing the import: financing and transporting. You must decide how to pay for the goods you have purchased as well as how to transport them to your waiting domestic market. The two processes often overlap.

Processing the import may not be the glamorous end of the business, but it offers many rewards. This is where the acquaintances that you formed on your shopping expeditions turn into friendships as you and your foreign supplier work out the nitty-gritty details of the exchange. This is where you learn about a complex worldwide network of transportation and financing that, working in conjunction, can move 150 fragile sequined tops purchased in Hong Kong in March and two gross of perfume bought in southern France in early May and, literally, deliver them to your loading dock on October 5th, in time for you to have a successful holiday selling period.

FINANCING THE IMPORT PURCHASE

As soon as you have agreed to buy an imported product, you will turn your attention to arranging its payment. Most of the time, you will not be able to take possession of the goods until you have completed this process.

Persons who have traveled outside the United States have had the experience of going to a foreign currency exchange and buying another country's money. Sometimes this can give rise to images of planes flying around the world loaded down with money to pay off international debts.

Enjoyable as the image may be, it is pure fantasy. In fact, no planeloads of money fly around the world paying off foreign businesses' bills. Often, no money at all moves from one part of the world to another during international exchanges. The only time money changes hands in such a literal way is when tourists like yourself go to a currency exchange to buy spending money for a trip abroad.

The actual process is far more complicated—and also in an odd way, far simpler—than you could perhaps ever imagine.

BANKING AND THE INTERNATIONAL BUSINESS COMMUNITY

In addition to meeting the banking needs of local businesses and consumers, **commercial banks** provide a financial network that services the international marketplace. It is through commercial banks that payments for imported goods are arranged.

RELATIONSHIPS BETWEEN BANKS These banks, operating as they do in an international milieu, often form special relationships with one another so they can offer their customers even better worldwide banking services. A commercial bank may work with a **correspondent bank.** Two banks form a correspondent relationship when they agree to provide services to one another that will facilitate the payment of international debts. Such banks typically have secret codes and authorized signatures they use to identify one another and also to provide confidentiality in their exchanges.

Depending on the demands of their communities, banks form correspondent relationships in various parts of the world. For example, the First Fifth Bank of Ft. Wayne, Indiana, may have a correspondent relationship with the Thirty-Second Royal Bank of Hong Kong to service the account of an entrepreneur who sells imported beaded evening wear in her shop.

Banks also form **account relationships,** which tie them together even more closely. In an account relationship, each bank actually keeps funds on deposit with the other. When the evening dress importer in Ft. Wayne, for example, asks her bank—the First Fifth Bank of Ft. Wayne—to pay for her most recent order of beaded dresses, no funds need change hands. The Thirty-Second Royal Bank of Hong Kong simply debits the account of the First Fifth Bank of Ft. Wayne.

Sometimes, a banker at the Hong Kong bank does walk into the vault and physically move a chunk of money from one corner of the room, that belonging to the First Fifth of Ft. Wayne, to another corner, that reserved for the Thirty-Second Bank's own funds. But this is the extent of how far money moves in most foreign exchanges, and this is why planeloads of money don't fly around the world from bank to bank and from importer to exporter.

SERVICES PROVIDED BY COMMERCIAL BANKS On the surface, commercial banks provide the same services to importers and exporters, but in reality, importers, who are the buyers, and exporters, the sellers, have different needs and goals. The importer seeks a saleable product, timely delivery, and advantageous payment terms. The exporter, in contrast, wants to be sure to get paid, and also wants favorable payment terms—which may not necessarily be the same as those desired by the importer.

Commercial banks provide the following services to importers:

1. Credit reports on foreign suppliers.
2. Advice on payment terms.
3. Rendering of payment, including currency exchange.
4. Loans to finance purchases.
5. References.
6. New supplier contacts.

It is surprising to most businesspeople that a commercial bank will provide new contacts or business leads; yet, it is not unusual and is certainly in the bank's best interests. For the Thirty-Second Royal Bank to put together its exporter client in Hong Kong with its correspondent bank's importer client in Ft. Wayne benefits all parties involved.

CHOOSING THE CURRENCY TO USE

The most routine, and at the same time, valuable, work of commercial banks is arranging for payment of goods bought and sold by their customers. One of the first decisions that must be made early in the payment process is whose currency will be used for payment.

To understand why this decision is important, take a moment to consider the problems inherent in buying a product in one currency and paying for it with another. As an American, you are used to dealing in U.S. dollars. Other money looks funny, almost unreal, and it has strange names, at least by your reckoning.

INTER- NATIONAL COMMERCE HAS *ALWAYS* HAD AN ELEMENT *of the* UNKNOWN.

A plunge into foreign markets can be fraught with uncertainties. But if you'll pardon a little salesmanship on our part, U.S. Bank has several ways to help you. For example, your international credit needs are addressed by personnel who specialize in international trade banking. In addition, we have country officers who frequently travel to the countries they represent and understand the individual cultures, business practices and economies of these countries. To find out more call 1-800-645-1126. In the era of the global village, we're all in this together. **U.S. BANK.**

©1991 U.S. Bank. Member FDIC.

©1992 U.S. Bank. Member FDIC.

Commercial banks offer a wide range of services that cater to the particular needs of importers and exporters. *Courtesy of U.S. Bank.*

More relevant to our discussion, foreign currency is also usually worth more or less than the U.S. dollar. A U.S. dollar may equal .45 in British pounds, or 5 French francs, or 126 Japanese yen.

Some currencies even exist that cannot be translated into other currencies. This usually happens in developing countries with so little capital that it is not circulated on the world market. Legal tender that cannot be translated into other monies are called **soft currencies.** A **hard currency,** in contrast, is one that is accepted everywhere, such as the U.S. dollar, the Japanese yen, the British pound, the German mark, and the French franc. Much of the world's business, in fact, is happily conducted in U.S. dollars.[1]

The currency that is used in an international sale matters because money has a price beyond its face value. Money is bought and sold every day on a world market just like corn or soybeans. Two hundred British wool sweaters may be priced 5000 U.S. dollars and 11,000 pounds sterling on the day an importer and exporter arrange a sale. But three months later, when the goods are delivered, the dollar may have dropped in value, making the sweaters worth $4700 rather than $5000, or it may have risen, putting the cost of the sweaters at $5300. An importer, therefore, not only has to have the money to pay for the sweaters but must also have the money to pay for the money.

Playing with international currency is a very sophisticated business, one that is best left to the experts. Importers do have a few options, however. They can arrange for a **forward exchange,** a request for their banks to cover the costs of the purchase on a specific date, usually the delivery date. If all goes smoothly and the goods are delivered on time, the importer may come out ahead, that is, with a lower rate of exchange than when the purchase was agreed to. On the other hand, the importer loses if the goods are not delivered on time, because he or she can no longer use the money or earn interest from it once the forward exchange takes effect.

Alternately, an importer can wait until payment is due and take the chance that the currency exchange rate will be favorable, making the goods less expensive than the original price. The rate may, however, work against the importer, making the goods more expensive than the quoted price.

Once you have developed some understanding of the currency market, it is smart to consider making sales in currencies other than your own. The currency you use may be a strong selling point. For example, one way to sweeten a sale is to promise a client that you will pay in his or her currency.[2]

Currencies will also probably become more stable in the future as the world continues to divide itself into large free trade regions of the types that were described in Chapter 2. The European Community, Japan, and the United States are already working to keep the dollar stable for trading purposes.

TIMING THE PAYMENT

Payment is normally made at one of three times during the process of exchanging goods: (1) before the goods are shipped, (2) while the goods are in transit, or (3) after shipment. The first option pleases exporters because they take no risks to get their money, and the third option pleases importers because they owe no money until they have seen the goods and assured themselves that they are undamaged and clean.

Foreign Exchange
MONDAY, AUGUST 24, 1992

Rates for trades of $1 million minimum.

	Fgn. currency in dollars		Dollar in fgn. currency	
	Mon.	Fri.	Mon.	Fri.
f-Argent (Peso)	1.0100	1.0100	.9900	.9900
Australia (Dollar)	.7225	.7225	1.3841	1.3841
Austria (Schilling)	.1012	.0975	9.881	10.26
c-Belgium (Franc)	.0334	.0334	29.91	29.91
Brazil (Cruzeiro)	.00021	.00022	4655.00	4545.45
Britain (Pound)	1.9910	1.9515	.5023	.5124
30-day fwd	1.9784	1.9405	.5055	.5153
60-day fwd	1.9675	1.9290	.5083	.5184
90-day fwd	1.9554	1.9183	.5114	.5213
Canada (Dollar)	.8410	.8384	1.1891	1.1928
30-day fwd	.8398	.8372	1.1907	1.1945
60-day fwd	.8388	.8360	1.1922	1.1962
90-day fwd	.8379	.8351	1.1935	1.1974
y-Chile (Peso)	.002801	.002803	356.96	356.76
China (Yuan)	.1845	.1839	5.4211	5.4412
Colombia (Peso)	.001709	.001709	585.00	585.00
c-Czechosl (Koruna)	.0376	.0376	26.57	26.62
Denmark (Krone)	.1783	.1783	5.6095	5.6095
z-Ecudr (Sucre)	.000635	.000635	1575.00	1575.00
ECU	1.42600	1.38830	.7012	.7203
d-Egypt (Pound)	.3001	.3053	3.3325	3.2750
Finland (Mark)	.2584	.2514	3.8705	3.9778
France (Franc)	.2074	.2057	4.8225	4.8605
Germany (Mark)	.7123	.6978	1.4040	1.4330
30-day fwd	.7082	.6939	1.4121	1.4411
60-day fwd	.7047	.6901	1.4190	1.4491
90-day fwd	.7008	.6869	1.4270	1.4558
Greece (Drachma)	.005747	.005522	174.00	181.10
Hong Kong (Dollar)	.1293	.1293	7.7320	7.7345
Hungary (Forint)	.0133	.0133	75.43	75.19
y-India (Rupee)	.0352	.0352	28.409	28.409
Indnsla (Rupiah)	.000493	.000493	2029.01	2029.00
Ireland (Punt)	1.8900	1.8325	.5291	.5457
Israel (Shekel)	.4192	.4183	2.3856	2.3906
Italy (Lira)	.000932	.000918	1073.00	1089.00
Japan (Yen)	.008013	.007949	124.79	125.80
30-day fwd	.008010	.007945	124.85	125.87
60-day fwd	.008007	.007941	124.89	125.92
90-day fwd	.008007	.007941	124.89	125.93
Jordan (Dinar)	1.5230	1.5230	.65660	.65659
Lebanon (Pound)	.000426	.000426	2350.01	2347.00
Malaysia (Ringgit)	.4004	.4004	2.4973	2.4973
z-Mexico (Peso)	.000324	.000322	3083.00	3105.00
Nethrinds (Guilder)	.6109	.6109	1.6370	1.6370
N. Zealand (Dollar)	.5395	.5395	1.8536	1.8536
Norway (Krone)	.1744	.1744	5.7340	5.7340
Pakistan (Rupee)	.0400	.0400	25.00	25.10
y-Peru (New Sol)	.8026	.7782	1.250	1.285
z-Philips (Peso)	.0413	.0400	24.20	25.00
Poland (Zloty)	.000077	.000077	13004	13038
Portugal (Escudo)	.008107	.007871	123.35	127.05
Saudi Arab (Riyal)	.2667	.2667	3.7495	3.7498
Singapore (Dollar)	.6223	.6223	1.6070	1.6070
So. Korea (Won)	.001267	.001265	789.00	790.50
So. Africa (Rand)	.3660	.3613	2.7325	2.7678
Spain (Peseta)	.010834	.010724	92.30	93.25
Sweden (Krona)	.1889	.1889	5.2945	5.2945
Switzerlnd (Franc)	.8060	.7843	1.2407	1.2750
30-day fwd	.8028	.7814	1.2457	1.2798
60-day fwd	.7999	.7782	1.2501	1.2850
90-day fwd	.7967	.7752	1.2551	1.2900
Taiwan (NT $)	.0401	.0398	24.91	25.13
Thailand (Baht)	.03954	.03953	25.29	25.30
Turkey (Lira)	.000144	.000144	6967.04	6955.94
U.A.E. (Dirham)	.2723	.2723	3.6727	3.6727
f-Uruguay (Peso)	.000305	.000305	3275.51	3278.69
z-Venzuel (Bolivar)	.0147	.0147	68.0000	67.9400
Yugoslav (Dinar)	.00500	.00500	200.00	200.00

ECU: European Currency Unit, a basket of European currencies. The Federal Reserve Board's Index of the value of the dollar against 10 other currencies weighted on the basis of trade was 79.02 Monday, off 1.17 points or 1.45 percent from Friday's 80.19, A year ago the index was 93.87.
Prices as of 3:00 p.m. Eastern Time from Telerate Systems and other sources.
c-commercial rate, d-free market rate, f-financial rate, y-official rate, z-floating rate.

Because the price of foreign currency against the U.S. dollar changes daily, dealing with international currency is a sophisticated business best left to experts. (Reprinted by permission of *The New York Times*.)

As a compromise the most commonly used method of payment is while the goods are in transit. Occasionally, a new customer is required to pay before the goods are delivered. Occasionally, too, goods are paid for after delivery is made, but this is a more common practice in the United States than in international trade.

GLOBAL GLIMPSES

DUELING BILLS

Two pieces of legislation, each designed to take the U.S. Customs Service into the twenty-first century of computer wizardry, are dueling it out in the halls of Congress.

One piece of legislation was drafted by the Customs Service, the other by a coalition of businesses and trade associations whose products are subject to custom rules. Given the often different interests and viewpoints of the Customs Service and the importing public, similarities between the two bills are few. The final outcome, however, may be the basis for doing business with the Customs Service for many years to come.

Both the bill drafted by the Customs Service, which is entitled "The Customs Modernization Act" (CMA), and the bill prepared by the Joint Industry Group (JIG), called "The Customs Informed Compliance and Automation Act," seek to update outmoded laws that assume all transactions are handled in person and written on paper. Each bill includes provisions expressly recognizing the existence and potential of electronic technology and authorizing its use in processing the entry of goods.

However, neither bill limits itself to such basics. Both the Customs Service and JIG have broader agendas. Each bill also addresses a wide variety of procedural and substantive issues completely unrelated to automation. These issues highlight some of the conflicts that have been simmering between the Customs Service and the public, including importers, domestic producer interests, customs brokers, and customs attorneys.

The two bills even vary in basic definitions of terms. Under these circumstances, passing any form of customs reform legislation will not be an easy task for Congress. Although some in Congress seek to reach a "neutral" compromise by limiting legislation to the minimum necessary to authorize electronic data transmissions, such a result would provide limited satisfaction to either Customs or JIG. Expect both contenders to fight to the finish for major changes in customs law.

Based on Brenda Jacobs, "Dueling Customs Bills Vie For Attention," *Bobbin*, June 1991, pp. 10–15.

FINANCING THE PAYMENT

After determining when goods will change hands, the next step is to settle on the method of payment. Importers' goals are to obtain terms helpful to themselves. In the fashion industry, payment is usually rendered through one of two methods: letter of credit and open account. Factors who specialize in international financing are also used to provide extended payment.

LETTER OF CREDIT

The usual method of arranging for payment is a letter of credit, which is a written promise that the goods will be paid for on presentation of certain documents.[3]

To arrange a letter of credit, the importer asks his or her commercial bank to draw up the letter and forward it to the exporter's bank. The letter promises to pay on presentation by the exporter of certain export documents. Once the documents are forwarded to the importer's bank, the letter of credit can be executed and payment rendered. The importer's bank then turns over the documents to the importer, who needs them to claim the goods, that is, to take title to them. Banks charge the importer a fee, ranging from .25 percent to 1 percent of the transaction price, for arranging and executing a letter of credit.

An importer should understand that a letter of credit guarantees only that the bill will be paid. It is a guarantee of neither quality nor timely delivery. A letter of credit, in fact, cannot be used as a protection against fraud. Importers have arranged payment for goods only to discover that they have been shipped rags rather than garments or a product of vastly inferior quality to what they believed they were buying. The only way for the importer to avoid this kind of disaster is to know the exporter and to have careful background and credit checks made to be sure the exporter can be counted on to deliver the goods.

OPEN ACCOUNT

The second method of financing a payment is through an **open account,** a credit line opened in the importer-buyer's name that is used continuously for

GLOBETROTTING **Gaffes**

SEVEN WAYS TO LOSE A LOVER—OR A LETTER OF CREDIT

Like the little girl with a curl in the middle of her forehead—when she was good, she was very, very good—but when she was bad . . . she was horrid! The same adage appears to work with letters of credit. When the letter of credit deals are good, they are very, very good; when they are bad—disaster!

The disasters are to:

1. Accept time versus sight drafts.
2. Ignore language requirements.
3. Allow payment holdbacks.
4. Ignore extra paperwork requirements.
5. Don't read the letter of credit against your checklist.
6. Let sales win out over finance—or vice versa.
7. Surprise your banker.

Even for companies that pay close attention to all the rules, problems can arise. The best advice is to keep your eyes open and allow the letters of credit to function as they were designed to be.

Based on Virginia J. Rehberg, "Seven Ways to Mess Up a Letter of Credit," *Export Today*, April 1992, pp. 22–23.

different purchases and for extended payments. In comparison, a letter of credit is good only for one specific shipment and payment is made at one specific time. In the United States, goods are most often purchased on open account, but this method of financing is used less often in foreign transactions.

When the goods are to be paid for after delivery, the exporter and importer must agree on the terms of payment. In the fashion industry, typical terms are 30, 60, 90, or 180 days.

The expressions used to describe payment terms vary around the world. In the United States, for example, "net 60" means pay in sixty days with no discount. In much of Europe, however, the German interpretation of "net 60" prevails, which is "net 60, 2.5 percent discount if paid in 30." Importers and exporters should discuss what the terms they are using mean to them—as well as negotiating any discount—before a final settlement is reached.

The due date is probably the most contentious part of doing business globally, and it should be discussed early to avoid confusion. Most of the confusion results from disagreement over shipping dates. Consider, for example, a shipload of Italian leather jackets made in Florence. The jackets leave the Florence factory on May 15, but they must travel to Naples, where they are shipped out on May 25. The exporter and importer have agreed that payment for the jackets is "net 60," that is, payment will be rendered within sixty days of shipment.

But the question that then arises is, sixty days from which shipment? The bill of lading is dated May 25, the day the jackets were loaded on the ship

at Naples. Is payment due on July 25, as the U.S. buyer will insist or on July 15, as the Florentine seller will insist? Add to this the fact that checks take a week to ten days longer than domestic mail to travel from one country to another, and the payment period has been stretched another ten days, or a total of twenty days beyond the period expected by the now very disgruntled seller.

There are solutions to these problems. A seller can ask for the money to be wired, which insures delivery within one to two days. Both exporter and importer can build the extra time into the schedule from the start. Finally, the exporter can factor the cost of money into the cost of the goods, that is, the price can be increased to take account of the interest he will lose by not being paid promptly because the goods are traveling halfway around the world.

FACTORING

Factoring is a method of financing whereby exporters sell their invoices to a financial specialist—called an international factor—who then takes responsibility for collecting payment. Factors, widely used in the U.S. fashion industry, are even more valuable in international transactions.

The most important thing international factors offer their clients is their skill with languages. They speak the languages of the countries where they do business, thus reducing the opportunity for misunderstandings all the way around.

An international factor begins by checking the potential buyer's credit (again, language is helpful here). He or she then buys the credit receivable from the seller, just as in the United States. As an additional service, an international factor is often able to arrange payment in the seller's own currency.[4]

The use of a factor is another way of obtaining credit because a factor may be willing to work out longer term payments than any individual seller will be.

INTERNATIONAL AGENCIES

Several organizations also help with extended payments. In the United States, the Export-Import Bank, more commonly referred to as the Exim Bank, will help an importer work out a more extended payment by either lending the money or guaranteeing a loan from a bank. The Exim Bank is an agency of the U.S. government.

An association of insurance companies, called the Foreign Credit Insurance Association (FCIA), also offers loan guarantees to importers who need extended credit. FCIA tends to handle smaller loans, whereas the Exim Bank handles large loans, but in a move that many consider good for the fashion industry, both organizations have instituted programs in recent years to assist new and small importers and exporters.

Organizations in other countries often offer similar programs to promote exports from their countries. Consulates can provide information about these programs.

TRANSPORTING THE IMPORT PURCHASE

The second important process that is required to complete an international sale is transporting the import to the place where it will be offered for sale, most typically, the importer's store or shop. To transport foreign goods into the United States, an importer must consider traffic, that is, how the goods will be moved physically from one place to another; modes of transportation; documentation, or the papers that are required to bring the imported goods into the country; and insurance, which is necessary to protect the goods as they travel thousands of miles.

TRAFFIC

International shipping is rarely a smooth process, because it is never a one-stop process. The average imported product is loaded out of the factory, which may be in some small town or city buried deep within a country. It is loaded onto an **inland freight carrier,** as ground transportation is called, which then takes the fashion product to a port. This may be an airport, typically located near a large city, or it may be a seaport.

At the port, the goods are unloaded and reloaded onto an **international freight carrier**, which conveys them from their point of origin to their destination, yet another port, where they will again be unloaded. At that point, if all the documentation is in order, the importer may begin the rather lengthy process of claiming the goods, which is described in detail in the next chapter.

Or the importer may decide it is not advisable to claim the goods right away. The products may be Christmas stock that has been delivered in July, and the importer cannot possibly earn any money on the product until November, when the holiday buying season begins. Furthermore, the importer will have to pay taxes, or duties, on the goods when claiming them.

An importer may not be able to claim goods immediately upon arrival because the documentation is incomplete, or the goods may be slated for reexport, which means they will be shipped out to a third country as soon as possible. In the latter case, no duty will be owed on them.

Importers who do not want to claim imported goods right away can store them in a **bonded warehouse,** a special storage area under the strict supervision of the U.S. Customs Service.

PHYSICAL QUALITY OF FASHION GOODS

One factor works in the importer's favor when shipping fashion goods and that is the physical nature of the goods. Shipping fashion goods is easier than shipping, say, construction cranes or automobiles, both of which are extremely heavy and occupy a lot of space.

International shippers measure goods by volume and weight, and fortunately for the cost of the product, fashion products are, for the most part, low bulk and low weight.

All goods being shipped internationally are weighed by ton, a term used to describe a large unit of weight. Ton measure is not the same everywhere in the world. A **short ton,** most commonly used in the United States, weighs 2000 pounds. A **metric ton,** used in the many parts of the world on the metric system of measurement, weighs 2204 pounds. A **long ton**, often used in the Caribbean, weighs 2240 pounds. One of the things an importer must check into before choosing the final method of transporta-

Freight carriers are a vital component in the globalization of fashion merchandising. Courtesy of DHL. *Robert Riccardi, acct. supervisor; John Donahue, casting dtr.; Jim McDonogh, art dtr.; Irene Bowen, prod. mgr.; Catherine Moore, traffic supervisor.*

tion is which kind of ton is used in the area of the world from which the goods will be transported.

MODES OF TRANSPORTATION

Fashion goods usually travel by a combination of truck and air; occasionally, they move by ship.

TRUCKING Trucking is an excellent method of transportation for fashion goods, especially for the inland lap. Unlike trains, trucks provide door-to-door delivery to the smallest town in America and even on busy Seventh Avenue. Trucks transport goods across the United States, from port to port, and also are the chief kinds of carriers for exports from Canada and Mexico.

Because so much of their business has an international lap, trucking companies have learned to make it easy for importers to use their services. They often are set up to handle the overseas shipping as well as

GLOBAL *Goodies*

GLOBAL LOGISTICS—WHO CARRIES THE GOODS? AND HOW?

In today's increasingly competitive global marketplace, it is quite possible that the top-performing companies of tomorrow will not be "American" or "European" or "Asian," they may not even be importers and exporters as we know them now.

Tomorrow's top companies will be global. They will source raw material, manufacture, distribute products, expand markets and service accounts more efficiently. Because of worldwide sourcing, the role of procurement and purchasing will grow. As companies deal with greater distances, supply and distribution chains will expand along with time and people devoted to handling inventory, transportation, and paperwork.

In the textile and apparel industries, management has to form a "global logistics pipeline" that joins raw materials, sourcing, manufacturing, order processing, customer service, and distribution. Managing international transportation is more difficult than domestic operations, mainly, because more people are involved. These include carriers, banks and insurers, freight forwarders, and customs agents and other governmental agencies. Also, the negotiated terms of sale are more complicated for exports and imports and must be carefully monitored.

In the midst of changes brought about by globalization, the need for capable logistics management is essential. The new logistics will not be business as usual among successful companies. For the successful, it will be important for management to challenge carriers to find better, faster, and cheaper ways to satisfy their expanding global business.

Based on Patrick M. Byrne, "A 1990's Issue for Senior Management," *Export Today*, October 1991, pp. 37–40.

the domestic lap. A trucking company will make arrangements for the air or ocean transport as well and present the shipper with one all-inclusive bill, another convenience.

AIR FREIGHT Air freight is hardly the least expensive way for goods to travel, but it still is often the most cost-efficient for fashion products.

Less packing is needed than for ocean travel, and because the travel time is smoother and shorter, there is less opportunity for damage. Less pilferage can be expected than there would be with train travel, because the goods are closely sheltered on a plane and because a plane makes fewer stops. Plane travel is also cleaner. It avoids the moisture, cold air, and humidity that can plague ship travel. Finally, despite its higher cost, air travel offers tighter inventory control because goods can be transported in a matter of days rather than weeks.

Air carriers also base their fees on the commodities transported. Each carrier has a price list.

OCEAN FREIGHT Shipping by sea offers the possibility of using containerization, a great modern advance in shipping. **Containerization** involves the use of a container specially designed to be filled with goods and then easily loaded, by crane onto a large

freight ship or a train. Containers can be locked for protection and sealed against the elements; they are easily handled by cranes and do not need individual crating—all of which cuts the cost of shipping and eliminates many of the other problems associated with ocean shipping as well.

Containers come in twenty- and forty-foot lengths. Because many fashion shipments are not large enough to fill an entire container, specialists have arisen within the fashion industry who help importers consolidate shipments.

Even though most fashion products travel by air, importers and exporters should be aware of the various other forms of transportation as well. Knowledge—and also flexibility—about all the forms of international transport is one more important sales tool in global business.

INSURANCE

The longer goods are in transit, and the farther they travel, the greater the need for insurance to cover lost or damaged goods.

International shipping insurance usually covers goods warehouse to warehouse, which means from the factory where they are made to the importer's dock. A policy covers a specific shipment and usually ceases to be effective a certain number of days after the goods are unloaded.

Shorter travel time, cleaner storage facilties, and less opportunity for damage and pilferage makes air freight the most cost-efficient means of exporting fashions. *Courtesy of Saudian Arabian Airlines.*

Insurance typically covers the value of the shipment, including the freight cost, plus ten percent for contingencies.

Because for decades international shipping always meant ocean travel, insurance on international shipments, whether by air or sea, is still often referred to as **marine cargo insurance.** Air cargo insurance is generally cheaper than ocean cargo insurance.

Once an insurance policy is purchased, a single document called an **insurance certificate** becomes part of the parcel of official papers that accompany a foreign shipment.

Because goods are sometimes purchased from countries that may not be stable politically, some importers like to take out extra coverage called war risk insurance. Both Exim Bank and FCIA offer policies to protect the importer against political instability. Ironically, this kind of insurance is cheap most of the time, becoming expensive only in times of international conflict.

TECH TALK

TRACKING YOUR TRANSPORTATION

In sports, it is said that the game is won in the trenches. This is also true for international trade. You have your star players, star salesperson, key negotiator, fantastic dealmaker, but once the deal is made, ultimate success is often dependent on the more ordinary, like transportation.

Transportation costs play a bigger role in international business transactions than in domestic sales. Often these costs are the sole factor that can make or break a sale: the costs of getting the goods to their final destination can push the total cost past the edge of competitiveness when compared with similar goods available from domestic suppliers or from manufacturers in countries closer to the buyer.

What is particularly frustrating is that, unlike many costs of doing business, transportation costs are largely beyond the control of the manufacturer who incurs them. This is why it is extremely important to constantly monitor the transportation industry to spot trends and services that can help the manufacturer keep costs down.

The development of EDI (electronic data interchange) and its rapid integration into the international movement of goods is but one trend that will benefit imports and exports in terms of cost savings and efficiency gains. An apparent greater focus on logistics by upper management is another sign that U.S. companies are becoming better prepared to meet the challenges of transporting goods around the world. Integrating the transportation function into the overall product marketing mix is allowing the prudent importer or exporter to offer an extra measure of price competitiveness and customer service.

Based on "Moving the Goods: Opportunities for Cost Cutting," Special Report, *Export Today*, October 1991, p. 24.

Some insurance companies offer international insurance programs designed to protect the products, premises, property, and employees of importers and exporters. *Reprinted with the permission of Kemper National Insurance Companies.*

DUTIES AND QUOTAS

✀ ✀

The importer must also take quotas and duties into account when deciding whether or not to import certain foreign products. They can literally make some goods impossible to import. Although the United States is among the few countries that does not impose many restrictions on imported goods, it has kept restrictions on many textile and apparel products.

DUTIES

A duty, or tariff, you will recall from Chapter 9, is a tax that is paid to import goods into a country. Du-

ties, which vary from product to product, can make some products too expensive to import.

An importer of perfumes and cosmetics who sells them in discount outlets, for example, probably cannot afford to buy the very top lines of French perfume because the duty required to bring them into the country would make them too expensive to sell at a discount.

QUOTAS

Quotas are limits on the amount of a product that may be brought into a country. A quota may mean that a product cannot be imported at all, or that only limited amounts can be imported each year. Some-

GLOBAL *GO-GETTERS*

TOMMY HILFIGER . . . TOMMY WHO?

Courtesy of Tommy Hilfiger.

Tommy Hilfiger, the Manhattan designer who used his retailing background and knowledge of the customer to spring seemingly out of nowhere to become a leading menswear designer and manufacturer, is one step closer to his dream of building an international fashion empire.

He entered into a joint venture agreement with one of Japan's largest trading companies, C. Itoh & Co. Together they formed Tommy Hilfiger Japan, which is projected to do in excess of $100 million in sales by 1997.

His deal was unusual because it gave Hilfiger's company an equity stake in the new Japanese business. Most designers merely license their names to Japanese manufacturers, sometimes losing control over the quality, distribution, and image of their products.

Back in 1979, Tommy was a complete unknown, but after heralding himself as the next great designer in a famous advertising campaign, he built a small menswear company that was almost put out of business in 1988 when his backer, Mohan Mujani of Hong Kong went out of business.

But soon after, he found a new financial partner, Silas Chou, a Hong Kong textile manufacturer. Since then, Tommy's star has been rising in stores all over the country. Retailers say his line is second only to Ralph Lauren. Much of this success he credits to having the right look for the times, all-American classics that are priced right for his customers.

Like Americans, the Japanese are trading in their power suits for chinos as their values change. Tommy feels that the Japanese have become more introspective and more life-style-minded.

Tommy Hilfiger Japan has already signed one licensing agreement with D'Urban, a major Japanese manufacturer. The Tommy Hilfiger men's sportswear collection produced by D'Urban debuted in 50 Japanese specialty stores in the fall of 1992.

Future plans call for free-standing Tommy Hilfiger stores as well as broader distribution in Japanese department stores. Over time, Hilfiger expects his Japanese business to account for half his total sales. So far, Tommy Hilfiger has been very successful with a little help from his friends in Hong Kong and Japan.

Based on Phyllis Furman, "Hilfiger mini-empire hits Japan," *Crain's New York Business*, April 6, 1992, p. 9.

times, after a specified amount of a product has been imported, the duty on it goes up. This makes some products too risky for importers, especially if they have access to other products that are not burdened with quotas.

MERGING THE TWO PROCESSES

Obviously with arrangements as complicated as sending goods and payment halfway around the world, small things can—and will—always go wrong. This is to be expected, perhaps even to a greater degree in international than in domestic business. But major things going wrong can spell disaster.

Clothing can literally rot in overheated, humid foreign warehouses. Goods can be stolen or delivery can be delayed; goods can be held up for months because a country has gone to war. Generally however, disasters of this magnitude do not come out of the blue. They happen because someone—often the importer—did not pay attention to detail. A letter of credit was not properly written; a delivery date was missed; proper insurance was not obtained—the list of things that can go wrong is endless.

But when all goes well, meaning that careful attention is paid to detail, the financing and transporting of imported goods often work beautifully in tandem. Goods are transported safely and in timely fashion to their destination. This is when the importing experience is most rewarding—and the only thing to prevent this happening on a regular basis is lack of know-how on the importer's part.

ENDNOTES

1. Sandra Kruzel and Frank Reynolds, *Import-Export Procedures.* Cincinnati, OH, and Dallas, TX: Southwestern Publishing Co., 1992, p. 39.
2. Irving Vigdor, *Exporting: Get Into It!*, Merrick, NY: Redwood Associates, 1989, p. 84.
3. Fashion Institute of Technology, *Glossary of International Trade Terms,* unpublished and undated pamphlet, p. 7.
4. Vigdor, *Op. cit.*, p. 42.

VOCABULARY

account relationship _____

_____

_____

bonded warehouse _____

_____

_____

commercial bank _____

_____

_____

containerization _____

_____

_____

correspondent bank

_____

_____

_____

factoring

_____

_____

_____

forward exchange

_____

_____

_____

hard currency

_____

_____

_____

inland freight carrier

_____

_____

_____

insurance certificate

_____

_____

_____

international freight
carrier

_____

_____

long ton

_____

_____

_____

marine cargo insurance

_____

_____

_____

metric ton

_____

_____

_____

open account _____
_____
_____

short ton _____
_____
_____

soft currency _____
_____
_____

GLOBAL REVIEW

1. What are the two important steps involved in processing your import orders?

_____
_____
_____
_____

2. In commercial banking, many relationships are formed. What is meant by account relationships?

_____
_____
_____

3. Commercial banks provide many services for importers. List five of these services.

_____
_____
_____
_____
_____

4. What is the major difference between soft currency and hard currency?

_____
_____
_____
_____

5. Why is it beneficial for an importer to arrange for a forward exchange? Under which circumstance would it not be beneficial?

    _____

    _____

    _____

    _____

6. When are the three times during the process of exchange goods that payment may be made?

    _____

    _____

    _____

    _____

7. Explain what a letter of credit means.

    _____

    _____

    _____

    _____

8. Which of the many forms of transportation are most used by fashion product imports? Explain why this form is used the most often.

    _____

    _____

    _____

    _____

9. What is the difference between a duty and a quota? Can a product be subject to both a duty and a quota?

    _____

    _____

    _____

    _____

10. What does insurance cover when it comes to shipping your product?

    _____

    _____

    _____

    _____

GLOBAL DIGEST

1. Because financing and transporting are the next important steps to be considered after the product has been selected, what are the steps to be taken in choosing and arranging the type of financing best suited for your product?

2. Describe the services offered to an importer by the following: an international factor, the Exim Bank, and the FCIA.

3. What are the benefits of using a bonded warehouse? What type of product benefits most from the use of a bonded warehouse?

CHAPTER 14

Import Procedures

I n many ways, importing and exporting *are* like flip sides of the same coin. Many of the tasks that exporters undertake—whether it is procuring certain documents or selling and promoting a product—are also done by importers. Despite this, some very real differences do exist between importing and exporting. They are never more apparent than when an importer is trying to bring a foreign product into the country. Import procedures, that is, the steps that are necessary to physically bring foreign goods into the United States, are the subject of this chapter.

The apparent similarities between physically exporting goods out of the United States and physically importing them into the United States include the fact that both exporters and importers must classify their products. Exporters work closely with the Commerce Department, and importers work closely with the Customs Service. But the classifications are not done for the same purpose, as you will see, and whereas the relationship between the Commerce Department and exporters is supportive, the same cannot be said of the relationship between importers and the Customs Service.

At times, especially if one does not know how the system works, this final stage of importing, the entry process, can feel downright adversarial. It is not, of course, and that is something you will learn as you read this chapter and discover the complex, ongoing relationship between importers and Customs.

WHY IMPORT PROCEDURES EXIST

There are several reasons why it is sometimes difficult to bring imported goods into the United States— or any country, for that matter, because all countries have their own import procedures. On the simplest level, the government wants to know what is coming into the country. It wants a count of goods coming in so it can measure imports against exports, its competitive strength against that of other nations. The government also wants to be sure that the goods are in compliance with its laws—usually regarding consumer goods, safety, and health. Some goods are illegal and cannot be brought into the country at all. Other goods can be brought in only in limited amounts or under certain conditions.

THE ROLE OF THE U.S. CUSTOMS SERVICE

The U.S. Customs Service is the government agency responsible for handling imports into the United

TECH TALK

WHO? OR WHAT? IS THERE!

With all the technology that international communications have installed, it is likely that the someone at the other end of an international telephone call could now be a something.

That is the information from the London-based International Institute of Communications. Their report says international telecommunications traffic is rising dramatically but that much of the traffic is "non-voice." In Japan, for example, "voice traffic"

will fall from about 46 percent of international traffic in 1990 to about 31 percent in the year 2000. Other media—data, video, image, and facsimile—will make up the difference.

One other sign of the times: U.S. "outbound traffic," including voice and data, has risen 18 percent a year since 1988. In the United States, as in Japan, "non-voice" traffic is rising faster than "voice."

Based on "London Calling," *World Trade*, March 1992, p. 40.

States. It classifies products, examines them, collects duty, and enforces any constraints on trade.

It is one of our oldest agencies, having been authorized by Congress in 1789, shortly after the new nation was formed. Until the income tax was instituted, Customs was the primary source of revenue for the United States. It is still an important source of revenue, however, as literally billions of dollars are collected each year in duties on goods brought into the country.

The Customs Service is an agency of the Treasury Department, and the Commissioner of Customs reports directly to the Secretary of the Treasury.

GEOGRAPHIC ORGANIZATION OF CUSTOMS

Customs is divided into nine regions, each with its own regional commissioner. The regions are divided into 42 districts—for a total of 400 stations and ports of entry. Customs also operates in eight foreign countries, plus the U.S. territories of Puerto Rico and the Virgin Islands.[1]

Stations and ports even vie with one another for business, as each promotes its conveniences or added services to "customers," or importers. Importers may choose the port of entry or station where they bring their goods into the United States, and importers do, indeed, sometimes foot the bill for added transportation to bring their goods into one station rather than another. The port of Charleston, for example, promotes its new sophisticated computer system as being able to speed cargo through faster than in the past. But an importer who was bringing in furs in

July, for example, might find the port of Baltimore, with its 9.5 cubic feet of cold storage, a necessity.[2]

SPECIALIZED OPERATIONS OF CUSTOMS

To do its job, Customs is organized into four main divisions.

The Uniformed Division consists of the front-line inspectors who examine cargo and baggage. These are the men and women who greet you when you return from a trip to a foreign country. They are extremely adept at what they do, which is to make value judgments about the values of people and the values of objects passing through Customs.

The Classification and Valuation Section determines the classification for products, that is, what kind and type of product is being brought in. They also review importers' valuations of the goods to determine whether they are fair.

Laboratory Facilities are advanced laboratories whose workers are capable of determining the exact composition of an import's substance, should this kind of testing be required. Obviously, the laboratory is most busy testing for drugs, but it can also determine, for example, whether wool is 100 percent wool, as claimed, and whether silk is actually silk or microfiber.

The Agency Service investigates abuses of Customs. It has the right to telephone or call on an importer during ordinary working hours and to review records of past import shipments to determine a pattern of abuse. Abuse of Customs is subject to criminal penalties.

U.S. CUSTOMS SERVICE

Map of nine U.S. Customs regions. *Courtesy of U.S. Customs Service.*

An importer who is not attempting to conceal anything from Customs and is not misrepresenting the goods being brought into the United States will never have contact with the latter two divisions. With experience and knowledge, importers usually enjoy amicable relations with the agents with whom they work.

THE ENTRY PROCESS

The primary task of Customs is to facilitate the **entry.** An entry refers to the set of documents that is required to bring goods into the United States. All goods entering the United States require some kind of documentation. You will recall from Chapter 9 that the exporters prepare certain documents— commercial invoice, a bill of lading, shipping papers,

a packing list—as they ready the goods for shipping. These documents are mailed to the importer, who uses them to claim the goods at U.S. Customs. Entries are one of two types: informal and formal.

INFORMAL ENTRY

An **informal entry**, the most common, least complicated, and fastest procedure, can be used for any commercial shipment valued at under $1000 and for all noncommercial shipments. All goods imported with the intention of reselling them are considered a **commercial shipment.**

The documents required for an informal entry are the bill of lading or an air waybill and a commercial invoice. The value of the goods must be described in the invoice.

To claim the goods, the importer fills out an **Entry Summary Form.** This document identifies the

DEPARTMENT OF THE TREASURY
UNITED STATES CUSTOMS SERVICE

ENTRY SUMMARY

1. Entry No.	2. Entry Type Code	3. Entry Summary Date
4. Entry Date	5. Port Code	
6. Bond No.	7. Bond Type Code	8. Broker/Importer File No.

9. Ultimate Consignee Name and Address	10. Consignee No.	11. Importer of Record Name and Address	12. Importer No.
		13. Exporting Country	14. Export Date
		15. Country of Origin	16. Missing Documents
	State	17. I.T. No.	18. I.T. Date

19. B L or AWB No.	20. Mode of Transportation	21. Manufacturer I.D.	22. Reference No.
23. Importing Carrier	24. Foreign Port of Lading	25. Location of Goods/G.O. No.	
26. U.S. Port of Unlading	27. Import Date		

28. Line No.	29. Description of Merchandise 30. A. T.S.U.S.A. No. B. ADA CVD Case No.	31. A. Gross Weight B. Manifest Qty.	32. Net Quantity in T.S.U.S.A. Units	33. A. Entered Value B. CHGS C. Relationship	34. A. T.S.U.S.A. Rate B. ADA/CVD Rate C. I.R.C. Rate D. Visa No.	35. Duty and I.R. Tax	
						Dollars	Cents

36. Declaration of Importer of Record (Owner or Purchaser) or Authorized Agent		**U.S. CUSTOMS USE**		TOTALS	

I declare that I am the ☐ importer of record and that the actual owner, purchaser, or consignee for customs purposes is as shown above.

OR ☐ owner or purchaser or agent thereof.

I further declare that the merchandise was obtained ☐ pursuant to a purchase or agreement to purchase and that the prices set forth in the invoice are true.

OR ☐ was not obtained pursuant to a purchase or agreement to purchase and the statements in the invoice as to value or price are true to the best of my knowledge and belief.

I also declare that the statements in the documents herein filed fully disclose to the best of my knowledge and belief the true prices, values, quantities, rebates, drawbacks, fees, commissions, and royalties and are true and correct, and that all goods or services provided to the seller of the merchandise either free or at reduced cost are fully disclosed. I will immediately furnish to the appropriate customs officer any information showing a different state of facts.

Notice required by Paperwork Reduction Act of 1980. This information is needed to ensure that importers/exporters are complying with U.S. Customs laws, to allow us to compute and collect the right amount of money, to enforce other agency requirements, and to collect accurate statistical information on imports. Your response is mandatory.

A. Liq. Code	B. Ascertained Duty	37. Duty
	C. Ascertained Tax	38. Tax
	D. Ascertained Other	39. Other
	E. Ascertained Total	40. Total

41. Signature of Declarant, Title, and Date

Form 16-758 Printed and Sold by UNZ&CO. 190 Baldwin Ave., Jersey City, NJ 07306 • (800) 631-3098 • (201) 795-5400

Customs Form 7501 (030984)

Entry Summary Form. *Reprinted by permission of Unz & Co., 190 Baldwin Avenue, Jersey City, NJ 07306.*

importer and gives such details of the import transaction as the transport carrier and the size, quantity, and value of the shipment.

If the Entry Summary Form is acceptable to the Customs agent, it is approved. Any taxes that are owed must be paid at this point.

FORMAL ENTRY

Commercial shipments larger than $1250 must go through **formal entry**. Unless a formal entry qualifies for immediate delivery privileges, it must be covered by a bond and must go through a process that involves an examination process.

IMMEDIATE DELIVERY PRIVILEGE Importers with impeccable records may be able to qualify for immediate delivery privileges. The Customs Service tries to extend this convenience to anyone bringing in perishables, shipments from Mexico and Canada, and articles for trade fairs, to name just a few of the categories that routinely qualify for immediate entry.[3] Immediate entry both simplifies and shortens the entry process.

The first step to immediate delivery occurs when the importer learns that the shipment has arrived in the United States. At the port or entry station, the importer fills out an Entry/Immediate Delivery Request, a form that asks Customs to release the goods immediately to the importer. There is one form for shipment by land and another for shipments by air or ocean.

A documents package, including the commercial invoice, which must be in English, a copy of the transport bill (the bill of lading or the air waybill), and the packing list is presented to Customs along with the request for immediate delivery.

If the package is in any way unacceptable, Customs may return it for further processing. Entry packages have been returned because documents were missing or because a form was illegibly written. An entry, either formal or informal, immediate or through the usual channels, is not to be done piecemeal or haphazardly. The importer who submits a problematic documents package risks delaying the shipment for weeks, if not months.

Once the entry packet is presented to Customs, the Service decides whether or not to inspect the shipment. Customs—usually represented by the agent you are working with—has the right to inspect as intensively as it likes, to conduct a routine spot check, or to waive any inspection. At this point, importers can take custody of their shipments. Within five working days, an importer must file an Entry Summary and mail it to Customs along with any duties or other taxes that are owed on the shipment. The Entry Summary is a much more detailed version of the Entry/Immediate Delivery Form.

The privilege of immediate entry is just this—a privilege. It can be revoked for a variety of offenses on the importer's part: late payment, incomplete records, consistently sloppy papers in the entry packet.

BONDS All formal entries must be covered by a bond. Issued by special insurance companies, these **bonds** guarantee payment of duties and other entry fees. Depending on the financial stability of the importer and how well known he or she is to the company, the insurance company may require **collateral**, or security, from the importer. An irrevocable letter of credit is acceptable for this purpose. Bonds cost about 2 percent of the value of the shipment, with a minimum purchase of $100.

The bond can be issued for one shipment, called a single entry bond. These bonds are issued by Customs and reimbursed subsequently by the U.S. Treasury. An importer can purchase a **continuous**, or **term**, **bond** that can be used for several similar shipments. Term bonds cost about 5 percent of the value of the goods.

FORMAL ENTRY WITHOUT IMMEDIATE DELIVERY On paper, the steps to formal entry without immediate delivery look fairly simple: An Entry Summary Form is required up-front; the goods are inspected (or not) and then released. In reality, this kind of formal entry takes far longer than an immediate delivery. Even filling out the Entry Summary, a form that can be delayed five days with immediate delivery, requires more time and effort. But the major disadvantage of a formal entry is that duties and other taxes are owed before the shipment can be claimed, thus depriving importers of a few more days' interest on their money.

THE EXAMINATION PROCESS

Customs has the right to examine any and all shipments of foreign goods entering the United States. Because it does examine so many shipments passing through its offices, a savvy importer needs to thoroughly understand all phases of the examination process. The examination process usually consists of the following five steps, which may or may not be required of all goods:

1. Classification.
2. Valuation.
3. Physical inspection.
4. Agency certification.
5. Liquidation.

CLASSIFICATION OF FOREIGN GOODS

Classification of foreign goods is an important substep in the examination process, one that involves assigning the goods to a descriptive category that determines, in turn, how much tax will be owed on them, and sometimes whether they can be imported at all.

The importer and his or her agent are the first to classify a shipment. No smart importer would arrange to import anything without first checking its classification category—usually long before making the final decision to import. Importers sometimes go to great lengths to modify products in order to avoid a more highly taxed or banned classification.

TSUS AND TSUSA   Importers use one of two sources, or schedules as they are called, to classify products. The first, and older of the two, is the Tariff Schedule of the United States (TSUS) or the Tariff Schedule of the United States Annotated (TSUSA). You will also sometimes hear reference to Schedule B, an older version of the tariff schedule that these two sources replace.

HARMONIZED SYSTEM   There is also a newer schedule that supplants TSUS and TSUSA. In 1989, as was noted earlier in Chapter 7, the United States joined the European Community, Canada, and Japan in using a new tariff schedule called the **Harmonized System.**

The Harmonized System (HS) has many advantages. It is an international document, used not only by many countries but also by importers and exporters. This has led to greater standardization and uniformity in the import/export business. For importers, the Harmonized System replaces TSUS and TSUSA. Some products, however, still may be listed in the older schedules, so importers will need to be familiar with both documents for a few more years.

The HS, as well as TSUS and TSUSA, are published in loose-leaf form by the Government Printing Office at a cost of about $60 each to individual importers. Because importers frequently use special agents to guide them through the entry process, they usually do not have to buy the books themselves, unless they do a great deal of importing and process their own imports. Although importers and their agents will seek to classify their products before they go through Customs, only one official source can issue a binding classification for a product, and that is the Customs Service.

They will issue a binding classification on a product on request, at no charge. Once a classification has been formally issued by Customs, it is rarely changed. Thus, it behooves the smart importer to take the time to obtain a binding classification on his or her goods *before* they arrive in the United States.

VALUATION OF FOREIGN GOODS

Valuation is another important substep in the examination process. It consists of determining the value of the goods for purposes of figuring out what, if any, tariffs or duties are owed on them.

The Customs value of a shipment generally is considered to be the transaction value plus shipping costs, any selling commission paid by the buyer to the exporter, the value of any royalty or licensing fee, and the anticipated profits the importer expects to make on the goods.

If, for some reason, Customs cannot determine these values from the entry documents, then it may compare the merchandise with identical or even similar merchandise, or a Customs agent, as a last resort, may simply estimate the perceived value, based on personal experience. Obviously, there is room for debate between importer and Customs over this process.

INSPECTION OF FOREIGN GOODS

In recent years, with the help of a powerful mainframe computer located in Franconia, Virginia, Customs has been able to intensify its **inspection**, or investigation, process. The increased number of imported goods coming into the United States since the 1970s left Customs short of staff in many ports and stations. To counter this, it has opted to inspect fewer shipments and to do a more intense inspection than in the past.

Importers can expect intense scrutiny under certain circumstances. Shipments of any product from countries suspected or known to be involved in the drug trade will garner intense inspections.

When an importer's past record is troubled—if for example, he or she has previously been caught falsifying information or consistently has been undervaluing goods—a more intense inspection will be warranted.

Some classes of goods warrant more ardent inspections simply because of what they are. These change from year to year, depending on where Customs finds trouble areas. One year, Customs may inspect all crates of shoes because they have reason to believe shoes are being misrepresented by importers. Another year, their interest may focus on silk t-shirts from China.

Before conducting the physical inspection, a customs officer dials the mainframe computer to get a printout that shows the history of the importer's operations, a history of the product being imported, and any recent changes in duty or tariff, special taxes.

A Customs agent can enforce any level of inspection he or she chooses. An agent can have an importer or importer's agent open one crate, several crates, or an entire shipment. Customs can even detain

GLOBAL *Goodies*

STOPPING UNFAIR TRADE PRACTICES OR "DUMP ON SOMEONE ELSE!"

In today's global economy, there is much talk of trade agreements and trade negotiations. Most U.S. companies are aware of official government efforts to achieve a better, and fairer, balance in world trade.

Through Import Administration, a branch of the Commerce Department's International Trade Administration, companies can actively seek relief from unfairly traded imports that they feel are damaging to their industry. Any company can do this by concurrently filing a petition with both the Commerce Department's Import Administration and the International Trade Commission (ITC), another government agency.

In the petition, the U.S. industry would claim that the imported product was being either "dumped" (sold in the United States at a lower price than it sells for in its home or other export markets) or subsidized by the exporting country. The Commerce Department and the ITC then begin an investigation to determine whether the product is providing unfair competition to comparable products made by the domestic industry.

When a foreign country dumps a product in the United States, it is essentially maximizing its profits through price discrimination, charging different customers different prices for the same products. It is selling the product in the United States for less than "fair value" or less than it sells it for in its home market or other export market. A foreign company could also be considered dumping if it is selling its products in the United States at a price below the cost of producing the goods.

When unfair or extensive subsidization is the charge, it generally means that a foreign government is subsidizing an industry's exports to the United States either directly or indirectly through grants on the production or exportation of the goods. Subsidies take many forms such as direct cash benefits, credits against taxes, and artificially low interest rates on loans. For the U.S. government to react, the subsidization must be found to be limited to a specific firm, industry, or group of firms or industries or to a firm's export activities.

The investigation begun by the U.S. industry's petition is carried out according to U.S. "antidumping" and "countervailing duty" laws. Any party involved in this process may contest any actual findings or legal conclusions that are the basis for final determinations. They may also contest decisions to suspend an investigation, decisions not to initiate an investigation, and the final results of administrative reviews. The Court of International Trade will hear the complaint and rebuttal and determine whether the findings are legally correct or whether they should be modified.

For further information regarding antidumping or countervailing duty cases, contact Import Administration, U.S. Department of Commerce, Washington, DC 20230, Telephone: (202) 377-1780.

Based on Cydney Louth and Edwina Rogers, "Import Administration: Stopping Unfair Trade Practices," *Business America*, November 5, 1990, pp. 2–5.

products to test them in its laboratory if it chooses to do so.

Customs agents are not unreasonable if they are treated politely and fairly by importers and their agents, but they are specially trained to look for bogus or illegal goods, and they know how to do their jobs.

They are looking for falsification, smuggling, and these days, drugs. Drug smugglers have created increasingly imaginative ways to bring in drugs, which makes many products tainted or suspect that would not ordinarily be. Any irregularities found between the shipping documents and the actual goods must

be resolved before the goods can be released. Often, inconsistencies are accidental; the exporter who packed the shipment may have miscounted or wrongly described the goods or erred in filling out documents, for example.

If the law has been deliberately disobeyed, if an importer is smuggling goods, for example, or attempting to bring in illegal goods, they will be confiscated and the importer will be subject to criminal prosecution and even prison. Even minor discrepancies, however, such as a miscount, can hold up a shipment for weeks.

U.S. Customs agents inspect incoming foreign fashion goods to search for both falsification and smuggling of goods. *Courtesy of U.S. Customs Service.*

AGENCY CERTIFICATION

To speed up the entry process, Customs, as a courtesy, checks to be sure importers are in compliance with other agencies' regulations regarding import products. Automobiles, for example, are subject to regulation by the Environmental Protection Agency. Firearms are subject to regulations of the Bureau of Alcohol, Tobacco, and Firearms.

In the garment industry, Customs checks to be sure that textiles, apparel, and furs meet with Federal Trade Commission regulations. Gold and silver fall under the auspices of the National Stamping Act, a section of the Department of Justice. Cosmetics are regulated by the Food and Drug Administration under Health and Human Services.[4]

LIQUIDATION PROCESS

The final step in the entry process is the **liquidation,** or dispatching, of the imported goods. Before this can happen, the classification and valuation reports, plus any other documents, are reviewed for correctness and properness.

If the documents are accepted without change, the goods are liquidated, or released to the importer or his agent. Notices of liquidation were once posted on a public bulletin board but, now, they are entered in a computer, and interested parties have access to frequently updated printouts.

Liquidation can take up to several months, but it must be finalized, by law, within one year. At the time of liquidation, any duties or other taxes that are owed must be paid.

After liquidation, an importer may pursue any claims for adjustment or refund for up to ninety days

by filing a special form of protest. A local ruling that does not satisfy an importer can be appealed to the U.S. Customs Court of International Trade.

DUTIES AND QUOTAS

Throughout this chapter, you have heard about duties that must be paid on imported goods. A duty, as you will recall, is a tax that must be paid to bring foreign goods into a country. It is a source of revenue for governments and also serves to protect domestic manufacturers from cheap imports by equalizing the price of the goods. Duties vary from product to product. Perfume, considered a luxury item, may have a higher duty than a raw textile that American manufacturers need to make products they will sell. Duties are typically a percentage of the total value of the imported goods.

QUOTAS

Quotas, or limits on the amount of a product that may be brought into a country, are established by law and administered by Customs.

For goods entering the United States, one of two kinds of quotas may be imposed: absolute or tariff rate. An **absolute quota** means that no more than a specified number of the product may enter the country during any one period, usually one year.

Some absolute quotas apply to all products in a certain category. Others apply only to the product when it is brought from certain countries. For example, if Singapore is flooding the United States with cheap scarves, Congress may declare that only 20,000 scarves can enter the country from Singapore. Exporters may send in as many scarves from other countries as they like. To protect the U.S. athletic shoe industry, as another example, Congress may limit the number of athletic shoes that may be imported from any other country.

A **tariff-rate quota** permits some specified quantity of imports to enter the country at one duty rate. Any quantity above that rate is charged a higher duty.

OTHER IMPORT FEES

In 1985, Congress enacted an import-user fee to cover the cost of operating the Customs service. It is a small percentage of the total value of the imported goods.

Excise taxes are also sometimes levied on top of duties. Sometimes called "sin taxes," they are typically imposed on domestic and imported luxury goods. Fashion imports that are most often subject to luxury taxes include furs, perfumes, and jewelry.

OTHER CONSTRAINTS ON TRADE

Apart from duties and quotas, the two primary means of restricting imported goods, the government also denies access to goods on a variety of other grounds, some of which, admittedly, are purely political.

A **boycott,** for example, is a ban on trade imposed by one government on another, usually for political reasons. It may be total or partial. A partial boycott prohibits only certain goods from entering the country. A total boycott bans all goods.

Because the United States does not have diplomatic relations with the government in Cuba, it has imposed a total boycott on Cuban-made products. In another example, it has imposed a partial boycott on Kruggerands, a gold coin used to finance the racist government of South Africa. It does not ban the import of South African diamonds or certain minerals, such as chromite and manganese, that are scarce and virtually unobtainable elsewhere.

ANTIDUMPING DUTY

As was mentioned in Chapter 7, an antidumping duty is imposed when the price of an imported good is lower than the price in its country of origin. Some countries try to "dump" their cheap imports in other countries where they hope to sell them for a greater profit than they would otherwise earn. When U.S. Customs determines that foreign goods are being dumped in this manner, it imposes the antidumping duty.

COUNTERVAILING DUTY

Similar to antidumping duties are countervailing duties, which are imposed on foreign products that have been subsidized by their governments. Importers hoping to bring in cheap imports whose price has been artificially reduced with a government-subsidized program will find that the U.S. Government has ways of equalizing the prices, namely, by imposing a countervailing duty.

TRADEMARKS AND LICENSES

After nearly a century of not being overly interested in protecting trademarks, the United States has become stricter, largely due to pressure from the fashion industry. The new interest arises from the increasing number of fashion imports in the past two decades—decades that saw increasing ripoffs of many kinds of American-made fashion products.

Manufacturers of everything from Cartier and Rolex watches to Izod and Hard Rock Cafe t-shirts have felt the pain of seeing their products produced in cheaper, often tawdry versions, to say nothing of the further pain of being deprived of deserved profits from the manufacture of these items by unauthorized sources.

At minimum, such unlicensed items cheapen the product. Too many Cartier watches selling for $25 make many customers less interested in the real thing for $2500. In addition, the genuine manufacturers are often held responsible by people who bought their product, believing it was real and expecting to have it serviced by the company with the name on the product.

In the face of shifting government concern, lawsuits over trademarks have proliferated in recent years. High-end accessory designer Barry Kisselstein-Cord estimates he has been involved in 50 to 60 lawsuits to protect his unique products, which include his distinctive belt buckles.[5]

In its efforts to become more serious about trademark protection, the U.S. Government finally joined the 100-year-old Berne Convention, an international treaty that provides added trademark protection to its 80 member nations. The United States has also worked to broaden GATT talks so they cover trademarks, patents, and copyrights. And finally, the government announced that respect for foreign trademarks would be dependent on how U.S. trademarks were protected in other countries. Do not protect our trademarks, the government seemed to be saying, and we will be less diligent about protecting yours.[6]

COUNTERFEIT GOODS

In addition to increased vigilance over trademarked goods, Customs is authorized to confiscate counterfeit goods. These are goods that are obviously intended to fool customers into thinking they are buying the original, trademarked item, thus depriving profits to the rightful owner of the license.

GRAY MARKET GOODS

A newer and less well-known area of protection is that of **gray market goods.** Gray market goods are genuine products, licensed by the manufacturer to be made outside the United States. Because these goods are produced outside the United States, they are of-

GLOBAL *GO-GETTERS*

ROBERT TALBOTT—THE TIES THAT BIND

Courtesy of Robert Talbott Company.

In dramatic contrast to the age of high-tech heros, stands neckwear maker Robert Talbott. Talbott is the world's only neckwear maker that still retains its handcrafted, renowned seven-fold tie. On the best days, only 10 or 12 seven-fold ties are finished. Handcrafted from a huge piece of exquisite silk and without a separate lining, the seven-fold name stems from its architecture. Instead of separating lining, the silk is carefully hand-folded into itself seven different times. At strategic folds, the narrowing single piece of silk fabric, once nearly the size of a woman's blouse, is slip stitched and hand sewn. When finished, the several overlaid silk folds will create an all-silk, self-lining. The virtues are a perfect drape, a superb knot, and a dimple at the knot that is unmatched.

Along with Ralph Lauren, Robert Talbott was among the U.S. top fashion labels to recognize America's overseas cachet and capture a market share foothold in the Orient and Europe. Marketing the image of quality, style, and Made-in-America, the Talbott label has been widely accepted all over the world. In a surprising fashion reversal, the American-made Talbott studio collection is now considered by most neckwear aficionados to be even more directional and more fashion-forwarded than many of the top European designer names.

Staying faithful to its original marketing vision, Talbott targets only the most discriminating of fashion-conscious men and refuses to sway from handcrafted production. Robert Talbott has successfully maintained its mystique as the world's sole remaining maker of handmade neckwear and shirts while meeting the pressures of selling in a world market.

Based on Andy Stenson, "Talbott Ties Up the Market," *Bobbin*, December 1991, pp. 85–91.

---

ten cheaper than U.S.-produced goods. They are not intended for sale in the United States, however.

Picture a scenario where a large supply—or rather oversupply—of cheap gray market goods is made. To keep from taking a loss, the foreign manufacturer unloads them by selling them to an importer. Through this unauthorized channel, they wend their way back to the United States, where they are purchased in bulk, usually by an importer intending to sell them for as much as 25 to 40 percent less than their list price. They are good in every way except one: The manufacturer will not honor warranties or service these products.[7]

The number of gray market goods, also sometimes called **parallel imports,** has increased dramatically in recent years, to the point where they are now worth upward of $10 billion a year in annual sales. Several popular gray market goods, such as t-shirts and jewelry, touch on the fashion industry.[8]

Although they are legal, a 1991 Supreme Court ruling will make it harder for importers to bring gray

market goods into the country. The ruling was unclear about which goods would now be protected, but new stricter laws regarding gray market goods will undoubtedly be written in the next few years.[9]

WORKING YOUR WAY THROUGH THE MAZE

Although the Customs Service provides considerable printed information to guide the inexperienced importer through its maze of rules and regulations, even experienced importers have trouble keeping up-to-date on all the rules and regulations. One importer learned the hard way, by bringing a shipment of shoes 6000 miles from Asia to New York and having it land in what might best be described as Customs limbo, because U.S. law bans the entry of goods made in prison.[10]

GLOBETROTTING **Gaffes**

PIRATES ON THE HIGH SEAS—AGAIN!

Thousands of U.S. companies are fighting the "pirates" around the world to keep them from "knocking-off" their products. In 1990/1991 the U.S. Customs Service nabbed a record 522 shipments worth an estimated $90 million.

As more and more cheap foreign-made copies of trendy or fashionable products like Chanel handbags, Hard Rock Cafe t-shirts, Rolex watches, and designer jewelry show up on street corners or in retail shops, businesses are trying a tougher approach. In a recent study of piracy, the International Trade Commission reported that losses to U.S. companies are as high as $63 billion a year. Also, the commission has estimated that foreign piracy has cost the United States about 131,000 jobs. Although international piracy is no longer conducted by swordsmen swinging from the mast, flying the skull and cross-bones, these modern "pirates" are gaining more riches than was ever imagined by Captain Morgan and his buccaneers.

Now, the U.S. Government is using treaties with other nations to combat the problem. Recently, the government has been successful in broadening the General Agreement on Tariffs and Trade (GATT) talks to include protection of intellectual property: copyrights, trademarks, and patents. In 1989, the United States joined the Berne Convention, an international treaty that greatly expands copyright protection. All this should be a warning to an unsuspecting importer. Make sure that the famous goods you import are the "real" and not the "pirated" version of the product.

Based on John Delman, "Are Pirates Cutting Into Your Sales?" *International Business*, July 1991, pp. 30–33; Marlene C. Piturro, "Global Spies, Lies and Videotape," *World Trade*, March 1992, pp. 43–46.

Fortunately, a specialist exists to help the importer through the complex web of import law. A **customs broker**, also sometimes called a customhouse broker, acts as a liaison between the importer and Customs and works to move the importer's foreign goods quickly and efficiently through Customs.

It is not necessary to hire a broker, but most importers do—not least because they are also well-informed about freight handling and transportation. Although many reputable brokers are one-person operations, the larger brokerage houses also issue

bonds and prepay shipment taxes, billing the importer later.

Although the nitty-gritty, physical procedures of bringing a fashion import into the country may not be the most intriguing aspect of the overall importing process, they are not without their reward. Customs entry, after all, is the last step in the import chain. At last, after months of researching, planning, creating, modifying, and rethinking the import product, the importer can finally take possession of his or her dream.

GLOBAL GLIMPSES

IS IT REAL? OR IS IT COUNTERFEIT?

Jeffrey Harris is a private detective and his beat is Asia. His specialty is catching counterfeiters. Not the ones that print money—the ones that print other people's names and designs. His clients are primarily U.S. companies and include names like Reebok and Microsoft.

The work can be dangerous—round-the-clock surveillance, night raids on warehouses, and keeping undercover factory workers undetected. His original office was opened in Taiwan, long the capital of counterfeiting in Asia. As the textile and apparel labor-intensive industries moved from Taiwan to Southeast Asia, the counterfeiters moved with them. Mr. Harris has recently set up another office in Thailand to catch counterfeiters in these new areas.

Information based on "To Catch a Thief," Gregory J. Millman.

ENDNOTES

1. Sandra L. Kruzel and Frank Reynolds, *Import/Export Procedures*, Cincinnati, OH: Southwestern. 1992, p. 124.
2. "Infofile: Port Profiles, North American Ports/East Coast (Part One of Two)," *North American International Business*, May 1991, p. 56.
3. Carl A. Nelson, *Your Own Import-Export Business: Winning the Trade Game*, Chula Vista, CA, 1988, pp. 128–30.
4. *Ibid.*, p. 144.
5. John Delman, "Are Pirates Cutting into Your Sales?" *International Business*, July 1991, pp. 31–33.
6. Kruzel, *Op. cit.*, p. 154.
7. Ellen Klein and J. D. Howard, "Gray Market Rules: Strings Attached." *North American International Business*, May 1991, pp. 54–55.
8. *Ibid.*, p. 53.
9. *Ibid.*, p. 54.
10. "U.S. Ignored Notice of Chinese Prison Goods," *Newsday*, March 25, 1992, p. 33.

VOCABULARY

absolute quota

_____

_____

_____

bond

_____

_____

_____

boycott

_____

_____

collateral

_____

_____

commercial shipment

_____

_____

_____

continuous or term bond

_____

_____

_____

customs broker

_____

_____

_____

entry

_____

_____

_____

Entry Summary Form

_____

_____

_____

formal entry

_____

_____

_____

gray market goods

_____

_____

_____

informal entry

_____

_____

_____

inspection

_____

_____

_____

liquidation

_____

_____

_____

parallel imports

_____

_____

_____

tariff-rate quota

_____

_____

_____

valuation

_____

_____

_____

GLOBAL REVIEW

1. Why is it sometimes difficult to bring imported goods into the United States?

   _____

   _____

   _____

   _____

2. The U.S. Customs Service is an agency of which government department?

   _____

   _____

   _____

   _____

3. What are the four major divisions of the U.S. Customs Service?

   _____

   _____

   _____

   _____

4. There are dollar amounts that qualify a shipment for informal entry or formal entry. What are these designated dollar amounts?

   _____

   _____

   _____

5. Who is usually granted immediate delivery privilege and under which circumstances?

   _____

   _____

   _____

   _____

6. Because Customs has the right to examine all foreign goods shipments, it is important to know what the examination process involves. What are the five steps usually involved in this examination process?

   _____

   _____

   _____

   _____

   _____

7. What is the Harmonized System of Tariffs?

_____

_____

_____

_____

8. Explain the difference between an absolute quota and a tariff-rate quota.

_____

_____

_____

_____

_____

9. What is meant by gray-market goods and how do they affect domestic manufacturers?

_____

_____

_____

_____

_____

10. Who is the specialist that helps an importer and acts as a liason between the importer and Customs? What services does this specialist perform?

_____

_____

_____

_____

_____

GLOBAL DIGEST

1. All formal entries of imported goods must be covered by a bond. What is a bond and what does it guarantee? If the insurance company asks for collateral, what can the importer use to serve this purpose?

_____

_____

_____

_____

_____

_____

_____

2. During the inspection of foreign goods many things are scrutinized. What circumstances may lead to a more intense scrutiny on imported goods?

_____

_____

_____

_____

_____

_____

_____

_____

3. Protecting trademarks has become more important in recent years. What reasons have contributed to this protection and why has the fashion industry supported it so strongly?

_____

_____

_____

_____

_____

_____

_____

_____

UNIT 4 READING

CHANGES AFOOT IN TEXTILES/ APPAREL SOURCING PATTERNS

By Julie Ritzer Ross

The times, they are still "a-changing." While politics and accusations of wrongdoing continue to render some textiles and apparel markets difficult to tap, liberalized quotas, reasonably priced labor and increasingly sophisticated manufacturing capabilities are creating new opportunities for shippers and carriers. Here's the latest developments within specific markets:

CHINA

While China's share of U.S. textile and apparel imports now stands at 15 percent ($3.5 billion), myriad legislative and non-legislative developments could soon deflate these figures.

Notably, Most Favored Nation (MFN) status still permits China to remit the lowest possible general import duties. However, in June, the U.S. Congress will be reviewing a bill that would deprive China this privilege and impose higher Column II rates. Should the legislation pass, ad valorem duties may rise as much as 100 percent, thereby forcing shippers to source elsewhere.

"Whether China stays in the MFN realm with stipulations, as I believe will happen, or is indeed stripped of its rights, recessionary conditions make it impossible to absorb the cost increases higher duties necessitate," said Sally Wread, import/export manager, Totes Inc., Loveland, Ohio. "Consumers are hurting and won't tolerate the higher prices we would consequently have little choice but to impose."

George Horowitz, president of Total Impact, New York City, expressed similar views. To him the idea of paying stiffer duties for Chinese goods gives shippers a rationale for patronizing nations with underutilized quotas. "The only product that could not be replaced elsewhere is silk," he observed.

Actions being taken by the United States under a law known as Special 310 are also expected to clog Chinese clothing/fabric pipelines. Enactment of Special 310 would permit American retaliation against continued Chinese patent and copyright piracy with punitive tariffs of 100 percent on silk blouses, silk dresses and footwear. Although a spokesperson for U.S. Trade Representative (USTR) Carla Hills said the final list of items facing trade sanctions is still being formulated, importers appear fearful to await the final verdict. "President Bush has promised to get tough on China about infringement. With the election coming up, he won't skirt the issue," one retail conglomerate's import director said. "As a result, we—like many organizations in our industry—are actively looking at places to find product at a rate we can bear."

Additionally, a statement issued by USTR purported, "political necessity" will prevent a lifting of China's textile and apparel import quotas no matter what the outcome of future Uruguay Round trade talks.

The Multi-Fibre Arrangement (MFA), which governs the bulk of world fabric and clothing commerce via a quota system, was extended this past July 31 through year end 1992. If Uruguay Round participants strike an agreement, though, MFA and its requisite quotas would be phased out over a 10-year interval and the textile trade, incorporated into General Agreement on Tariffs and Trade (GATT). "If a deal is struck, we'll have no incentive to remain on the Chinese side and every reason to gravitate where there's a quota-free situation," the retailer commented.

Recent U.S. Customs allegations linking importers to the illegal practice of selling prison-made products may shrink Chinese import potential even further. Approximately 12 to 16 million prisoners are interred in some 3,000 camps across China. About 50 percent of the merchandise they turn out is eventually exported, said Harry Wu, a researcher at California's Stanford University and author of *Laogai: The Chinese Gulag*.

"We're prepared to withdraw Chinese business the minute we see evidence that what's being shipped to us isn't being made legitimately," revealed the vice president of one apparel concern. "Distinguishing between legal and illegal is tough, but when we hear we can't see a subcontractor, we think *prison*."

Interestingly, a few importers interviewed reported that they are taking precautions against this problem in other ways as a means of preventing themselves from being compelled to drastically reduce Chinese imports. For instance, Wread stated, Totes' vice president and international purchasing manager visit China's factories annually, then bring home photographs and videocassettes documenting that no prison laborers are involved in its production processes. Similarly, Nike, Inc., Beaverton, Ore., has procured statements from its factories certifying the same situation, claimed Dale Watanabe, director of customs.

HONG KONG

Sourcing here remains somewhat sensible because product transit time from the Far East averages 12 to 14 days, versus 25 to 30 days from Bangladesh and the Philippines, said Jim

Langlois, executive director, National Apparel and Textile Association in Seattle.

"Unfortunately, though," countered the manager of foreign merchandising services for a large retail chain, "the majority of clothing created in Hong Kong is produced when more lucrative electronics manufacture and petroleum export processing suddenly began proceeding at a slow pace. Buyers must order goods far in advance. They can't wait for the lulls any longer. Only by going outside Hong Kong are they presently able to have goods on the shelves when customers want them."

THE PHILIPPINES

Importers believe the Philippines is destined to suffer trade repercussions because of underhanded business practices. Several apparel and textile manufacturers headquartered there were recently charged with illegally smuggling large volumes of Chinese textiles into the United States. In light of this situation, investing in Filipino resources would, prove tantamount to supporting China and, indirectly, sanctioning its unconscionable attitudes about human rights, insisted Wolf Finkelman, chairman of Houston-based Scope Imports.

Scope has not been importing much from China since the Tiananmen Square incident several years ago. "Competition compels us to be politically correct, and if that means cutting the Filipinos loose from our [clothing and fabric] loop, so be it," agreed an import specialist for one garment manufacturer.

THAILAND

Unlike some of its Far Eastern neighbors, Thailand is seeing a boom in U.S.-bound textiles and apparel. Volume garnered during the first eight months of 1991 rose 9 percent over that recorded for the same period in 1990, according to U.S. Department of Commerce (DOC) statistics. Some $594 million worth of Thai textile shipments reached American destinations in the fiscal year ending last June, up from $407 million received within the previous 12 months.

CHANGES AFOOT IN TEXTILES/APPAREL SOURCING PATTERNS
CONTINUED

Currently, hot commodities include fabric, polyester and cotton yarns; ready-made garments; brassieres; socks and gloves. Sources expect this trend will continue, citing that some of the country's quotas are underutilized.

"Better luck with quotas is making Thailand a popular spot; it will, not surprisingly, be among the first nations to see [enhanced] demand should China not maintain MFN status," observed Laura Jones, executive director, United States Association of Importers of Textiles and Apparel (USA-ITA).

Additionally, while Thai manufacturing technology has yet to develop fully, shippers deemed the country an increasingly viable clothing and fabric market based on its still-reasonable labor costs.

"Korean and Taiwanese production expenditures are going up, but that's not true of Bangkok," Watanabe remarked.

WESTERN ASIA

Under terms of a bilateral agreement signed with the United States late last November, India will adhere to the same 1992 textile and apparel quotas. Quotas for 1993 will remain unchanged if a Uruguay Round textile pact has not been ratified at that point, U.S. trade officials announced.

The greater availability of clothing and fabric rendered possible by such an agreement is slated to push India's shipments of these commodities to more than $795 million this year, up from $793 million in 1990, according to a DOC report. Actual textile volume will increase by 15 percent, from 392 million square yards to 450 million square yards.

"India and Bangladesh have definitely become important markets for us since [obtaining material] there became easier," proclaimed Horowitz. He anticipates doing "deeper" sourcing in both nations if China's MFN renewal does not reach fruition.

Meanwhile, Bangladeshi manufacturers' willingness to produce quality fabrics rather than focusing on tea and jute is creating even wider routing opportunities for carriers interested in the region, shippers' comments indicate.

"Product from Bangladesh no longer comes with the automatic stigma of shoddy, so we do not have as much of a reason as before to consider it a less-than-desirable source," stated a spokesperson for a children's sportswear manufacturer. Further, price-squeezed producers are setting their sights on Malaysia, Sri Lanka and Indonesia, where an extensive labor pool permits clothing to be turned out at very low cost.

"The recession is strapping our vendors, and the price limitations that satisfy their demands are best met not in the Far East, but in Western Asia and particularly the latter two nations," said a spokesperson for Wrangler, Inc., Greensboro, N.C.

MEXICO

U.S. imports of apparel from Mexico have risen consistently, from 91.7 million square meters in 1985 to 174.1 million square meters in 1990, according to the American Textile Manufacturers Institute (ATMI). The North American Free Trade Agreement (NAFTA), would vastly relax tariff restrictions on the latter nation," said Carlos Moore, executive vice president, ATMI.

Some shippers support NAFTA, insisting it will not only yield better access to more reasonably priced materials than may be available elsewhere, and enhance the selection of textiles and apparel offered for import to the United States.

Other companies oppose the pact, claiming they do not want to be associated with what they perceive as the exploitation of Mexican workers earning the equivalent of 63 cents per hour.

CARIBBEAN BASIN

Shippers' overwhelming adoption of "just-in-time" delivery methodologies aimed at enabling them to bow to mercurial fashion trends has given this region a strong shot in the arm.

Several individuals interviewed said they either plan to or have already begun relying upon basin nations as primary textile/apparel sources. They explained that while orders from the Far East require six months' lead time, operations in Guatemala, Jamaica, Haiti, Costa Rica and the Dominican Republic generally fill them within eight weeks.

CHANGES AFOOT IN TEXTILES/APPAREL SOURCING PATTERNS
CONTINUED

Parties contacted also pointed toward low factory worker wages and favorable trade policies as rationales for their enhanced interest in Caribbean fabrics and clothing. Pay scales run roughly $1 per hour, versus somewhat higher in other regions and around $6 plus benefits in the United States. Under the 807 tariff program, American apparel makers may avail themselves of lower rates and pay duty only on costs incurred offshore by cutting fabric domestically, then sending it to the basin for stitching. Stitched materials are returned to the United States where manufacturers label, package and distribute them.

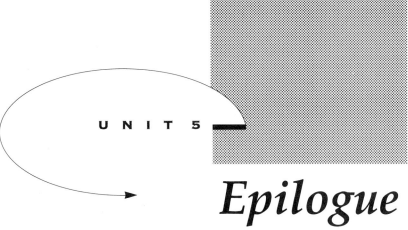

UNIT 5

Epilogue

CHAPTER 15

Your Career and the Future of Global Fashion Marketing

When you travel, do you insist on staying in one place long enough to really drink in the local customs and culture rather than hitting 12 cities in 10 days?

Even when you are at home in the United States, are you interested in meeting people from other countries, and is your interest based on an intense desire to learn how other people live?

If you answered yes to these questions, you might enjoy working in global fashion.

Not everyone is suited to this kind of work. Not everybody will have the training or, for that matter, the personality to undertake this kind of work. But global fashion is the most exciting, new area of the fashion business in the 1990s. The demand for trained professionals to work in international fashion has been growing for several years now, and will probably reach an all-time high in the next decade. There will be more opportunities than ever before.

WHY THE INTERNATIONAL WORK FORCE WILL EXPAND

Partly, the demand for workers willing to live and work in countries other than their own is tied to

changes both in U.S. industry in general and in the fashion industry specifically.

For much of the past decade, the United States lagged behind other countries in exporting. At the moment, only 6 percent of the U.S. gross national product comes from exports, compared with 25 percent for West Germany and a whopping 35 percent for South Korea. But the United States is finally preparing to compete in the world market, and the 1990s will be the decade when it becomes a strong international presence. When it does, there is no reason that the fashion industry should not lead the effort. A world that has long admired U.S. fashion eagerly awaits the day when it is exported around the world.

Meanwhile, there is also little chance that the importing boom will slow down. Two-way trade in the world currently tops a staggering 550 billion, with no sign of a slowdown in sight.[1]

These two trends have great significance for anyone interested in working in international fashion. They mean that new positions will be created and old ones expanded to fill the growing demands of the global market.

Jobs in the international fashion world will require people with special skills and training. In the past, exporters and importers brought relatively few specialized skills to their jobs. The vast majority, in fact, had no training at all other than what they got on the job. Some experts have speculated that this may be one reason that the United States has not been a major player in the current expansion of the global marketplace.

But in the future, in the intensely fast-paced, sophisticated world of international fashion, the United States will need a competitive edge—and that means that its workers will have to be specially trained for the new jobs in foreign markets.

FASHIONING A CAREER IN INTERNATIONAL FASHION

The training you get will determine the kinds of careers that will be open to you. A **career** is a person's chosen life's pursuit as well as progress in that pursuit. Anyone can have a job, but to have a career usually takes some special advance planning and skills. It is up to you to write your own plan and then put it in motion.

The direction that a career takes is called a **career path.** This is a road map of the jobs you hold, as well as the jobs you plan to hold, to reach your ultimate goal.

Career paths can take one of several forms. Almost everyone in any field begins with an **entry-level,** or training, **position**. The next step is to progress to a **mid-management** position, where you have increased responsibilities but are still learning about the business. Many carefully planned careers culminate in a **management,** or top, position. In a management position, you will no longer be a learner, and people will pay you for the knowledge you bring to the job.

Most people try to follow this kind of career path, but in international fashion and among creative people, careers sometimes move in another direction as well. That is why human resources experts speak of a **vertical,** or upward, **career path** versus a **lateral,** or more horizontal, **career path**.

A vertical career path moves upward in a straightforward line. You begin with an entry-level job, move through mid-management, and advance to a management position.

In a lateral career path, the road is a little less straight. You would probably still begin with an entry-level job—because these are required in almost every business. But you might then take a series of jobs often—but not always—involving more pay but not necessarily greater responsibility. Each job would move you closer to your career goal, either by teaching you more about a specialty you were developing or by moving you closer to a part of the world in which you hope to work.

In many traditional industries, it is important to have a vertical career path. A lateral move is considered a setback. But in less rigid industries, and fashion is certainly one of those, career paths more often tend to be lateral. This will be especially true for those seeking global fashion careers.

Why, you may ask? The reason is that if you want a career in international fashion, you have two, not just one, primary career goals. You want to reach a certain level, usually a management position; on top of that, however, and equally important, you want to reach that position in another part of the world other than where you now live. That is your second important career goal. To achieve both, a little zigging and zagging may be necessary. In fact, a zigzag route may be the fastest path to the top.

Consider the not atypical career path of one young fashion graduate who hoped to work as a product developer in Japan. As a child, she had traveled there with her mother, an international businesswoman, and had fallen in love with the country and its culture. She vowed she would one day live and work there.

Despite her training—she had studied Japanese business practices and was fluent in the language—she found that no jobs were open to her in the mid-1980s, largely, because women were not welcome in the Japanese workplace at that time.

Finally, after months of searching, she was offered a job in Brazil, as an assistant plant manager in a shoe factory. About half of the shoe manufacturer's clients were, in fact, Japanese. Even so, Brazil seemed farther away from Japan than the United States, but her guidance counselor encouraged her to take the job for the experience.

She did and promptly set about learning Spanish and Portuguese, as well as keeping up with her Japanese, while she waited for a chance to work in Japan. Periodically, she traveled to Japan for her South American employer. On these forays, she was able to develop contacts and test the waters.

For several years, the tests proved futile. No one offered her a job in Japan. None of the largely male-dominated Japanese companies seemed interested in employing a young, inexperienced American female—even one who spoke Japanese. Gradually, however, the taboo against women loosened up. Her break came in 1990, and then it came unexpectedly from an American company.

A U.S. branch of a specialty shoe store was making plans to open in Japan and sought a Japanese-speaking American who was familiar with Japanese culture to manage the operation. Everything about

GLOBAL SOURCING PROFESSIONALS

As a supplier to many successful mass merchants in America, our customers expect us to provide the very best product values. We do this by hiring the best and the brightest talent in the business, and empowering them to do the job.

Due to the strength of our business and continued aggressive entry into Global Sourcing markets, we are seeking outstanding candidates for the following key positions:

**DIVISIONAL VICE PRESIDENT
OF PRODUCTION**

Position requires a minimum of 10 years of wide-ranging apparel global sourcing experience which must include solid understanding and experience in: line development calendar methodology; product: fabrications, looks, garment construction, quality and cost; sourcing in most of the world's supply markets; purchase order negotiation and placement; and WIP control. Factory management and quality assurance background a big plus. The successful candidate will have managed a staff of buyers and coordinators; and must be prepared to demonstrate achievements in terms of FOB responsibility, and cost/quality/delivery performance.

**MEDITERRANEAN REGIONAL DIRECTOR and ASIA
& MEDITERRANEAN COUNTRY DIRECTORS**

Positions require a minimum of 10 years' experience as the manager in an off-shore operation doing $20 million or more. Successful candidates need the skills to negotiate aggressive pricing, place business, and follow-up on both work-in-progress and quality assurance. Proven track record of consistently achieving superior results and willingness to relocate permanently to assigned region or country a must.

PRODUCTION ASSOCIATES & BUYERS

Positions require a minimum of 5 years' procurement experience with a solid understanding of merchandising concepts, product development, fabrications, construction, pricing, cost components, countries of production, makers, etc. Strong track record of verifiable achievements a must.

If you are qualified and want to join an aggressive Global Sourcing Team. We'd like to hear from you. For prompt, confidential consideration, forward your resume which MUST INCLUDE position of interest and salary history to:

Meryl Wendreti
VICE PRESIDENT/DIRECTOR OF GLOBAL SOURCING
FASHIONS UNLIMITED, INC.
200 Broad Street, Dept. WWd., NY, NY 10001

Principals only, please.
We're sorry, but we cannot accept telephone calls

An equal opportunity employer M/F

International fashion offers a vast array of jobs aimed at all levels of skill and experience.

this woman was right, including her experience in the South American shoe factory. She landed the job.

The moral of the story is simple: It pays to go where the opportunities are, even if they are not exactly where you want to be. In fact, it may be necessary to do so while you wait for your big break. Any experience you can get in international merchandising and marketing will only make you a stronger candidate for the next job.

EXPORTING OR IMPORTING— WHICH WILL IT BE?

The skills required to be an exporter or an importer are very much the same, and anyone with training in international business will probably find it fairly easy to move between the two areas of global business.

In terms of finding a job, however, it often pays to buck trends or be a bit "contrarian," as they say on Wall Street. These days, with all the emphasis on importing, that may mean looking for a job in exporting while everyone else is looking for one in importing. Those who go to work in exporting now will be in a good position to capitalize on the coming expansion.

Keep in mind, however, that trends have a way of reversing themselves. In another few years, the life of an exporter might be the hot job area.

GETTING THE TRAINING YOU NEED

What exactly are the kinds of skills you will need to have a career in global fashion? The first step is to get training in a fashion career that would work

GLOBAL *GO-GETTERS*

ANNE MARINO: REVERSING ROLES

Courtesy of J. Crew International.

Reversing roles was not difficult for Anne Marino. Most of her career had been spent helping foreign companies to set up headquarters in the United States and assisting them to market their products to the American customer. These companies include Simint SpA of Modena, Italy; Stefanel Corp. based in Ponte di Piave, Italy; and D'Urban, a subsidiary of Renown, the Tokyo-based men's wear manufacturer.

Because of this international experience and her global outlook she was the perfect choice for Arnold Cohen, President of the J. Crew Group, when he hired her to fill a new position, vice-president of international development.

In its first overseas venture, J. Crew Group signed a licensing agreement with C. Itoh Co. Ltd. and Renown, Inc. to retail J. Crew merchandise in Japan. In the general plan, Renown will build shops ranging from 1200 to 2100 square feet inside the high-end department stores. These "shops-in-shops" will have the same merchandise and decor as J. Crew stores in the United States, and the agreement provides controls to ensure that the presentation and merchandise are identical to their U.S. appearance. Although the look will be the same, the specifications will be different to fit the Japanese consumers. The merchandise will be made in many factories currently contracted by J. Crew around the world.

Cohen believes that the Japanese customer is sophisticated, style-conscious, and quality-minded. Anne Marino agrees that there is a trend in Japan for consumers to move away from high-priced European designs.

J. Crew specializes in moderate-to-better priced casual yet sophisticated looks. In addition to stores and licensing, there is a possibility of establishing foreign operations for the catalog. The overseas catalog would have the same look as the U.S. catalog. The expectation is that they will be exporting the image as it is in America.

"If you look at the trends in Europe and Japan, in particular, you see a strong acceptance of the American fashion statement," says Anne Marino adding, "I've always dreamed about taking an American company abroad." And so she has!

Based on David Moin, "With Overseas Venture, J.Crew Sees Net Sales Doubling in Five Years," *Women's Wear Daily*, February 13, 1992, p. 2; David Moin, "J. Crew Licenses Itoh, Renown to Open Shops and Stores in Japan," *Women's Wear Daily*, April 7, 1992, p. 15.

IMPORTERS OR MANUFACTURERS' REPS, WHICH SHALL IT BE?

It takes nerves of steel and the spirit of a gambler to make it in the tricky business of importing and representing international ready-to-wear collections. So say the members of firms that struggle daily with foreign manufacturers for the early deliveries and salable silhouettes American retailers demand.

But as the demand for foreign fashion remains strong among U.S. specialty stores, the rewards make the game worth playing, according to importers and manufacturer reps. In fact, many handle both the selling and importing responsibilities, with some extending their roles into partnership ventures or licensing pacts with the vendor. Others prefer to specialize in one area.

Sales reps simply market international lines in showrooms or at trade shows, whereas importers act as the liaison between the foreign manufacturer and the U.S. selling agent. Importers negotiate with makers in pricing a line, relay orders from reps to the firm, verify credit and receive payment from retailers, bring the merchandise through customs, and distribute goods to the appropriate store. They also arrange their own credit terms for compensating a manufacturer, ranging from a letter of credit through a bank to payment plans of thirty to sixty days with a vendor.

It is not easy being the U.S. face of a foreign company. Differences in language and deliveries are only the start of it. Importers and manufacturers' reps say overcoming these difficulties is crucial. Their reputations depend on it!

Based on Debra Michals, "The Rep of a Eurorep," *Children's Business*, Fall 1990, p. 168.

anywhere—as a designer, in fashion and business management, whatever interests you most. Along the way you can also prepare yourself for a career in international business.

To do so, you will need to learn at least one, if not more than one, language. For years, Americans have gotten along speaking only English, but in the coming global market, they will need to be multilingual. Speaking other languages will be necessary to compete effectively. Admittedly, English is becoming the language of international business, but it does not make sense to live and conduct business in a country if you do not understand what is being said all around you.

Beyond that, you will need to take some courses in international business practices. Not everyone around the world conducts business in the same way. Sales practices, retail practices, even accounting practices vary from one country to another. You will need an understanding of how business is done around the world—especially in the part of the world where you hope to work—to work successfully in the international marketplace.

Finally, and most indispensably, do everything you can to get experience with the culture where you hope to work. Join a student-exchange program and live abroad for a semester or a year. (It is also a good way to test whether you would really like living in another country.)

Invite someone from another culture to live with you. Get a summer job with a foreign-run company.

Join the Japan Club or Spain Club or any group you can find that will help you keep up with your language skills and also teach you about the other culture.

You cannot have too much contact with the people of a country where you plan to work, and even social contacts have a way of turning into professional contacts when the time is right.

SPECIAL OPPORTUNITIES: MINORITIES AND WOMEN ENCOURAGED TO APPLY

Special opportunities exist for both minorities and women in international business. An African-American, for example, may find that doors open to him or her in Africa and in Latin and South America because of his or her ethnic background. Similarly, an American Hispanic will find a special welcome in Spanish-speaking parts of the world.

The situation for women is less clearly defined. Throughout most of the rest of the world, with the exception of some parts of Western Europe, women have not made the inroads they have in the United States. Now, women are becoming more welcome in

Numerous business opportunities are available for both minorities and women in the international fashion industry. *Reprinted by permission of Unz. & Co., 190 Baldwin Avenue, Jersey City, NJ 07306.*

many parts of the world, but there are still problems, the primary one being the separation of sexes that exists to one degree or another in many cultures.

Japanese men, for example, now do business with women more willingly than in the past, but even so, not all the barriers are down. Japanese men conduct much of their business dealings over evening entertainments, and although they now extend the invitation to American businesswomen to join them, women are still expected to refuse the invitation. Not to do so would be a breach of Japanese etiquette. However active you might be in promoting social change at home, it is difficult, if not impossible, to conduct business in another culture if you do not acknowledge its customs and folkways. Still, changes have occurred and they will continue to occur in the future.

THE JOB MARKET

Some fashion jobs can be done anywhere in the world with little or no extra training, whereas others require a great deal of extra training.

A designer's work is the same, for example, anywhere in the world. In contrast, a store manager working in a foreign environment needs special training and skills. Many aspects of business operations vary from country to country: pricing, inventory, delivery schedules, even the fashion calendar, to name but a few of the areas with different practices. One international buyer was surprised to learn that European stores still stock wool sweaters in January when U.S. stores are full of bathing suits and resort wear. Another was amazed to learn that delivery times were much looser in many countries than in the United States.[2]

Similarly, some jobs will never be available to a foreigner seeking employment in the international market. A low-level position like a patterncutter, for example, would rarely be filled by anyone other than a local worker.

Apart from this, in each of the major categories of employment—manufacturing, retailing, and auxiliary services—many interesting jobs are open to the ambitious international job-seeker.

MANUFACTURING

The number of manufacturing jobs will increase as U.S. producers continue to relocate their operations overseas. Although they can hire nationals to carry out the low-level jobs, most manufacturers, in the start-up stage if nothing else, tend to feel more confident if they have one or more persons in on-site management. Communication feels easier, and there is shared understanding of U.S. methods of operations. A U.S. employee working in a foreign plant can also perform a valuable function as a scout seeking out interesting foreign methods of production.

Among the specific jobs that are to be available in manufacturing in foreign countries are plant manager, assistant plant manager, product manager, and sourcer. Manufacturers will also hire U.S. professionals as retail sales coordinators and quality control analysts.

RETAILING/WHOLESALING

More retailing than wholesaling has gone abroad. As the world becomes one big global market, individual stores have been eager to try their luck in the international arena. It goes both ways, of course, as Americans recently watched one French department store fold in Denver, Colorado, while another, Galeries Lafayette, opened in Manhattan.

No major U.S. department store has opened a foreign branch yet (although inevitably one will), but when Americans travel abroad these days, they are no longer surprised to turn the corner of a medieval village in Italy and encounter a Gap or some other well-known specialty store.

When U.S. specialty stores open abroad, they often like to take at least some of their selling methods with them. This translates into a need for U.S. employees in such jobs as production assistant, merchandise assistant, fashion director, fashion coordinator, import coordinator, store manager, assistant store manager, and, sometimes, even department manager.

Major U.S. department stores have always maintained some ties in Europe and Asia through active buying offices. Jobs such as buyer and assistant buyer are often open to interested U.S. personnel.

AUXILIARY SERVICES

Several auxiliary businesses—most notably, journalism, banking and finance, and shipping and transportation—service the fashion industry. These are often excellent training grounds for people who eventually want to work more directly in the fashion industry. Some people even find work in auxiliary areas so interesting that they never move on.

Journalists have always covered the French fashion shows, sending back lively descriptions of new styles. In recent years, their coverage has been expanded to include other European countries and, in-

GLOBAL *Goodies*

YOUR HOME IS YOUR EMPIRE

It is certainly not for everyone, but working from the home could be ideal for world traders.

Right now you are 30,000 feet over Somewhere, The World, headed for a U.S. international airport. You've been on the road for two weeks straight visiting markets in Brussels, Bangkok, or Brazil. You feet are swollen. Your eyes are bloodshot and your suit is so wrinkled it looks like it was pressed between two corkscrews. There has to be a better way to do international business. Working from your home might just be the answer.

More and more international consultants, sales reps, brokers, and designers are setting up in-home centers for themselves. The benefits are many. Working from home, international professionals can work through the night, when their foreign clients are working and ready to receive calls and do business.

In Sandy Hook, Connecticut, Marlene Gaberel works as an import/export consultant to a number of clients too small to afford an in-house global professional. Her clients do not care where her office is. They just want her to help them export and sell products.

But for all its advantages, there are still some disadvantages to working from your home. You must be disciplined and methodical in your approach if you want to make a home office work.

In the reality of today's high-tech business place, most home-based international professionals will need a computer, a fax, and a modem. A reliable telephone-answering machine or service is also imperative. Remember, your clients buy you and your expertise. They are not interested in where you work or when. If you get results, you can work from anywhere and thrive in the international business.

Based on Greg Matusky, "An International Empire in Your Home," *World Trade*, October 1991, pp. 52–54.

creasingly, the rest of the world as well. Fashion is also no longer covered exclusively on the women's pages of newspapers and in women's magazines but is, instead, turning up regularly on the business pages.

Positions for editors, assistant editors, and news reporters are among those open to anyone interested in working in fashion journalism.

Banking and financial institutions that service the fashion industry are a traditional, time-honored way to hone skills in international business. An array of jobs, from an entry-level position like executive trainee to a mid-management position like loan officer, are available to anyone interested in working in international finance.

Shipping and transportation, arguably the most important of the auxiliary businesses, offer a variety of positions, from training through management lev-

els, to the interested international businessperson. The two most specialized posts are customs broker and freight forwarder, but a host of other jobs are available as well to those who want to acquire some background in these two vital areas.

The outlook for jobs in auxiliary services will remain good throughout the 1990s. As growing numbers of U.S. fashion businesses enter the export market, additional jobs will open to meet the demand.

GETTING AN ENTRY LEVEL JOB

Hardest of all is to get a first job anywhere. Getting a job in international fashion requires a couple of strategies that would not be used for a domestic job interview. These may vary depending on the kind of job

TECH TALK

THE FUTURE IS NOW

The global office can be anywhere and everywhere. With more services at lower prices, international telecommunications can be had by everyone.

Telecom consultants can help you analyze your communications patterns and help you choose the right mix of carriers and services. International direct is becoming commonplace, but take a look at the following international services that just yesterday were nothing more than a gleam in a global marketer's eye.

INTERNATIONAL 800 SERVICE: It works domestically, why not try it internationally? All three major carriers offer service in selected countries with no monthly or recurring charges.

INTERNATIONAL WATS: Comparable to the staple of domestic telephone-dependent businesses, International WATS is now offered by all the major carriers.

ENHANCED FAX SERVICES: All three carriers will instantly broadcast your fax to literally hundreds of fax machines worldwide.

ON-LINE OPERATORS AND INTERPRETERS: All three major carriers provide operators fluent in English and a foreign language. AT&T offers on-line interpreters for business conversations. "Language Line" interpreters are available for more than 140 languages, 24 hours a day, seven days a week.

VOICE/DATA SWITCHING: All three carriers offer digital capabilities and optional broadband capabilities for data as well as voice communication.

VIDEOCONFERENCING: All three carriers are filling this explosive market niche.

FAVORITE-NATION CALLING: If you call one country more often than any other, you can get a substantial discount for that country.

CREDIT CARD CALLING: When calling outside the United States, you can charge your calls in U.S. currency. And remember: Telex, electronic mail, and EDI services offer additional possibilities when a telephone call is just not enough.

Based on Eric J. Adams, "Phone Rome," *World Trade*, January/February 1992, pp. 40–42.

one is seeking, but two approaches can help any job-seeker get through an interview with a prospective foreign employer.

First, strange as it may sound, try not to be a typically aggressive American. Americans are known around the world for their can-do spirit, and it serves new workers well when they are trying to impress future employers. To foreign prospective employers, however, Americans often seem too aggressive, and there are many cultures around the world where this trait is not as valued as it is in the United States. Be as low key as you can and still manage to convey a willingness to work hard.

Second, forget—for the moment, at least—the theories you learned in school. They will be helpful to you on the job, of course, but hard-core skills are more impressive in a job interview.

Can you read a letter in French? Prospective employers have been known to hand a letter in a foreign language to prospective employees and ask them to read it as a means of testing their language skills.

Even better, can you translate the letter? Answer it? Help an employer find information that is needed to answer the letter? These are what employers need from any employee—and what they especially want

from a new, inexperienced one whom they know they will have to train. Do not try to be impressive during the interview. Instead, try to be valuable, and you will have a much better chance of landing the job.

Another bit of advice about finding a job in a foreign country: Look outside the industry, if necessary. Embassies and consulates, as well as trade centers, banks, and Chambers of Commerce all offer jobs that service the fashion industry and will help you build valuable contacts within it. The training you get in such jobs will prove invaluable, and may be exactly what you need to eventually land a job in fashion.

And last but hardly least, do not be unwilling to take an entry-level position, such as executive trainee, administrative assistant, assistant to the president, or sales trainee. The access these jobs provide for you to more experienced persons in the industry can prove invaluable. In conclusion, few experts doubt that the 1990s will be the decade when the United States, quite possibly led by the fashion industry, enters the international arena in a big way. For the well-trained, skilled, and experienced professional, the export boom will be a wonderful route to a highly successful career.

Individuals with drive and perseverence can succeed in getting jobs in the world of global fashions. *Reprinted by permission of Unz. & Co., 190 Baldwin Avenue, Jersey City, NJ 07306.*

GLOBETROTTING Gaffes

GRADUATES NEED NOT APPLY

Despite the proliferation of global trade programs in America's colleges and universities, graduates are finding overseas jobs elusive. Only 20 of the 549 U.S. companies surveyed by Michigan State University have plans to fill overseas jobs with U.S. college graduates.

Michigan State University's Collegiate Employment Research Institute says that multinationals will staff overseas jobs with a combination of local nationals and long-time U.S. employees.

The roadblocks recent American graduates face are foreign employment quotas, lack of international business experience, and lack of language skills beyond English.

Yet opportunities exist for students who structure their programs with foresight. Advice to undergraduates include: do pursue an overseas internship program, do not pick a discipline like finance or management, unless you are prepared to go on to graduate school.

Patrick Scheetz, director of MSU Research Institute says, "When you're 18 or 19, you tend to think that a degree in international trade or relations will be your ticket. But if all you have is the degree, you'll have a tough time getting hired." So, word to the wise, broaden your scope and work, work, work in the field.

Based on Warren Stugatch, "Trends-Job Search," *World Trade*, October 1991, p. 14.

ENDNOTES

1. David Win. *International Careers: An Insider's Guide,* Charlotte, VT: Williamson Publishers, 1987.
2. Debra Michals, "The Rise of the Eurorep," *Children's Business.* Fall 1990, p. 68.

VOCABULARY

career   _____

_____

_____

career path   _____

_____

_____

entry-level position   _____

_____

_____

lateral career path   _____

_____

_____

mid-management position   _____

_____

_____

management position   _____

_____

_____

vertical career path   _____

_____

_____

GLOBAL REVIEW   1. Why do you think the international work force will expand?

_____

_____

_____

_____

2. What is the difference between a job and a career?

_____

_____

_____

_____

3. How does a vertical career path differ from a lateral career path?

_____

_____

_____

_____

4. Why is it important to learn about international business practices?

_____

_____

_____

_____

_____

5. Some special opportunities exist for minorities and women in international trade. Explain why this is true.

_____

_____

_____

_____

_____

6. Name the different levels of the fashion business that have jobs available overseas.

_____

_____

_____

_____

7. List at least three jobs from each level that will include overseas living or assignments.

_____

_____

_____

_____

8. What are other areas that can be considered, outside the industry, as an entry to overseas employment?

_____

_____

_____

_____

9. An entry-level job is usually rejected by college graduates. Explain why this should not be true in international trade.

_____

_____

_____

_____

10. Why would a student-exchange program be helpful for someone hoping to enter international trade?

_____

_____

_____

_____

GLOBAL DIGEST

1. Why is it important to be able to speak another language? Which language, other than English, would you think will be the most important international language? Give reasons why you think this language will be helpful.

_____

_____

_____

_____

_____

_____

_____

_____

2. If given a choice, would you choose to have a career in exporting or in importing? Explain and give reasons for your choice.

_____

_____

_____

_____

_____

_____

_____

_____

3. Explain the different paths open to someone interested in working in international trade; in manufacturing, in finance, in government, and in retailing.

_____

_____

_____

_____

_____

_____

_____

_____

UNIT READING FOR EPILOGUE

CAREERS IN INTERNATIONAL TRADE AND MARKETING

The world is quickly becoming one large marketplace. This trend towards "globalization" is expected to increase during the '90's; and with the expansion of the "global market" comes new career opportunities in the international field. In fact, employment opportunities abroad, especially in Europe in the business fields, will very likely increase in the near future. While American firms are expanding into the European and Asian community, many of these companies are actively engaged in mergers and acquisitions as a part of their own economic expansion plans.

WHAT IS AN INTERNATIONAL JOB?

"International" does not necessarily mean "abroad." You can work for the international division of a large corporation in the US and never travel overseas; or you can work for a manufacturing company where international travel is required 50–75 percent of the time!

The field of International Trade and Marketing is difficult to define because job opportunities cover such a broad spectrum. Career possibilities in the field of International Trade and Marketing may be found in the federal government, non-profit organizations and foundations, manufacturers, import/export, retail, law, banking, finance, engineering, economics, medicine, communications, teaching, researching and educational development, agriculture, etc. The diversity of occupations in the International arena is tremendous; and each field has its own special qualifications for hiring and rules for advancement. But one thing is certain—the US seems firmly committed to "internationalism" and this orientation is shared by many European and Asian countries alike.

QUALIFICATIONS FOR INTERNATIONAL JOBS

Opportunities to work abroad remain tight and competition is keen. Most international jobs are available to individuals who are proficient in a specific area, fluent in foreign languages, or who have advanced academic credentials. Companies generally require that candidates have at least a BA/BS degree and sometimes even an advanced degree such as, Master of Business Administration (MBA), Master of International Affairs (MIA), or an LD (Law Degree). Excellent verbal and written skills as well as the ability to handle details and follow-up are also important attributes. Knowledge of or fluency in foreign languages is preferred; willingness to travel or live abroad is sometimes required, depending upon the demands of the job.

Americans working abroad must develop an understanding and appreciation for the country's culture and traditions. Lifestyles and work habits abroad are different from the American way of life. You must make an effort to understand cultural traits and be flexible and adaptable to a variety of new situations.

Many companies specifically seek individuals with international and overseas experience. It is expensive for businesses to send Americans abroad, so the few that go usually have been with the company for a number of years and have a proven track record.

Summer or part-time international work experience may be obtained through internships with government offices and agencies, trade association companies, commodity trading companies, consulting firms, etc.

You must also keep in mind that in most countries abroad, a work permit is required before you are allowed into the country for employment purposes. Work permits may not always be available in the country where you wish to work. Furthermore, foreign countries are usually required to hire their own nationals unless another person can show that they have special skills not readily available locally. Basic regulations within each country ensure that a certain percentage of the jobs are held by citizens of that country.

The procedures for obtaining a work permit vary among nations; therefore, you should get detailed information from the Washington, DC embassies or consulates in New York, before you leave the United States.

INTERNATIONAL JOB HUNTING

The best route to an overseas career is via a successful domestic career with a company expanding its international business. Being an outstanding performer in your domestic position and making certain that management knows of your desire for an international assignment are key ingredients. Understanding the industry and the company before entering a foreign country should facilitate cultural adjustments. Also, firms may be more likely to offer a position abroad to an experienced and trained employee.

Before you consider a career in the international arena, you must evaluate what you have to offer an employer i.e., your skills, abilities, areas of special knowledge, etc. Then you must research the international market to decide where these skills and interests may be applied. Research those countries you would like to pursue, in order to facilitate the job search.

Since the lead time for international jobs is often longer than for other types of work (often 5–12 months for the job campaign process), it is best to begin the job hunt at home. The possibilities of foreign employment vary and need research and preparation. Explore possibilities with headquarters of the American companies with branches in countries you wish to visit. To get lists of American companies with foreign branches, go to the reference desk of the library and ask for *The Directory of American Firms Operating in Foreign Countries* published by Simon and Schuster.

GOVERNMENT POSITIONS

For recent college graduates in International Trade, a good place to begin a foreign career is with one of the domestic or foreign-oriented government agencies. One especially good domestic agency is the Department of Commerce. This agency is an important center for information about International Trade in general and United States' International Trade in particular. All positions are obtained through the Civil Service system, an exam and specific ranking procedure.

CAREERS IN INTERNATIONAL TRADE AND MARKETING
CONTINUED

The following publications will give you additional information on each government agency, its functions, organizations and top personnel:

US Government Manual
write to:
US Government Printing Office
Washington, DC 20402

Washington Information Directory
write to:
Congressional Quarterly, Inc
1414 22 Street, NW
Washington, DC 20037

The Federal Yellow Book Directory
write to:
Washington Monitor, Inc
National Press Building
Washington, DC 20045

ORGANIZATIONS FOR FURTHER INFORMATION

The following organizations, both in the US and Europe, may be helpful in your international job search campaign. American embassies and consulates have commercial and/or economic sections that can provide you with business information and explain aspects of the local economy. Chambers of Commerce consist of firms in both countries interested in international trade. Trade Centers usually include many foreign companies operating in the country. Foreign government missions in the US such as the National Tourist Offices, embassies, and consulates can furnish visas and information on work permits as well as other important regulations. They may also offer economic and business information about the country.

Many summer or temporary jobs can be found in areas catering to the tourist and hospitality industry. The National Tourism office of each country can often provide information on hotels, resorts, restaurants, and other tourist areas. Simply write or call each office, requesting information on that country or region of the country and the vacation areas within it.

(Courtesy of Fashion Institute of Technology Placement Department)

Exporting Procedures Simulation

Hariel, Inc. of Queens, New York is a manufacturer of women's sportswear with a decidedly American flavor to its styling.

Hariel's sportswear items—jackets, pants, skirts, and vests—were selling well in specialty store chains throughout the United States. Their unique styling and top quality workmanship combined to make them best-sellers in the stores and sought out by consumers.

While on vacation trips to cities such as Paris, Rome, Tokyo, Hong Kong, and Brussels, Harriet King, the owner of Hariel, noticed that typical "American" items such as hamburgers, Cokes, and jeans were much desired by the local population and sold extremely well. Therefore, reasoned Harriet, I should be able to sell my products overseas to customers who have already shown a preference for things American.

When she returned to the United States, she had already made her decision to export her products. But—where? In what country or countries should she try to enter the foreign market? Taking a page from her domestic marketing plans, she proceeded to do some market research about the various countries she thought would be perfect for her products. Much of this information was available from business libraries and from the Department of Commerce. Also helpful were country-specific studies supplied by the various foreign embassies or consuls located in New York City.

Issues to be considered in her export decision included the following:

OBJECTIVES

- What are the company's reasons for pursuing export markets (e.g. increasing sales volume or developing a broader, more stable customer base)?
- How committed is the company's management to an export effort? Is exporting viewed as a quick fix for a slump in domestic sales? Will the company neglect its export customers if domestic sales pick up?
- What are the company's expectations for the export effort? How quickly does management expect export operations to become self-sustaining? What level of return on investment is expected from the export program?

PAST EXPERIENCE

- With what countries has business already been conducted, or from what countries have inquiries already been received?
- Which product lines are mentioned most often?
- Are any domestic customers buying the product for sale or shipment overseas? If so, to what countries?
- Is the trend of sales and inquiries up or down?
- Who are the main domestic and foreign competitors?
- What general and specific lessons have been learned from past export attempts or experiences?

PERSONNEL

- What in-house international expertise does the firm have (international sales experience, language capabilities, etc.)?
- Who will be responsible for the export department's organization and staff?
- How much senior management time (a) should be allocated and (b) could be allocated?
- What organization structure is required to ensure that export sales are adequately serviced?
- Who will follow through after the planning is done?

PRODUCTION CAPACITY

- How is the present capacity being used?
- Will filling export orders hurt domestic sales?
- What will be the cost of additional production?
- Are there fluctuations in the annual work load? When? Why?
- What minimum order quantity is required?
- What would be required to design and package products specifically for export?

FINANCIAL CAPACITY

- What amount of capital can be committed to export production and marketing?

What level of export department operating costs can be supported?

How are the initial expenses of export efforts to be allocated?

What other new development plans are in the works that may compete with export plans?

By what date must an export pay for itself?

When the export decision has been made based upon the needed research, the next decision Harriet King must make is to determine which distribution channel should be used. If it is determined that a foreign representative will distribute the product, there are many factors that must be considered before choosing a foreign representative. The following simple checklist would help Ms. King determine if a representative is qualified:

An outstanding reputation with suppliers and banks

Solid financial strength and reputation

Experience with the product or a similar product

An existing sales organization

A sales record of growth

Customers and accounts who are the target market for the product

Warehouse capacity

After-sales service capability

Understanding of international business practices

Knowledge of both English and the language of the country

Knowledge of marketing techniques (promotion, advertisement, etc.)

Harriet King must also realize that there are equally important considerations and factors that the foreign representative wants from her. These include:

Excellent products

Exclusive territories

Training available about product if needed

Reorder availability

Advertising and merchandising support

To make available credit terms, discounts, and deals

Commissions on direct sales by the manufacturer in the distributors' territory

Minimum control and/or visits from the U.S. producer

To determine for what price they will sell product in the foreign country

To be able to deal with only one person

Security that the product will not be taken away once it is established in the territory

The right to terminate the agreement when he or she pleases

No matter which distribution channel Harriet King decides to use in her exporting efforts, there are many forms that are an integral part of the exporting procedure. On the following pages, many of these forms are shown with a description about their uses and how and when they must be issued.

FORMS

Shipper's export declaration (Figure A-1) is used to control exports and compile trade statistics. It must be prepared and submitted to the customs agent for shipments by mail valued at more than $500 and for shipments by means other than mail valued at more than $2,500. In addition, an SED must be prepared for all shipments covered by an IVL (individual validated licenser), regardless of value.

Shipper's letter of instructions (Figure A-2) is a written statement from the exporter to the forwarder explaining how the shipment should be handled. In turn, the forwarder provides the exporter with this multi-part form with, in many cases, the remainder of the information completed.

Pro forma invoices (Figure A-3) are not for payment purposes but are essentially quotations in an invoice format. In addition to the following list of items, a pro forma invoice should include a statement certifying that the pro forma invoice is true and correct and a statement describing the country of origin of the goods. A pro forma invoice includes the following:

1. Buyer's name and address.
2. Buyer's reference number and date of inquiry.
3. Listing of requested products and brief description.
4. Price of each item. (It is advisable to indicate whether items are new or used and to quote in U.S. dollars to reduce foreign-exchange risk.)
5. Gross and net shipping weight (in metric units where appropriate) packed for export.

6. Total cubic volume and dimensions (in metric units where appropriate) packed for export.
7. Trade discount, if applicable.
8. Delivery point.
9. Terms of sale.
10. Terms of payment.
11. Insurance and shipping costs.
12. Validity period for quotation.
13. Total charges to be paid by customer.
14. Estimated shipping date to factory or U.S. port (it is preferable to give U.S. port).
15. Estimated date of shipment arrival.

Certificates of origin (Figure A-4) are documents declaring the country in which the goods in a particular shipment were produced. This is important to the buyer, as his or her customs authorities need to know the origin in order to establish the rate of duty.

Many countries charge different rates of duty depending on where the goods were made. Examples of this are the preferential rates for "MFN" or "Most Favored Nation." There are specific certificates of origin used for U.S. shipments to Canada and Israel. The United States has free trade agreements with both countries. Both countries have designed forms which only U.S. exporters use. These special certificate of origin forms entitle the shipments they cover to the lower duty rates.

The shipper usually prepares the certificates of origin and signs them in the presence of a notary public. Once the certificates are signed and notarized, they are taken to the chamber of commerce in the shipper's city. An authorized person at the chamber of commerce will then sign them.

Insurance certificate (Figure A-5) shows that insurance coverage has been obtained for a particular shipment. The insurance certificate forms are issued by the insurance company and are completed by the party providing the insurance. This can be either the seller or the buyer. When the seller supplies the insurance coverage, he or she provides the buyer with a certificate of insurance.

Additional forms include:
Standard form for presentation of loss or damage claims (Figure A-6)

Canada customs invoice (Figure A-7)

U.S. DEPARTMENT OF COMMERCE—BUREAU OF THE CENSUS—INTERNATIONAL TRADE ADMINISTRATION

FORM **7525-V** (1-1-88)

SHIPPER'S EXPORT DECLARATION

OMB No. 0607-0018

1a. EXPORTER *(Name and address including ZIP code)*		
Hariel, Inc. 48-30 Garfield Blvd. Maspeth, NY	ZIP CODE 11356	2. DATE OF EXPORTATION 8-22-93

3. BILL OF LADING/AIR WAYBILL NO.
992

b. EXPORTER EIN (IRS) NO. 13-245187	c. PARTIES TO TRANSACTION ☐ Related ☒ Non-related

4a. ULTIMATE CONSIGNEE
Grovner's
Montreal, P.Q., Canada

b. INTERMEDIATE CONSIGNEE
NONE

5. FORWARDING AGENT

6. POINT (STATE) OF ORIGIN OR FTZ NO.
U.S.A.

7. COUNTRY OF ULTIMATE DESTINATION
Canada

8. LOADING PIER *(Vessel only)* 41	9. MODE OF TRANSPORT *(Specify)* VESSEL
10. EXPORTING CARRIER S.S. Anita	11. PORT OF EXPORT NYC
12. PORT OF UNLOADING *(Vessel and air only)* Montreal	13. CONTAINERIZED *(Vessel only)* ☒ Yes ☐ No

14. SCHEDULE B DESCRIPTION OF COMMODITIES. *(Use columns 17-19)*

15. MARKS, NOS., AND KINDS OF PACKAGES

D/F (16)	SCHEDULE B NUMBER (17)	CHECK DIGIT	QUANTITY—SCHEDULE B UNIT(S) (18)	SHIPPING WEIGHT *(Kilos)* (19)	VALUE (U.S. dollars, omit cents) *(Selling price or cost if not sold)* (20)
	1		3	50	2,889
	2		5	164	6,300
	3		2	16	1,782

21. VALIDATED LICENSE NO./GENERAL LICENSE SYMBOL LIC 3422	22. ECCN *(When required)*

23. Duly authorized officer or employee — The exporter authorizes the forwarder named above to act as forwarding agent for export control and customs purposes.

24. I certify that all statements made and all information contained herein are true and correct and that I have read and understand the instructions for preparation of this document, set forth in the "Correct Way to Fill Out the Shipper's Export Declaration" (available Bureau of Census, Wash., DC 20233). I understand that civil and criminal penalties, including forfeiture and sale, may be imposed for making false or fraudulent statements herein, failing to provide the requested information or for violation of U.S. laws on exportation (13 U.S.C. Sec. 305; 22 U.S.C. Sec. 401; 18 U.S.C. Sec. 1001; 50 U.S.C. App. 2410).

Signature

Title Export Mgr.

Date 8-22-92

Confidential—For use solely for official purposes authorized by the Secretary of Commerce (13 U.S.C. 301 (g)).

Export shipments are subject to inspection by U.S. Customs Service and/or Office of Export Enforcement.

25. AUTHENTICATION *(When required)*

Figure A-1 Shipper's Export Declaration

Source: Reprinted with permission of Unz & Co., 190 Baldwin Avenue, Jersey City, NJ 07306, USA.

© Copyright 1987 UNZ. CO.

SHIPPER (Name and address including ZIP code)		INLAND CARRIER (See note #2 below)	SHIP DATE	PRO NO.
	ZIP CODE			

EXPORTER EIN NO.	PARTIES TO TRANSACTION ☐ Related ☐ Non-related	

ULTIMATE CONSIGNEE

INTERMEDIATE CONSIGNEE

FORWARDING AGENT

	POINT (STATE) OF ORIGIN OR FTZ NO.	COUNTRY OF ULTIMATE DESTINATION

SHIPPER'S LETTER OF INSTRUCTIONS

NOTE:
① IF YOU ARE UNCERTAIN OF THE SCHEDULE B COMMODITY NO.—DO NOT TYPE IT IN—WE WILL COMPLETE WHEN PROCESSING THE 7525-V.

② IF YOU HAVE SHIPPED THIS MATERIAL TO US VIA AN INLAND CARRIER—PLEASE GIVE US THE INLAND CARRIER'S NAME, SHIPPING DATE, AND RECEIPT OR PRO. NO. (IF AVAILABLE). THIS WILL HELP US EXPEDITE YOUR SHIPMENT WITH THE INLAND CARRIER.

③ BE SURE TO PICK UP TOP SHEET AND SIGN THE FIRST BUFF EXPORT DECLARATION WITH PEN AND INK.

SHIPPER'S REF. NO.	DATE	SHIP VIA ☐ AIR ☐ OCEAN	☐ CONSOLIDATE	☐ DIRECT

D F	MARKS, NOS., AND KIND OF PKGS. SCHEDULE B NUMBER	SCHEDULE B DESCRIPTION OF COMMODITIES				VALUE (U.S. dollars, omit cents)
		QUANTITY— SCHEDULE B UNIT(S)	SHIPPING WEIGHT (Kilos)	SHIPPING WEIGHT (Pounds)	CUBIC METERS	(Selling price or cost if not sold)

VALIDATED LICENSE NO./GENERAL LICENSE SYMBOL	ECCN (When required)	SHIPPER MUST CHECK ♦ ☐ PREPAID OR ☐ COLLECT
Duly authorized officer or employee	The exporter authorizes the forwarder named above to act as forwarding agent for export control and customs purposes.	C.O.D. AMOUNT $

SPECIAL INSTRUCTIONS

BE SURE TO PICK UP TOP SHEET AND SIGN THE FIRST BUFF EXPORT DECLARATION WITH PEN & INK.	SHIPPER'S INSTRUCTIONS IN CASE OF INABILITY TO DELIVER CONSIGNMENT AS CONSIGNED: ☐ ABANDON ☐ RETURN TO SHIPPER ☐ DELIVER TO
	SHIPPER REQUESTS INSURANCE ☐ NO ☐ YES $	If Shipper has requested insurance as provided for at the left hereof, shipment is insured in the amount indicated (recovery is limited to actual loss) in accordance with the provisions as specified in the Carrier's Tariffs. Insurance is payable to Shipper unless payee is designated in writing by the shipper.

NOTE The Shipper or his Authorized Agent hereby authorizes the above named Company in his name and on his behalf, to prepare any export documents, to sign and accept any documents relating to said shipment and forward this shipment in accordance with the conditions of carriage and the tariffs of the carriers employed. The shipper guarantees payment of all collect charges in the event the consignee refuses payment Hereunder the sole responsibility of the Company is to use reasonable care in the selection of carriers, forwarders, agents and others to whom it may entrust the shipment.

Form 15-305 Printed and Sold by UNZ & CO. 190 Baldwin Ave., Jersey City, NJ 07306 • (800) 631-3098 • (201) 795-5400

SHIPPING RETAIN THIS COPY

Figure A-2 Shipper's Letter of Instructions

Source: Reprinted with permission of Unz & Co., 190 Baldwin Avenue, Jersey City, NJ 07306, USA.

EXPORTER'S PRO FORMA INVOICE

S O Grovner's L 10 Blvd. St. Germain D Montreal, P.Q., Canada T O	INVOICE DATE 8/21/93 | INVOICE NO. PRO-592B OUR ORDER NO. 359745A | CUSTOMER ORDER NO. 92326B TERMS 3/10/EOM | DATE SHIPPED 8/22/93 SHIPPED VIA ocean freight

SAME AS SOLD TO UNLESS INDICATED BELOW

S
H
I   MARKS:
P
T
O   GROSS WEIGHT:

QUANTITY	DESCRIPTION	UNIT PRICE	AMOUNT
108	Ladies 100% wool-pants-rayon lined inset waist band-belt loops slim leg.	26.75	2,889.
180	Ladies 100% wool-jackets-cotton lined notched lapel collar-botton sleeve with knit ribbed cuff.	35.00	6,300.
72	Ladies 100% wool-skirts-rayon lined inset waist band-belt loops slim-line cut.	24.75	1,782.

These commodities licensed by U.S. for ultimate destination are made of U.S. materials in U.S. production
Diversion contrary to U.S. law prohibited.   facilities.

"WE HEREBY CERTIFY THIS INVOICE IS TRUE AND CORRECT AND
THAT THE MERCHANDISE DESCRIBED IS ORIGIN OF THE U.S.A."

AUTHORIZED SIGNATURE

Figure A-3 Exporter's Pro Forma Invoice
Source: Reprinted with permission of Unz & Co., 190 Baldwin Avenue, Jersey City, NJ 07306, USA.

CERTIFICATE OF ORIGIN

The undersigned   Hariel, Inc.
(Owner or Agent, or &c)

for   Niva Shipping Co.   declares
(Name and Address of Shipper)

that the following mentioned goods shipped on S/S   Anita
(Name of Ship)

on the date of   8-22-93   consigned to   Grovner's

are the product of the United States of America.

MARKS AND NUMBERS	NO. OF PKGS., BOXES OR CASES	WEIGHT IN KILOS		DESCRIPTION
		GROSS	NET	
RD-293	3	50	49	ladies' 100% wool pants
RD-297	5	164	163	ladies' 100% wool jackets
RD-298	2	17	16	ladies' 100% wool skirts

Sworn to before me

Dated at   N.Y.C.   on the   22   day of   Aug.   19   93

this   22   day of   Aug.   19   93

(Signature of Owner or Agent)

The   New York City Cham. of Commerce   , a recognized Chamber of Commerce under the laws of the State of

New York   , has examined the manufacturer's invoice or shipper's affidavit concerning the
origin of the merchandise and, according to the best of its knowledge and belief, finds that the products named originated in the
United States of North America.

Secretary

Figure A-4   Certificate of Origin
Source: Reprinted with permission of Unz & Co., 190 Baldwin Avenue, Jersey City, NJ 07306, USA.

INSURANCE CERTIFICATE

EXPORTER (Principal or seller-licensee and address including ZIP Code)	DOCUMENT NUMBER	BL OR AWB NUMBER
Hariel, Inc. 48-30 Garfield Blvd. Maspeth, NY	359745A	3

ZIP CODE 11356

EXPORT REFERENCES

CONSIGNED TO	FORWARDING AGENT (Name and address—references)
Grovner's 10 Blvd. St. Germain Montreal, P.Q., Canada	

POINT (STATE) OF ORIGIN OR FTZ NUMBER
Maspeth, New York

NOTIFY PARTY INTERMEDIATE CONSIGNEE (Name and address)	DOMESTIC ROUTING EXPORT INSTRUCTIONS
	Palermo Trucking from Maspeth on 8/21/93 to Marine Terminal in Manhattan, New York

PRE-CARRIAGE BY	PLACE OF RECEIPT BY PRE-CARRIER	
Palermo Trucking	Maspeth, Queens	

EXPORTING CARRIER	PORT OF LOADING EXPORT	LOADING PIER TERMINAL
Nina Shipping	New York City	Marine Terminal

FOREIGN PORT OF UNLOADING (Vessel and air only)	PLACE OF DELIVERY BY ON-CARRIER	TYPE OF MOVE	CONTAINERIZED (Vessel only)
Montreal		ocean	XX Yes ☐ No

MARKS AND NUMBERS	NUMBER OF PACKAGES	DESCRIPTION OF COMMODITIES in Schedule B detail	GROSS WEIGHT (Kilos)	MEASUREMENT	D OR F
	3	cartons ladies' 100% wool pants	50		
	5	cartons ladies' 100% wool jackets	164		
	2	cartons ladies' 100% wool skirts	16		

DATE OF POLICY	SUM INSURED	AMOUNT IN WORDS
8/1/93	$10,971	Ten thousand nine hundred seventy one

SPECIAL TERMS AND CONDITIONS: SHIPMENTS ON DECK or AIR CARGO when Insured Under this Policy are subject to terms and conditions specified on the reverse side hereof. SHIPMENTS SUBJECT TO AN UNDER DECK BILL OF LADING are insured.

THIS INSURANCE IS ALSO SUBJECT TO THE FOLLOWING AMERICAN INSTITUTE CLAUSES CURRENT ON THE DATE OF ISSUANCE OF THIS POLICY
MARINE EXTENSION CLAUSES   **S.R. & C.C. ENDORSEMENT**   **WAR RISK INSURANCE**

WHEN GOODS ARE SO DESTINED THIS INSURANCE IS SUBJECT TO:
SOUTH AMERICAN 60 DAY CLAUSE

This Policy not transferable unless countersigned by an authorized representative of this Company or the Assured undersigned.

IN WITNESS WHEREOF, this Company has executed and attested these presents

_____ Secretary   _____ President

Form 80-340 Printed and Sold by UNZ 190 Baldwin Ave. Jersey City, NJ 07306 · (800) 631-3098 · (201) 795-5400

Figure A-5   Insurance Certificate
Source: Reprinted with permission of Unz & Co., 190 Baldwin Avenue, Jersey City, NJ 07306, USA.

STANDARD FORM FOR PRESENTATION OF LOSS OR DAMAGE CLAIMS

Approved by
THE INTERSTATE COMMERCE COMMISSION
THE NATIONAL INDUSTRIAL TRAFFIC LEAGUE
THE FREIGHT CLAIM ASSOCIATION

_____

(Address of Claimant

_____

(Date)

Claimant's Number §

_____
(Name of person to whom claim is presented)

$\binom{\text{Name of}}{\text{carrier}}$ _____

(Carrier's Number

$\big(_{\text{Address}}\big)$ _____

This claim for $ _____ is made against the carrier named above by $\binom{\text{Name of}}{\text{claimant}}$ _____

_____ for $\binom{\text{Loss or}}{\text{damage}}$ _____ in connection with the following described shipment:

Description of shipment _____

Name and address of consignor (shipper) _____

Shipped from $\binom{\text{City, town}}{\text{or station}}$ _____ , To $\binom{\text{City, town}}{\text{or station}}$ _____

Final destination $\binom{\text{City, town}}{\text{or station}}$ _____ Routed via _____

Bill of Lading issued by_____ Co.; Date of Bill of Lading _____

Paid Freight Bill (Pro) Number _____ . Original Car number and Initial _____

Name and address of consignee (to whom shipped) _____

If shipment reconsigned enroute, state particulars: _____

DETAILED STATEMENT SHOWING HOW AMOUNT CLAIMED IS DETERMINED
(Number and description of articles, nature and extent of loss or damage, invoice price of articles, amount of claim, etc.)

Total Amount Claimed

**IN ADDITION TO THE INFORMATION GIVEN ABOVE, THE FOLLOWING DOCUMENTS
ARE SUBMITTED IN SUPPORT OF THIS CLAIM.***

(   )   1. Original bill of lading, if not previously surrendered to carrier.

(   )   2. Original paid freight ("Expense") bill.

(   )   3. Original invoice or certified copy.

        4. Other particulars obtainable in proof of loss or damage claimed.

_____

_____

Remarks: _____

_____

_____

_____

_____

The foregoing statement of facts is hereby certified to as correct.

_____
(Signature of claimant)

§ Claimant should assign to each claim a number, inserting same in the space provided at the upper right hand corner of this form. Reference should be made thereto in all correspondence pertaining to this claim.

* Claimant will please check (×) before such of the documents mentioned as have been attached, and explain under "Remarks" the absence of any of the documents called for in connection with this claim. When for any reason it is impossible for claimant to produce original bill of lading, if required, or paid freight bill, claimant should indemnify† carrier or carriers against duplicate claim supported by original documents.

† Indemnity agreement for lost bill of lading.

Figure A-6   Standard Form for Presentation of Loss or Damage Claims

Source: Reprinted with permission of Unz & Co., 190 Baldwin Avenue, Jersey City, NJ 07306, USA.

Revenue Canada Customs and Excise	Revenu Canada Douanes et Accise	**CANADA CUSTOMS INVOICE** *FACTURE DES DOUANES CANADIENNES*	Page 1 of 1 de

1. Vendor (Name and Address)/Vendeur (Nom et adresse)

Hariel, Inc.
48-30 Garfield Blvd.
Maspeth, NY 11356

2. Date of Direct Shipment to Canada/Date d'expédition directe vers le Canada

8-22-93

3. Other References (Include Purchaser's Order No.)
Autres références (Inclure le n° de commande de l'acheteur)

359745A

4. Consignee (Name and Address)/Destinataire (Nom et adresse)

Grovner's
10 Blvd. St. Germain
Montreal, P.Q., Canada

5. Purchaser's Name and Address (If other than Consignee)
Nom et adresse de l'acheteur (S'il diffère du destinataire)

6. Country of Transhipment/Pays de transbordement

7. Country of Origin of Goods
Pays d'origine des marchandises
U.S.A.

IF SHIPMENT INCLUDES GOODS OF DIFFERENT ORIGINS ENTER ORIGINS AGAINST ITEMS IN 12
SI L'EXPEDITION COMPREND DES MARCHANDISES D'ORIGINES DIFFERENTES, PRECISER LEUR PROVENANCE EN 12

8. Transportation: Give Mode and Place of Direct Shipment to Canada
Transport: Préciser mode et point d'expédition directe vers le Canada

Niva Shipping Co.
Vessel - S.S. Anita

9. Conditions of Sale and Terms of Payment
(i.e. Sale, Consignment Shipment, Leased Goods, etc.)
Conditions de vente et modalités de paiement
(p. ex. vente, expédition en consignation, location de marchandises, etc.)

10. Currency of Settlement/Devises du paiement

U.S. Dollars

11. No. of Pkgs N^bre de colis	12. Specification of Commodities (Kind of Packages, Marks and Numbers, General Description and Characteristics, i.e. Grade, Quality) Désignation des articles (Nature des colis, marques et numéros, description générale et caractéristiques, p. ex. classe, qualité)	13. Quantity (State Unit) Quantité (Préciser l'unité)	14. Unit Price Prix unitaire	15. Total
3	cartons of ladies' 100% wool pants	108 ea.	26.75	2,889.
5	cartons of ladies' 100% wool jackets	180 ea.	35.00	6,300.
2	cartons of ladies' 100% wool skirts	72 ea.	24.75	1,782.

18. If any of fields 1 to 17 are included on an attached commercial invoice, check this box
Si les renseignements des zones 1 à 17 figurent sur la facture commerciale, cocher cette boite ☐

Commercial Invoice No. _____

16. Total Weight/Poids Total

Net	Gross/Brut
504 lb.	530 lb.

17. Invoice Total
Total de la facture

10,971.

19. Exporter's Name and Address (If other than Vendor)
Nom et adresse de l'exportateur (S'il diffère du vendeur)

20. Originator (Name and Address) Expéditeur d'origine (Nom et adresse)

Hariel, Inc.
48-30 Garfield Blvd.
Maspeth, NY 11356

21. Departmental Ruling (If applicable) Décision du Ministère (S'il y a lieu)

22. If fields 23 to 25 are not applicable, check this box
Si les zones 23 à 25 sont sans objet, cocher cette boite ☐

23. If included in field 17 indicate amount:
Si compris dans le total à la zone 17, préciser:

(i) Transportation charges, expenses and insurance from the place of direct shipment to Canada
Les frais de transport, dépenses et assurances à partir du point d'expédition directe vers le Canada

$ _____

(ii) Costs for construction, erection and assembly incurred after importation into Canada
Les coûts de construction, d'érection et d'assemblage après importation au Canada

$ _____

(iii) Export packing
Le coût de l'emballage d'exportation

$ _____

24. If not included in field 17 indicate amount:
Si non compris dans le total à la zone 17, préciser:

(i) Transportation charges, expenses and insurance to the place of direct shipment to Canada
Les frais de transport, dépenses et assurances jusqu'au point d'expédition directe vers le Canada

$ _____

(ii) Amounts for commissions other than buying commissions
Les commissions autres que celles versées pour l'achat

$ _____

(iii) Export packing
Le coût de l'emballage d'exportation

$ _____

25. Check (If applicable):
Cocher (S'il y a lieu):

(i) Royalty payments or subsequent proceeds are paid or payable by the purchaser
Des redevances ou produits ont été ou seront versés par l'acheteur ☐

(ii) The purchaser has supplied goods or services for use in the production of these goods
L'acheteur a fourni des marchandises ou des services pour la production des marchandises ☐

☐

DEPARTMENT OF NATIONAL REVENUE—CUSTOMS AND EXCISE   MINISTERE DU REVENU NATIONAL—DOUANES ET ACCISE

FORM NO. 10-726

Figure A-7   Canada Customs Invoice
Source: Reprinted with permission of Unz & Co., 190 Baldwin Avenue, Jersey City, NJ 07306, USA.

Importing Procedures Simulation

American fashion retailers constantly shop the global marketplace for creative, innovative styles and items to offer their customers.

Foreign merchandise often adds a special "look" and distinction to the merchandise mix of a store. Whenever possible, buyers will buy foreign merchandise that will make their stores appear unique and special. The major reasons retailers seek imports are to create an image of prestige and uniqueness or to obtain lower prices for items that will interest their customers and give their stores a better margin for profit.

Whitney Mallot, a small chain of department stores located in the southwest and throughout California, have a policy of including a wide mix of imports in their stores. All departments, from shoes to small appliances, feature a special international mix in their assortments. The junior sportswear and the accessories departments are particularly well-known for their imports.

Ilana Bethel and Tania Rachell are the buyers for the sportswear areas. Ilana buys all the bottoms, skirts, pants, jeans, and shorts, and Tania buys all the tops, blouses, shirts, jackets, and sweaters. Both buyers are experienced and have bought merchandise from countries around the world. They shop both the European markets and the markets in the near and far East.

Even though both Ilana and Tania have traveled abroad many times, before buying plans are made for each year's import purchasing, they conduct current research on what is needed and review the past selling records on imported merchandise bought previously. Among the important factors to be considered each time are:

- What is the level of domestic competition in the products being imported?

- What are the salable advantages of the proposed import?

- If the major advantage is price, will the quality be sustained?

- If the main advantage is quality, will the overseas supplier maintain that quality?

- Are there government restrictions on the type of product being imported?

- Is the country that produces the imported product stable both politically and economically?

- Is the potential supplier reliable in the production of wanted or specified goods and does the supplier also have a good credit rating?

There is much market research and study of past sales done before Ilana and Tania put together their merchandise open-to-buy plans. Constant contact with foreign buying offices or commissionaires aids them in determining the mix of styles and prices needed for an outstanding import purchase.

It is after the foreign buying trip has been completed and orders have been placed overseas that the entry process of imports becomes the main point of interest and attention.

The United States Customs Service is the federal government agency that is in charge of regulating imports and the collection of import duty. When Ilana's and Tania's shipments of goods reaches the United States, their goods may not legally enter the country until:

- They enter the port of entry

- Estimated duties have been paid

- Delivery of the merchandise has been authorized by customs

This entry process has five essential steps. They are:

1. Entry
2. Examination and inspection
3. Valuation
4. Classification
5. Liquidation

Entry

Within five working days of arrival of a shipment at a U.S. port of entry, entry documents must be filed. They are:

- Entry manifest (special permit for immediate delivery)

- Commercial invoice or a pro forma invoice

- Packing list

- Bill of lading

- Surety insurance

Examination and inspection

Prior to release of the goods, the port director will choose designated representative qualities of goods for examination. This is done to determine:

- The value of the goods for Customs and their dutiable status

- That the proper markings of the goods with the country of origin is evident

- Whether the shipment contains prohibited items

- Whether the goods are correctly invoiced

⊕ Whether the goods are short or in excess of the invoiced quantities

Valuation

Valuation determines the value of the goods for purposes of applying any tariffs or duties. Generally, the customs value will be the transaction value, or the price actually paid or payable for the merchandise when sold for exportation to the United States, plus amounts for the following items if not included in the price:

⊕ The packing cost incurred by the buyer

⊕ Any selling commission paid by the buyer

⊕ Any royalty or license fee that is required from the buyer as a condition of the sale

⊕ Any proceeds from the sale of the imported goods that accrue to the seller

Classification

Classification is initially the responsibility of the importer, custom house broker, or other person preparing the entry papers. Familiarity with the Tariff Schedule of the United States and Harmonized System Tariff Schedule of the United States facilitates the process.

Classification and, when ad valorem are applicable, appraisement are the two most important factors affecting dutiable status.

Liquidation

The classification and valuation, as well as other required import information, are reviewed for (a) correctness, (b) as a proper basis for appraisement, and (c) for agreement of the submitted data with the merchandise actually imported. If it is accepted without changes, it is liquidated "as entered."

After the liquidation, an importer may pursue claims for adjustment or refund by filing, within 90 days, a protest. Time limits do not begin to run until the date of posting. If, after further review, the importer is still not satisfied, the summons may be filed with the United States Customs Court of International Trade. In order to guarantee fast customs clearance, the following ten points, although seemingly very basic and simple, will guarantee the smooth processing of imported goods.

1. Inclusion of all information required on customs invoices.
2. Careful preparation of invoices. They should be typed clearly, with sufficient space between lines, and the data within each column.

3. Invoices should contain the information that would be shown on a well-prepared packing list.
4. Packages should be marked and numbered so that they can be identified with the corresponding marks and numbers appearing on their invoice.
5. A detailed description of each item of goods contained in each individual package should be shown on the invoice.
6. Goods should be marked legibly and conspicuously with the name of the country of origin, unless they are specifically exempted from the country of origin marking requirements, and with such other marking as required by the marking laws of the United States.
7. Any special laws of the United States which may apply to goods should be complied with.
8. The instructions with respect to invoicing, packaging, marking, labeling, etc. should be observed closely.
9. U.S. Customs should be consulted in developing packing standards for commodities.
10. Sound security procedures should be established at facilities and while transporting goods for shipment. Narcotics smugglers should not be allowed the opportunity to introduce narcotics into shipments.

FORMS

Entry summary and entry/immediate delivery forms (Figures B-1a and B-1b) are filed by the store or a customs broker when a shipment that has been ordered by the store buyers reaches the United States. Imported goods are not legally entered until after the shipment has arrived within the port of entry, delivery of the merchandise has been authorized by Customs and estimated duties have been paid. It is the responsibility of the importer to arrange for examination and release of the goods.

Goods may be entered only by the owner, purchaser, or a licensed customhouse broker. When the goods are consigned "to order," the bill of lading properly endorsed by the consignor may serve as evidence of the right to make entry. An airway bill may be used for merchandise arriving by air.

The entry of merchandise is a two-part process consisting of (1) filing the documents necessary to determine whether merchandise may be released from Customs custody and (2) filing the documents which contain information for duty assessment and statistical purposes. In certain instances, such as the entry of merchandise subject to quotas, all documents must be filed and accepted by Customs prior to the release of the goods.

If the goods are to be released from Customs custody on entry documents, an entry summary for consumption must be filed and estimated duties deposited at the port of entry within 10 working days of the time the goods are entered and released.

The **delivery order with a bill of lading** (Figure B-2) is used by the customs broker to authorize a stevedore or airline to release goods to a third party. This form is occasionally used to transfer title from one broker to another.

The **bill of lading** (Figure B-3) is a document used in transporting goods. It can be an air waybill for a plane carrier or an ocean bill of lading for ship. It serves as a receipt for the shipper, indicating that the shipment has been made.

Straight bills of lading are nonnegotiable bills that consign the goods to an importer or other party named on the document. Once consigned, the seller loses title control because the goods will be delivered to anyone who can be identified as the consignee.

Order bills of lading are negotiable.

Standard form for presentation of loss or damage claims (Figure B-4)

DEPARTMENT OF THE TREASURY
UNITED STATES CUSTOMS SERVICE

ENTRY SUMMARY

Form Approved OMB No. 1515-0065

(1) Entry No. **01**	(2) Entry Type Code **13**	3. Entry Summary Date
4. Entry Date	(5) Port Code **LB/CA**	
6. Bond No.	7. Bond Type Code	8. Broker/Importer File No. **WM/23679**

9. Ultimate Consignee Name and Address

Whitney Mallot
One Embarkadero Place
Long Beach, Calif.

10. Consignee No.

(11) Importer of Record Name and Address

Whitney Mallot
One Embarkadero Place
Long Beach, Calif.

(12) Importer No. **126-26-9187**

(13) Exporting Country **Taiwan**   14. Export Date

(15) Country of Origin **Taiwan**   16. Missing Documents

State

(17) I.T. No.   (18) I.T. Date **None**

(19) B/L or AWB No. **B/L 2273**   20. Mode of Transportation   21. Manufacturer I.D.   (22) Reference No. **None**

(23) Importing Carrier **Niva Shipping**   24. Foreign Port of Lading   25. Location of Goods/G.O. No.

26. U.S. Port of Unlading   (27) Import Date **6/1/93**

(28) Line No.	30. (A) T.S.U.S.A. No. (B) ADA/CVD Case No.	(29) Description of Merchandise	31. (A) Gross Weight (B) Manifest Qty.	(32) Net Quantity in T.S.U.S.A. Units	33. (A) Entered Value (B) CHGS (C) Relationship	34. (A) T.S.U.S.A. Rate (B) ADA/CVD Rate (C) I.R.C. Rate (D) Visa No.	(35) Duty and I.R Tax Dollars	Cents
1	11314879			5,000	65,150	7% None	4,560	50

(36) Declaration of Importer of Record (Owner or Purchaser) or Authorized Agent

I declare that I am the

[X] importer of record and that the actual owner, purchaser, or consignee for customs purposes is as shown above.

OR

[ ] owner or purchaser or agent thereof.

I further declare that the merchandise

[X] was obtained pursuant to a purchase or agreement to purchase and that the prices set forth in the invoice are true.

OR

[ ] was not obtained pursuant to a purchase or agreement to purchase and the statements in the invoice as to value or price are true to the best of my knowledge and belief.

I also declare that the statements in the documents herein filed fully disclose to the best of my knowledge and belief the true prices, values, quantities, rebates, drawbacks, fees, commissions, and royalties and are true and correct, and that all goods or services provided to the seller of the merchandise either free or at reduced cost are fully disclosed. I will immediately furnish to the appropriate customs officer any information showing a different state of facts.

Notice required by Paperwork Reduction Act of 1980: This information is needed to ensure that importers/exporters are complying with U.S. customs laws, to allow us to compute and collect the right amount of money, to enforce other agency requirements, and to collect accurate statistical information on imports. Your response is mandatory. (Continued on back of form.)

↓ U.S. CUSTOMS USE ↓		TOTALS	
A. Liq. Code	B. Ascertained Duty	(37) Duty **4,560**	50
	C. Ascertained Tax	(38) Tax **0**	
	D. Ascertained Other	(39) Other **4,560**	50
	E. Ascertained Total	(40) Total	

(41) Signature of Declarant, Title, and Date

SIGNATURE OF INDIVIDUAL

Customs Form 7501 (081790)

*U.S. Government Printing Office: 1992 — 321-118/60235

Figure B-1a   Entry Summary Form
Source: U.S. Government Printing Office

DEPARTMENT OF THE TREASURY
UNITED STATES CUSTOMS SERVICE

Form Approved
OMB No. 1515-0069

ENTRY/IMMEDIATE DELIVERY

19 CFR 142.3, 142.16, 142.22, 142.24

1 ARRIVAL DATE	2 ELECTED ENTRY DATE	3 ENTRY TYPE CODE/NAME	4 ENTRY NUMBER
June 1, 1993	June 6, 1993		

5 PORT	6 SINGLE TRANS. BOND	7 BROKER/IMPORTER FILE NUMBER	
Long Beach, Calif.			

	8 CONSIGNEE NUMBER		9 IMPORTER NUMBER

10 ULTIMATE CONSIGNEE NAME	11 IMPORTER OF RECORD NAME
Whitney Mallot One Embarkadero Place Long Beach, Calif.	Whitney Mallot One Embarkadero Place Long Beach, Calif.

12 CARRIER CODE	13 VOYAGE/FLIGHT/TRIP	14 LOCATION OF GOODS—CODE(S)/NAME(S)
NIVA/MIN	302	container - NM 212

15 VESSEL CODE/NAME	
S.S. Minnie M	

16 U.S. PORT OF UNLADING	17 MANIFEST NUMBER	18 G.O. NUMBER	19 TOTAL VALUE
Long Beach, Calif.			65,150

20 DESCRIPTION OF MERCHANDISE

Ladies Sportswear Apparel

21 IT/BL/ AWB CODE	22 IT/BL/AWB NO.	23 MANIFEST QUANTITY	24 TSUSA NUMBER	25 COUNTRY OF ORIGIN	26 MANUFACTURER ID

27. CERTIFICATION	28. CUSTOMS USE ONLY
I hereby make application for entry/immediate delivery. I certify that the above information is accurate, the bond is sufficient, valid, and current, and that all requirements of 19 CFR Part 142 have been met.	☐ OTHER AGENCY ACTION REQUIRED, NAMELY:

SIGNATURE OF APPLICANT

X SIGNATURE OF BROKER FOR WHITNEY MALLOT

PHONE NO	DATE

☐ CUSTOMS EXAMINATION REQUIRED.

29. BROKER OR OTHER GOVT. AGENCY USE

☐ ENTRY REJECTED, BECAUSE:

DELIVERY AUTHORIZED:	SIGNATURE	DATE
	SIGNATURE OF CUSTOMS AGENT	

Paperwork Reduction Act Notice: This information is needed to determine the admissibility of imports into the United States and to provide the necessary information for the examination of the cargo and to establish the liability for payment of duties and taxes. Your response is necessary.

Form 16-461 Printed and Sold by UNZ 190 Baldwin Ave., Jersey City, NJ 07306 • (800) 631-3098 • (201) 795-5400

Customs Form 3461 (112085)

Figure B-1b Entry/Immediate Delivery Form
Source: Reprinted with permission of Unz & Co., 190 Baldwin Avenue, Jersey City, NJ 07306, USA.

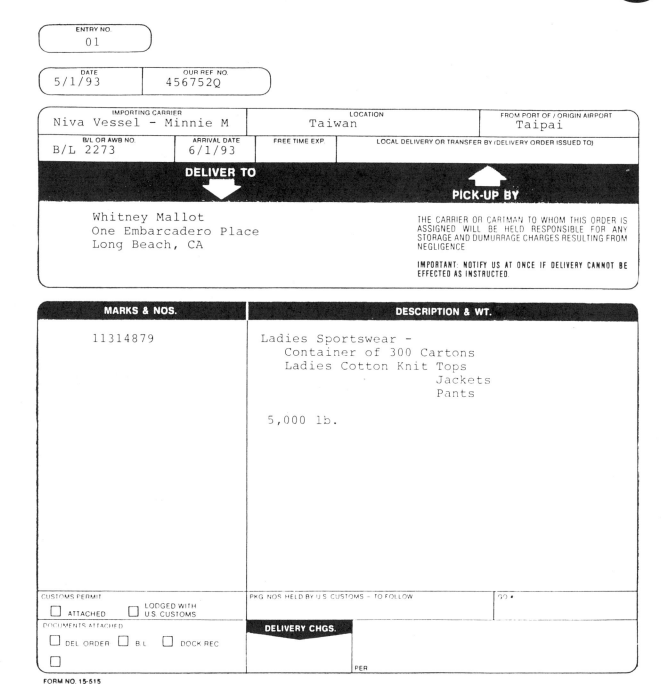

DELIVERY INSTRUCTIONS

Figure B-2   Delivery Order With Bill of Lading
Source: Reprinted with permission of Unz & Co., 190 Baldwin Avenue, Jersey City, NJ 07306, USA.

RECEIVED, subject to the classification and tariffs in effect on the date of the issue of this Bill of Lading.

AGENTS NO. _____

DATE	OUR REF. NO.
5/1/93	456752Q

FOR A/C OF SHIPPER

R.W. Wong
4 Tong Terrace
Taiwan, R.C.

UNIFORM STRAIGHT BILL OF LADING
ORIGINAL—NOT NEGOTIABLE

Uniform Domestic Straight Bill of Lading, adopted by Carriers in Official, Southern, Western and Illinois Classification territories, March 15, 1922, as amended June 15, 1941.

IT IS CERTIFIED THAT THE PROPERTY IN THIS RECEIPT WAS IMPORTED IN THE: _____ AT

IMPORTING CARRIER
Niva Vessel - Minnie M

the property described below, in apparent good order, except as noted (contents and condition of contents of packages unknown), marked, consigned, and destined as indicated below, which said carrier (the word carrier being understood throughout this contract as meaning any person or corporation in possession of the property under the contract) agrees to carry to its usual place of delivery at said destination, if on its route, otherwise to deliver to another carrier on the route to said destination. It is mutually agreed, as to each carrier of all or any of said property over all or any portion of said route to destination, and as to each party at any time interested in all of any of said property that every service to be performed

FROM PORT OF / ORIGIN AIRPORT
Taiwan   Taipai

hereunder shall be subject to all the terms and conditions of the Uniform Domestic Straight Bill of Lading set forth (1) in Official, Southern, Western and Illinois Freight Classifications in effect on the date hereof, if this is a rail or a rail-water shipment, or (2) in the applicable motor carrier classification or tariff if this is a motor carrier shipment. Shipper hereby certifies that he is familiar with all ther terms and conditions of the said bill of lading, including those on the back thereof, set forth in the classification or tariff which governs the transportation of the shipment, and the said terms and conditions are hereby agreed to by the shipper and accepted for himself and his assigns.

ORIGINATING CARRIER

CONSIGNED TO	ROUTE
Whitney Mallot One Embarcadero Place Long Beach, CA	Ocean Conference Ship

DELIVERING CARRIER
Niva Vessel - Minnie M

CAR INITIAL	CAR NO.

THE BELOW DESCRIBED MERCHANDISE HAS NOT BEEN IN A PRIVATE WAREHOUSE

NO. OF PKGS.	DESCRIPTION OF ARTICLES, SPECIAL MARKS & EXCEPTIONS	WEIGHT	CLASS OR RATE	CHECK COL.
	Ladies Sportswear - Container of 300 Cartons Ladies Cotton Knit Tops Jackets Pants	5,000		

Subject to Section 7 of conditions, if this shipment is to be delivered to the consignee without recourse on the consignor, the consignor shall sign the following statement:
The carrier shall not make delivery of this shipment without payment of freight and all other lawful charges.

SIGNATURE
(Signature of consignor)

If charges are to be prepaid write or stamp here, "To Be Prepaid."

Received $ _____
to apply in prepayment of the charges on the property described hereon.

Agent or Cashier

Per _____
(The signature here acknowledges only the amount prepaid.)

Charges advanced:

$ _____

*If the shipment moves between two ports by a carrier by water, the law requires that the bill of lading state whether it is "carrier's or shipper's weight." NOTE—Where the rate is dependent on value, shippers are required to state specifically in writing the agreed or declared value of the property. The agreed or declared value of the property is hereby specifically stated by the shipper to be not exceeding

_____ per _____

_____ Agent

PER:

FOR THE SHIPPER
Permanent Post Office Address

Per _____

1

FORM 16-717—printed and sold by Unz & Co.,
190 Baldwin Ave., Jersey City, NJ (201) 795-5400/(800) 631-3098

Figure B-3   Bill of Lading

Source: Reprinted with permission of Unz & Co., 190 Baldwin Avenue, Jersey City, NJ 07306, USA.

General Order No. 41   P. DF. D.G. D.G.

STANDARD FORM FOR PRESENTATION OF LOSS OR DAMAGE CLAIMS

Approved by
THE INTERSTATE COMMERCE COMMISSION
THE NATIONAL INDUSTRIAL TRAFFIC LEAGUE
THE FREIGHT CLAIM ASSOCIATION

_____
(Address of Claimant

_____
(Date)

Claimant's Number §
_____

_____
(Name of person to whom claim is presented)

(Name of carrier) _____

(Carrier's Number)

(Address) _____

This claim for $ _____ is made against the carrier named above by (Name of claimant) _____

_____ for (Loss or damage) _____ in connection with the following described shipment:

Description of shipment _____

Name and address of consignor (shipper) _____

Shipped from (City, town or station) _____ , To (City, town or station) _____

Final destination (City, town or station) _____ Routed via _____

Bill of Lading issued by_____ Co.; Date of Bill of Lading _____

Paid Freight Bill (Pro) Number _____ . Original Car number and Initial _____

Name and address of consignee (to whom shipped) _____

If shipment reconsigned enroute, state particulars: _____

DETAILED STATEMENT SHOWING HOW AMOUNT CLAIMED IS DETERMINED
(Number and description of articles, nature and extent of loss or damage, invoice price of articles, amount of claim, etc.)

Total Amount Claimed

IN ADDITION TO THE INFORMATION GIVEN ABOVE, THE FOLLOWING DOCUMENTS
ARE SUBMITTED IN SUPPORT OF THIS CLAIM.*

( ) 1. Original bill of lading, if not previously surrendered to carrier.

( ) 2. Original paid freight ("Expense") bill.

( ) 3. Original invoice or certified copy.

   4. Other particulars obtainable in proof of loss or damage claimed.

_____

_____

Remarks: _____

_____

_____

_____

The foregoing statement of facts is hereby certified to as correct.

_____
(Signature of claimant)

§ Claimant should assign to each claim a number, inserting same in the space provided at the upper right hand corner of this form. Reference should be made thereto in all correspondence pertaining to this claim.
   * Claimant will please check (×) before such of the documents mentioned as have been attached, and explain under "Remarks" the absence of any of the documents called for in connection with this claim. When for any reason it is impossible for claimant to produce original bill of lading, if required, or paid freight bill, claimant should indemnify† carrier or carriers against duplicate claim supported by original documents.
   † Indemnity agreement for lost bill of lading.

Form 30-048 Printed and Sold by UNZCO 190 Baldwin Ave., Jersey City, NJ 07306 • (800) 631-3098 • (201) 795-5400

Figure B-4   Standard Form for Presentation of Loss or Damage Claims

Source: Reprinted with permission of Unz & Co., 190 Baldwin Avenue, Jersey City, NJ 07306, USA.

GLOSSARY

9802 Production (Formerly called 807 Production) Permits some stage of production, usually assembly, to be done outside the United States (usually done in the Caribbean) and brought back into the country with tariff paid on the value added (or assembly value) portion of the garment only.

Antidumping duty Charged if the price of an imported good is lower than the price in its country of origin.

Assortments The number of styles, number of fabrics per style, number of colors per fabric, number of sizes, and number of units.

Attitudes A customer's basic opinions and emotions about a product.

Authoritarian When people or governments are controlled by one person or one small group.

Balance of trade Difference between what a nation sells to other countries (exports) and what it buys (imports).

Bills of lading Transportation documents. *Lading* means cargo, or freight. The different types are *air waybill* for air transport, *ocean bill of lading* for ship movement, and *inland bill of lading* when goods are transported from a port of entry to a destination somewhere within a country.

C&F Seller pays cost and freight only.

Cartel A group of similar businesses that work together to regulate production, promotion, and pricing. Usually illegal (unfair competition) but to bolster foreign trade, the U.S. Commerce Department issues certificates providing antitrust immunity to cartel members.

Centrally planned economies Not geared to profit and not run by consumer demand. Usually go hand in hand with authoritarian government.

Certificate of origin Document that states where the good is produced.

Chain organizations A group of centrally owned stores, usually four or more, that carry similar goods and merchandise.

C.I.F. Seller pays cost, insurance, and freight.

Classic A style or design that satisfies a basic need and remains in general fashion acceptance for an extended period of time.

Commercial invoice A document detailing the terms of sale. This is a bill for the goods as well as a description of the order.

Commissionaires (Also known as independent agents) Specialists who act as agents for producers or retailers who do not have their own foreign buying office.

Competitor's profile A report that describes each competitor's market share, profitability, industry position, and likely future activities.

Confirmed letter of credit Exporter's bank guarantees payment. An unconfirmed letter of credit is guaranteed only by the issuing bank.

Consular invoice May be required by the importing country. It becomes a means of identifying and controlling goods and may be used to determine what the duty will be on the goods. Must be written in importing country's language.

Consumer expenditures How much people are spending on fashion products.

Cost-value quotas A quota based on the cost of the goods imported.

Counterfeit Fake versions of trademarked and licensed fashion products.

Countervailing duty Imposed on foreign products that have been subsidized by their governments.

Credit terms Outlines the responsibilities of the buyer to the seller regarding how payment will be rendered.

Culmination stage Height of popularity and the fashion is mass-produced in prices that make it acceptable and affordable to most customers.

Cultural traits (Distinguishing qualities) Considered to be shared among the people of a nation.

Customer profile A written description that is derived from studying the variables of demographic studies, psychographic, and buying behavior patterns of consumers in a given market.

Cut, Make, and Trim *Cut* is the cost of the rise of the materials used to make a garment. *Make* is the cost of labor and production. *Trim* is the number, size, and expenses of "extras" such as buttons, zippers, appliques.

Decline stage Period when the fashion begins to fade because of boredom resulting from widespread use of the fashion.

Democratic When everyone is involved and there are many constituencies, or groups, who can influence the political process.

Details Individual elements that include trimmings, length, width, and affect the inside line.

Developed countries Includes all members of the Organization for Economic Cooperation and Development (OECD) which is the United States.

Canada, Japan, Western Europe, Australia, and New Zealand.

Direct exporting When manufacturers take complete responsibility for all aspects of marketing their products in a foreign market. They sell their product directly to a wholesaler or a consumer.

Dispersion retailing Form of merchandising in which the retailer handles both the manufacturing and selling functions. It allows tight control of the store's image as well as the distribution channel and sales promotion. (Type of vertical marketing.)

Distribution The process of getting the product to the ultimate customer.

Duties Special taxes on imported goods.

Ethnocentric pricing Universal pricing that does not take national or regional differences into account.

Ethnocentrism Is the belief, held by virtually every nation in the world, that its way of life is best or even superior to the way others live.

EX Used to convey the end of the seller's responsibility (as in Ex-mill or Ex-factory).

Exclusive distribution Gives an importer a great deal of control over the product and its distribution.

Export management company (EMC) Handles exports for foreign producers who, in turn, are its clients.

Export strategy A business plan specifically slanted toward the selection and development of a particular international market.

Export license A general decree permitting the export of general categories of goods to specific destinations.

Export trading company (ETC) Performs same function as EMC but takes title to the product whereas EMC does not.

Exports When a country sends its goods or products abroad, usually for purposes of selling them to other countries.

Extensive distribution Puts imported goods into a large number of outlets diluting the control that the importer can exercise over the product.

Extroverted culture A culture where people are outgoing and direct in their communication. Americans are prime examples of an extroverted culture.

F.O.B. (Free on Board) An agreement in which the seller agrees to deliver the merchandise to a specific point without added charges to the buyer.

Factors Financial institutions that act as credit and collection departments for a manufacturer. For their services the factors receive fees known as factoring commissions.

Fashion cycle Follows an orderly pattern: introduction, rise, culmination, decline, obsolescence.

Fashion importer A specialist who assumes responsibility for bringing foreign fashion goods into the country.

FAX (facsimile) Machine that makes a copy of your transmission and sends the copy electronically over telephone wires into a receiving FAX machine.

Fiber consumption How much fiber was used during a given period. (Used in determining global consumption.)

First cost The wholesale or factory price of merchandise in the country of origin.

Foreign buying offices Usually store owned and located in foreign markets. Their purpose is to facilitate the purchase of goods from a particular trade region.

Franchising An agreement between a producer (franchisor) and distributor or dealer (franchisee) to sell the franchisors products in a store that bears the original producer's name and image. The franchisor receives a share of the profits and in return, supplies products, managerial advice, and image.

Free trade regions Geographic areas in which there are few or no barriers to trade. These zones are secure areas, usually located in or near customs ports of entry, which are regarded as legally outside a nation's custom territory.

Free traders Support international trade with no or few limitations.

Free trade zone An enclosed or isolated area of a port of entry that provides shipping and loading facilities for goods that are being reexported.

Full-line wholesaler An importer who offers a full assortment of many different kinds of warehoused products.

General merchandisers Retail stores that sell a number of lines of merchandise under one roof. Stores included in this group are commonly known as department stores, mass-merchandisers, variety stores, or general merchandise stores.

Geocentric pricing Local intermediaries are allowed to set price in their regions independent of other markets.

Global sourcing Purchasing production from markets around the world.

Global retailing When retail fashion operations in many countries expand into other countries.

Global product development The process of screening and judging products to be sure they suit the international market for which they are intended, meet the legal requirements of the importing countries, and can be developed and delivered in a timely fashion.

Globalization A process whereby the nations of the world are becoming more interlinked with one another.

Harmonized System (HS) The U.S. revised classification system for information after 1989.

Import penetration The degree to which imports have saturated a market.

Import sourcing The business of buying and processing imports.

Import-transfer price Value is the price a foreign manufacturer charges the importer.

Imports When a country brings in goods or products from another country for the purpose of selling them.

Indirect exporting When manufacturers use a management company, a trading company, or a broker to market their products. These foreign agents, who work on commission are responsible for the selling and promotion of the exporter's product.

Intermediary A middle person who helps an exporter communicate with foreign customers.

Intermodal A method involving two or more modes of transportation, such as plane and truck, for the movement of goods.

International orientation A perspective that encompasses an overview as well as specific strategies required to perform well in the international marketplace.

Introduction stage Worn initially by fashion pacesetters, usually produced in high-priced lines, and production is relatively limited.

Introverted culture A culture where people are inward-looking, contemplative, and reserved. Much of the Asian world is made up of introverted cultures.

Isolationists Advocates of limited trade who believe imports should be severely limited.

Joint venture A U.S. manufacturer is part-owner of a trading operation. Sometimes the foreign government is the trading partner; sometimes the partner is another business.

Knockoff A copy, often line-for-line, of a higher-priced style that is mass-produced at a lower price.

Landed cost The cost of an imported product that has added shipping costs, duties, forwarding costs, and insurance cost to the first cost.

Lead time The amount of time between ordering goods and receiving them in a store.

Less developed countries (LDCs) Suffer from a lack of resources and competitive industries. Cannot participate in world trade, depend on imports. LDCs include most of the African nations and Bangladesh, Afghanistan, Laos, and Nepal in

Asia. Haiti is the only LDC in the Western Hemisphere.

Letter of credit A financial document issued by an importer's bank declaring that payments will be made to an exporter regarding a specific shipment of goods, accompanied by the shipping documents. The letter of credit is usually cashed when the goods are loaded on to the chosen mode of transportation.

Licensing An agreement where firms are given permission to produce and market merchandise that carries the name of the licensor, who receives a royalty for each item sold under the licensing agreement.

Life stage A psychological profile based on the customer's psychological age, which may or may not match chronological age.

Limited-line wholesaler An importer who offers only a few products, which are drop-shipped to customers.

Market strategy report Summarizes the size, structure, and dynamics of the overall market as well as your target markets; describes the characteristics that distinguish your product from the competition—from the customer's point of view.

Market segmentation The division of markets into specialized niches.

Market-oriented economy Geared to making profit and satisfying consumers.

Matchmaker programs Provide an opportunity for small business trade delegations to travel to foreign markets specifically for the purpose of meeting potential distributors, agents, and licensing and joint venture partners.

Merchandise plan Describes what must be done to create an acceptable finished product delivered to its ultimate destination.

Model The garment or product to be shown to the trade.

Modifications May involve product's basic design, its quality, its cost, and ultimately, its price.

National brands Nationally advertised and distributed brand owned by a manufacturer and identified with that specific manufacturer.

Newly developed countries (NICs) These include Hong Kong, South Korea, Taiwan, South Africa. The Eastern bloc nations are now considered NICs; they are Romania, Poland, Estonia, Hungary, Czechoslovakia, and Lithuania.

North-south dialogue Series of ongoing talks between the north (the richest nations are in the Northern Hemisphere) and the south (the poorest nations occupy the Southern Hemisphere) about how to help the LDCs through reduced trade barriers, investment, and improved exports.

Note draft A bill designating a specific date for payment. The exporter holds title until the bill is paid.

Obsolescence stage When distaste and disinterest occurs and a style can no longer be sold at any price.

Offshore production Having products entirely made in another part of the world.

Perceptions A customer's immediate intuitive feeling about a purchase is based on all the senses.

Polycentric pricing Takes national and regional differences into account in setting prices.

Portfolio fit Describes how well any new product will work within an established product line.

Preferred origin countries Imports from these countries are favored over the imports from other countries because of special status.

Price averaging A technique of mixing different cost-priced goods together at one retail price. In this way you can average the retail price, making less on some and more on others.

Pricing strategy Process of evaluating and setting the price of a product, taking into account such factors as cost, competition, and other elements of the marketing factors.

Private label Merchandise that meets standards specified by a retail organization and which belongs exclusively to it; Stores design and produce their own line of products under their own store-brand label.

Product restrictions Enforced requirements for label identification including manufacturer's name, country of origin, and the fiber content.

Product liability Either the manufacturer or the importer is legally obligated for any defects in a product.

Product developers Staff specialists who create products, test them, and follow through on all aspects of their production.

Promotion The process of letting the customer know the product is available.

Psychographics The study of peoples' attitudes and values.

Purdah The ultraconservative, head-to-toe, black garments dictated to Muslim women by their religious leader.

Quick response A U.S. fashion industry strategy for delivering fashion products in timely fashion to consumer demand.

Quotas Limits on the amount of a product that may be brought into a country.

Reexporting Importer who buys unfinished products and then sells them to another foreign country.

Rise stage Becomes accepted by more people and is a version of the introductory designer style. These changes supply the customer with the same "look" for less money.

Sales terms Outline the responsibilities of the seller to the buyer and specify, from a legal standpoint, title to the goods changing hands

Samples A prototype that is tested and modified if necessary.

Scouting trip Locating suppliers by participating in a fact finding or trade mission for purposes of scouting out potential products.

Selective distribution When the imported goods will be sold through a limited number of outlets.

Shippers' export declaration (SED) Used by the Census Bureau to compile trade statistics.

Sight draft Bill for immediate payment, equivalent to a cash-on-delivery (COD) in the United States.

Silhouette The overall outline of a garment sometimes referred to as "shape" or "form."

Social communication To communicate with others by understanding their culture and customs.

Specialty merchandiser Store that carries limited lines of merchandise.

Specification buying Retailers create and manufacture lines to their own standards or specifications rather than the manufacturers.

Standard Industrial Classification (SIC) The domestic system of classification of products.

Standard Industrial Trade Classification (SITC) The international system of classification of products.

Target market A group of potential customers, identified according to their needs and buying habits, that a business is attempting to turn into regular customers.

Telex Communication method sometimes called a "written telephone." Sender types message on special tape and the tape is sent to the recipient who answers in the same way.

Time draft Bill of exchange that specifies a number of days within which payment is due. The exporter officially holds title until the bill is paid.

Trade deficit When a nation buys (imports) more than it sells (exports) it will have a trade deficit.

Trade surplus When a nation sells (exports) more than it buys (imports) it will have a trade surplus.

Unfinished products Goods whose production was begun somewhere outside the United States.

Unit-quotas A quota based on unit of goods or number of pieces imported.

Validating license Issued to individuals on a case by case basis for a single transaction or a specific time period.

Value-added The increase in the value of a product contributed by each producer or distributor as the product progresses through stages of production and distribution.

Value-in-use Allows the customer to save money by substituting an imported product for one currently in use.

Vertical marketing When firms at different marketing levels merge or are acquired, as when a retailer becomes both manufacturer and seller.

INDEX